WAITING FOR DISASTER

WAITING FOR DISASTER

Earthquake Watch
in California

Ralph H. Turner
Joanne M. Nigg
Denise Heller Paz

UNIVERSITY OF CALIFORNIA PRESS
Berkeley   Los Angeles   London

University of California Press
Berkeley and Los Angeles, California

University of California Press, Ltd.
London, England

Library of Congress Cataloging in Publication Data

Turner, Ralph H.
Waiting for disaster.

Includes index.
1. Earthquakes—Social aspects—California.
2. Disaster relief—California—Planning.
3. Earthquake prediction—Social aspects—California.
4. Disasters—Research.
I. Nigg, Joanne M. II. Paz, Denise Heller. III. Title
HV599.T87 1986   363.3'495   85–8447
ISBN 0–520–05550–0 (alk. paper)

Printed in the United States of America

1 2 3 4 5 6 7 8 9

Contents

Acknowledgments

The research proposal for this investigation was developed jointly by the authors and Barbara Shaw, who remained a full coinvestigator until the project's third year. Her contributions were extensive. Two research associates, K. Jill Kiecolt and Gerald Goetsch, joined us early to service our computer needs and advise on statistical matters. They participated actively in our weekly research conferences and contributed many unacknowledged ideas to the final report. James Goltz took charge of the newspaper analysis halfway through the project and likewise became a major participant and contributor.

Shelley Garcia, Cynthia Hollos, Kathryn Kremer, Denise Nardi, Vicki Lee Rasson, and Eric A. Sas served helpfully as student assistants on the project. Sharon Stevens initiated the newspaper study and made other contributions during the early phases of data-gathering and analysis. Christine H. Turner assumed responsibility for investigating the response to current earthquake threat in the Los Angeles County schools. Kathleen Carothers, while taking an independent study course under the senior author's direction, made an important contribution to our analysis of newspaper treatment of earthquake prediction topics.

Eve Fielder, Director of the Survey Research Center, supervised the massive data-gathering and data-reducing operations, and was always responsive to our special requests. Vi Dorfman, as field supervisor, took charge of the actual interviewing, with the help of Suzy Chapman and Kathy Thompson. We cannot begin to name the dozens of interviewers who conscientiously and diplomatically conducted our interviews under Vi Dorfman's watchful eyes. Rita Engelhardt, head of Statistical Services for the Institute of Social Science Research, frequently helped us with unfamiliar problems. Also on the staff at the Institute, Donald Witzke helped us develop appropriate sampling designs, Cheryl Groves and Kathleen O'Kane supervised coding of interview protocols, and Matthew Futterman and Jack Katola developed programs to enable us to conduct our final interview waves by a computer-assisted procedure.

Howard Freeman, director of the Institute, was ever-accommodating to our needs. Ann Cinderella, assistant director of the Institute during most of the project, was helpful in many ways. Whenever we encountered difficult administrative problems we turned to Madeleine De Maria, administrative assistant and subsequently assistant director of the Institute. Invariably, we received the kind of careful attention that we might have expected had there been no other projects similarly housed in the Institute.

As principal consultant to the project, Charles Wright made inestimable contributions during the initial questionnaire development stage and again in commenting on draft reports of preliminary findings. Howard Kunreuther took unusual interest in the project and made discriminating suggestions at different stages. Helpful commentaries on our progress report were also received from Lewis M. Killian and Robert Stallings. Enrico L. Quarantelli welcomed the coinvestigators for a week of study at the Disaster Research Center of Ohio State University at the start of the investigation. Our colleagues, Philip Bonacich and David McFarland, gave freely of their time in answering questions about appropriate statistical procedures.

The project would never have been launched without the strong encouragement and help of Charles C. Thiel, Jr., of the National Science Foundation. And the special interest that William Anderson took in the project, in his official capacity as program manager for NSF and also as a coprofessional in the study of social aspects of natural disasters, made him a source of constant support and counsel.

The willingness of Dr. Robert M. Hamilton, then chief of Earthquake Studies in the U.S. Geological Survey, to provide us with initial funding until the National Science Foundation review could be completed accounts for the relative timeliness of the investigation. And Peter Ward, in charge of earthquake prediction studies for the U.S. Geological Survey in Menlo Park, was constantly available and helpful throughout the course of the investigation.

Anita Anderson was our diligent and perceptive secretary and editor during two years of the project. Marcus Hennessy and Nancy Siris-Rawl carried on the secretarial responsibilities until the project's conclusion. In the early stages of the project, Nannette Littlestone typed some of the interview schedules. The final manuscript was typed cheerfully and with dispatch by Ceil Mirsky and Rieko Imai.

Funding for the research was provided under National Science Foundation Grants NSF ENV76–24154 and NSF–PFR78–23887 and U.S. Geological Survey Grant 14–08–00001–G–347.

PART ONE

Background for the
Investigation

CHAPTER ONE

A Bulge on the
San Andreas Fault

The Developing Prospect of
Earthquake Prediction

As recently as 1973, a report on public response to the 1971 San Fernando-Sylmar earthquake was issued under the title *The Unpredictable Disaster in a Metropolis.*[1] Forecasting earthquakes had commonly been relegated to fiction writers and seers, such as those who warned that much of California would fall into the Pacific Ocean in June of 1969. But as early as 1968, a working group of the Federal Council for Science and Technology, impressed by progress in Japan, had recommended earthquake prediction as a valuable tool for saving lives in case of an earthquake. And in late 1973 and 1974, a spate of articles by leading seismologists optimistically recounted progress toward the practical realization of scientific prediction capability. In May 1975, a popular article by Frank Press bore the following headline: "With adequate funding several countries, including the U.S., could achieve reliable long-term and short-term forecasts in a decade."[2]

Some of the optimism was stimulated by the report from an American scientific delegation to the People's Republic of China in 1974 that their hosts might have successfully predicted as many as eleven substantial earthquakes. The most impressive, and certainly the most extensively verified Chinese success, came the following year, when a Richter scale magnitude 7.3 earthquake in the vicinity of Haicheng on February 4 was predicted with almost pinpoint accuracy just a few hours before it happened.[3]

Early optimism was also based on the conviction that seismologists were close to finding a theoretical model that would adequately account for the various signs often observed before an earthquake. The model would permit quantitative analysis as a means of specifying the place, time, and magnitude of the expected quake. Building especially on Soviet findings, American seismologists formulated the dilatancy theory, which promised a framework in which all the pieces of the puzzle could be fitted neatly together. In the meantime, American scientists were having some encouraging practical success. Peter Ward of the U.S. Geological Survey reported that five small earthquakes had been predicted with varying degrees of accuracy in the United States between 1974 and 1977. In a definitive analysis of the state of the art released in 1976, the National Research Council's Panel on Earthquake Prediction was appropriately cautious about current progress. But the panel reiterated the conclusion that "With appropriate commitment, the routine announcement of reliable predictions may be possible within ten years in well instrumented areas, although large earthquakes may present a particularly difficult problem."[4]

Enthusiasm for earthquake prediction was occasionally muted by anxiety over the potentially unsettling social and economic effects of warning the public about a coming earthquake. Especially if the warning involved weeks, months, or years of advance notice, might not disruption in the social and economic fabric of community life exceed whatever benefit could be anticipated from knowing when to expect an earthquake? In a witty and polemical essay that attracted wide attention, Garrett Hardin imagined all of the worst possibilities. Hardin warned that a prediction would change Californians' happy denial to pathological anxiety as they approached the fateful day, that real estate values would plummet, and that we would eventually be driven to destroy the prediction facility as a desperate last chance to end the mounting chaos.[5] Other writers either echoed these forecasts or took the opposite position, that denial and apathy would render the prediction inconsequential. And many responsible scientists and public officials, fearing that a false alarm would nullify the effectiveness of a subsequent valid prediction, recalled Aesop's fable about the shepherd boy who cried wolf once too often.

More serious efforts to estimate possible effects began with a working paper by J. Eugene Haas entitled "Forecasting the Consequences of Earthquake Forecasting," prepared for the University of Colorado Institute for Behavioral Science in 1974. Haas and Dennis S. Mileti then launched the first empirical study in which key decision makers in commercial and noncommercial sectors of the community tried to anticipate what measures they would adopt in the event of a prediction, taking into account the decisions that were being contemplated in other community sectors. Their conclusions were that lives would indeed be saved, but that this would very likely be at the cost of a crippling economic recession.[6]

With a mandate to review the full range of social, economic, and legal aspects of prediction, the Panel on Public Policy Implications of Earthquake Prediction was established within the National Research Council in early 1974 as a counterpart to the Panel on Earthquake Prediction. Drawing widely on experience with warnings of other types of disaster, this panel offered tentative recommendations for both action and research. Central to several of the research recommendations was the need to study response to actual instances of earthquake prediction and warning as they occurred. In 1978 a report from the National Research Council Committee on Socio-economic Effects of Earthquake Prediction presented a more fully elaborated outline for research. The committee underlined the importance of studying response to *near predictions* as well as to predictions, reminding investigators that people may not distinguish between near predictions and scientifically adequate predictions.[7]

A near prediction is an announcement that approximates a prediction, but either the place, time, and magnitude cannot be specified with sufficient precision or plausible alternative interpretations of the evidence make an outright prediction unwarranted. Announcement of the southern California uplift, or Palmdale bulge, in 1976 constituted just such a near prediction under both criteria. Our investigation was launched in 1976, soon after the announcement was released, in order to accumulate timely evidence on public response. The investigation was intended as a first step toward understanding how communities respond to the announcement of near predictions, and by inference, how they may respond to earthquake predictions in the future.

EARTHQUAKE HARBINGERS IN
SOUTHERN CALIFORNIA

In its title, a perennial best-seller proclaims that California is *Earthquake Country*.[8] The great San Francisco earthquake of 1906 is a landmark in California history, much like the great Chicago and London fires. Although the last "great" earthquake in southern California predates living memory and occurred when the region was thinly populated, the memory of more recent destructive earthquakes remains vivid for many residents. The Long Beach-Compton quake of 1933, the Bakersfield-Tehachepi earthquake of 1954, and the San Fernando-Sylmar quake of 1971 were all quite destructive, and the tremors were strongly felt over wide areas where no destruction occurred.

As early as November 1973, Dr. James Whitcomb of the prestigious California Institute of Technology (Caltech) predicted an earthquake of at least 5.5 magnitude within three months for the populated region just beyond the eastern boundary of Los Angeles County. A weaker quake of 4.1 did occur in January in that region, but the possibility of coincidence could not be ruled out in this single case. In 1974 the much-publicized book *The Jupiter Effect*, by astronomers John Gribbin and Stephen Plagemann, predicted major earthquakes in California and around the world in 1982, when all nine planets would be aligned on the same side of the sun.[9] On Thanksgiving Day 1974, a magnitude 5.2 earthquake near Hollister in northern California confirmed an informal prediction by U.S. Geological Survey scientists. Throughout 1975, the local media discussed these events and reported American and international progress in the art of earthquake prediction, speculating on its possible social and economic implications.

On February 4, 1976, news of the tragic Guatemalan earthquake in which more than 20,000 people were killed and 200,000 left homeless heightened awareness of earthquake hazard. But whatever meaning this disaster may have had to southern Californians, it did not directly stimulate increased attention on problems of earthquake preparation and survival in Los Angeles-area newspapers. But on February 13, before the Guatemala disaster ceased to be news, a front-page story in the *Los Angeles Times* announced the discovery that the earth's surface was uplifted over a vast area with Palmdale near its center. The precise meaning of the uplift remained a puzzle to seismologists, and scientists admitted that alternating uplift and subsidence can occur without accompanying earthquakes. However, four circumstances could not be ignored, namely: (1) an uplift of this nature is one important hypothetical precursor to an earthquake; (2) if the uplift were a precursor, its extent—covering approximately 100 miles along the fault—could indicate an earthquake in the magnitude 8 range; (3) the National Oceanic and Atmospheric Administration (NOAA) study published in 1973 had estimated that a quake of similar magnitude centered in approximately the same location could cost as many as 12,000 lives in the greater Los Angeles area, with astronomical injuries and property loss; (4) seismologists had long warned that a serious earthquake was overdue in the southern portion of the San Andreas fault. While acknowledging the uncertain meaning of the uplift, the California Seismic Safety Commission officially declared on April 8 that "the uplift should be considered a threat to public safety and welfare in the Los Angeles metropolitan area."

Although nothing approaching a true prediction had yet been issued, the early treatment of the southern California uplift might well serve as a prototype for the first stage of eventual prediction of a highly destructive earthquake affecting a major metropolitan area. The U.S. Geological Survey rapidly increased instrumentation and observation in the uplifted area. A succession of further developments might well have occurred, culminating in a positive prediction, a reinterpretation of the uplift as benign, or an actual earthquake that could strike while scientists and responsible community leaders were still debating the significance of the anomaly.

Subsequent events justified the assumption of a developing scenario, though not yet the anticipation of a true earthquake prediction. On April 21, 1976, another front-page story in the *Los Angeles Times* reported that Whitcomb of the Caltech's Seismology Laboratory had "predicted" that a quake between the magnitudes of 5.5 and 6.5 would occur at some time between that date and April 1977. The quake might occur on any of several faults in the area and anywhere within an irregularly shaped circle some eighty-seven miles in diameter. It could not be determined at once whether this qualified prediction referred to the same phenomenon as the southern California uplift or whether Los Angeles now faced the prospect of two earthquakes. In subsequent discussion, Whitcomb made it clear that he was merely engaged in testing a controversial hypothesis rather than issuing a confident prediction, though the distinction was much too subtle to be clear to people not experienced in the intricacies of scientific method.

On May 28, the *Los Angeles Times* again carried a front-page story, with the headline "Palmdale 'Bulge' Higher, Wider Than First Thought." This story suggested that the uplift might relate to a fault on the Los Angeles side of the San Gabriel Mountains rather than to the San Andreas fault, and it reported a growing conviction at the U.S. Geological Survey that the uplift indeed presaged an earthquake.

The year following the first announcement of the uplift was marked by an abundance of earthquake-related news. There were more destructive earthquakes around the world than usual, with the May 6 quake in northern Italy and the July 28 Tangshan quake in the People's Republic of China receiving the most attention. Just about the time when Whitcomb was canceling his near prediction, a forecast from outside the established scientific community attracted nationwide attention. Henry Minturn, a self-styled geophysicist unknown to the scientific community, was given a hearing by KNBC-TV on November 22, 1976. He claimed to have predicted many earthquakes successfully, including a small one that occurred while he was in the studio. On the air he forecast an earthquake for the Solomon Islands on December 7, to be followed by a quake in Los Angeles on December 20. Although recognized earthquake scientists consistently disparaged Minturn's methods and his predictions, interest in the forecast mushroomed. Media coverage was extensive and ranged from positive to inquiring to devastatingly critical. After December 20 had passed without an earthquake, most of the media simply dropped further mention of Minturn, without so much as a recapitulation and assessment. It was approximately a month after this disconfirmation and Whitcomb's cancellation that our first and principal field survey was conducted.

The Purpose of the Investigation

The general purpose of our investigation was to gather a wide range of information concerning individual and community response to these events as they developed. The time required to develop a research proposal and the time required for review before a grant could be awarded precluded our conducting a sample survey until approximately one year after the first announcement of the southern California uplift. We were able, however, to monitor newspaper and other media treatment of relevant events from the time of the original announcements and to conduct sample surveys as events unfolded during the second and third years after public notification of the uplift.

Data were gathered with two general aims in mind. One was to assemble as rich a case study as possible of a series of events whose eventual outcome could not be known at the time of the investigation. The uncertain and open-ended but severe threat of earthquake disaster represented by the uplift was a unique event at the time, yet one likely to be repeated in the future. The second aim was to provide a basis for refining our understanding of what community response will be when true earthquake predictions are released to the community sometime in the future. While it would be foolhardy to assume that community response to an earthquake prediction would be merely an intensified version of the response to a near prediction, we can profitably examine which aspects of the response to a near prediction are in accord with prior assumptions and which are not. And it is likely that the issuance of true earthquake predictions will in many instances be preceded by announcements of near predictions similar to the recent discussions of the uplift.

In more specific terms, our objectives included finding answers to such questions as these: How have near predictions and other earthquake matters been communicated to the general public? How aware were people of relevant developments, and how well did they understand them? How fearful were people, and how salient a concern was the earthquake threat? What steps did people take to protect themselves and their families? What do they expect of their government, and what is their attitude toward what governments are already doing? How do people feel about the release of earthquake predictions and other earthquake information? To what sources do people turn in making up their minds about all these matters? And, specifically, to what extent do they trust scientific as compared with nonscientific sources? To what extent has altruistic concern been aroused in the community by the earthquake threat? To what extent are attitudes changeable over the period of waiting? To what extent can changed attitudes be linked to changing events as reported in the media?

In dealing with all these questions, we will be searching for individual and group differences of many kinds. In order to interpret public response, we must first outline the major visible actions of local governments and of large-scale organizations in dealing with the earthquake hazard.

Sociological Implications

DISASTER STUDIES

The most obvious wider implications of this investigation are for the sociological study of natural disasters. This work has been well summarized, so there is no need to recapitulate the major problems and findings from studies of tornadoes, hurricanes, floods, earthquakes, fires, and volcanic eruptions as well as from studies of disasters resulting at least partly from human error, such as dam failures, explosions, and leakages of radiation and poisonous substances.[10] The direct effects of disaster are obvious: essential roadways and other lifelines are destroyed, homes and workplaces are rendered unusable, lives are lost, and many people are injured.

Mobilization of the community to prepare for such exigencies and to deal with them after the disaster constitutes one critical set of sociological problems. But the social and economic effects of disaster as well as the problems in preparing for potential disaster are deeply affected by the *social meanings* embedded in existing social structures and relations and held by individuals. A major focus of disaster research is on the meanings attached to the disaster agent. These meanings do not stand alone, however; as an exceptional or crisis event, the disaster is viewed in its relationship to ordinary events and states of affairs. For example, it is critical to know if river dwellers view floods as recurrent but manageable crises, like domestic end-of-the-month cash-flow problems, and if denizens of "earthquake country" prepare for earthquakes by pushing their best bottles of scotch to the rear of the cupboard shelf or whether in contrast they view the disaster as heralding a sacred or secular Armageddon.[11]

The crucial meanings are not strictly cognitive but rather meld cognitive with affective components into more of a *feeling* than an intellectual image. A major theme linking this investigation to sociological research on disasters is the emphasis on social meanings, in both their cognitive and affective aspects, as they convey feelings about the relationship of the disaster event to ordinary life.

Sociological research on disasters has emphasized either the responses of organizations or the responses of individuals, families, neighborhoods, and informal groupings. The organizational response has been admirably summarized by Russell Dynes.[12] Our major emphasis has been on individuals and associated social units. While we have given some attention to the response of governmental agencies and especially to the mass media of communication, it has been primarily in relation to how they help shape the responses of individuals, families, and neighborhoods. But causation does not flow simply in one direction. Organizational responses take into account what decision makers correctly or incorrectly perceive as actual and potential public responses, and there is a continuous interaction that constantly modifies both organizational and individual responses. A key observation by Joanne Nigg, made early in the investigation, was that organizations take longer to react to new information and events than do individuals and families, so the periodicity of the interaction is affected by *organizational lags* that are different for different organizations and different problems. Because we emphasize public response, a major theme of this investigation is the continuing interaction between public and organizational response.

Again, disaster research deals either with response to disaster or response to anticipation and warning of disaster. Our investigation concerns the latter. We have not studied the response to imminent warnings, such as air-raid sirens sounding under ambiguous circumstances or the authoritatively communicated rumor that an upstream dam has broken.[13] We deal instead with a general awareness that the time for a great earthquake is inevitably coming closer, coupled with frequent reminders and punctuated by near predictions and events that periodically serve to make the threat of disaster more tangible. The study of disaster warnings has dealt with a variety of questions, from how widely a warning message is received and comprehended to whether comprehension is converted into action and what kind of action is taken. In the kind of situation we have studied, there are few instances of either complete unawareness of danger or of drastic responses. Hence, our emphasis is on variations in the kind and quality of awareness, thresholds for minor action response and support for government action, and readiness for action in case of a credible imminent warning.

Another important theme comes from disaster research. Investigators have been repeatedly impressed with the spontaneous outpouring of altruism that pervades the community in the immediate aftermath of natural disaster.[14] Unpremeditated compassion and disposition to self-sacrifice are largely responsible for the success of emergency rescue and rehabilitation. But we do not know why altruistic responses prevail, nor do we understand the conditions that foster or impede altruism. For example, a 1965 blackout in New York City caused by electrical failure evoked community solidarity and protectiveness of an admirable sort, while a similar blackout in 1977 triggered a night of vandalism and looting.[15] A National Research Council panel speculated that even a fairly definite and credible earthquake prediction would not evoke widespread altruism, for the following reasons: the damaging effects indicated by the prediction are not tangible, visible, instantaneous, or dramatic; a prediction lacks the emotional impact of a near miss; losses from the prediction itself are more like an intensification of the normal hazards of life than like the uniquely catastrophic evidence of a collapsed or burned building; and there would be ambiguity over responsibility and blame, since issuance of a prediction is a human rather than a strictly natural event.[16] By looking for dispositions toward altruism in the pre-earthquake situation, we hope to add to the understanding of conditions that foster or impede the altruistic response in pre- and post-disaster situations.

A final disaster concept of relevance to our research is that of *disaster subculture*. It has been proposed that in regions recurrently subjected to the impact of a specific disaster agent (such as the hurricane, tornado, or flood), a pattern of awareness that includes conventional ways of viewing and dealing with the disaster agent comes to be part of the local culture. These disaster subculture elements include both adaptive and maladaptive practices, such as practical survival knowledge on the one hand and, often, an attitude of unjustifiable bravado on the other hand. Because the interval between destructive quakes in southern California is relatively long and because there has thus far been no forewarning of disastrous earthquakes, it is uncertain whether a true earthquake disaster subculture could have developed here.[17] One of our aims is to examine the concept of disaster subculture as it may apply to earthquake country in order to contribute to the growing body of research dealing with a wide range of disaster agents.

COMMUNICATION AND THE
MASS MEDIA

The implications of the investigation and the theory upon which we draw go far beyond the confines of disaster studies and into general sociology and behavioral science. Much of our concern is with the processes of communication in urban communities and with the part played by the mass media.[18] Except in the infrequent case of felt earthquakes, the events that make news all originate outside of direct public experience, so they only become generally known through the mass media. Consequently, we are dealing with a situation in which media discretion and media interpretation of events are especially crucial. While there is controversy over earthquake prospects and appropriate responses, only rarely is such controversy polarized between competing organized interest groups. The citizen does not have an organized political party or social movement to turn to for help in sifting media messages or to use to pressure the media and stage newsworthy events.

One of the earliest problems in the sociological study of the mass media, propounded by Robert Park, was the question of what makes an item newsworthy.[19] We find, for example, that newspapers aimed at the Mexican-American and black communities in southern California treat the prospect of a great earthquake locally as much less newsworthy than papers aimed at the Anglo community. And we find that similar stories are assigned grossly different news value at different periods of time. We hope to add to the existing understanding of the social determinants of newsworthiness.

If an item is newsworthy, the question still remains of how the media convey and interpret it. In the political arena, students of the mass media devote much attention to the bias injected when the media excerpt and summarize public pronouncements. Bias similarly arises in reporting earthquake news. However, the relative importance of two other features of the communication we are studying makes this situation different from political communication. First, media have the special problem of communicating technical information that is seldom popularly comprehensible in its original form and often only partly comprehensible in most felicitous translation. This is a growing problem with many topics of communication in contemporary society, but it is particularly acute in the case of scientific assessments of potential earthquake precursors. Second, the media are confronted with the special problem of stating the implications of earthquake news for individual and collective action. An augury of disaster provokes the question, What should be done? But the answers are seldom clear and must be gleaned from sources other than that announcing the danger. How the media translate technical news and how they deal with the implications for action are critical questions in understanding the impact of the mass media in modern society.

However important the media, they do not monopolize the communication process. Mass communication researchers have long stressed that interpersonal communication sifts and supplements—and sometimes substitutes for—media messages. Informal discussions in the family, among friends and neighbors, and at the workplace are integral to the communication process. Populations differ in their relative dependence upon different kinds of communication, and there may be affinities between topics and communication modes; too, circumstances can alter the relative importance of a communication mode from one occasion to the next. Our investigation will attempt to shed light on such variations in the use of different communication modes, and differences in the effects of communication through different modes.

One version of the relationship between the media and interpersonal communication is the venerable theory of a two-step flow.[20] According to this theory, people refer what they hear and see in the mass media to locally based opinion leaders before making up their own minds. The opinion leaders are thought to be experts on the topic in question, and the personal relationship supplies credibility that is complementary to the impersonal authority of media spokespersons. Like many other communications theories, this one was developed in the study of public opinion on political questions. By examining the applicability of the idea of opinion leader, or "local expert," to earthquake communication, we hope to extend our understanding of the way communications from the media are sifted in a way that results in individual acceptance or rejection of the message.

Finally, the individual is not merely the passive recipient of communication, no matter what the source. A great deal of attention has been devoted in communications research to the credibility assigned to different messages according to source, content, and other cues. Again, different populations employ different standards and criteria for credibility, and changing circumstances have their effects. An even more active stance for the individual is recognized in the study of information seeking. Often, the individual is impatient and goes looking for news rather than waiting for media initiative. How such efforts are conducted and the circumstances that foster such intiatives constitute an important realm of communications research, to which we shall attempt to make some additions.

COLLECTIVE BEHAVIOR

The study of collective behavior overlaps the study of communication, but with a different emphasis. Collective behavior concerns the dynamics of large-scale collaborative activity when organizational or institutional patterns either are absent or are insufficient to provide the framework for the collaboration or to identify the goals and means for action. The study of public opinion as a form of collective behavior is a different way of looking at much that we have already spoken of. But sociological conceptions of the public center around normatively defined issues that divide the interested public into factions.[21] The less focused phase of public concern, when issues and alignments are incipient rather than formed, has received minimal attention.

Rumor is a more frenzied and episodic collective effort to establish the social meanings of events or states of affairs. Although rumor is generally feared and decried, sociologists see it as an effort to achieve some clarification of inadequately defined circumstances that are the intense mutual concern of many people.[22] If ambiguity is an essential precondition for rumor, a period of vague earthquake warnings should provide a favorable occasion for clarifying its conditions and character.

Collective behavior can be purposive, developing into social movements. An early stage in such a sequence is small-scale grass-roots organization to promote an objective of common concern. Such grass-roots collaboration, in the form of self-help groups to foster neighborhood earthquake preparedness or of pressure groups to encourage governmental action to mitigate earthquake hazard, has been the object of special study in this investigation. The flourishing of self-help groups in recent decades has attracted much social science attention, although relatively little is yet known about the circumstances fostering this type of collective behavior.[23] Social movements have been the subject of investigation for a longer period of time, but the field is currently marked by debate over the extent to which social movements have genuinely grass-roots origins.[24]

Besides these movements, resistance movements of various sorts have grown apace in the United States. In spite of slogans such as "You can't fight City Hall!" and citizen passivity in the face of taxation, bureaucratization, and many other forms of regimentation, instances in which groups have banded together to resist the application of modern technology are especially frequent. Such movements include organized resistance to the implementation of earthquake-hazard mitigation efforts. However, little is also yet known about conditions that foster this kind of collective behavior.[25] We shall pay special attention to the conditions that facilitated the rise of resistance movements in southern California during our study period.

DECISION MAKING UNDER UNCERTAINTY AND RISK

Theories in almost every branch of sociology depend upon assumptions about how individuals and groups of individuals will make decisions in the face of uncertainty about future events and about the consequences of their actions. Approaches to this problem have included theories of habituation-conventionalization, of reality construction, and of sequential decision making that imply a quasi-rational assessment of probable risks, costs, and benefits.[26] The more sophisticated theories of rational decision making seem to be most applicable to situations in which the components can be quantitatively assessed on fairly objective grounds. For the assessment of earthquake risk and most other situations of uncertainty in daily life, we believe that a more adequate approach combines a theory of reality construction with a model of bounded (rather than maximizing) rationality, coupled with the rejection of any purely cognitive model of decision making. This view returns us to the emphasis stated at the outset on the meanings that people attach to events.

In the attempt to deal with these problems of earthquake risk in terms that can be generalized to other conditions of uncertainty, we must consider such problems as the following: Under what circumstances do people handle uncertainty by assuming that things will continue as usual, and when is this tendency overcome? How is the assessment of acknowledged risk affected by the existence of an implicitly understood level of acceptable risk and by the relative salience of competing areas of risk?[27] How do time spans and time perspectives affect the assessment of risk?[28] How do patterns of social integration and isolation—including family, neighborhood, and institutional support systems—affect risk assessment?

RELATIONSHIP OF ACTION TO
AWARENESS AND ATTITUDE

The question of how decisions are made under conditions of uncertainty overlaps with the classic problem of the extent to which awareness and attitude are translated into action. The well-known observation that people often do not put into action either their ideals or their prejudices has been identified in sociological literature as the problem of *words and deeds*.[29] One orienting hypothesis is that action results when awareness and attitude pass a threshold of intensity, but that most of our attitudes and states of awareness are at low levels of intensity. According to this principle, the way to stimulate action is to augment the force of the conditions that sustain awareness and appropriate attitudes until the threshold is crossed. According to an alternative orienting hypothesis, some threshold of awareness and attitude is a necessary, but not a sufficient, condition for action. According to this view, there is a different set of conditions that trigger action, so that no amount of intensification of awareness and attitude will lead to action. We shall address this general question in the theory of action directly.

Of special relevance to this issue are the many investigations of the relationship of affect to action. The evidence suggests that affect must be added to attitude and awareness to produce action, but that affect alone is not a sufficient addition. Affect must be coupled with knowledge about courses of action and, indeed, excessive levels of affect can be counterproductive.[30]

Another set of variables that affect action tendencies consists of self-confidence, fatalism, and ability to respond. Actions that deviate from normal routines are intrinsically risky and hence require appropriate levels of self-confidence. Fatalistic attitudes are global counterparts to individual lack of self-confidence and should impair the translation of attitudes into action. More objectively, one's ability to act on one's attitude is often low. Sociological theory and research indicate that this complex of causes is especially likely to vary by age, socioeconomic status, ethnic group, sex, and other social categories.

Finally, while conceptions of reality are largely constructed collectively rather than individually, action is probably even more of a social product. Both community and primary-group leadership are critical for action. The sociological study of social control has most often addressed the suppression of action tendencies, but the principles are equally applicable to the stimulation of action. Informal social control, especially among peers, ranges from the force of example to the imposition of coercive pressures.

STABILITY AND CHANGE IN ATTITUDE,
INTEREST, AND ACTION

A problem in all realms of social life is the stability of human response. Children are taught many things in school on the often doubtful assumption that what they have once learned will be a continuing resource throughout life. Advertisers make the opposite assumption, and that is that repeated exposure to fresh appeals is necessary to maintain product preferences among their customers. While there are no experimental controls in our investigation, we can look at the pattern of responses during a two-year period of reduced stimulation following the initial year of exceptional earthquake news. A further effort will be made to sort out the persistence patterns based on events of 1976 from the effects of new items during the following two years.

The Nature of the Investigation

The active period of the investigation extended over three and a half years and included the gathering and analysis of several kinds of data. The pivotal data for the entire investigation were responses to a series of sample surveys of adult residents of Los Angeles County. The most important of these was the *basic field survey*. From late January until early March of 1977, a representative sample of 1,450 adults was interviewed in their homes by trained personnel of the UCLA Survey Research Center. Some selective oversampling was added to these cases to enable us to make separate comparisons by ethnic group and by residential zones marked by special earthquake vulnerability. Telephone interviews with smaller samples of Los Angeles County residents were conducted four times, at five- to six-month intervals after the basic survey, and these supplied the data for assessing stability and change. Each of these four waves included 500 or more new respondents, and three of the waves included samples of previously interviewed subjects. The former enable us to plot changes in public response, while the latter enable us to sort out the kinds of people most and least likely to change. A final telephone survey of 519 new respondents was conducted immediately after the occurrence of a moderate earthquake on New Year's Day, 1979. We asked how the quake had been interpreted in relation to earlier earthquake warnings and what effect it had on the aspects of awareness, attitude, and action that we had been following for the two previous years.

A more informal kind of focused field research was conducted in order to study collaborative grass-roots activities related to earthquake threat. From questions on our surveys and lists of persons requesting speakers on earthquake topics, we located as many instances of such activities as possible and then interviewed people who were instrumental in bringing about the collaboration.

Complementary to the field surveys was a program to monitor the treatment of earthquake topics by the local media of mass communication for the full three years of 1976, 1977, and 1978. Comprehensive monitoring of all media would be a gargantuan task, far beyond the scope of this investigation, and so our program was constructed as follows: For quantitative analysis, we copied every item dealing with earthquakes—news, editorials, letters, advertisements, and so on—in the two major metropolitan dailies, three large-circulation "community" dailies in different parts of the metropolis, and the leading Spanish-language daily. We recorded or took notes on nearly all television and radio specials dealing with earthquakes, and we regularly watched the prime-time evening news on the three major network television channels. With the help of a wide circle of friends, we located relevant magazine articles and were informed of other television and radio items. Using the newspaper record as the framework, we were able to prepare a detailed descriptive account of earthquake coverage for three years, beginning six weeks before the southern California uplift was announced. In addition, we have a quantitative record of the changing rate of attention to earthquake topics and of the relative attention to different kinds of earthquake topics.

Finally, we prepared an account of major governmental and other organizational responses to the earthquake threat on the basis of interviews with key informants and of reports gleaned from our newspaper files.

Outline of This Book

Part Two reports on our examination of the state of public awareness of the earthquake threat and of the communications process contributing to that awareness. Chapter two looks at the beginning of the process in organizational activity and media content. Chapter three takes up the communications process by which earthquake awareness is transmitted to the public, including the complementary relationship between media and interpersonal discussion. Chapter four considers the fact that people do not always wait passively for the media to initiate the transmission but instead often engage in rumoring and in other information-seeking activities. Chapter five reviews the survey findings concerning the state of awareness one year after the announcement of the uplift.

Part Three addresses the translation of awareness into action. Chapter six examines the evidence of fear and concern and the difference between merely being aware and taking things seriously. Chapter seven asks what people think can be done, taking note of widespread fatalism about earthquake effects, and reports the extent to which individuals and households have taken the simple precautionary measures often recommended by experts. Chapter eight explores the prospects for altruism and reports on the abundant evidence that people often look to government in coping with the earthquake threat. The disappointing record of grass-roots collaborative activity, except as resistance to earthquake-safety measures, occupies chapter nine.

Part Four covers two special problems. Chapter ten examines whether people discriminate between earthquake notices from scientific and nonscientific sources and what credibility and respect they assign to science. Chapter eleven explores whether people living in especially vulnerable zones or in neighborhoods recently subjected to severe earthquake damage exhibit distinctive patterns of awareness and action or of distinctive earthquake subcultures.

Part Five deals with stability and change over the two years following the basic survey. Chapter twelve searches for evidence that intervening events, such as new forecasts and an earthquake in nearby Santa Barbara, have affected local awareness and action patterns. The two-year trends in major forms of awareness and action are examined in chapter thirteen. The aftermath of the magnitude 5 earthquake on New Year's Day, 1979, is analyzed in chapter fourteen. Chapter fifteen reports on the search for patterns of stability and change during the first three years following the announcement of the Palmdale bulge.

Chapter sixteen (Part Six) offers some conclusions and suggests the existence of some new problems.

PART TWO

Communicating the

Crisis or Business as Usual? Government, Organizations, and the Media

There are no direct lines of communication between the scientists who study earthquake precursors and the general public, unless we count the contorted paths of rumor that sometimes emanate from scientific laboratories. And even with access to the mass media, few scientists are expert in communicating information and advice to the public. Consequently, television, radio, newspapers, and other mass media are crucial in determining what the public can hear and read, with what seriousness and comprehensibility scientific reports are presented, how often and with what prominence people are reminded of unfinished business, and what advice is offered. But the media seldom take the initiative. Except when the newsworthiness of dramatic events is obvious, the media look to government agencies, public service organizations, and prominent individuals for their cues. Hence, we cannot understand media coverage without also looking at organizational responses.

The purpose of this chapter is to prepare the ground for examining public awareness of the earthquake threat by exploring media treatment of the topic, as that in turn is related to responses by government agencies and other public interest organizations. We shall begin with a brief review of organizational response, followed by a more extended account of media coverage.

Our data cover principally the years 1976, 1977, and 1978. We break this time span into two periods: the *year of the bulge*, from February 1976 to January 1977; and the *period of reassessment*, from February 1977 to the end of 1978. The break between these two periods is a natural one, because there was nothing later to match the excitement of the first announcement of the uplift, the publication and cancellation of the Whitcomb "hypothesis test," and the release and disconfirmation of the Minturn forecast, which came in succession during the year of the bulge. Nor was there a worldwide rash of disastrous earthquakes to match the sequence of those in Guatemala, northern Italy, Indonesia, China, the Philippines, Iran, and Turkey in 1976. The two periods also separate the events preceding our first and major survey, on which most of the analyses are based, from the events contributing to the changes we found in subsequent surveys. In most of Parts Two, Three, and Four, we shall deal only with the year of the bulge, leaving the reassessment period for Part Five.

Overcoming Organizational Inertia

Our review of agency and organizational response to the uplift is guided by several questions.

1. Were government agencies and service organizations spurred into action by announcement of the uplift, or did business as usual prevail? Which agencies responded, how promptly, and with what vigor? Were initiatives chiefly from local agencies, or from state and federal agencies?

2. When agencies responded, did they do so by devising new programs or simply by accelerating and augmenting existing programs?

3. Did the near prediction stimulate shifts in emphasis from emergency preparedness toward hazard-reduction strategies?

4. Was thought given to possible side effects of prediction, such as economic disruption or emotional stress during the waiting period?

5. Did agencies actively publicize their actions, fostering community awareness and establishing leadership patterns in preparation for an earthquake emergency, or did they carry out their tasks with minimal publicity? Did they foster widespread community participation in earthquake preparedness, or did they view preparedness as a set of tasks to be performed by technically qualified professionals?

A full month elapsed before there was an audible governmental response to the announcement of the uplift. On March 17, scientists from the U.S. Geological Survey briefed state officials on the implications of the Palmdale bulge. Survey Director McKelvey emphasized the inevitability of a great earthquake in the Los Angeles metropolitan area in the near future and the presumptive significance of the uplift as an earthquake precursor. It was revealed that the USGS, the State of California Division of Mines and Geology, and several universities had already initiated studies and installed additional instrumentation to expand data gathering in the uplifted zone.

Within two weeks after the briefing, the state Office of Emergency Services (OES) had written to local government officials, reporting on the briefing, transmitting maps of the uplifted zone, and urging officials to review and update local earthquake emergency preparedness and response plans. A few days later a similar letter went to all state agencies. OES had been established in the governor's office as the Office of Civil Defense in 1950. It soon became involved in natural disaster operations, and received its present name in 1970. OES is responsible for issuing disaster warnings, assisting local government agencies in preparing for disasters, and helping local governments in the wake of disaster. During an emergency, the director acts for the governor to coordinate emergency activities of all state agencies and to carry out the state's responsibilities under applicable federal emergency statutes.

Complementing the OES emphasis on emergency management and preparedness is the California Seismic Safety Commission's (SSC) responsibility for earthquake hazard-reduction planning. Five years of study by a joint committee of the state legislature under the cochairmanship of Senator Alfred Alquist and Assemblyman Paul Priolo convinced the legislature to establish the commission in 1975. The SSC is advisory to the governor and the legislature in developing programs and long-range strategies for dealing with earthquake hazard throughout the state. It consists of seventeen unpaid experts, who meet monthly, and a small support staff.

The commission took an activist and expansionist view of its responsibilities from the start. On April 8, 1976, commissioners adopted a resolution that was to be cited repeatedly in the months ahead as the warrant for taking the uplift seriously. Acknowledging the uncertain meaning of the uplift, but emphasizing the potential for a devastating earthquake, the SSC called on state agencies to initiate a wide range of disaster-mitigating activities. Included was the following clause: "Resolved, the Seismic Safety Commission finds that the uplift should be considered a possible threat to public safety and welfare in the greater Los Angeles metropolitan area."

In something of an anticlimax, the California Earthquake Prediction Evaluation Council (CEPEC) met at Stanford University on April 14 to render the finding of a select body of earth scientists:

> In our judgment, the uplift is probably a manifestation of the gradual buildup of earthquake producing stresses, and it should serve to give us a renewed sense of urgency in preparing for the large earthquake that someday inevitably will occur in this region.

CEPEC consists of nine earthquake scientists who are on call to provide prompt technical evaluation of any prediction or near prediction of a potentially damaging earthquake. Members are appointed by and are responsible to the director of OES, who in turn advises the governor on whether to issue a public warning.

On April 20, the OES Advisory Panel on State Government Response to Earthquake Prediction met to review implications of the CEPEC evaluation. At the same time, OES established liaison with the USGS headquarters for earthquake prediction studies in Menlo Park, California, and sent a second set of letters to local government officials, including eleven earthquake planning recommendations.

Thus, it took from one to two months after the announcement of the uplift for the principal state agencies to launch their responses. During these two months, nothing was heard from local government agencies or public service organizations, and political leaders such as the governor of California and the mayor of Los Angeles kept mum on the subject of earthquake threat.

CEPEC's evaluation of Whitcomb's "hypothesis test," forecasting a moderate earthquake within a year, came more promptly than their evaluation of the earlier uplift announcement. On April 30, nine days after Whitcomb had made newspaper headlines, the council assembled at Caltech, where Whitcomb worked, to examine his evidence and analyses. CEPEC members remained

PART TWO

Communicating the Threat

interpersonal discussion. Chapter four considers the fact that people do not always wait passively for the media to initiate the transmission but instead often engage in rumoring and in other information-seeking activities. Chapter five reviews the survey findings concerning the state of awareness one year after the announcement of the uplift.

Part Three addresses the translation of awareness into action. Chapter six examines the evidence of fear and concern and the difference between merely being aware and taking things seriously. Chapter seven asks what people think can be done, taking note of widespread fatalism about earthquake effects, and reports the extent to which individuals and households have taken the simple precautionary measures often recommended by experts. Chapter eight explores the prospects for altruism and reports on the abundant evidence that people often look to government in coping with the earthquake threat. The disappointing record of grass-roots collaborative activity, except as resistance to earthquake-safety measures, occupies chapter nine.

Part Four covers two special problems. Chapter ten examines whether people discriminate between earthquake notices from scientific and nonscientific sources and what credibility and respect they assign to science. Chapter eleven explores whether people living in especially vulnerable zones or in neighborhoods recently subjected to severe earthquake damage exhibit distinctive patterns of awareness and action or of distinctive earthquake subcultures.

Part Five deals with stability and change over the two years following the basic survey. Chapter twelve searches for evidence that intervening events, such as new forecasts and an earthquake in nearby Santa Barbara, have affected local awareness and action patterns. The two-year trends in major forms of awareness and action are examined in chapter thirteen. The aftermath of the magnitude 5 earthquake on New Year's Day, 1979, is analyzed in chapter fourteen. Chapter fifteen reports on the search for patterns of stability and change during the first three years following the announcement of the Palmdale bulge.

Chapter sixteen (Part Six) offers some conclusions and suggests the existence of some new problems.

Crisis or Business as Usual? Government, Organizations, and the Media

There are no direct lines of communication between the scientists who study earthquake precursors and the general public, unless we count the contorted paths of rumor that sometimes emanate from scientific laboratories. And even with access to the mass media, few scientists are expert in communicating information and advice to the public. Consequently, television, radio, newspapers, and other mass media are crucial in determining what the public can hear and read, with what seriousness and comprehensibility scientific reports are presented, how often and with what prominence people are reminded of unfinished business, and what advice is offered. But the media seldom take the initiative. Except when the newsworthiness of dramatic events is obvious, the media look to government agencies, public service organizations, and prominent individuals for their cues. Hence, we cannot understand media coverage without also looking at organizational responses.

The purpose of this chapter is to prepare the ground for examining public awareness of the earthquake threat by exploring media treatment of the topic, as that in turn is related to responses by government agencies and other public interest organizations. We shall begin with a brief review of organizational response, followed by a more extended account of media coverage.

Our data cover principally the years 1976, 1977, and 1978. We break this time span into two periods: the *year of the bulge*, from February 1976 to January 1977; and the *period of reassessment*, from February 1977 to the end of 1978. The break between these two periods is a natural one, because there was nothing later to match the excitement of the first announcement of the uplift, the publication and cancellation of the Whitcomb "hypothesis test," and the release and disconfirmation of the Minturn forecast, which came in succession during the year of the bulge. Nor was there a worldwide rash of disastrous earthquakes to match the sequence of those in Guatemala, northern Italy, Indonesia, China, the Philippines, Iran, and Turkey in 1976. The two periods also separate the events preceding our first and major survey, on which most of the analyses are based, from the events contributing to the changes we found in subsequent surveys. In most of Parts Two, Three, and Four, we shall deal only with the year of the bulge, leaving the reassessment period for Part Five.

Overcoming Organizational Inertia

Our review of agency and organizational response to the uplift is guided by several questions.

1. Were government agencies and service organizations spurred into action by announcement of the uplift, or did business as usual prevail? Which agencies responded, how promptly, and with what vigor? Were initiatives chiefly from local agencies, or from state and federal agencies?

2. When agencies responded, did they do so by devising new programs or simply by accelerating and augmenting existing programs?

3. Did the near prediction stimulate shifts in emphasis from emergency preparedness toward hazard-reduction strategies?

4. Was thought given to possible side effects of prediction, such as economic disruption or emotional stress during the waiting period?

5. Did agencies actively publicize their actions, fostering community awareness and establishing leadership patterns in preparation for an earthquake emergency, or did they carry out their tasks with minimal publicity? Did they foster widespread community participation in earthquake preparedness, or did they view preparedness as a set of tasks to be performed by technically qualified professionals?

A full month elapsed before there was an audible governmental response to the announcement of the uplift. On March 17, scientists from the U.S. Geological Survey briefed state officials on the implications of the Palmdale bulge. Survey Director McKelvey emphasized the inevitability of a great earthquake in the Los Angeles metropolitan area in the near future and the presumptive significance of the uplift as an earthquake precursor. It was revealed that the USGS, the State of California Division of Mines and Geology, and several universities had already initiated studies and installed additional instrumentation to expand data gathering in the uplifted zone.

Within two weeks after the briefing, the state Office of Emergency Services (OES) had written to local government officials, reporting on the briefing, transmitting maps of the uplifted zone, and urging officials to review and update local earthquake emergency preparedness and response plans. A few days later a similar letter went to all state agencies. OES had been established in the governor's office as the Office of Civil Defense in 1950. It soon became involved in natural disaster operations, and received its present name in 1970. OES is responsible for issuing disaster warnings, assisting local government agencies in preparing for disasters, and helping local governments in the wake of disaster. During an emergency, the director acts for the governor to coordinate emergency activities of all state agencies and to carry out the state's responsibilities under applicable federal emergency statutes.

Complementing the OES emphasis on emergency management and preparedness is the California Seismic Safety Commission's (SSC) responsibility for earthquake hazard-reduction planning. Five years of study by a joint committee of the state legislature under the cochairmanship of Senator Alfred Alquist and Assemblyman Paul Priolo convinced the legislature to establish the commission in 1975. The SSC is advisory to the governor and the legislature in developing programs and long-range strategies for dealing with earthquake hazard throughout the state. It consists of seventeen unpaid experts, who meet monthly, and a small support staff.

The commission took an activist and expansionist view of its responsibilities from the start. On April 8, 1976, commissioners adopted a resolution that was to be cited repeatedly in the months ahead as the warrant for taking the uplift seriously. Acknowledging the uncertain meaning of the uplift, but emphasizing the potential for a devastating earthquake, the SSC called on state agencies to initiate a wide range of disaster-mitigating activities. Included was the following clause: "Resolved, the Seismic Safety Commission finds that the uplift should be considered a possible threat to public safety and welfare in the greater Los Angeles metropolitan area."

In something of an anticlimax, the California Earthquake Prediction Evaluation Council (CEPEC) met at Stanford University on April 14 to render the finding of a select body of earth scientists:

> In our judgment, the uplift is probably a manifestation of the gradual buildup of earthquake producing stresses, and it should serve to give us a renewed sense of urgency in preparing for the large earthquake that someday inevitably will occur in this region.

CEPEC consists of nine earthquake scientists who are on call to provide prompt technical evaluation of any prediction or near prediction of a potentially damaging earthquake. Members are appointed by and are responsible to the director of OES, who in turn advises the governor on whether to issue a public warning.

On April 20, the OES Advisory Panel on State Government Response to Earthquake Prediction met to review implications of the CEPEC evaluation. At the same time, OES established liaison with the USGS headquarters for earthquake prediction studies in Menlo Park, California, and sent a second set of letters to local government officials, including eleven earthquake planning recommendations.

Thus, it took from one to two months after the announcement of the uplift for the principal state agencies to launch their responses. During these two months, nothing was heard from local government agencies or public service organizations, and political leaders such as the governor of California and the mayor of Los Angeles kept mum on the subject of earthquake threat.

CEPEC's evaluation of Whitcomb's "hypothesis test," forecasting a moderate earthquake within a year, came more promptly than their evaluation of the earlier uplift announcement. On April 30, nine days after Whitcomb had made newspaper headlines, the council assembled at Caltech, where Whitcomb worked, to examine his evidence and analyses. CEPEC members remained unconvinced by Whitcomb's analysis but sought to support legitimate prediction research, fearing that an unqualifiedly negative verdict would lull the public into a false sense of security. Their mixed emotions were apparent in the resolution they adopted:

> After limited study of the data, theory, and methods of analysis involved, the Council did not conclude that the probability of an earthquake in the area in question is *significantly* higher than the average for similar geological areas of California. Nevertheless, the data are sufficiently suggestive of such an increased probability as to warrant further intensive study and testing of the hypothesis presented by Dr. Whitcomb. It remains possible that a moderate or major earthquake could occur in the area at any time, as is true for many other geologic areas of California.

At the reported insistence of Governor Brown, the meeting was open to the press. As a result, journalists who could not understand the essentially technical discussion often featured the most controversial exchanges and the most negative statements made during the meeting.

From late April through the summer months, the OES and SSC continued their campaigns to mobilize state and local government agencies. The SSC urged the Southern California Association of Governments to encourage their member local governments to step up earthquake-preparedness actions and supplemented their earlier resolution with a new one calling for help from Congress and from federal agencies. During this period, many of the state agencies reported back to the SSC concerning actions they had taken. Often, this consisted of transmitting the SSC resolutions to local government agencies with the state agencies' added suggestions for action. The OES sent a third round of communications to local governments, took steps to improve communication with the Department of Water Resources in an earthquake, and held a conference in the San Fernando Valley on a proposed but unfunded computer bank for recording all facilities, equipment, and trained personnel that could be used in responding to a disaster or other emergency.

Locally, Whitcomb's near prediction created a furor in the Los Angeles City Council. Councilman Louis Nowell demanded that the city attorney file legal suit against Whitcomb and Caltech to secure reimbursement to his San Fernando Valley constituents for losses in property values because of the "prediction." The council referred the matter to the city attorney for a decision on legal actionability. The city attorney reported a negative judgment, citing no evidence that property values had been affected by the announcement. As usual in such cases, the city attorney's report received much less press attention than had the councilman's original charges, although some newspapers featured their own investigations showing that the boom in property values was unabated.

In one of the first positive responses of local government noted in the press, the Los Angeles County Board of Supervisors ordered that safety-procedure notices be posted in county buildings because of the threat posed by the uplift. In late June proposals on earthquake safety were formulated in the northern San Fernando Valley by police, clergymen, businessmen, and relief agency representatives.

During this same period, California Senator Alan Cranston's $150 million earthquake research bill, given special urgency because of the uplift, was debated and passed in the U.S. Senate but was subsequently defeated in the House of Representatives.

On July 8, Los Angeles County School Superintendent Richard Clowes wrote to the ninety-sixth district superintendents in the county, calling attention to the uplift. He relayed a request from the state's Office of Architecture and Construction calling for a resurvey of school building safety and evacuation plans, and he ordered each district to submit a reconsidered and revised emergency plan to his office. Emergency plans had already been filed in compliance with a post-San Fernando quake provision of the state administrative code, but Superintendent Clowes now required that these be revised in light of the uplift.

Another type of local government activity was expanded in late spring and summer, not through local or state government initiative, but by public demand. Community requests for information and for speakers on earthquake preparedness were routinely referred to the Los Angeles Civil Defense Office. Requests burgeoned during this period; information packets were mailed out in large numbers, and the civil defense coordinator began a grueling schedule of public presentations to local groups which continued for several months (see chapters four and eight).

From July to September we began to hear from a few local government agencies. In July, the Downey City Council sponsored an open all-day conference on "Disaster Preparedness in the Home," conducted by a newly formed grass-roots organization called Creative Home Economics Consultants (see chapter eight). The stress was on how the family unit could prepare for an earthquake or other natural disaster, with the goal of achieving self-sufficiency during a period when crucial lifelines were disrupted.

In September the Los Angeles County Emergency Preparedness Commission chose several hypothetical earthquakes of increasing magnitude as the scenario for their second countywide disaster exercise, "Operation Ring of Fire." Eight hundred people participated in the exercise, representing fourteen county departments, twelve cities, the Red Cross, utilities, the OES, the California Highway Patrol, and the volunteer Radio Amateur Civil Emergency Services (RACES). Concurrently, the Los Angeles Police department held their own earthquake emergency drill, with headquarters in the Hollywood Bowl. About the same time, a Southern California Earthquake Response Planning Guide, prepared under the auspices of the Federal Disaster Assistance Administration and the California OES, became available. It was to serve local governments as a guide to immediate postimpact response.

During the fall months, local government attention to earthquake preparedness increased visibly. September and October meetings of the Los Angeles County Earthquake Preparedness Council were devoted to problems of dam safety and evacuation, with participation by a wide range of agencies and organizations. UCLA's Extension Division offered a one-day, noncredit seminar called "Earthquakes: Prediction, Risk, and Survival," which was attended by representatives from the Los Angeles Fire Department, civil defense, the Red Cross, and other organizations, as well as by interested individuals. In November the Earthquake Preparedness Commission arranged a seminar on earthquake preparedness for Los Angeles County supervisors, other local government officials, civic groups, and the press. Across town, the University of Southern California also held an earthquake prediction conference. The Los Angeles civil defense coordinator arranged for the Creative Home Economics Consultants to make their presentation at a meeting of the Emergency Preparedness Commission meeting and separately at meetings for twelve city agencies at the Los Angeles City Hall.

The earliest and most ambitious school program began in September, with a conference arranged by the Sulphur Springs district. Sulphur Springs is near the center of the uplift, and an OES official who lived in the district was a prime mover. Enthusiasm waned, however, when two evening PTA meetings on earthquake preparedness attracted only twenty-eight people. A November PTA program in Beverly Hills, with the title "When an Earthquake Strikes," was better attended. Plans were afoot in many other districts, but they did not come to fruition until well into 1977.

Word that the U.S. Geological Survey had established its own internal earthquake prediction council (paralleling CEPEC) came out in October. In early November, at the state level, the National Guard held exercises featuring an evacuation center near Paso Robles (200 miles north of Los Angeles), to which "evacuees" from the destructive impact of a great earthquake were brought from both Los Angeles and San Francisco. Also in November, Mayor Bradley of Los Angeles appointed a task force on earthquake prediction "to explore and evaluate the range of possible city responses to an earthquake prediction and provide recommendations for alternative contingency programs that would be adaptable to the specific magnitude, urgency, and confidence level of a given prediction." The task force included both city employees and civilian members. The report was issued about two years later.

Direct efforts by the OES during the fall to promote public awareness and concern had immediate and dramatic effects. An earthquake safety pamphlet was included in all September billings by the Pacific Telephone Company; it suggested contacting the OES, SSC, and USGS for more information. Eight professionally prepared spot features on earthquake safety were distributed to sixty-one television stations in California during September and October, and ten public service announcements went to 400 radio stations. Requests for information to the three agencies shot up nearly sixfold from previous levels in October and rose even higher in November.

Henry Minturn's November 22 forecast that an earthquake would strike Los Angeles on December 20 added fuel to this growing concern. When information requests in December continued to escalate above November levels, there was no way to separate the effects of public service announcements and telephone bill enclosures from concern aroused by the new forecast. Supporting evidence submitted by Minturn for his forecast was examined by Thomas Gay, State Geologist and Chairman of CEPEC, who adjudged it unworthy of council consideration.

December brought reports of more meetings at which the uplift was discussed, and there was particular press coverage of the American Geophysical Union meeting in San Francisco. Other information meetings in southern California continued the fall trend into December and January.

From August 1976 until late January 1977, the Los Angeles City Council was the scene of intense controversy raised by the prospect of local government action. Soon after the disastrous 1971 San Fernando-Sylmar earthquake, the threat posed by buildings constructed before the 1934 seismic safety ordinances had taken effect became a concern for the Building and Safety Committee. In January 1976, a proposed ordinance requiring that certain pre-1934 structures be brought into compliance with earthquake safety standards was referred back to the Building and Safety Committee following tumultuous public hearings. From August until January 1977, the council considered various proposals, including the posting of warnings on potentially unsafe structures. Finally, in late January an ordinance was adopted that in effect postponed definitive action for another two years. (This controversy will be discussed more fully in chapter eight.)

The picture we have painted is one of slow but cumulative response. Learning from the uplift, agencies could respond more promptly to Whitcomb's later near prediction. But the novel character of Minturn's pseudoscientific forecast again seemed to catch agencies unprepared and unable to deliver timely responses. Throughout the year, initiative came principally from two state agencies with headquarters outside the threatened region and with primary responsibility for fostering earthquake safety. Local agencies began to accelerate and augment emergency safety programs belatedly, and they did so chiefly in response to pressures from state agencies rather than because of local initiative. Officials from safety and welfare agencies, such as the sheriff's department, police and fire departments, and the Red Cross, told us that their standard emergency procedures were already designed to cope with any anticipated earthquake—the near predictions didn't really change anything. There was also very little disposition to see the uplift as the occasion for adding new hazard-mitigation measures to their customary programs of emergency preparedness.

Direct popular demand prodded some agencies into supplying more public information, but it seems to have had a negligible effect in fostering preparedness actions.

Two observations are important in understanding the pattern of response. First, earthquake-preparedness initiatives undertaken in the aftermath of the 1971 San Fernando–Sylmar earthquake were still active or were evolving tortuously. The vague and uncertain near predictions of 1976 underlined existing and recent concerns rather than opening up new concerns. The response of most agencies, therefore, was to resume or intensify attention to measures previously contemplated or in process.

Second, without meaning to be pejorative, we can distinguish between *working* agencies and *goading* agencies. The staff and resources of a typical working agency are fully committed and are insufficient to meet all of the goals normally set for the agency. Unless the plea of new responsibilities can bring augmented funding, new initiatives mean chiefly new problems for the agency. Agencies such as the Seismic Safety Commission and the Office of Emergency Services, however, are evaluated largely by what they can goad working agencies into doing. Hence, the more dramatic initiatives start with them. Their dire warnings, too, are more newsworthy than are working-agency tasks (such as the accelerated inspection of local dams or the painstaking reassessment of lifeliness for seismic safety). But with disaster a real possibility, the working agency cannot afford to be totally unresponsive to appeals from goading agencies. Through this two-stage process, then, of goading agency to working agency, the delayed response to earthquake prediction and near prediction begins to take shape.

The Media: Learning to Make News of the Earthquake Threat

To find out what southern Californians were being told about the earthquake threat, we devised a simple but time-consuming plan. For our primary data, we copied and filed every item dealing with earthquakes (news reports, editorials, letters, advertisements, and so on) from six newspapers, from January 1, 1976, through the end of January 1979. The two major metropolitan dailies in Los Angeles are the *Los Angeles Times* and the *Herald Examiner*. Three large-circulation dailies in different communities within the metropolis were included. The *Valley News* (now the *Daily News*) serves the 1 million-plus suburban residents of the San Fernando Valley, northwest of the city center, where the impact of the last destructive earthquake was most acute. The *San Gabriel Valley Tribune* serves another vast suburban region, to the northeast and mostly outside the city limits. Although untouched by destructive earthquakes within living memory, this region became a prime candidate when the uplift was interpreted as presaging destructive earthquakes along the southern edge of the San Gabriel Mountains. The *Santa Monica Evening Outlook* serves the socioeconomically relatively high-status west side of Los Angeles and the city of Santa Monica. Our sixth paper was *La Opinion*, the Spanish-language daily serving the largest ethnic minority in the metropolis.

The *Sentinel*, the leading newspaper aimed at the black community, was monitored for six months. Only one item dealing with earthquakes was located during this entire period. When our survey data indicated that most blacks read the *Times* or the *Herald Examiner*, we discontinued monitoring the *Sentinel*.

Each newspaper item was classified as reporting a current earthquake, as dealing with predictions and warnings of earthquakes, or as addressing earthquake safety and preparedness. Items were further subclassified and were listed under more than one major category or subclassification whenever appropriate. These operations gave us a quantitative record of rising and declining attention to earthquakes as well as of shifting attention from one aspect of earthquake concern to another.

We also listened regularly to prime-time newscasts on the major network television channels, recorded or secured scripts of all earthquake specials on television and radio, and collected magazine articles and book notices with the help of a large network of interested friends. The following brief account of media coverage in the year of the Palmdale bulge combines the quantitative analysis of newspaper coverage with the qualitative review of all media coverage.

How adequate are the newspaper tabulations as a basis for estimating all media coverage? Qualitatively, our review suggests that newspapers, television, and radio rely on standard sources for news. Hence, the same major events are usually covered by all media outlets. Newspaper coverage differs chiefly in that it consists of more extended and penetrating accounts and more frequent reporting of minor events. Similarly, differences of coverage by different newspapers or different television stations appear to be more accidental than systematic, except in ways that we shall note as the account proceeds.

Sixty-nine percent of the respondents in our basic survey said that they read a newspaper on a regular basis, including 24 percent who read two or more papers. The *Times* dominates, with 43.5 percent readership, followed distantly by the *Herald Examiner*, with 13.2 percent. The largest community daily, the *Valley News*, is read by 4.8 percent, *La Opinion* by 3.2 percent, the *Tribune* by 2.6 percent, and the *Outlook* by 1.8 percent. Eighty-eight percent of *Outlook* readers, 69 percent of *Valley News* readers, and 65 percent of *Herald Examiner* readers also follow another paper, mostly the *Times*. Only 39 percent of *Tribune* and 30 percent of *La Opinion* readers follow a second paper, with the *Times* leading but the *Herald Examiner* following closely. Forty-nine percent of the *Times* readers follow other papers.

When we look at this information in combination with the importance of television viewing (chapter three), there is evidently a great deal of media redundancy. We can thus safely assume that the omission of an important item of news by a particular newspaper or by a particular television or radio station does not preclude exposure to that item for most of their audience. We shall assume that the ensuing account of the main outlines of media coverage describes what most Angelenos were exposed to during the year of the bulge.

THE SOUTHERN CALIFORNIA UPLIFT

Initial attention to the uplift in February was meager, and even less in March (fig. 1). But attention soared in April, when the Seismic Safety Commission and the California Earthquake Prediction Evaluation Council rendered their verdicts, and the

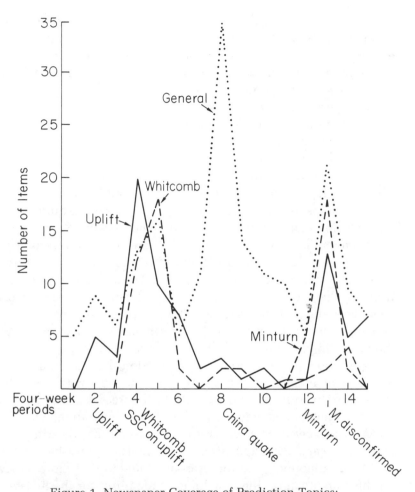

Figure 1. Newspaper Coverage of Prediction Topics:
January 1, 1976 to February 26, 1977

Whitcomb hypothesis reminded people of the earlier persisting earthquake threat. For three months, coverage remained higher than the initial response, and then it dropped to a low level from July until December. Minturn's forecast in November and a meeting of the American Geophysical Union in San Francisco in December then brought the uplift back into the news. Both the rise and fall of attention to Whitcomb's "hypothesis test" were steeper than those of attention to the uplift. The prompt response reflected the media's two months of accumulated experience with the uplift, association of the new warning with a local person rather than with a remote agency, and the political controversy stirred up by Councilman Nowell's attack on Whitcomb. The equally quick demise of interest resulted from the media's negative interpretation of CEPEC's prompt evaluation and from the lack of continuing developments comparable to the periodic reports of changes in the configuration and interpretation of the uplift. Attention to Minturn's pseudoprediction was even more short-lived, though the peak was of comparable height, and even higher if we count television and radio coverage.

Like a shadow cast by each new warning, more general discussion of earthquake prediction techniques, experience, and possible consequences peaked and declined in a similar pattern, with one notable exception. In midsummer, when the uplift and Whitcomb's hypothesis were seldom in the news, general discussions peaked higher than at any other time. Testimony in the campaign to enact Senator Cranston's earthquake research measure first triggered the rise, which was sharply accelerated by postmortems over the failure of the vaunted Chinese prediction program to anticipate the disastrous Tangshan earthquake of July 28 and by the predictions of aftershocks issued subsequently.

The *shadow pattern* of general prediction discussion and the reawakened interest in the uplift in connection with both the Whitcomb hypothesis and the Minturn forecast illustrate the media tendency to augment topical coverage by drawing on their recent past experience. Progress toward developing an earthquake prediction capability had been news for two years before the uplift was announced, so the press was able to find more to say on this topic than on the new topic of the uplift for the first two months. Three months of experience with the uplift as well as general prediction discussion then supplied material and leads for stories that capitalized on the interest aroused by Whitcomb's hypothesis test. In December, the media again dipped into the bag of past experience, often in lieu of directly acknowledging Minturn's forecasting.

That the uplift was initially newsworthy is hardly surprising. Indeed, the U.S. Geological Survey was forced to release the announcement several days before officials had planned to do so when their report was "leaked" to the *Los Angeles Times* science editor, George Alexander, by a third party. But why was the uplift consistently taken seriously and treated as a great-earthquake precursor? The initial reports and subsequent discussions conscientiously reiterated the scientific disclaimers. And occasional items, such as some that appeared in May, December, and January of 1977, presented alternative scientific interpretations. The uplift could be a continuation of the normal mountain-building that had created the 10,000- and 11,000-foot mountain ranges at the locked bend in the San Andreas Fault during past eons. Yet the sense that the uplift was the augury of a coming dread earthquake prevailed. And there was none of the ridicule that surfaced five years later in a *Los Angeles Times* article (April 9, 1981) discussing an earthquake forecast issued by investment advisor Joseph Granville under the headline "Quake 'Doomsday' Time Again":

> Rumors of a Big One about to hit also circulated in April, 1969, supposedly based on a death-bed prediction by the mystic Edgar Cayce. Then there was the more recent alarm over the Palmdale Bulge, a lump in the desert supposedly indicative of strain along the San Andreas Fault.

Several circumstances may have accounted for the relatively unquestioning acceptance of the dire meaning of the uplift. Two years of prior discussion of Chinese success and American progress in earthquake prediction techniques made the discovery of a great-earthquake precursory sign in southern California a natural and even expected development. Issuance of the announcement after ten days of media preoccupation with the tragic Guatemalan earthquake was inadvertently timely. The standard of serious exposition and respect for the science establishment set by *Los Angeles Times* science editor Alexander in the first account and in his continuing reportage influenced media treatment throughout the metropolis. And by inference from the "slant" in most articles and from the orientations of journalists we talked to, we concluded that the media personnel had a sense of mission. Earthquakes are an ever-present threat in southern California. After five years, many of the lessons from the San Fernando earthquake were already being forgotten, and anything that would dramatically reawaken people to the need for earthquake preparedness was a good thing.

But why did the newsworthiness of the uplift persist with a new surge of attention in December and, as we shall see in Part

Five, at later intervals? First, the stamp of authenticity from the USGS, California state earthquake preparedness agencies, and Caltech drew respect from media personnel who overwhelmingly looked favorably toward the professional and scientific establishments. And, unlike the one-shot announcements by Whitcomb and Minturn, the uplift was a developing phenomenon, generating new items of news at frequent intervals. In late May and early June, USGS scientists reported that the uplift was higher and wider than had previously been thought. Continuing research suggested that the 1971 San Fernando quake and the 1973 Point Mugu tremor were associated with the uplift. In December scientists reported discovering land subsidence on the coastal side of the San Gabriel Mountains, which they related to the uplift. The start of the reassessment period was marked by the first of several reports of subsidence over portions of the original uplift, a development that was not soon interpreted as meaning that the earthquake threat had diminished.

Also keeping interest alive was the intimate connection between the presence of the uplift and the need for action to reduce the loss of life and property in a great earthquake. This connection was established in the original release for the USGS and was reinforced by official pronouncements from the Seismic Safety Commission and the Office of Emergency Services. We shall say more about that connection later in this chapter.

Finally, the open-endedness of uplift warning kept it newsworthy, in contrast to the closed-endedness of Whitcomb's and Minturn's forecasts. Minturn's December 20 forecast might have remained newsworthy in spite of disconfirmation, like the belief systems of many religious cults that have survived and even thrived after a forecasted "second coming" failed to materialize, if a cult had formed around Minturn.[1] But the zero-lead-time, open-ended time window character of the near prediction made the uplift itself an object of interest as a continuing source for new signs that the threat had grown or receded.

The actual reports on the uplift and many of the general prediction discussions followed an *alarm-and-reassurance* pattern.[2] As if to jolt people out of their complacency, story after story reiterated that 14,000 dangerously unreinforced buildings remained in the Los Angeles area and that between 3,000 and 12,000 people could be killed and 48,000 injured, with $25 billion in property damage sustained, in a quake that generated 540 times as much energy as the San Fernando earthquake. Much of the standard fare was taken from the USGS's briefing to the governor's office in March. The stress each time was on the worst that could be expected. And although words such as *could* were faithfully used, the reasoning proceeded as though *could* was the same as *would*. Because of this, the coverage might often have been called sensationalistic, and the sense of inevitability it conveyed may have made the recommended actions seem trivial or pointless.

As though fearing the negative consequences of unduly alarming their readers and listeners, journalists typically included in the same news item information that was designed to be reassuring. Reminders that most southern California buildings fare well in earthquakes, that legislation would be enacted to deal with unsafe structures, that government agencies were making necessary preparations for the quake, that scientists were closely monitoring the uplift, and that there was no reason to suppose that the great quake was imminent all served to offset the initial alarm. We will try to ascertain in later chapters to what extent the seeming contradiction of the alarm-and-reassurance pattern left people confused, fostered an unjustified sense of certainty and imminence about the earthquake, reinforced fatalistic attitudes, encouraged complacency, or promoted the conviction that new protective measures and a more precise prediction would come before the actual event.

There were exceptions to the more sensational treatments of the uplift. On various occasions, Clarence Allen, a geophysicist from Caltech, was quoted as reminding people that there was no reason to suppose that a great earthquake was imminent and that the ability to predict great quakes was still ten years in the future.

WHITCOMB'S HYPOTHESIS TEST

In the short span of sixteen days, during which there were newspaper items almost daily and frequent television and radio reports, the treatment of Whitcomb's hypothesis test forecast was more varied and controversial than treatment of the uplift had been. Early reports combined discussion of both announcements, even though Whitcomb carefully explained that his forecast was based on entirely different evidence from that concerning the uplift. Whitcomb himself quickly became a media personality as his background, disposition, and motives were probed in television interviews and newspaper features. A front-page streamer two years earlier (April 11, 1964) in the street edition of the Times had already heralded Whitcomb's successful prediction of an earthquake just east of the metropolitan region. Times writer Betty Liddick's portrayal of Whitcomb as a modest and committed researcher who suddenly felt the unaccustomed weight of public scrutiny, rather than as a hero or "wild-eyed scientist eager for the limelight," suggests the kind of stereotyped meanings that were often attached to Whitcomb's pronouncement. Readers and listeners were often reminded of Whitcomb's reassurance that he would not hesitate to remain in the epicentral zone and that only such commonsense precautions as removing heavy stereo speakers from the walls were recommended. The chance to air curiosity about the person of the predictor greatly enhanced the immediate newsworthiness of the forecast.

Controversy made the announcement more fun and gave the media more to talk about. In part, the controversy was made available to the media by the raging debate over whether Whitcomb was provoking needless panic and depressed property values, especially in the San Fernando Valley. Bankers, real estate brokers, and insurance agents were interviewed for their observations on whether property values were plummeting and on whether there was a rush to buy earthquake insurance. Answers to both questions were consistently negative.

But by now media personnel had had the benefit of two months to familiarize themselves with the realistic prospect of earthquake prediction. Caught unprepared by the uplift, the media handled the news passively and without editorial punctuation. But Whitcomb's announcement brought a series of positive editorials in the Times and an editorial in the Santa Monica Evening Outlook that was critical of Whitcomb for disregarding the danger of panic and of a supposed "countdown syndrome." The Valley News, serving the targeted area, steered a neutral course by criticizing neither Whitcomb nor Councilman Nowell but instead by urging valley residents editorially not to panic because of the prediction. The Times, the San Gabriel Valley Tribune, and La Opinion (which had ignored the uplift) also published "man-on-the-street" interviews displaying the range of public response to the announcement. Some were highly critical, such as the valley resident who said: "I think that's the most stupid, the craziest thing you people could do. We've got so many panicky people here in Sylmar. You want to bet we're going to have half of Sylmar putting up their homes for sale?" But most reactions echoed one man's resignation: "I'm not worried anymore. If it comes, it comes." Pulitzer Prize-winning *Times* cartoonist Conrad pictured a headless chicken running madly about, shouting "The earth is quaking! The earth is quaking!"

One aspect of the media's active stance was the prompt featuring of action implications by all the monitored newspapers, television channels, and radio stations. The question of what we should be doing about the earthquake threat was a prominent feature of news coverage from the start.

Whitcomb's credentials as a scientist were not called into question, though the wisdom of his public announcement was hotly debated. But inherent ambiguities in the location and magnitude of the anticipated quake were "resolved" in media treatment by informally equating the quake with the 1971 San Fernando earthquake. The magnitude of the San Fernando quake slightly exceeded the upper limit of the magnitude range announced by Whitcomb, so discussions were premised (as with the uplift) on a worst-case eventuality. Although the idea of a hypothesis test was poorly understood and explained everywhere except in the *Times*, a careful reading of most news items would have conveyed to the reader the kinds of scientific qualifications attached to the announcement. But headlines often obliterated ambiguities, and early headlines conveyed the impression of an unqualified prediction. And CEPEC's hedged evaluation of Whitcomb's forecast was headlined as an outright repudiation.

The alarm-and-reassurance pattern was again prominent. By now, officials from public utilities and disaster relief agencies could offer well-rehearsed assurances that they were prepared for an earthquake. Always quotable, Whitcomb reminded people that the quake hazard was less than the risk one assumes in driving on a southern California freeway. And humor, strikingly absent from early consideration of the uplift, cropped up to leaven the moods of doom or indignation. Both the *Times* and *Tribune* quoted a man whose wife proposed that they buy a pair of motorcycle helmets and wear them as protection at home. Another citizen declared his intention to continue playing tennis during any tremor, "but not to a fault!" Popular *Times* columnist Jack Smith wrote a humorous account of the odd selection of belongings people try to salvage during an earthquake or other disaster. Acceptance of the earthquake threat as an appropriate subject for humor was a critical step in *normalizing* it—that is, treating it as something that could be acknowledged without substantially disrupting normal life routines.

The peak of interest in Whitcomb's forecast made the sudden termination of media attention that followed even more dramatic. Besides the reasons we have already cited, two other circumstances may have hastened the end of the attention. First, Whitcomb himself was disillusioned after going public by the violent criticism heaped upon him from some quarters and by bombardment with hostile telephone calls. Hence, he made himself less available. Second, beginning May 6, concern over casualties and destruction wrought by the earthquake and aftershocks in the Friuli region of Italy and in neighboring Yugoslavia seemed to monopolize the interest in the subject of earthquakes. As we shall see in chapter four, the void that followed in discussion of the local earthquake threat may have spurred grass-roots information-seeking and rumor.

CONVEYING SCIENTIFIC CONCEPTS

The problem of conveying a complex set of scientific ideas to the lay public was handled differently by different media. Television and radio generally featured brief, bare-bones items as part of the news. Except in the occasional earthquake "special," there was no time for explanation or subtlety. Except for a series of reports on the American Geophysical Union meetings in San Fernando in December, the Spanish-language daily ignored the uplift altogether. The three English-language community papers relied on Associated Press and United Press International wire services for reports that made only cursory efforts to convey an understanding of the basis for the alarm over the uplift, for the theory being tested by Whitcomb, and for other aspects of earthquake dynamics. In contrast, stories in the *Los Angeles Times* were written by full-time science editor George Alexander, who had early developed an interest in earthquake prediction. His accounts were skillful expositions, free from jargon or unnecessary oversimplification and effective in conveying a reasonable understanding of geological processes. He also tried to convey an understanding of the nature of the scientific process, as in one notable article featuring the way in which the public had been allowed a glimpse into the inner workings of science in the case of Whitcomb's hypothesis test. And it was Alexander who thoroughly unmasked Henry Minturn in an exhaustive examination of Minturn's claimed credentials and previous successes and of the bases for his current forecasts. Because of the dominance of the *Times* in the Los Angeles metropolis, a large share of the population had access to several installments of high-grade popular science writing. Alexander's articles were also usually prominently placed in the paper, rather than hidden on back pages as so often is the lot of scientific essays.

Except for Alexander's articles, the items in newspapers and on radio and television tended to be repetitive of what had been reported earlier. While each story did have something new to say, the novelty was often lost in the repetition of old news. The practice of starting from the beginning each time left little time to develop a more profound understanding in readers and listeners. In addition, repetition often meant the perpetuation of obsolete conclusions. For example, although in May it was reported that USGS scientists now saw the earthquake threat from the uplift as applying to lesser faults on the coastal side of the San Gabriel Mountains, subsequent reports uncritically repeated the initial assumption that the threat was an earthquake on the San Andreas Fault. In part, the practice of reporting each new development as though readers and listeners were innocent of prior knowledge is a matter of editorial policy. But often it is the consequence of assigning a different reporter to each new development, so writers may have only superficial acquaintance with previous news on earthquake prediction and dynamics.

THE MINTURN FIASCO

On November 22, after several months of relative media silence about earthquake forecasts, Henry Minturn was presented to southern California audiences during the 11 P.M.

news on KNBC-(TV). Addressed as "doctor," he was identified as a geophysicist who had accurately predicted a small quake felt over much of the Los Angeles basin only that morning. During the interview, he forecast an earthquake in southern California on December 20. His predictions were said to be based on the gravitational pull of the moon on "weak arches" in the earth's crust. And he carried affidavits testifying to a string of previously confirmed predictions, especially in Latin America.

Minturn, as a maverick scientist unconnected with the earthquake establishment, became an instant celebrity. He was featured not only on local television and radio but also eventually in the national network news. The regular Metromedia television news at 10:30 P.M. on November 29 reported an earthquake that day in Santiago, Chile. The commentator remarked that "Dr. Minturn" had predicted this quake on the news and that it had occurred as predicted, adding: "Remember, he predicts a quake to occur in southern California December 20." On the 11 P.M. NBC-TV news that same evening, viewers were told: "A California man's prediction for an earthquake in South America today came true. Tonight, his prediction for December involves us." Minturn was interviewed on the program to confirm his success in predicting several earlier quakes and to reiterate his predictions for December 7 and 20. At one point the interviewer commented, "Many scientists question Minturn's technique, but they cannot question his results." The following day on KFI radio, Hilly Rose, moderator of a popular daytime talk show, was critical of Minturn's predictions, mentioning Peter Ward from the USGS as an authority but basing his skepticism mostly on his long personal experience as a resident of earthquake country.

Our six area newspapers studiously ignored Minturn for nine days, until public interest had escalated to a level they could no longer ignore. Then their perspectives were uniformly critical, although they did not at first question Minturn's credentials. On December 1 the *Tribune* quoted Peter Ward of the USGS as having said that Minturn had apparently "learned enough code words to make himself sound authentic" and that the television network featuring him had been "taken for a ride" (also reported in the *Herald Examiner*, December 5). On December 2 both the *Valley News* and the *Santa Monica Evening Outlook* quoted Caltech's Clarence Allen as saying that reliable prediction was still ten

years in the future. The *Outlook* avoided specific mention of
Minturn in its article, headlined "Quake Forecast Said Pointless
Until Accurate." Allen was again quoted on December 5 by the
Herald Examiner as saying that Minturn's claim that his predic-
tion for an earthquake south of Mexico City was confirmed by a
quake on the border between Chile and Peru was "like saying
that an earthquake in Boston satisfies a prediction for southern
California."

December 5 also brought George Alexander's lengthy article in
the *Times* that devastatingly unmasked Minturn by reporting that
his employment record showed no evidence of more than a high
school education or of relevant professional experience and by
demonstrating that the plausible basis for his prediction technique
had been discredited by scientific research in past years. Many of
Alexander's points quickly found their way into the other newspapers, which also stopped referring to Minturn by the title of
doctor. The *Times* followed up on December 8 with an editorial
critical of both Minturn and the broadcast media that had given
him his forum.

During prime-time (7:30 P.M.) on December 7, Clete Roberts,
well known for many years on Los Angeles television, devoted
his hour-long weekly program on the public service channel to
interviewing Minturn. He questioned Minturn about documents
from his actual working history but did not confront him with his
earlier claims that he held a Ph.D. or was a qualified geophysicist.
In discussing his predictions, Minturn claimed that a quake 900
miles north of the Solomon Islands on December 5 satisfied his
December 7 prediction. In this and in subsequent discussions, the
prediction was said to have been made for the Solomon Islands,
while our transcripts of earlier programs contain reference only
to a location north of Australia. Thus, by inadequate verification
of past announcements, the media seem to have allowed the gap
between the locations of prediction and occurrence to narrow.
When questioned by Roberts about "the fact that you missed it
[by] a day and a half and 900 miles," Minturn retorted: "Well,
may I say that the only other current forecast made by any
geophysicist that I know of is for one to occur in California within
one year. So I don't think missing it a day and a half is too far
off!" Concerning the forecast for December 20, Minturn offered
what was probably his first hint concerning magnitude, saying,

"Now, I do not anticipate a large earthquake in this area. . . . I think we'll be lucky if we feel it." Our own impression from viewing this program was that Minturn came out rather well and that the moderator was pulling his punches.

Once the declaration by the director of the state Office of Emergency Services that Minturn's prediction was "so vague it is useless" had appeared in all the sampled newspapers between December 11 and 16, Minturn vanished from the press except for reports about the failure of his forecast after December 20. Indeed, the disconfirmation provoked so little in the way of postmortems that most of the public were probably sheltered from the lessons that might have been learned from this fiasco.

Why NBC and some of the other local television and radio stations gave Minturn a respectful public hearing without first investigating his credentials is a question we cannot answer satisfactorily. But the announcement was preceded by two periods of exceptional rumoring about imminent disastrous local earthquakes (chapter four). Calls to Caltech were so numerous and urgent that a standard disclaimer was prepared, and the *Times* reluctantly acknowledged the prevalence of the rumors and attempted to refute them on November 4 and 25. The popular demand for earthquake prediction news after the post-Whitcomb hiatus, along with the widespread disposition to believe that news of impending danger was being withheld from the public, probably contributed to an uncritical media response. The same public hunger for news quickly propelled what might have been a flash-in-the-pan exposure into a media event. We have been told, but cannot verify, that local television personnel soon recognized their error but were overruled in their desire to downplay Minturn by eastern-based national network editors who saw only news value and confirmation for stereotyped views of California. Newspapers that had tried not to fuel the rumors by acknowledging them in print and even by denying them continued the same strategy when calls to local earthquake "authorities" made them dubious of Minturn's forecast. In belatedly acknowledging the forecast, all the sample papers made a point of the tremendous public concern it had stirred up.

Aside from the propitious moment of his appearance, Minturn was newsworthy in several ways. His predictions were specific as to time. Furthermore, his simultaneous prediction of three successive and contingent events gave viewers two chances to score a hit or a miss in distant locations before watching the climax at home. His reference to the gravitational effect of the moon on opposite sides of the earth was superficially understandable and plausible. His television manner and appearance inspired confidence.

The ambiguity of the uplift and of Whitcomb's hypothesis test was often disturbing. To many people, the fact that scientists admitted they didn't really know whether there would be an earthquake or not, or just when it would occur, was translated into the feeling that the scientists did not really know what they were talking about. Minturn's simple assurance and his willingness to name specific dates impressed many people who felt that at last, here was someone who knew what he was talking about. It is the scientist's burden that informed uncertainty will often be interpreted as muddleheadedness.

Minturn was an apt symbol for the well-known populist theme in American culture. He was a maverick, not associated with "big science." He showed the world that truth was much simpler than the experts make it seem. He demonstrated that a resourceful person relying substantially on common sense could solve problems that remained insoluble to professionals whose methods and laboratories kept them out of touch with the real world. To the most confirmed populists, he was even more impressive when stripped of his educational credentials, for he now became the truly self-made man. And he asked only to be judged by his success in predicting earthquakes, not by theories and professional collegiality. Once this image was set, one could hardly be surprised that the experts, still unsuccessful in their own efforts to predict earthquakes, should attempt to discredit Minturn. Again, when it was approached in a predisposing frame of mind, the fact that scientists were unwilling to assert equally categorically that there would *not* be an earthquake on December 20 confirmed suspicions that they realized Minturn knew things that they did not or that he was predicting the disaster they knew was coming but were afraid to announce.

As our survey data show (chapter five), another sizable population, believing that Minturn was a credentialed scientist and in some cases mistaking Minturn for Caltech's Whitcomb, were only confused and dismayed by the outcry against him.

The confusion was not lifted when the newspeople who had first sponsored Minturn simply discontinued mentioning him rather than publicly confessing their error. The powerful authentication by prime-time television news personalities was never explicitly withdrawn.

Much of the public criticism of Minturn was addressed neither to his deliberate falsification of credentials nor to the vulnerability of his claims to a record of successful predictions. Instead, the familiar questions addressed to all forecasters were pulled out of the media's bag of past experience—namely, that it is irresponsible to publish a prediction that may strike terror into the hearts of many, many people. The recurrent question of whether predictions should be announced at all became a red herring, diverting attention from the question of whether Minturn's forecasts were justified at all. And media personnel lacked the initiative to obtain from the USGS lists of earthquakes with which to demonstrate that anyone forecasting at random in seismically active zones and counting as success events of any magnitude within a radius of a thousand miles or more would nearly always be right.

The shadow pattern for general prediction items can be observed here as it was with the uplift and Whitcomb's hypothesis test. In addition, items of earthquake preparedness and safety escalated during this period, though not exclusively in response to interest in Minturn's forecasts. This media saturation with earthquake items may have enhanced public conviction that something awesome was imminent. Unconvinced media personnel may have inadvertently fanned the flames by attempting to satisfy the heightened interest, even though only four out of twenty-seven preparedness items specifically mentioned Minturn or his forecasts.

In comparison to the February and April announcements, treatment of Minturn did not clearly follow the alarm-and-reassurance pattern. Minturn was vague about earthquake magnitude from the start, but his forecast was treated as a warning of disaster. Only after two weeks of a crescendo of concern was Minturn seen as reassuring people that the earthquake would be a mild one.

SEERS

Before leaving predictions and forecasts, we must take notice of the occasional forecasts by seers. These do not appear in our charts because they were usually ignored by main-line newspapers and were featured instead on television and radio, in books, and in periodicals, such as the *National Enquirer,* that are sold at supermarket checkout counters. At intervals throughout the year, one or more of these large-circulation, "supermarket" papers featured forecasts for the coming year by several seers. Earthquakes were usually included among the forecasts. Perhaps the most significant event of this kind was the personal appearance of well-known seer Clarissa Bernhart on the popular *Merv Griffin Show* on Wednesday evening, October 6. In a familiar format, Bernhart reported previously successful earthquake forecasts and conveyed the impression that the USGS paid special attention to her forecasts. The discourse then featured vague references to a great deal of future earthquake activity, with repeated mention of March 8, 1978 (without specification of what was to happen then), a strong suggestion that California would sink beneath the sea, and the forecast that by 2025 we should be able to drive overland to Hawaii.

IMPLICATIONS OF THE EARTHQUAKE THREAT:
ORGANIZATION AND HOUSEHOLD PREPAREDNESS

Like discussion of the uplift itself, attention to its implications was slow in coming. Again, the Seismic Safety Commission provided stimulus in its March meeting, identifying the high-priority tasks confronting the community. The *Times* faithfully reported on the meeting, but the *Valley News* offered the most comprehensive attention to earthquake preparedness, citing the uplift, in a six-part series from April 4 to 13. Actions most often advocated in light of the uplift were to review and fine-tune local government preparedness programs; to draft and pass hazard mitigation legislation at local, state, and national levels; and to foster scientific progress in quake prediction techniques. The April 8 SSC meeting, calling for action by various agencies, turned news media attention to agency and organizational preparedness. Newspaper coverage of this kind of preparedness was higher during April and May than at any other time during the year (fig. 2). A lesser peak followed in December, when Minturn spurred renewed attention to the adequacy of government agency earthquake preparedness. A majority of these items included reports from

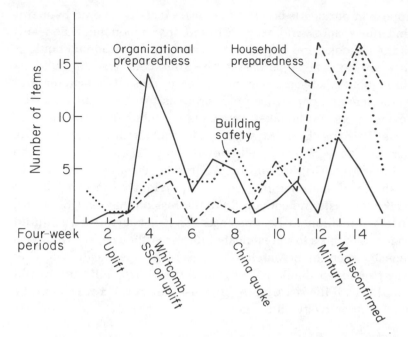

Figure 2. Newspaper Coverage of Earthquake Preparedness and Safety:
January 1, 1976 to February 26, 1977

various agencies concerning their preparations, reassuring the
public that everything was under control.

The most striking feature of the graph is the difference in the
curves for organizational (and agency) preparedness and for individual and household preparedness. After the initial delay, organizational preparedness peaked quickly, declining somewhat
while attention to Whitcomb was peaking, and never again approaching the initial high level. Advice to households and individuals responded only weakly to the uplift and Whitcomb
notices, dropping to nothing, then rising slowly from midyear and
suddenly soaring to a high peak in November, December, and
January. The high rates at year's end are partly explained by a
series entitled "Common Sense and Earthquake Survival," included serially or as a special supplement in several newspapers.
The author was Fil Drukey, a private citizen who was reportedly
concerned with the lack of advice for families and who privately
researched and wrote the series for general distribution.

This difference brings us back to an earlier observation, that the
media are heavily dependent upon organizational input for their

news and features. With some notable exceptions, in elaborating on newsworthy events media personnel turn to government agencies, universities, and other organizations to tell them what themes they should develop and to provide the material to use in developing the themes. Organizations often assume the initiative by calling the press and by issuing press releases. The goading agencies use their leverage on working agencies that already include earthquake planning in their patterns of organization.

These working agencies have mechanisms through which to develop reasonably prompt responses. Each agency has specialized responsibilities and reports back after a necessary lag for organizational planning. The reports of these agencies, such as utilities, police and fire departments, communication facilities, the Red Cross, and public schools, are necessarily restricted to their own specialized functions. And since the proposals originate mostly within the affected agencies, they deal more conspicuously with what has already been done than with what ought yet to be done.

But who speaks to or for families and individuals? Without grass-roots organization to encourage family preparedness and without a responsible agency, there is no one to encourage the media and to provide them with material to use in featuring household preparedness. As a consequence, we saw occasional sketchy sets of recommendations addressed to households, but no comprehensive treatment until nine months had elapsed. And the Drukey series remains largely a onetime document, not a program to be revised and supplemented periodically.

Besides the Drukey series, there was a substantial increase in items on household preparedness during the Minturn interlude and immediately after. We believe that the OES media "spots" and the notices enclosed with telephone bills may have fostered thinking along these lines. Here was a goading agency attempting to stir households as well as organizations to protective action. And the continuing public demand for survival advice may have had a cumulative effect on the media by this time.

BUILDING SAFETY

The safety of several thousand buildings that predated the 1934 seismic safety codes was both a continuing theme in earthquake prediction discussions and a topic of independent concern. A campaign to do something about this hazard began in the aftermath of the San Fernando-Sylmar earthquake of 1971 and was limping along at the beginning of 1976. In January, before the uplift was announced, the Los Angeles City Board of Building and Safety Commissioners received a proposal to eliminate or renovate an estimated 300 old "assembly" buildings. Responding to vocal opposition from church and theater spokespersons, the board referred the measure back to the Building and Safety Department manager for extensive revision. Newspaper coverage was perfunctory, and the issue was largely forgotten in February and March. Then, from April to August, treatment of building safety was principally linked to discussion of the uplift and of Whitcomb's forecast or to general prediction discussions. Ten articles during this period combined the themes of prediction and building safety. By August, the media had conveyed an emerging consensus among engineers, scientists, and government officials that potentially unsafe old buildings presented the most significant threat to public safety in an earthquake. After August, attention to building safety dealt primarily with proposals and debates in the Los Angeles City Council on December 9 and January 17. The peak of attention came a month after the Minturn disconfirmation and just as our field survey was being launched.

Newspapers, television, and radio were consistent in reporting and accepting the consensus, but they also reported the objections raised against each new proposal to deal with the problem. The hub of the controversy was whether the threat of a massive earthquake was sufficiently great to justify dislocation of thousands of area residents and economic hardship for hundreds of small businesses. Only the *Times* took sides, urging strong action in a series of editorials.

DAM AND NUCLEAR SAFETY

The safety of dams and nuclear power plants is affected by earthquakes, but the issues are different from those present in questions of organizational and household preparedness and of building safety. The construction of a dam is an environmental and a safety issue, although the safety of existing dams in California is questioned principally in relation to earth-quakes. The main opposition to nuclear power applies equally to regions with and without earthquakes. In each case, the earth-quake threat becomes an aggravating circumstance. In addition, the popular environmental movement and a vigorous antinuclear movement lead the opposition to unacceptable projects. The movement organizations supply material and attempt to influence the media, and there is polarized controversy. Our question concerns how earthquake threat and the issues of dam and nuclear power safety intersected in the year of the Palmdale bulge.

Dam safety received little attention during the year. What little discussion there was dealt mostly with the significance of earth-quake faults near the site of the proposed Auburn Dam, 500 miles away in northern California. These stories did not mention the situation in southern California. Only the *Valley News*, serving the 1971 evacuation area, paid more than perfunctory attention to the threat of dam collapse in southern California in the event of an earthquake, and it linked the discussion to the uplift. In spite of the dramatic days of suspense over the fate of the Van Norman Dam during the 1971 quake and the disastrous col-lapse of the Idaho Teton Dam in June of 1976, dam safety in an earthquake remained one of the most neglected topics for media discourse.

Nuclear safety received considerable attention until midyear and then vanished from the press for the remainder of the year. The discussions dealt principally with a continuing debate over the threat posed by an earthquake fault near the Diablo Canyon nuclear power plant, under construction about 135 miles north of the metropolis, and over Proposition 15 on the June 8 state ballot. Proposition 15 would have placed severe restrictions on the con-struction and operation of nuclear power plants. Its supporters frequently stressed the threat from earthquakes and occasionally mentioned the uplift. There was, however, no real joining of forces between earthquake safety and antinuclear power constituencies, perhaps because no nuclear plant was sited in the vicinity of the uplift. As a result, after the measure was defeated in the June election, no further connections were drawn between the two concerns until mid-1977.

In general, then, public controversy about dam safety and nu-clear safety meant temporary attention to the earthquake threat.

But it had no enduring effect on either the level or the nature of the concern for earthquake safety, as conveyed in the media.

EARTHQUAKES AT HOME AND ABROAD

We conclude our account by mentioning briefly the most numerous news items. Throughout our study period, the accounts of earthquakes in the United States and abroad outnumbered all other coverage combined. The reports ranged from the lengthy, daily, human-interest coverage of such tragedies as the Guatemalan and Friuli quakes, with pictorial enhancement, to the one-sentence "filler" reporting a small quake in a California desert region. The significant observation for our purposes is how seldom any connections or lessons were drawn from earthquakes in the news for local earthquake safety and preparedness. Perhaps three circumstances account for this failure. First, while minor quakes are simply taken in stride, disastrous earthquakes evoke a response of compassion, marked each time by an outpouring of gifts for the victims. The sentiment and norm of altruism on such occasions may preclude a more "selfish" concern for our own safety. Second, newspaper reporting is departmentalized, so different staffs are responsible for the two kinds of items. Third, dependent as the media are on material prepared for them by government agencies and other organizations, it is only when the Earthquake Engineering Research Institute or similar organization sends a study delegation to the site of a foreign quake that the connection is made.

Summary and Conclusions

Response to announcement of the uplift by government agencies, organizations, and the media began slowly. After six or seven weeks, the California Office of Emergency Services launched communications with local and state government agencies, and the Seismic Safety Commission publicly declared the uplift "a possible threat to public safety and welfare in the greater Los Angeles metropolitan area." But response to Whitcomb's earthquake "forecast," two months after announcement of the uplift, was speedy if marked by controversy. The OES and SSC actions, accented by Whitcomb's announcement, overcame community inertia to inspire a flurry of governmental and organizational activity that lasted for most of the year and soon provided grist for the news mills. After first insisting that the languishing earthquake safety programs initiated following the 1971 San Fernando–Sylmar earthquake were adequate for dealing with the new earthquake crisis, most public and private agencies concerned with public safety had announced new preparedness programs before year's end, as had the county schools.

The media were as ill prepared as government and private agencies to deal with the newly intensified earthquake threat, responding equally slowly and relying largely on the work of these agencies for their material. Only after two months of desultory coverage did media attention to the uplift soar, and it remained high for three months. Media attention to the Whitcomb forecast and other prediction topics was also high during this period. By July, both announcements had receded into the background. They remained there until a combination of events, including Minturn's forecast, brought them back to front stage in December. The more general discussion of earthquake prediction generally rose and fell like a shadow cast by the attention given to specific warnings and forecasts, except in midsummer, when attention to proposed federal earthquake preparedness legislation and the disastrous unpredicted Tangshan earthquake in China stimulated the highest level of general prediction discussion of the entire year.

Because of the controversy and because the media had by then accumulated some experience, the brief period of peak attention to Whitcomb's forecast was more exciting and certainly much more fun than the attention to the uplift. The media were now ready to take sides on the issue of whether such forecasts should be publicly released or not, and the first reports from various agencies on what they had done or could do to prepare for an earthquake provided material for "what-to-do-about-it" discussions. The media shared in a prevalent tendency to diminish the ambiguities in Whitcomb's announcement by translating "hypothesis test" into "prediction" and rendering place and time more specific. But the fun stopped rather suddenly when the media similarly glossed over the contrived ambiguities in a somewhat negative pronouncement on Whitcomb's forecast by the California Earthquake Prediction Evaluation Council.

Reasons for the sudden play of media attention in late November and December to a forecast by Minturn remain in some respects a mystery. NBC first provided him a stage and de facto authentication for his forecast of December 20 earthquake in Los Angeles. Other television and radio stations quickly followed suit. Major newspapers were skeptical, but they remained silent long enough for Minturn fever to reach a high pitch. Eventually, a carefully researched unmasking by the Los Angeles Times science editor encouraged other media to publish their reservations. In all probability, a public hunger for news—manifested in two unparalleled rumor surges in October and November—and the chance of a scoop undercut normal media caution. The definiteness and specificity of Minturn's forecast, in contrast to the ambiguity of the uplift and Whitcomb warnings, were publicly appealing. Minturn was dignified and self-assured in public appearance, explained his method simply, and supplied affidavits to authenticate successful prediction of many previous earthquakes. As his repudiation by the seismology establishment became well advertised, he gained additional appeal as a populist hero. Furthermore, without mentioning Minturn, the media often capitalized on the reawakened interest in the earthquake threat to create a new surge of attention to earthquake prediction and preparedness, reinforcing a widespread suspicion that something must be brewing.

Despite the inauspicious beginning, the uplift remained newsworthy while other prediction items had their days and dropped out of public attention. The stamp of authenticity from key government agencies, the occurrence of periodic new developments in the uplift saga, the intimate connection made between the uplift and the need for action to reduce the loss of life and property in a great earthquake, and the open-endedness of the uplift drama all helped to sustain its newsworthiness, at least for a year and probably for three to four years.

People may have been confused by an alarm-and-reassurance pattern in many media presentations. Typically, news and feature stories began with dramatized accounts of worst-possible scenarios, as though to shake readers out of their lethargy, and concluded with reassurances about the seismic resistivity of most local construction and other mitigating circumstances, as though to quiet the alarm so deliberately generated.

Except for outstanding science reporting in the *Los Angeles Times,* much of the reporting on the earthquake threat was superficial, repetitive, and lacking in scientific perspective. Although the media conscientiously quoted leading experts in the earthquake field, they tended to shift discussion from substantive issues to personalities and to such ethical issues as whether earthquake forecasts *should* be made public.

Media attention to earthquake preparedness was of three principal kinds, each of which followed a distinctive pattern. Organizational preparedness peaked early, as public and private agencies were goaded into action by the Office of Emergency Services and the Seismic Safety Commission. As agencies complied with the demand to reassess preparedness, their reports provided material on organizational preparedness for the media. Building safety discussions peaked at different times, reflecting the course of debate in the Los Angeles City Council over a proposed ordinance for dealing with seismically unsafe structures. Individual and household preparedness items did not peak until nine months after the uplift announcement, and then principally because one private citizen took the initiative in assembling a comprehensive set of suggestions. Because the media depend upon public and private agencies for most of their material and because no organization has primary responsibility for individual and household safety in an earthquake, this vital area of family concern was given short shrift for most of the year by the media.

Politically charged controversies over dam safety and nuclear power plant safety both had frequent reference to earthquake danger. However, there was no real joining together of dam and nuclear power safety issues with earthquake safety issues in the Los Angeles region.

Although the absolute amount of coverage was not great, the people of southern California were widely exposed at repeated intervals throughout the year of the Palmdale bulge to the existence and potentially threatening significance of the uplift, the more general questions of earthquake prediction and warning, the unsolved problem of what to do about 14,000 old and potentially unsafe buildings, and evidence that many government agencies were at least talking about being prepared for a great earthquake. For one brief period, they were invited into the controversy over a peculiar announcement that a Caltech researcher called a hypothesis test, and for four weeks they shared suspense and apprehension over a series of down-to-earth forecasts by a man who was widely credited with an unparalleled record of successful predictions.

Depending upon how people used the media, the groundwork was laid for widespread heightened awareness of earthquake threat and the need for both public and private preparedness. The existence of much confusion would also not be surprising.

CHAPTER THREE

The People Listen and Talk

In the preceding chapter we reviewed the treatment of prediction and other earthquake topics by the local mass media. We must now ask to what extent people actually relied on the mass media in forming their opinions about the earthquake threat. It would be surprising if the media were not the principal source of information and imagery. However, students of mass communications agree that media messages are often filtered through preexisting interpersonal networks by informal discussion for verification and further interpretation. Certain intermediaries play crucial roles in this filtering process. Before deciding upon a course of action, people frequently seek confirmation of the information disseminated by the media through face-to-face consultation with an *opinion leader*.[1] According to the classic *two-step flow* model, information from the mass media is disseminated first to socially recognized opinion leaders, who in turn relay it to less active segments of the public.[2] While prior research has not addressed the significance of opinion leaders in shaping disaster response, many investigators have reported that people often turn to others for advice and information before deciding to evacuate or to make other adaptive responses.[3] In this chapter we shall address the following three questions: How much have people relied on the media? How important is the filtering of communication through informal discussion? What part is played by opinion leaders?

The Mass Media

In order to find out where people acquired the information and misinformation they had, we posed the following question:

> We'd now like to ask you some questions regarding where you have heard about earthquakes. During the past year, have you heard about earthquakes or earthquake predictions or earthquake preparedness from *any* of the following sources?

Respondents answered "yes" or "no" to each item on a list of sources, as given in figure 3. The sources "people" and "organizations" were not on the list that was read to the respondents, but they were frequently mentioned in response to the query, "Any other source?"

Not unexpectedly, television news ranked first as a source of information. This is consistent with recent evidence that increasing percentages of the U.S. population receive most of their news about world events from television.[4] A 1974 Gallup Poll also reported that television is the most credible news medium in the United States. In studies conducted for the Television Information Office between 1959 and 1976, 51 percent of the people said that in case of conflicting reports from radio, television, magazines, or newspapers, they would be most inclined to believe television reports.[5] With its large and credulous audience, television ensured a hearing in 1976 for at least one earthquake forecaster who bypassed scientific authorities, with television news acting as the chief source of information about Henry Minturn's forecast from November 22 until December 1, when newspapers first acknowledged it.

Newspapers ranked second as an information source. Over three-fourths of the people who acknowledged receiving earthquake information from newspapers said that they read a newspaper regularly. Nevertheless, the remaining 23 percent had read something about earthquakes in a newspaper, even though they were not regular readers. Newspapers and other print media offer a perspective on and an interpretation of events that are not possible in brief television news reports.[6] Whether people took advantage of the greater detail and depth in newspaper coverage or read only headlines and lead paragraphs, we cannot say.

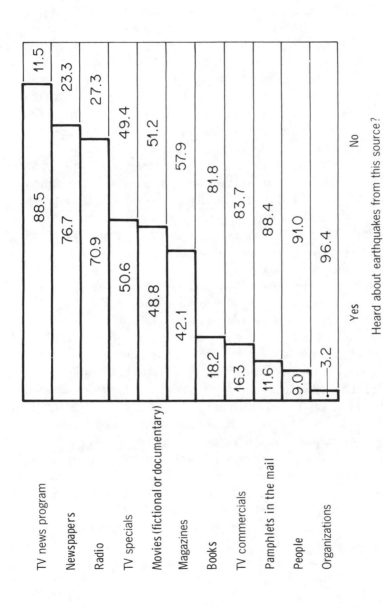

Figure 3. Sources of Information about Earthquakes, Earthquake Predictions, and Earthquake Preparedness

Most of the respondents also heard about earthquakes on the radio. Radio coverage is similar to television news programming in that it reaches all population segments and usually deals with each topic only briefly. But radio is unique in two important respects. First, the radio usually provides background entertainment for a listener whose primary attention is focused on another activity; this pattern of inattention probably works against accurate recall and retention of information from radio programs. Second, many radio stations feature talk shows, which often provide a forum for airing public concerns and discussing reports on the earthquake threat in an informal manner. Both the circulation and evaluation of rumors can be fostered through this medium.

Half of our respondents acknowledged watching television specials dealing with earthquakes. The specials we monitored dealt mostly with earthquake events and earthquake preparedness. They highlighted building safety and home preparedness, lent credibility to scientific earthquake prediction, and legitimized public concern by presenting dramatic scenarios on the possible effects of future earthquakes.

The entertainment value of earthquakes was illustrated by the nationally televised showing of the movie *Earthquake*. While we do not know how many people in our sample actually watched this movie, about 50 percent obtained earthquake information from a movie source of some kind. Film as a medium commands more exclusive attention from viewers than do radio or TV news programs. The sensationalistic depiction of events in movies such as *Earthquake* may have contributed to public misunderstanding of predictions and helped to perpetuate myths about panic and looting during a postdisaster period.

About two-fifths of our respondents acknowledged receiving earthquake information from magazines. Like newspapers, magazines provide more extensive accounts of earthquake topics and address themselves to smaller, more specialized audiences than do television or radio. Many popular magazines featured scientific prediction and research as well as major earthquake events and emphasized the urgency of the current earthquake threat.

Only small numbers of respondents acknowledged obtaining information from books, television commercials, and pamphlets in the mail. In a 1977 mail survey of reference librarians in city of Los Angeles branch libraries, we found that the number of earthquake references available to the public varied from three to forty. The average number of references was fourteen. Only fourteen of the thirty-nine librarians indicated that their branches had received new earthquake materials in 1976. Of the ten *books* reported as being available through the library system, eight dealt with earthquake folklore and nonscientific prediction, while only two had scientific orientations. Therefore, individuals requesting earthquake information from books in the public library were limited both in the number of sources and the type of information available. This, along with the fact that earthquake prediction is a relatively new area of interest, may explain why books were not a major source of earthquake information at that time.

In listing television commercials and pamphlets in the mail as sources, we were thinking of the short cartoons on earthquake preparedness distributed by the California Office of Emergency Services and of the home-preparedness pamphlets distributed with utility bills. These two media sources were used to arouse public awareness of earthquake safety, increase factual knowledge, and encourage participation in the diffusion of information. While the two campaigns served basically the same purpose, they employed different strategies of information diffusion. Sending pamphlets as enclosures with utility bills was relatively inexpensive compared to broadcasting public service announcements. Pamphlets were directed toward a reading audience, while television commercials were directed toward television viewers. While the information presented on television was transitory in nature, the pamphlets could be kept, periodically reviewed, and passed along to others. Despite the serious effort that went into preparing these communications, they did not command the public attention that items on regular television news programs might have commanded.

Finally, people and organizations appear to have played a rather insignificant part of the information process, though more respondents might have mentioned these sources if they had been listed in the interview.

It is important to remember that most people do not rely exclusively on one source for their information. Nearly half of the respondents had heard or read about earthquakes from five or more of the sources. Nearly two-thirds used four or more sources. Only one person in every fourteen had heard of earthquakes from just one media source.

Which segments of the public used the media most extensively? Men were more likely than women to obtain earthquake information from several media. Younger respondents heard about earthquakes from more varied media sources than did people over fifty. Anglos used a wider range of media than did either blacks or Mexican-Americans, who were quite similar in average exposure, but blacks were more polarized between high and low media use. Higher educational attainment and income also meant more diversified use of the media.

Contrary to our expectation, media use was unrelated to involvement in community social networks, as measured separately by marital status, the presence of school-age children in the home, and attachment to the local community.

Informal Discussion of Earthquake Topics

Most people in our sample heard about earthquakes from the mass media. How many took the next step of entering into informal discussion of the earthquake threat?

A series of questions was devised to let us know how much discussion occurred, with whom it took place, and on what aspect of the earthquake concern it centered. Questioning began as follows:

> To this point, we have discussed public sources of information on earthquakes. We would now like to know whether, within the last year, you have talked with anyone about the possibility of an earthquake happening in southern California.

A large majority (72.8 percent) said they had participated in such a discussion.

DISCUSSION PARTNERS

All respondents who answered affirmatively were then asked the following question:

With whom did you discuss the possibility of an earthquake happening in southern California in the near future?

The question was open-ended, but the interviewer was given a list of six types of discussion partners under which to code the replies. The categories are listed in figure 4. The schedule also allowed space in which to specify more precisely some of the answers that fell into the six categories. After the respondent had mentioned all of the applicable types of partners in earthquake discussion, he or she was then asked:

Within the past year, how often have you discussed the possibility of a future earthquake with——? Frequently, occasionally, or seldom?

The responses to these questions, indicating the partners with whom the respondents most frequently discussed earthquake matters, are summarized in figure 4. So few people gave responses that could not be coded into the six preestablished categories that we have omitted the seventh category of "Others" from the graph. As would be expected, adults in the household are most often partners in discussion. Children are either sheltered from these

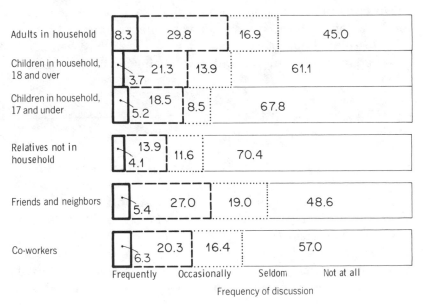

Figure 4. Partners in Informal Discussion of Earthquake Matters

discussions or are considered less interested or knowledgeable. Friends and neighbors are next in importance after adults in the same household, and coworkers come third.

In computing the percentages used in the graph, we have made adjustments for the number of people who could possibly have discussion with each type of partner.[7] If we were measuring the contribution that discussion with each type of partner made to total public consideration of earthquake matters, the rank order would be changed. Conversations with friends and neighbors make the greatest contribution to total public discussion (51.4 percent), followed (in order) by conversations with adults in the same household (35.8 percent), with relatives not in the house- hold (29.6 percent), and with coworkers (26.2 percent). Children make only a minor contribution to public discussion, with 13.3 percent of respondents discussing earthquakes with children under eighteen and only 2.9 percent doing so with children eighteen years and older.

Two observations are warranted by this analysis. First, although there is a good deal of discussion within the family or household, discussion is important in establishing linkages between the household and the neighborhood, the extended family, and the workplace. All of these linkages can be important in supplying perspective from which to interpret the news. Second, children are less often mentioned than might have been expected if they were learning things of relevance at school or if they were regu- larly part of the planning for family well-being in case of disaster.

RANGE OF INTERPERSONAL
COMMUNICATIONS CHANNELS

The six categories of discussion partners provided a way of assessing the range of interpersonal relations within which the concern over earthquakes was expressed and through which information was received, transmitted, and sifted. An index was computed to measure the range of interpersonal channels used by each respondent in discussions of earthquake topics. Someone who had not entered into a discussion of earthquake topics with anyone received a score of zero. Someone who had talked only with a spouse or only with coworkers, for example, received a low score. Someone who had talked about earthquakes both in and out of the household and family, with coworkers and with friends and with adults as well as with children, received a high score.

The index was not intended to measure the absolute range of discussion partners but rather the extent to which *available* partners were used in discussion. The index ranged from a possible value of zero, for those who engaged in no discussion, to one, for those who discussed the possibility of an earthquake with all types of partners available to them. As with the percentages reported in figure 4, the index incorporated adjustments for the presence or absence of other adults or of children in the household and for involvement in full- or part-time employment.

Young adults, Anglos, and people with more education and higher income discussed the earthquake threat with a wider range of partners, just as they heard about earthquakes from a greater variety of media sources. These four variables affected media usage and discussion patterns similarly, except in one respect, and that is that blacks were much less involved in discussion than were Mexican-Americans.

Women used fewer media sources than men, but they discussed the earthquake threat with a wider range of partners. Women and men differed not so much in the level of communication as in the affinity for formal or informal communication.

We again looked for evidence that involvement in stable social networks fosters communication. Allen Barton found support in several disaster studies for the conclusion that the level of informal communication in a community depends upon how well kinship and friendship ties are developed.[8] Among our respondents, married people engaged in discussion of earthquakes with more of their available types of partners than did single people. Similarly, people who participated in local organizations used more of their available discussion partners than did people without local organizational participation. But community attachment and the presence of school-age children in the home were not related to communication patterns. Thus, there is evidence that some kinds of integration into social networks, while not affecting media usage, foster informal discussion of the earthquake threat.

INFORMAL DISCUSSION TOPICS

After the interviewer had recorded each of the types of discussion partner used by the respondent and the frequency of discussion, he or she then inquired about discussion topics. The interviewer presented the respondent a card on which seven topics were listed, along with space for other topics not explicitly mentioned. The interviewer then went down the list of partners checked, asking the same question for each, as follows:

Looking at this card, please tell me which of these issues you've discussed with——.

The frequency with which each topic was discussed is reported in figure 5 without respect to discussion partner. Again, too few people took advantage of the opportunity to name "other" earthquake topics to warrant its inclusion as a separate discussion topic. The relative frequencies for the seven topics are surprising from one point of view. If we assumed that people are most interested in immediately practical matters, we might have expected more discussion of family preparedness. Because of the sensationalistic character of news about the earthquakes in Tangshan, northern Italy, and elsewhere during the preceding year, it is not surprising that "earthquakes around the world" was a popular topic for conversation. But it is striking that 83 percent have discussed predictions and that half the people say they have discussed "why earthquakes occur." Many people apparently want to understand what is going on around them rather than limiting their discussions to immediately practical questions.

Comparative Reliance on Information Sources

Our review of media usage and discussion has paid no attention to the importance or credibility attached to each source. Is the frequency with which television or books or discussion with friends mentioned a fair measure of the importance attached to what is learned through each medium? Answers to another set of questions in the basic survey indicate the relative importance of sources.

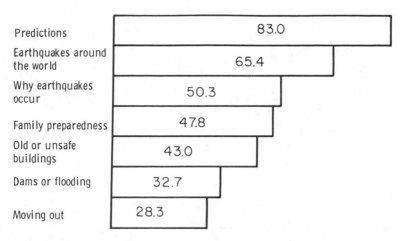

Figure 5. Informal Discussion by Earthquake Topic

As explained more fully in chapter five, each respondent was asked to describe up to five "predictions, statements, or warnings about earthquakes in the southern California area" heard "in the past year or so." For each announcement remembered, the respondent was asked:

Do you remember what your *chief source of information* about this prediction was?

Specific answers were not suggested to the respondents, and the interviewer recorded only one chief source. Since the question was asked about each of the announcements the respondent mentioned, the question was not asked at all of people who did not remember any announcement. For others, it could be asked as many as five times.

The graph based on this question cannot be precisely compared with the previous graphs, because percentages are based on the 1,788 reports of announcements rather than the 1,450 respondents and because the volunteered answers could not be broken down into exactly the same categories (fig. 6). However, it is possible to make a general comparison between where people hear about earthquake matters most frequently and which sources they rate as most important.

The three primary sources and their order remain the same. But

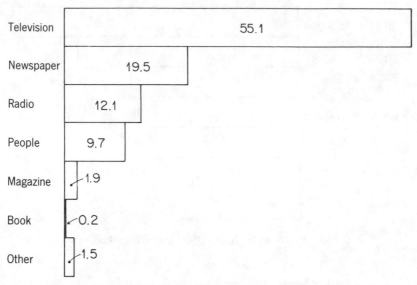

Figure 6. Chief Source of Information about Earthquake Predictions,
Forecasts, and Cautions

the differences in relative importance are greatly accentuated. Television is named by nearly three times as many people as newspapers are and by more than four times as many as radio is. "People" sources assume greater importance than before, surpassing magazines and books. While not many respondents think of their family, friends, and associates as a source of information on earthquakes, many of those who do are inclined to accept people as their chief source of information. Thus, in spite of preponderant reliance on the three principal media of mass communication, it may still be necessary to reach some people through personal networks.

Patterns of Communication Use

The similar effects of age, ethnicity, education, and income on the use of media and informal discussion suggest a positive correlation, and that is that wider media exposure to earthquake messages means discussion with a wider range of partners. But the effects of marital status and attachment to the community on discussion but not on media use and the reverse

effects of sex on the two kinds of communication suggest important individual and group differences in the way media use and
discussion are combined. If a combination of media use and discussion is the normal communication pattern, there may still be
people who rely disproportionately on one or the other form of
communication.

By combining indexes, we shall distinguish between people
who rely exclusively on the media, those who get their information principally from informal sources, and those who use informal discussion to sift and extend what they receive from the mass
media. The first group is easy to identify as being the respondents
who learned about earthquakes from media sources but did not
engage in discussion of earthquake topics. The second and third
groups are more difficult to distinguish. The number who rely
exclusively on discussion is too small for separate analysis. But
we can combine those few with all respondents who mention
family members, friends, coworkers, or other discussion partners
as the chief source of information about one or more earthquake
predictions, near predictions, or forecasts. The result of this sorting process is to separate respondents who identify the media as
their chief source of information and use informal discussion to
sift and extend their understanding from respondents who place
greater than customary reliance on informal discussion as an
authoritative source of information.

The incidence of these three patterns is presented in table 1.
Two-thirds of our respondents reported using interpersonal dis-

TABLE 1

PATTERNS OF COMMUNICATION USE

Pattern of use	Frequency	Percentage
Exclusive reliance on media	352	24.6
Discussion supplementing media	952	66.4
Disproportionate reliance on discussion	128	8.9
Total	1432	100.0

cussion to supplement the mass media, confirming the applicability of the two-step or multistep flow model. About a quarter of the respondents said they rely exclusively on the mass media. A sizable minority are not exposed to the important effects of interpersonal forecasts. A relatively small number (9 percent) of the respondents said they are willing to accept interpersonal discussion as a primary source of information about earthquakes. It is worth noting that only 18 people out of the 1,450 who constituted the complete sample were omitted from this analysis, either because they had not heard about earthquakes from the media or discussed earthquake topics informally, or because they supplied incomplete information and could not be classified. One way or another, nearly everyone had heard about earthquakes.

The filtering process, in conjunction with principal reliance on the mass media, is thought to have several important functions. First, discussion helps to imprint media content in memory and to make its content relevant to one's life situation. Second, discussion permits confirmation and correction of media communications that are imperfectly heard or understood. Third, discussion alerts people to media communications that they have not personally heard or seen.

The quantity and quality of earthquake awareness should be impoverished for people in the first category, who rely exclusively on the mass media. Several groups of people are overrepresented in this category. Twice as many blacks as Anglos relied only on the media, and an intermediate number of Mexican-Americans did so. Older people and people with less than a high school education were overpresented. As people whose social networks are often restricted, the unmarried, people living in households without school-age children, and people who are not in the labor force or who are unemployed more often rely exclusively on the media.

Experience with earthquakes was related to the communication pattern in a more complex fashion. Two measures of experience were used and compared. The first was simply the number of earthquakes experienced personally, from none to five or more. The second measure was the extent of physical injury and property damage experienced personally or vicariously in an earthquake. Damage and injury to the respondent and to close personal associates were combined on the assumption that vicarious experience within one's primary group has the same effect as personal experience. Five items were used to create the index of personal and vicarious earthquake loss:

> During any of these earthquakes, was the home you were living in then damaged enough to need repairs?
> Did you have any *other* personal property damage during these earthquakes?
> Have you ever been personally injured in an earthquake?
> Have you ever had a relative, family member, or close friend injured in an earthquake?
> Has any relative, family member, or close friend ever suffered any property damage in an earthquake?

The five items calling for simple "yes" or "no" answers were combined to produce a score that can range from zero for no intimate experience with earthquake damage to *five* for intense intimate experience with earthquake damage. Results using the two measures of earthquake experience are presented in table 2.

The notable effect of having no experience, a little experience, or considerable experience is on the tendency to rely disproportionately on discussion rather than to combine attention to the media with discussion. There seems to be a naive reliance on interpersonal sources and probably a hypersusceptibility to rumor among the inexperienced that is rare among people who have experienced three or more earthquakes. The effect of personal and vicarious experience of earthquake damage is just as clear and dramatic, but this effect is on the tendency to supplement media information with clarifying interpersonal discussion rather to rely exclusively on media reports.[9] These two relationships suggest something about the differing effects of quantity and quality of earthquake experience. Just the fact of experiencing earthquakes, without, in most cases, experiencing personal loss, reduces naive susceptibility to rumor and to accepting neighborhood and office talk as gospel truth. But the more personal experience of an earthquake's fury motivates individuals to seek clarification and evaluation of what they hear or read in the media through discussion with friends, family members, and work associates.

TABLE 2
PATTERNS OF COMMUNICATION USE
BY EARTHQUAKE EXPERIENCE

	% Number of earthquakes experienced			
Pattern of use	None	One	Two	Three or more
Exclusively media	31.4	22.6	21.0	28.7
Discussion supplementing media	54.8	69.1	71.2	69.4
Disproportionate reliance on discussion	13.7	8.4	7.7	1.9
Total	100.0	100.0	100.0	100.0
Total number	299	740	271	108
Exclusively media	30.5	23.8	14.9	13.4
Discussion supplementing media	61.4	66.9	75.1	76.5
Disproportionate reliance on discussion	8.2	9.3	10.0	10.1
Total	100.0	100.0	100.0	100.0
Total number	709	354	221	149

Local Experts in the Diffusion of Earthquake Information

Do certain individuals play a special role in the widespread discussion that supplements media communication? According to the classic studies of voting behavior, the opinion leaders to whom people turned for information and advice were generally thought to have some special knowledge or wisdom on the subject under debate. They were not merely prestigious figures or intimate friends.[10] It is this attribution of expertness in which we are especially interested. Do people find among their friends and associates someone whose special knowledge and wisdom about earthquakes inspires their trust? Personal influence is known to have a notable effect on decision making in highly uncertain situations.[11] The presence of a great many folk experts (or local experts) scattered throughout the community could aid in the formulation of unambiguous public views and decisive action in this area of uncertainty.

Each interviewee was asked the following question:

Including yourself, is there *anyone* in your circle of friends who seems *most* knowledgeable about earthquakes or earthquake predictions?

If the answer was "yes," respondents were asked:

Who is that?

A total of 257 respondents, or 17.8 percent of the entire sample, could identify a local expert (table 3). When we separate the 36 respondents who named themselves from the rest, 15.2 percent of the sample knew someone among their circle of friends whom they regarded as expert. About half of the local experts were identified as friends, about a third as relatives and members of the immediate household, and about one-eighth as work associates. The overwhelming majority of respondents said they had no one in their social circle to whom they could turn for expert counsel on earthquakes and earthquake predictions. While discussion plays an important part in earthquake communication, it is primarily a sifting process among peers. If reliance on opinion leaders has been essential to the crystallization of public opinion on political matters, the dearth of local experts could be a serious impediment to the crystallization of viewpoints concerning the earthquake threat.

As we look for personal characteristics that distinguish our local experts from other people, it is important to remember that the experts are strictly self-designated. The self-image of experts may or may not be recognized and accepted by others. Obversely, when the respondent identifies someone as a local expert, we

TABLE 3
PERSONS MOST KNOWLEDGEABLE ABOUT EARTHQUAKE TOPICS

Most knowledgeable person	Percent of total sample	Percent of "other"
Self	2.5	
Other:	15.2	
Friend/neighbor	(7.1)	46.6
Other relative	(3.5)	22.6
Adult in household	(2.1)	14.0
Coworker	(1.9)	12.2
Child in household	(.3)	2.3
Other	(.3)	2.3
No one named	81.9	
Don't know or no answer	.4	
Total	100.0	100.0
Total number	1450	221

cannot say whether the designated individual would make a corresponding self-designation. And in neither case can we tell whether there is truly expert knowledge involved or whether the attribution is without objective justification. We are dealing strictly with images of self and other, which past research leads us to believe are important in the formation of opinion and of the decision to act.

To facilitate analysis, we have labeled the three groups of respondents as follows: *local experts; associates*—individuals who identified someone in their circles as "most knowledgeable"; and *peers*—individuals who could identify no one in their circles as most knowledgeable." The statistical method of stepwise discriminant function analysis was used to determine what characteristics distinguished respondents in each category from respondents in the other two categories. A battery of twenty-six variables was entered into the analysis.[12] The statistical procedure first selects a smaller number of variables from the battery as most significantly discriminating among the three categories of respondents. It then factors these variables to see if they can be understood as measures of a still smaller number of underlying variables that distinguish among local experts, associates, and peers.

The statistical procedure selected ten variables as discriminating significantly among the groups of people. These variables are listed, from most to least discriminating, in table 4. But the variables did not discriminate equally among the three categories. Some variables set the local experts apart from the other two

TABLE 4
SUMMARY TABLE OF THE DISCRIMINANT ANALYSIS

Step number	Variable entered/removed	F to enter or remove	Wilks's lambda
1.	Extent of interpersonal discussion of earthquake possibility	24.49997	0.96199
2.	Favorability toward science	13.74760	0.94110
3.	Years of education	12.34180	0.92270
4.	Acknowledged hearing about earthquakes from books	9.62851	0.90856
5.	Number of group meetings attended	9.17995	0.89526
6.	Sex	4.52303	0.88875
7.	Marital status	5.57107	0.88080
8.	Awareness of endangered groups	5.26933	0.89332
9.	Acknowledged hearing about earthquakes from TV specials	5.42420	0.86570
10.	Employment status	3.39110	0.86095

groups, while other variables separated out the peers but failed to distinguish between experts and associates. Hence, we shall look first at the variables that make self-designated local experts a distinctive group of people, and then we shall take up the other important distinctions revealed by the analysis.

The local experts have more years of education and are more often male, unmarried, and not working than are either associates or peers. Associates and peers are indistinguishable on these four variables and on all other demographic background characteristics. The experts are more likely to say that they have gleaned information about earthquakes from books; in other respects their communication behavior is not distinctive. They endorse a more favorable set of attitudes toward science and scientists, based upon a six-item index explained in chapter ten. The use of books, the higher level of education, and the more favorable attitude toward science suggests an intellectual orientation that sets the self-designated local experts apart from others. The fact that they are more often male and have more education but are not distinguished by their occupations suggests that a traditional *status* element may have entered into these self-conceptions. Because of traditional status biases, being male and being well educated often serve as justifications for presenting one's views authoritatively. We should also note that some of the single, not employed, well-educated respondents who consider themselves experts are students.

Experts and associates together are distinguished from peers on the basis of three communication variables. They are more likely to have gleaned information about earthquakes from television specials, to have discussed the "possibility of an earthquake happening in southern California" with someone, and to have attended a meeting dealing with earthquakes and earthquake preparedness.

The more active involvement in communication indicated by these differences confirms the importance of the relationship between local experts and associates in the dissemination and filtering of earthquake information. While the three groups are indistinguishable on the basis of routine exposure to earthquake information through television and radio news programs and from newspapers, the greater interest that experts and associates share is indicated by their use of television earthquake specials and attendance at earthquake meetings.

The associates also stand apart from both the experts and the peers in three interesting respects. While they resemble the experts in having discussed the earthquake prospect, their discussions encompass a wider range of partners. And while they resemble experts in having attended meetings, they have attended *more* meetings. In addition, associates are distinguished from both experts and peers in being able to identify a larger number of groups of people who are especially at risk because of the earthquake threat (see chapter eight). Thus, the associates play a more substantial part in the process of interpersonal communication on the earthquake threat, and they are more sensitive to the *social* implications of the situation than are the self-designated experts or the peers. In some sense, the associates, who may have sought out local experts, are more socially aware and exhibit a more responsible concern for fostering communication than are either the experts or the peers.

Prior research has found that opinion leaders often utilize the mass media more extensively than do other members of the public.[13] Our data suggest a qualitative rather than a quantitative distinction, as indicated by the use of books and television specials as compared with the use of routine news reports. The associates are as clearly distinguished from the peers in this respect as are the experts. The suggestion by Katz and Lazarsfeld that opinion leaders are more active in the dissemination of information through interpersonal channels and often serve as important links between the mass media and less active segments of the public applies even more clearly to the associates than to the local experts.[14] Clearly, we cannot understand the flow of earthquake communications by making a simple twofold distinction between local experts or opinion leaders and the mass of opinion followers. Furthermore, the very small number of self-designated local experts in our sample is not an adequate indicator of the use of local experts in earthquake communications.

We shall mention the second step in the discriminant function analysis only briefly. Two major dimensions or functions were found to underlie the ten significantly discriminating variables. In general, the communications variables were most prominent in the first underlying dimension, which also accounted for most of the discrimination between the local experts and associates on the one hand and the peers on the other. The other and less important dimension featured employment status, marital status, and sex and applied more to the distinction between local experts and both associates and peers. This outcome is consistent with the emphasis we placed upon status factors in the tendency to identify oneself as an expert and with the importance of students among this group of respondents. It also concurs with our conclusion that the associates are as crucial to the communications process as are the experts.

The foregoing analysis leaves us wondering whether the local experts are really experts and whether the associates, by virtue of their access to local experts, really know any more than do the peers, who lack this access. Anticipating the topic of chapter five, which deals with the results of the communications process as measured by awareness of the earthquake hazard, we have included two awareness indexes in the comparisons among experts, associates, and peers. For technical reasons they did not appear among the ten most discriminating variables, but they do distinguish significantly among the groups in a consistent and meaningful fashion.[15] As indicated in table 5, more than twice as many peers as experts have not heard of the southern California uplift, and the associates take an intermediate position. When we asked people what "predictions, statements, or warnings about earthquakes in the southern California area" they had heard, the number they were able to give is similarly, though less consistently, related to the three categories. Thus there is some basis for believing that the self-designated local experts are generally the best informed, the peers are the least well informed, and the associates fall in between. At the same time, it is shocking that one in five of the people who regard themselves as "most knowledgeable" about earthquakes among their circle of friends and acquaintances had not even heard of the Palmdale bulge and that more than two out of five either had not heard of the bulge or did not understand that it might be an earthquake precursor. The identification of folk experts is at best prone to serious error, and a substantial minority of those identified as experts by themselves or by their associates may contribute a great deal of misinformation and misunderstanding to public discourse.

TABLE 5

EARTHQUAKE AWARENESS BY LOCAL EXPERTS,
ASSOCIATES, AND PEERS

Level of awareness	Local experts %	Associates %	Peers %
Awareness of the uplift:			
Heard, understood, relevant	33.3	30.8	24.2
Heard, understood	25.0	24.4	16.3
Heard, not understood	22.2	16.3	15.7
Not heard	19.5	28.5	43.8
Total	100.0	100.0	100.0
Predictive announcements heard:			
Three or more	11.1	11.3	4.9
Two	25.0	29.4	22.0
One	55.6	48.0	58.8
None	8.3	11.3	14.3
Total	100.0	100.0	100.0
Total number	36	221	1187

Conclusions

Nearly all our respondents had heard something about earthquakes in the past year or so. Most of them had gleaned earthquake information from several of the mass media; television news, newspapers, and radio were the most frequent sources. Nearly everyone had also discussed the prospect of an earthquake with friends. Most were clear in viewing the media as their chief source of information and any interpersonal discussion as supplemental. The classic two-step flow model, whereby information is disseminated through the mass media and then filtered for clarification and evaluation through interpersonal discussion in families, among friends and neighbors, and with work associates, fits the diffusion of earthquake information well.

Nevertheless, there are significant minorities who do not fully enter into this classic diffusion. A substantial minority learn from the media but participate in no discussion. They are disproportionately drawn from the black population and from the elderly, the unmarried, and other population segments with restricted social networks. The smaller minority who depend principally on interpersonal discussion rather than on the media are harder to distinguish, except that they are likely to have had little experience with earthquakes. Having been through some earthquakes makes people look to more authoritative sources of information than to interpersonal discussion only. Having actually suffered personal injury or property damage in an earthquake or having a close friend or relative who has suffered in this way motivates people to seek clarification and evaluation of what they hear and read in the media through informal discussion with family members, friends, and work associates.

Conversely, communication style affects the way people respond to the earthquake threat. People who supplement the media with interpersonal discussion are more aware of the earthquake threat and its social implications than are those who depend just on the media. Interpersonal discussion, whether alone or in conjunction with the media, seems crucial in making the earthquake threat real. Belief in the imminent probability of a damaging earthquake, the taking of steps to prepare for an earthquake, and fear are all greater among those who engage in discussion than among those who rely exclusively on the media.

Efforts to apply the classic theory of opinion leadership in the diffusion of mass communication led us to identify a more complex *expert-associate system,* in which *local experts* and *associates* are distinguished from *peers* and play special roles in the dissemination of earthquake awareness. While the local experts are somewhat better informed about the earthquake danger, have made use of books as a source of earthquake information, and are better educated, the distinctions between them and the associates may also be a matter of irrelevant traditional status dimensions, such as sex. As far as interpersonal communication is concerned, the associates are surprisingly more active than the experts, and both are more active than the peers.

The role of local experts fits a classic model. The experts provide a rare and valued service to others who seek clarification of the uncertainty generated by media reports of earthquake danger. Their accessibility as experts often facilitates discussion of earthquake topics. As persons with attributes of a higher status than that of many of their associates, incumbents of this role have prestige that supports their assumption of the expert identity and that is reinforced by others' appeals to them for information and clarification. Their serious interest and their claim to expertness is validated by their use of books as a source of information about earthquakes.

But the flow of influence is not principally from the local experts to the uninformed masses, as the simplest form of the two-step model indicates. Instead, influence flows most intensely between the opinion leaders and their highly interested associates. The experts and their associates may constitute a *social circle* within which opinions are sifted, issues defined, and some consensus reached. As Charles Kadushin and Robert K. Merton have suggested for other realms of opinion, informal social circles composed of experts and people who take a special interest in earthquake problems may form a crucial bridge from the media to the general public.[16]

There is support here also for A. W. Van den Ban's proposal that opinion leadership forms a hierarchy rather than a mere dichotomy.[17] The wide involvement of the associates in informal networks suggests that they may serve as opinion leaders for people outside of these informal social circles, even though they do not see themselves, nor are they seen by others, as experts. The information and viewpoints exchanged between experts and associates may eventually be disseminated via the associates to many of the less interested peers. Because there is less social distance and more informal communication between them and the peers, associates may constitute the crucial link between the book-reading local experts and the general public. Their less intellectual orientation to earthquakes and their more egalitarian contact with the general public allows them to appreciate more fully the potential human implications of the earthquake threat and to convey this understanding to others. The associates' greater awareness of especially endangered groups seems to reflect the distinctive nature of their bridging role.

While the diffusion of information and interpretation from associates to peers is probably a slow and very imperfect process, the existence of an earthquake circle consisting of experts and associates serves useful functions in the diffusion of earthquake awareness. First, lay people who are brought into such a circle pay attention to information and viewpoints that they would otherwise ignore, thus gaining a more comprehensive understanding of earthquake issues. Second, the circle ensures that there will be a reservoir of ordinary citizens who are better able to appreciate the significance of the earthquake threat than are most people outside of the social circles. While the system may not immediately succeed in disseminating this advanced understanding to large segments of the public, it may serve to keep public interest alive between crisis events.

In concluding this discussion of communication from the mass media through the local expert-associate system to the general public, two important qualifications should be mentioned once again. First, we have clear evidence that a substantial minority of self-conceived local experts and an even larger minority of the associates are not informed about the most widely featured current earthquake developments in southern California. The prestige accorded experts because they have read books about earthquakes may not distinguish between books that feature the occult and science fiction on the one hand and books that faithfully interpret science on the other. The pseudocircles in which ignorance and misinformation are sanctified as expertise may play as significant a part in the creation of popular conceptions of the earthquake threat as the circles that link the general public to valid information sources.

Second, the overwhelming majority of people cannot think of a friend or acquaintance who has special knowledge or wisdom on earthquake matters. Even though the links to the people we call associates undoubtedly bring many into indirect contact with local experts and provide them with a less obtrusive form of opinion leadership, vast numbers of people are probably untouched by the expert-associate system. If theories about the role of opinion leaders in public decision making are correct, this lack may contribute to public uncertainty and indecisiveness about the earthquake threat. Perhaps, too, it leaves public attitudes more directly at the mercy of the mass media than is true of other realms of public concern.

CHAPTER FOUR

But the People Won't Wait

As we have seen in the last chapter, a great deal of information about earthquake topics was exchanged through the informal networks in southern California during our study period. Attention to earthquake matters was not constant but instead waxed and waned irregularly. At certain times, people were unwilling to wait patiently for information to be made available to them and actively sought information from a variety of sources. In this chapter we will investigate *when* episodes of intensified information seeking took place and *where* people turned for expert information. The question—where people turned for expert information—becomes particularly important in light of the dearth of "experts" in the informal communication networks, as described in chapter three.

Episodes of intensified information seeking signify that the normalcy bias usually exhibited by people confronted with a potentially dangerous or threatening situation has been breached. Prior studies have found that people tend to interpret their situations as "normal" (i.e., not unusual) even though disaster warnings have been issued. These definitions do not change unless the person experiences social pressure to reinterpret the situation or is confronted with undeniable physical evidence that a disaster is imminent.[1] We shall attempt to identify the circumstances that drove many southern Californians to set aside the normalcy bias during peak periods of information seeking.

Questions will be asked about the following two types of information-seeking activities: First, when do people seek out expert evaluations and interpretations of predictions and the threat to which they are exposed? Under what conditions are the answers supplied by family members, friends, associates, and the popular media insufficient? Second, when do affirmative rumors of impending damaging earthquakes arise? How can rumor be explained as a collective, social process rather than as individualistic activity? What functions does rumoring serve, and how is it related to the availability of expert information?

An orienting hypothesis of this investigation is that the incidence of purposive information-seeking activities is strongly related to mass-media presentations. What people know about earthquake prediction, recent destructive earthquakes, and the actions being taken to reduce the hazard of earthquakes largely reflects the attention given to these topics and the way in which they are presented by the media. Initially, at least, the media were often responsible for the "newsworthiness" attributed to earthquake subjects. But too little is yet known about the dynamic relationship between the mass media and aroused individual and community concern.[2] Past research on media effects is sometimes criticized for proceeding from the wrong conceptualizations to study the wrong questions.[3] Recent thinking has produced a *dependency* model of mass media effects, stressing *mutual interdependency* among the media, the audience, and society as the key variables in understanding when and why media messages alter audiences' beliefs, feelings, and behaviors.

Employing this insight, the following discussion looks at how the media and its audience may be interdependent and how this relationship fluctuates over time. We shall not assume that the audience merely responds to the media and its presentations directly or passively. Rather, we will examine how the audience's needs and demands for certain kinds of "news" are reflected in media presentations and in the audience's subsequent actions.

Episodes of Information Seeking

Community requests for expert information on earthquake-related subjects were monitored over a three-year period. Relations were established with organizations that routinely provide pamphlets, books, speakers, movies, and experts on emergency planning and earthquake preparedness and with organizations that are contacted frequently for information on earthquake events and predictions. These organizations include the California Division of Mines and Geology, the California Institute of Technology (Caltech), civil defense offices, the Los Angeles City Fire Department, the Los Angeles County Sheriff's Department, the Los Angeles Public Library, the California Office of Emergency Services, the Red Cross, the California Seismic Safety Commission, and the U.S. Geological Survey. Periodic reinterviews were conducted with the organization members who routinely handle information requests, and the agencies' correspondence files were reviewed to determine the content and volume of inquiries received.

Information-seeking inquiries can be distinguished according to whether the inquirer seeks information on preparedness or on earthquakes and predictions. The first type of inquiry is usually addressed to officials who are responsible for the safety and welfare of local citizens, and the second is usually addressed to scientific experts.

PREPAREDNESS INQUIRIES

Figure 7 presents the requests for earthquake information which were directed to the civil defense office in Los Angeles over a period of twenty-four months. Almost all local requests for earthquake preparedness information are received by this office. Other agencies, such as fire and police departments, usually refer callers concerned about earthquake or disaster preparedness to the civil defense office, which provides free information and pamphlets.

Requests for information from individuals and organizations are listed separately in figure 7, as are requests for speakers to address groups (the subject of requests for speakers will be examined in more depth in chapter nine). Requests from organizations were infrequent during the eight months up to and including February, when the uplift was announced. Requests from individuals fluctuated during this period, but they did so at a low level compared with later peaks. Some of these early individual requests dealt with matters other than earthquake hazard (i.e., why an air-raid warning had sounded, where the nearest fall-

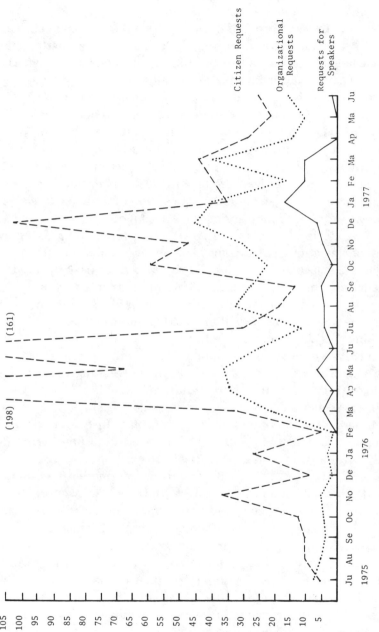

Figure 7. Individual and Organizational Requests for Earthquake Information

out shelter was located, and whether any general emergency-preparedness materials were available).

News of the southern California uplift was released on February 13, just nine days after the first reports of a disastrous earthquake in Guatemala. Nevertheless, the Los Angeles Office of Civil Defense received fewer information requests from individuals and fewer requests from organizations in February than in any of the seven previous months, and there were still no requests for speakers. The nadir in public information seeking parallels the weak response by the media to announcement of the uplift.

In March, information-seeking activities began to increase, although citizen inquiries were not unusually high in comparison to earlier levels. Organizational requests for information, however, showed a dramatic increase over earlier months.

It was during the month of April that information seeking by both organizations and citizens reached new high levels. Requests from citizens soared dramatically to the highest peak during the twenty-four months monitored. This increase in community interest and concern about earthquake preparedness corresponded with the increase in information-seeking inquiries to Caltech concerning the Whitcomb "prediction."

In May, while individual requests for information were declining slightly, organizational requests rose, reaching the second-highest peak during the entire monitored period. In June, organizational requests declined, and in July they reached their lowest level since the announcement of the uplift. In contrast to this decline, individual requests rose sharply again in June, stopping only a little short of the April peak. According to civil defense sources, several of those who asked for information mentioned the destructive Italian earthquakes as the reason for wanting to be prepared. In July, August, and September, requests from individuals plummeted to pre-Whitcomb levels. In August, however, organizational requests for information rose again.

To summarize the first half of 1976, individual inquiries regarding earthquake preparedness peaked in April and again in June and then continued to decline throughout the summer. It is not clear that announcement of the uplift alone stimulated disproportionate individual information seeking. But the Whitcomb announcement, perhaps in part because it followed the uplift announcement and occurred near the time of the Seismic Safety

Commission's declaration concerning the uplift, launched an epidemic of information seeking. Before such activity had returned to customary levels, dramatic news of the earthquake disaster in Italy reignited public concern to a second peak. With a few weeks of lag, organizational information seeking definitely responded to announcement of the uplift, was stimulated further by Whitcomb's "prediction" but peaked a month later, but did not respond to the Italian disaster.

An affirmative rumoring episode in October (to be discussed shortly) was paralleled by a substantial increase in inquiries from individuals for both preparedness and prediction information. Both the rumoring and the high level of requests for preparedness information from the general public continued in November.

In December, as the Minturn prediction was given extensive media coverage, an increase in requests to scientific institutions was paralleled by more requests for preparedness information. Both citizen and organizational requests for preparatory information peaked in this month. Organizational requests reached their highest level for the monitored period, and requests from citizens reached their highest level since June.

The beginning of 1977 saw a shift in the media's focus from earthquake predictions toward preparedness (see chapter two). Similarly, both individual and organizational levels of inquiry began to fall from their peaks in December but held at fairly high levels until March. After March, both media attention and community concern about earthquake threat and preparedness began to decline.

PREDICTION INQUIRIES

Clarification of an actual earthquake prediction—the uplift, Whitcomb's hypothesis test, and Minturn's prediction—took the form of an attempt to pin down the specific parameters of initially vague announcements or media discussions. Most of the inquiries about predictions were directed to scientific organizations, particularly Caltech.

Very little information-seeking activity was generated by the U.S. Geological Survey announcement of the Palmdale bulge in February 1976. Neither Caltech nor USGS mentioned receiving

more than one or two inquiries from the public relating specifically to the uplift.

By contrast, the Whitcomb announcement in April caused a
flurry of public response. Caltech, where Whitcomb was affiliated,
was inundated for two to three weeks with calls from people
attempting to clarify Whitcomb's "hypothesis test." Since the bulk
of incoming calls mentioned his name or referred to his recently
issued "prediction," the Caltech switchboard routed all calls directly to Whitcomb. He reportedly received five to ten letters per
day during this period, and two of his staff members screened all
calls and answered the majority of questions. Two-thirds of these
calls were reportedly from the public; the others came from
scientific or governmental agencies. Most of the inquiries from
the public were based on "misinformation," with callers believing that Whitcomb had predicted a 7.5 (or so) magnitude
quake for the San Fernando Valley. Caltech personnel attributed
most inquiries to misinformation from the press, which had
sensationalized Whitcomb's hypothesis test by treating it as a
prediction.

A resurgence of interest in Whitcomb's hypothesis test occurred
at an intersection of several events that began in late September 1976. These events were the distribution of an earthquake-
preparedness pamphlet that was included with September and
October telephone bills, a rumoring event (to be discussed in the
next section), and extensive media attention to destructive earthquakes and earthquake predictions.

The USGS public relations office received so many requests for
information on Whitcomb's "prediction" during the latter part of
1976 (many of which were in response to the phone companies'
mailings) that a special card was printed with specific information
on his announcement. The USGS enclosure on Whitcomb's prediction stated the following:

> James Whitcomb of the California Institute of Technology, Pasadena,
> made a tentative prediction for an earthquake, comparable to the 1971
> San Fernando event, to take place between April, 1976, to April, 1977.
> The State Earthquake Review Board, however, considered the data
> insufficient to issue an official warning. We have no information on
> earthquake predictions other than this one.

Two common examples of requests to USGS are as follows:

I have heard "experts," via TV talk shows, state that the Los Angeles area is due for a very major earthquake before April, 1977. Have you any information as to the substance of the prediction? (Dated October 20, 1976)

Where do you expect the big one to be if there is one? Do you feel that James Whitcomb is correct in his estimations, only you can't document it? What is the predicted date? (Dated November 6, 1976)

These requests illustrate two types of effort to pin down a prediction: getting the facts or seeking an "insider's" knowledge about the real threat behind the prediction.

The first example cited is a request for further clarification of the specifics of a prediction heard through the media. As confirmed by our questionnaire data pertaining to Whitcomb's announcement (chapter three), most people who had heard something about this "prediction" knew only that it was issued by a scientist (referred to as an "expert" in this letter) and that the quake would occur before or during April 1977. The inquirer's intent was to solicit further facts, or "substance," about the prediction itself.

The second writer, perhaps a bit better informed than the first, is also asking for clarification of the prediction's specifics; however, this writer is also seeking an expert's assessment of the prediction. He or she wants the scientist's "feelings" about the prediction, even if documenting or substantiating evidence is not available. By asking for an informal evaluation of the imminence of the earthquake threat, the inquirer may be seeking a private communication from an established authority, which would give additional personalized information with which to assess the threat and Whitcomb's announcement.

An additional type of information being sought during this period in relation to Whitcomb's announcement was the potential impact of the quake on the writer's geographic location. For example, one person asked whether the quake would harm a house located on the beach; another asked how strongly the quake would be felt in the city of Covina.

The prediction of a December 20 quake in southern California by self-proclaimed geophysicist Henry Minturn resulted in an immediate increase in calls to several Los Angeles County safety agencies and scientific institutions. This high level of local information seeking was sustained throughout the entire prediction period. Particularly between November 22 and 30, and again on December 13, the Los Angeles Office of Civil Defense was contacted by hundreds of callers asking for preparedness materials and trying to find out if any special measures were being taken by the government to prepare for the quake. For example, some callers wanted to know whether evacuation planning was being contemplated by government officials or where postquake shelters were going to be established. Most of these inquiries concerned the agency's readiness to handle a coming quake. Minturn's prediction of a pre-Christmas quake was taken seriously by most of these callers.

Caltech received between 100 and 500 calls per day throughout this period, particularly during the days immediately following the November 22 Minturn news interview and on December 7 and 20, the dates of his two predicted quakes. Almost all inquiries received by either the public relations office or the Seismology Laboratory during December pertained to Minturn's prediction, even though the media announced (albeit inconspicuously) that Whitcomb had canceled his hypothesis test during this period.

Several types of inquiries were received by Caltech's public relations office staff and the researchers in the Seismology Laboratory. The majority of callers wanted to know whether, in fact, an earthquake would occur on December 20; these callers were seeking confirmation of the much-discussed prediction from a credible scientific source. Following are examples of such calls:

A teacher from Palmdale called and said she had a class of hysterical kids who were afraid that the earthquake was going to occur, and she wanted to check to see if it was true or not.

Another woman called to see if she should leave town because of the earthquake. Her husband did not believe the prediction, but she did, so she said she was going to leave her husband in Los Angeles if the quake were really going to happen.

A man from Lancaster who owns a gas station called to find out about the quake since the gas company's trucks would not deliver to his station on the twentieth because of the coming quake.

A woman caller wanted to find out if there was going to be a quake that weekend. She said she wanted to leave town but would not want to leave her children alone if there was going to be a quake.

A large number of callers who had apparently already accepted the prediction as credible were seeking additional information. According to one staff member in the public relations office, many callers seemed frightened and wanted to know what they should do; some asked whether they should leave Los Angeles on December 20. A few asked whether a tidal wave was anticipated because of the December 20 quake. Some rather irate callers asked why Minturn's predictions were so accurate and yet Caltech, with its expensive labs and equipment, still could not predict earthquakes.

On December 20, Caltech received inquiries about the quake, which callers believed had occurred. As with clarification attempts related to earthquake events discussed earlier, callers asked, "When did the quake hit?" and "How large was it?" Some out-of-town callers asked whether it was safe to return yet.

AFFIRMATIVE RUMORING

Numerous rumors of predicted earthquakes arose during this time which could not be linked directly to any media-relayed earthquake predictions, whether scientific, psychic, or otherwise. For this reason they are being classified as affirmative rumoring events to differentiate them from actual prediction-related information seeking. However, the clarification attempts and content of inquiries are similar: in both instances callers are attempting to elicit further information on a prediction that holds a certain amount of ambiguity for them. The two differ significantly, however, in that rumoring episodes, unlike information seeking, are not directly stimulated by media attention to a prediction event.

Widespread rumoring occurred only during a two-month period, in October and November 1976. Successive episodes of rumoring seemed to begin with the same intersection of events that refocused attention on the Whitcomb announcement, about a month before Minturn's first prediction. Public clarification attempts and information-seeking activities seemed to peak twice during this period, during the third week in October and the third week in November. Each of these rumoring episodes will be discussed separately.

The October rumoring episode seems to have started early in October and peaked between October 19 and 22. Although the predicted magnitude of the rumored quake varied, Caltech was consistently cited as the source of the prediction.

Although information-seeking attempts to clarify this prediction do not seem to have begun in large numbers until the eighteenth or nineteenth of the month, there are indications that stories of an impending quake had already been circulating for two or three weeks. In mid-October, a USGS scientist mentioned during an interview about earthquake predictions that he had recently heard a rumor of an earthquake predicted for the San Fernando Valley, the site of the 1971 quake. He had received a call around the first of October from a San Fernando resident who had heard that a huge quake was going to strike her area about October 11. The caller said the source of the prediction was Caltech but that no official prediction was going to be made because Caltech had decided to withhold the information from the general public. She wanted verification that a prediction, even though unannounced, had actually been made. While attending a party, another USGS scientist had been told that the mother of one of the guests was a San Fernando resident and had packed all of the family's expensive crystal in boxes because a large earthquake was expected to strike the San Fernando Valley sometime around the fifteenth of October.

By October 19, Caltech's public relations office was receiving at least fifty calls per day, and the Seismology Laboratory was receiving upward of a hundred calls a day. At this time, someone from either the Jet Propulsion Laboratories or Caltech was said to have predicted a magnitude 8.0 earthquake for October 21. In addition, the National Guard was supposedly already on alert status for this event. Most clarification inquiries merely asked whether the prediction was true or not. As with the later Minturn inquiries, some callers were reluctant to accept the disconfirming information and became argumentative, stating that Caltech was just withholding the information.

On October 20, the information-seeking calls increased and the rumor intensified. The twenty-first was still the date of the predicted quake, but most callers now claimed that the magnitude would be 8.5 or 9.0. The National Guard was said to be evacuating people from the predicted impact area, which some callers identified as the San Fernando Valley and others as the area of the last big quake. Most of these inquiries were attempts to ascertain whether any quake was really predicted.

Caltech also started receiving calls on the twentieth from schools and hospitals about information received from an alleged "Caltech scientist." In the last day or two, a man identifying himself as a Caltech scientist had been calling schools and hospitals to warn them to be ready for a large, destructive earthquake that would occur around the twenty-first. He said that the quake prediction was not being released because it was feared that many people would panic. This type of anonymous communication to large institutions may have given rise to the intensification of information-seeking inquiries after the nineteenth.

Also on the twentieth, the Seismology Laboratory received several calls from angry parents who wanted to know why their children's school was to be closed on the twenty-first. They referred to the closure as "the trouble your prediction made." One of the laboratory researchers called the school's principal and explained the situation; the principal responded that he had not realized that the prediction was not authentic.

Another call to the laboratory on the twentieth came from a psychiatrist treating a child who was still having problems resulting from the 1971 San Fernando quake. He requested that someone from the laboratory call the child to reassure him that no earthquake had been predicted for the next day. Because of the prediction rumor, the child reportedly was unwilling to let his mother go to work the next day.

The large volume of inquiries on the predicted October 21 quake prompted Clarence Allen, representing Caltech's Seismology Laboratory, to issue a statement on October 20 to be read to all Caltech callers as an "official" disclaimer of the rumored prediction. That statement read:

> Dr. Clarence Allen of Caltech says: "No such prediction came out of Caltech or from any other responsible agency that we know about. It appears to be an unfounded rumor. Furthermore, specific predictions of this type are not yet possible."

Not until November 4 did any newspaper carry the story of the rumor along with Allen's disclaimer, although each paper that carried the story gave it front-page coverage.

During this time, Caltech was not the only organization to receive calls. The Los Angeles Office of Civil Defense received an unusually large number of calls between October 20 and 22 requesting manuals on preparedness in the home and on first aid. Inquiries to public agencies became so numerous at this time that on October 22, the civil defense office activated its Emergency Operations Center, a communications center with interagency tie-lines that is usually activated only during a disaster or under extreme conditions, to handle the earthquake-prediction inquiries.

The rumor had become "substantiated" by this time, with "confirming" evidence being cited by the callers, the majority of whom were not seeking to clarify the prediction but instead were seeking preparedness information to ready themselves for the quake. Confirming evidence cited by the callers included reports that ambulance drivers throughout the city had been put on alert, that recent citywide earthquake exercises by safety and emergency agencies had been held in preparation for this already predicted quake, that well-water temperatures had risen recently, that animal life was leaving the Newhall area, and that friends at Caltech had confirmed that a prediction had actually been made.

By October 25, all inquiries on this rumoring episode had subsided.

The November rumoring episode seems to have been much smaller in scope than the October incident; no dramatic increase was found in inquiries to civil defense or police agencies due to a rumored quake, and Caltech received only a few calls during the early part of the month.

As in the October rumoring episode, Caltech was cited as the source of the prediction, and the earthquake was said to be of magnitude 8.0 or above. The expected date was sometime after the fifteenth of the month. And, as in the October episode, it was said that the Caltech scientist who had made the prediction did not want to release it to the public.

By November 19, the rumoring episode had intensified, and the prediction had become more specific: an 8.0 or greater earthquake predicted by a Caltech scientist was to occur within the next thirty-six hours. On November 19, several discussions were overheard concerning whether or not people would come to work the next day, usually accompanied by nervously humorous references to the types of masonry in the buildings in which people worked.

On the twentieth, the rumor was elaborated. It was reported that Caltech or Jet Propulsion Laboratory staff had been sent home early from their jobs because of the prediction. A check with Caltech revealed that some inquiries had been received asking whether people had been dismissed early because of an earthquake prediction; however, these were few in number. Even on the date of the predicted quake, few clarification attempts had been received.

On November 27, however, the *Los Angeles Times* carried a front-page story debunking rumors of an impending great earthquake which had circulated "for the past several weeks." Don Anderson, director of Caltech's Seismology Laboratory, and Peter Ward and Jerry Eaton of USGS were all quoted as saying that they knew of no valid earthquake predictions issued by reputable scientists for the southern California area. This disclaimer, although it followed Minturn's prediction by a couple of days, was essentially directed toward the November rumoring episode.

How Widespread The Concern?

The wildly fluctuating episodes of rumoring and information seeking had easily demonstrable effects on the conduct of public officials, scientists, and media personnel. But the brief history that we have recounted does not indicate how large a fraction of the population was involved. An abrupt wave of twenty or thirty requests for speakers on earthquake preparedness overloads the small civil defense office. A few hundred telephone calls each day overloads Caltech's answering capacity. Yet both figures constitute negligible proportions of the several million people living in the metropolis of Los Angeles and Orange counties. From conversations with our own friends and associates throughout this period, we know firsthand that the rumors in October and November and the concerns in April and December reached a very substantial part of the population. The inquiries directed to authoritative sources are the very small tip of a great iceberg.

But since the numbers of recorded inquiries are so small, we must guard against an unwarranted assumption that they accurately reveal wider community concerns. They could reflect only the anxieties of a small and atypical population segment.

Fortunately, we have answers to two sets of questions from our surveys which can shed at least partial light on the generality of the concerns underlying information-seeking activity. First, a common theme, especially in rumoring, is the suspicion that scientists and public officials know a great deal that they are not revealing to the public. Three months after the rumoring episodes, we asked the following question in our basic survey:

Do you think scientists and public officials are giving us all the information they have on earthquake predictions, or are they holding back information?

Forty-six percent replied that scientists were holding back information, and 49 percent that public officials were less than candid. Of those who had opinions, majorities in each instance thought that information was being withheld. Clearly, in this respect, the rumor bearers are not unrepresentative of the general population. (Further analysis of this item appears in chapter ten.)

A second set of questions deals with public desire for expanded or contracted media coverage of earthquake topics. Unfortunately, we did not include these questions in the field survey of early 1977. However, we remedied this a year later by including a battery of five questions in our February 1978 telephone survey of 500 Los Angeles County residents. Residents were asked:

Now here are some questions about television, radio, and newspaper coverage during the last six months. We want your personal opinion on each of these questions. Would you say there has been too little coverage, just about the right amount of coverage, or too much coverage for each of the following?

A. Coverage on what to do when an earthquake strikes?
B. Coverage on how to prepare for an earthquake?
C. Coverage on the Palmdale bulge and scientific earthquake prediction?
D. Coverage on earthquake predictions by people who are not scientists?
E. Coverage on what government officials are doing to prepare for an earthquake?

The findings were overwhelmingly one-sided and the message surprisingly unambiguous (fig. 8). From 65 percent to 83 percent of respondents wanted *more* coverage of "the Palmdale bulge and scientific earthquake prediction," "what to do when an earthquake strikes," "how to prepare for an earthquake," and "what government officials are doing to prepare for an earthquake." The consensus that too little is reported about preparations by government officials was particularly striking. No more than 3 percent felt there had been too much coverage on any of these topics.

Only on the topic of "predictions by people who are not scientists" did a substantial number feel that the coverage had been excessive. But even on this topic, somewhat less than a majority (43 percent) said that the coverage had been excessive, and fully 25 percent would have liked more coverage.

These questions were repeated in the two subsequent surveys, with quite stable results. The episodic search for meaning that we have described in this chapter is the eruption of widely shared attitudes that remain latent between episodes.

As a footnote, we must caution that the demand for more information to clarify a situation made confusing by vague forecasts and by an absence of visible public leadership for coping with the earthquake prospect may be different from the attitude toward publicly announcing a specific, scientifically based earthquake prediction. Questions dealing with release of predictions were included in the initial field survey. The following question was read to the respondents:

> If there is information indicating that there will be a damaging earthquake in the near future, please look at this card and tell me how certain you think this prediction should be before a public announcement is made.

Simultaneously, repondents were handed a card containing the following choices:

90–100%	Definitely sure the earthquake will occur.
60–80%	Quite sure the earthquake will occur.
40–50%	A fifty/fifty chance the earthquake will occur.
20–30%	Somewhat sure the earthquake will occur.
0–10%	Not very sure the earthquake will occur.

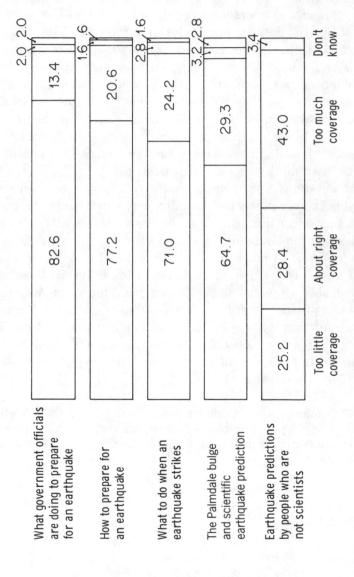

Figure 8. Amount of Earthquake News Coverage

In reading table 6, it is important to remember that answers are always biased to some degree by the choices people are given. We did not include in this question the option of not releasing the prediction at all, so we must assume that some of the people who said predictions should be released when scientists are 90 to 100 percent certain as well as some of those who were recorded under "don't know" might have said "never" if given the option. Furthermore, answers to ensuing questions showed that closeness to the predicted time of occurrence as well as degree of certainty affect people's judgments about releasing predictions.

TABLE 6

How Certain Should a Prediction Be before a Public Announcement is Made?

Degree of certainty	Percent	Cumul. percent
Don't know or no answer	3.5	—
Not very sure (0–10%)	4.3	4.3
Somewhat sure (20–30%)	9.1	13.4
Fifty-fifty chance (40–50%)	23.2	36.6
Quite sure (60–80%)	29.5	66.1
Definitely sure (90–100%)	30.4	96.5
Total percent	100.0	
Total number	1,450	

The easiest way to understand table 6 is to look at the cumulative percentages, reading down the table. Very few people favored the release of predictions about which the scientists themselves are quite unsure. Only 13.4 percent would have scientists publish predictions when they are no more than 30 percent confident that they are correct. Just over a third would have scientists publish predictions when the odds of being right are even. About two-thirds of the people favored publishing the prediction when the odds are solidly in favor of the prediction (60 to 80 percent certain). And if scientists can reach the magic 90 percent to 100 percent range of certainty, nearly everyone favored releasing the information. We can summarize by saying that if scientists are relatively confident of a prediction, the public wants to be told. But most of the public do not want to be told every time there are signs leading scientists to feel that there is a remote possibility of an earthquake. Without reviewing the further findings in detail, we can add that even with predictions about which scientists are 90 to 100 percent certain, fully a third would withhold public notice until, at most, six months before the predicted date.

This apparent discrepancy between wanting more media coverage of earthquake topics but favoring suppression or delay of prediction announcements highlights public hunger for information that is definite, reliable, and relevant to potential action. Much of the information seeking is undoubtedly an effort to supplant information that is vague, unreliable, and of unclear relevance to action with more satisfying kinds of information.

In the remainder of this chapter we shall attempt to speculate constructively about the meaning of these observations.

Rumor Theory and Information Seeking

Traditionally, the study of public opinion processes (such as the two-step flow model of communication) and collective behavior processes (such as rumoring) have been treated separately. It may be helpful, however, to think of them on a scale, with the October and November affirmative rumoring near the top. At the low end of the scale is simply hearing or reading about the disaster threat from the media without discussing it with anyone. In a small minority of instances, the low end of the scale is merely learning about the threat from discussion with family, friends, and work associates. A major step up the scale is the supplementing of media communication with informal discussion to sift, clarify, and confirm understandings from the media. A further step up the scale is the supplementing of the usual combination of media and discussion with inquiries directed to authorities, as in the waves of information seeking described in this chapter. Affirmative rumoring, in which informal discussion produces scenarios that are sharply detached from any obvious media sources and inquiries to authorities are centered on these scenarios rather than on media reports, completes the scale. One might imagine the scale being elongated further to include some kind of precipitant collective action. Since no such extension occurred, however, we shall limit our analysis to the four stages.

Arraying these phenomena on a scale enables us to think of them as differing more in degree than in kind. It also allows us to draw upon the theory of rumor to explain each step up the scale. The definition of rumor as "the process of forming a normatively relevant collective definition of a situation"[4] applies as much to the sifting of media content through informal discussion as it does to affirmative rumoring. Shibutani had defined rumor more elegantly as "a recurrent form of communication through which men caught together in an ambiguous situation attempt to construct a meaningful interpretation of it by pooling their intellectual resources. It might be regarded as a form of collective problem solving."[5] Indeed, the second and fourth stages are not as different in kind as is often assumed. While sifting media communications, people advance interpretations and suggest "facts" that the media are, allegedly, concealing. At the affirmative-rumoring stage, people continue to attribute their scenarios to the same authorities used by the media.

Gordon W. Allport and Leo Postman advanced a *basic law of rumor* whose elements are incorporated into most current theories of rumor: "The amount of rumor will vary with the importance of the subject to individuals concerned *times* the ambiguity of the evidence pertaining to the topic at issue. The relation between importance and ambiguity is not additive but multiplicative, for if either importance or ambiguity is zero, there is *no* rumor."[6] This formula is just as plausible in explaining the sifting of media communications through informal discussion as it is in explaining affirmative rumoring. For example, we found earlier that both experience with earthquakes and experience of personal or vicarious loss because of an earthquake increase the likelihood that people will look to the media for authority while sifting media communication through informal discussion. Earthquake experience probably enhances the personal importance of the topic. A direct application of Allport and Postman's basic law of rumor would lead us to look for increases in importance and ambiguity to explain movements up the scale from simply paying attention to the media to active information seeking and affirmative rumoring.

Ambiguity was rife from the beginning of stories about the southern California uplift. The media often downplayed its significance in their stories while featuring sensationalistic headlines. The uplift was frequently described as an anomaly that had scientists concerned but also confused; they were quoted as saying that they were unsure about the relationship of the bulge to actual seismic activity. However, in articles concerning building and dam safety and seismic-safety legislation, the uplift was routinely referred to as the reason for taking action. Also, a feeling of immediacy was frequently conveyed in these articles, giving the impression that the uplift might be more of a threat than scientists were willing to admit to the public.

But a review of the evidence immediately reveals that a straightforward application of the basic law of rumor does not work. The uplift, with its very plausible precursory sign, was certainly objectively important, and ambiguity was surely at a peak when the announcement was first made. Yet the threshold to widespread information seeking was not crossed for two months after the announcement was first featured on the front page of the *Los Angeles Times*. Neither ambiguity nor importance had been reduced when information seeking dropped to preuplift levels in July, August, and September. And it is not immediately apparent what dramatic increases in importance or ambiguity could have accounted for the October and November episodes of affirmative rumoring.

One obvious problem with the basic law is that ambiguity is in the eye of the beholder. When people had very little comprehension of the uplift, objective ambiguity was great, but subjective ambiguity was often minimal. As people learned more about the uplift, they became more aware of what they did not know. To say, however, that information seeking and rumoring increase as subjective ambiguity increases is to approach tautology.

At least four considerations demand our attention before we can develop a more refined understanding of the rise and fall of information seeking. First, most analyses of rumoring deal with actual events or authoritative information leaks as rumor sources: people feel the jolt of an earthquake or experience the deluge that could overfill the upstream dam, or past experience with information grapevines establishes the frequent credibility of rumor. But in the case of the uplift we have no event, nothing observable had happened. It was reported that people driving through Palmdale sometimes asked to be shown the bulge—but an uplift of no more than one foot, spread over thousands of square miles, could only be detected through the most sophisticated mapping techniques. And there are no established grapevines linking seismology laboratories to the public as there are linking political figures to their publics. Hence the determination that something important was happening was made in the first instance by the media. Since the media gave only perfunctory attention to the uplift in the first two months, the public perception was that nothing more important could have been happening.

Second, earthquake prediction and the uplift as a manifestation of accumulating seismic tension were new and unfamiliar ideas when the uplift was first announced. A certain amount of familiarization was necessary before people could begin to grasp the reality of the situation. At first, Palmdale seemed safely remote from the metropolis, and prediction evoked images ranging from fanciful prophecy to weather forecasting to precise identification of time and place. Just as the media could not initially assimilate and deal adequately with news of the uplift, so also the public could not grasp the reality of what might be in the offing.

Third, the acceleration of the rumor process from the mere sifting of media communications to the state of active information seeking constitutes a breach of the ordinary normalcy bias. Ambiguity often remains high after friends have discussed current media reports, but people wait to see whether later media items will bring clarification or else they continue to discuss the issues with friends and associates in the hope of achieving closure. When a great many people are no longer willing to wait or to live with remaining ambiguities, a threshold has been crossed.

Fourth, besides the cumulative effect of growing comprehension of the uplift, two qualitative differences in the April messages may have helped to carry the public across the threshold to information seeking. One of these was the specificity of time and place that marked the Whitcomb "prediction" as compared with the much vaguer uplift announcement. It's not that the Whitcomb report was more important—indeed, the anticipated earthquake was of lesser magnitude than the quake associated with the uplift. But the new report was more timely—the quake would occur within a year, rather than during some vague, much longer time span—and the location was specified more narrowly. The other difference came with the Seismic Safety Commission's official designation of the uplift as a threat. The threat was now authenticated. Objective ambiguity was reduced by each of these changes, but rumoring escalated nevertheless. Public authentication and the specification of time and place may have been the critical features.

The wave of information seeking that accompanied the Minturn prophecy is amenable to similar explanation. No lag in response occurred, because ample familiarization with the idea of earthquake prediction had already occurred. The forecast was specifically for December 20 and for Los Angeles, and it was authenticated both by the airing of it on NBC television and by the identification of Minturn as a qualified seismologist with a documented record of successful predictions.

As we shall report in chapter twelve, an earthquake prediction for southern California by a Soviet seismologist was reported in the *Los Angeles Times* in 1978 but stirred no flurry of information seeking. The prediction was as definite about location as Minturn's and as precise about the time window as Whitcomb's, but it was reported only briefly by the media and was accorded no American scientific authentication. Thus, while a fair degree of specificity of time and place may be *necessary*, it may not be *sufficient* to cause widespread breaching of the normalcy bias without the further stamp of authenticity.

The April, May, and June wave of information seeking ended as abruptly as it began. Failure of the California Earthquake Prediction Evaluation Council to confirm Whitcomb's "prediction," reported more negatively by most of the media than was warranted by the council's deliberations, served to deauthenticate the warning. On the other hand, deauthentication of Minturn's December 20 forecast was less dramatic in its effect on information seeking. The difference is probably in what constitutes authentication and deauthentication in the two cases. Whitcomb came from within the scientific establishment, so the failure of spokesmen for that establishment to endorse his prediction was a severe blow to his credibility. Because Minturn came from outside the scientific establishment, his forecast could not be so effectively discredited by testimony from within the establishment. Minturn's appeal to the large populist segment of the population (see chapter ten) could even be enhanced by vocal opposition from within the scientific establishment.

As a fourth consideration, we note that every wave of information seeking comes to an end, even without deauthentication. The pull of normalcy is strong. How soon that pull overcomes the rumoring impulse undoubtedly depends on many considerations, but one of the most important may be the exhaustion of ideas and sources. After a while, people are no longer hearing anything new. The known sources for information seem to have been fully milked. Although neither importance nor ambiguity are substantially reduced, exhaustion of ideas and sources allows the pull of normalcy to prevail.

We can summarize the discussion to this point by observing, first, that a topic must be both important and ambiguous to stimulate either informal discussion to sift media communication or escalated forms of information seeking. But the concepts of importance and ambiguity are of little help in determining when active information seeking will occur. In order for the threshold between informal discussion of media communication and active information seeking to be crossed, the following three factors must exist: a certain level of comprehension of the message; specificity concerning the time and place of the threat; and authentication of the message.

The fourth stage, in which a rumoring public creates and authenticates its own scenario while seeking further authentication and elaboration from established authorities, remains to be explained. We have associated escalation of the rumoring process with rising attention from the media. But the affirmative rumoring episodes in October and November came during a three-month period, from September through November, in which media attention to earthquake predictions as well as to all other earthquake topics dropped dramatically. Why, then, did the whole rumoring process not remain within normalcy limits?

Juxtaposition of two sets of circumstances may have been critical. First, the abrupt September drop in media attention followed an active summer. There was a spate of prediction of stories in August, many referring to the death of thousands in the unpredicted Chinese earthquake in July and to aftershock predictions. Stories also critically evaluated American progress in the art of earthquake prediction, often reminding readers of the need to refine prediction techniques because southern California was already overdue for a great earthquake. Throughout the summer the media assured people that the threat was real and perhaps imminent in spite of the welcome demise of Whitcomb's "prediction." And reports of devastating earthquakes in China and elsewhere supplied fuel for imagination.

Could the fairly sudden drop in media attention after mounting expressions of concern account for affirmative rumoring to fill the media gap? Perhaps not by itself. The second circumstance was the airing of television spot features on earthquake preparedness and the inclusion of leaflets on personal and household earthquake preparedness in telephone bill mailings. Both kinds of communication were probably too brief to satisfy the demand for information proportional to the earthquake threat, but they did serve as authenticators: "Something must be brewing," the public might conclude. "But what? What do they know that we are not being told?"

We suggest that affirmative rumoring took place when comprehension and authentication of the threat were at a high level and expectation had been aroused, but the media were no longer providing current material that could serve as the focus for informal discussion among family members, friends, and work associates and as the topic for direct inquiries to authorities. People were ready to believe that reluctance of the authorities and the media to tell what they knew meant that the truth could only be known through information leaks that bypassed established communication channels.

One further element in information seeking needs to be stressed. People have to know who to contact for information, and information sources must be accessible. The presence of Caltech in Pasadena undoubtedly facilitated a great deal of information seeking about earthquakes and earthquake prediction that would not have taken place elsewhere. Unlike scientific experts, preparedness experts were not so well known or widely advertised in the media. Seekers were frequently shuttled from agency to agency when they sought preparedness information. A strong latent demand for information became active whenever sources for preparedness information were publicized. According to the civil defense officer for the City of Los Angeles, each time he was interviewed concerning the city's level of earthquake preparedness on a local radio or television program, his office was inundated with requests for earthquake materials. When the *Santa Monica Evening Outlook* offered reprints of the Fil Drukey series on individual and household preparedness, the paper received 4,000 requests. When telephone companies offered preparedness information referrals to agencies for additional materials in their September and October bills, the four referral agencies were unprepared for the massive response.

Conclusions

Evidence presented in this chapter clearly demonstrates that many people took active steps to learn more than they were being told by public officials and the media during a disaster warning situation. Nearly half the people were convinced that information about the earthquake threat was being withheld from the public by scientists or public officials. The overwhelming majority of people wanted more rather than less information from the media. Yet the widespread doubts about the wisdom of releasing earthquake predictions to the public unless scientists are nearly certain a quake will occur, and then only fairly close to the anticipated date of occurrence, suggest that most people want not just more information, but more *precise* information.

In chapter three we distinguished between the public's simply reading or hearing about earthquakes from the media and a more active pattern, in which media communications are sifted and interpreted through discussion among family members, friends, and work associates. In this chapter we have added two more levels to a scale from passive to active involvement in communication. The third level is *information seeking*, in which people go directly to outside and supposedly authoritative information sources in search of confirmation, clarification, elaboration, and "inside" information. The fourth and most active level is *affirmative rumoring*, in which new "information" is generated collectively and disseminated informally as authoritative.

The two main variables in the classic Allport and Postman theory of rumor, *importance* and *ambiguity*, are not helpful in explaining the rise and decline of information seeking and rumoring at different times during the year of the bulge, except as underlying constants. Our evidence suggests that the threshold from information sifting to information seeking is crossed as comprehension of the threat message increases, when the nature of the threat is specified more precisely and immediately (e.g., time and place), when the threat is authenticated, and when people know of an accessible source for additional information. The threshold to affirmative rumoring is crossed when all but the last of these conditions exist and heightened expectations are frustrated by a decrease or dearth of information from the media and other authoritative sources. The key to affirmative rumoring is the shared conviction that something must be brewing but that authorities won't talk publicly.

Explanations for both information seeking and affirmative rumoring must be qualified by principles of exhaustion and disconfirmation. Information seeking subsides after a period in which nothing new is being learned, and affirmative rumoring tends to be self-terminating because it generates accounts and predictions that are sufficiently specific that events soon disconfirm them.

CHAPTER FIVE

What Have They Learned After All?

Routine communication through the mass media was extensively augmented by popular initiative in seeking information about the earthquake threat during 1976. Although the popular initiative was vigorous and even boisterous at times, it may have directly involved only a small fraction of the whole population. In this chapter we will ask how much people actually learned as a result of the two-way communication. First, we will ask how many of the people became aware of the southern California uplift and what its potential significance was for them. Next, we will ask similar questions about awareness of all kinds of earthquake predictions, forecasts, and warnings. Because these notices came from both scientific and nonscientific sources, we will make some comparisons: How do the remembered scientific forecasts and warnings differ from the nonscientific notices? Exploring the differences further, we can find affinities between certain kinds of announcements and certain communications channels. Whether people have heard scientific or nonscientific announcements depends partly on which media they rely on. We will attempt to "explain" differences in levels of awareness by asking what kinds of people are most aware and what kinds are least aware of the uplift and of the wider range of earthquake warning announcements. Finally, we will look briefly at some indications of how well people have come to understand the earthquake as a physical and social phenomenon.

Awareness of the Uplift

Amid the diversity of earthquake concerns aired in 1976, existence of a great uplift along the San Andreas Fault near California's largest metropolis was the constant that gave meaning and urgency to all discussions. After a year's exposure, how aware were people of the uplift?

We first approached this question indirectly, in order to see how often the uplift came to mind when people were asked about earthquake predictions and warnings. We use the term *salience* as distinguished from mere *awareness* to indicate that people think immediately of the uplift when the topic of earthquake predictions and warnings is broached. Respondents were asked the following question:

> In the past year or so, have you heard any predictions, statements, or warnings about earthquakes in the southern California area? That is, about specific locations, specific time, or from specific people?

If the answer was positive, the respondent was then asked:

> I'd like you to tell me about the predictions, statements, or warnings. *Any* specific ones, *anything* at all that you remember.

Respondents were encouraged to give more than one answer, and up to five different answers were recorded and coded for each respondent. The range of answers to these questions will be discussed later in the chapter. But only 110 people, or 7.6 percent of the sample, mentioned the uplift by one of its names or in vaguer but recognizable terms.

Later in the interview we asked the following question of everyone who had not volunteered a reference to the uplift:

> Do you remember hearing about a bulge in the earth near Palmdale in the Mojave Desert?

Combining the respondents who answered "yes" to this question with the respondents who mentioned the uplift in answer to the prior questions, we found that 857 people, or 59.1 percent of the sample, were at least minimally aware of the uplift.

Merely having heard about a bulge in the desert may not signify any real awareness of the uplift and its significance. Hence, we asked people if they remembered what scientists were saying was signified by the bulge. Endorsing the answer "There is definitely an earthquake coming," 10.8 percent of the entire sample over-estimated scientific confidence in this interpretation of the uplift but were at least on the right track. The 15.8 percent who said, "There is probably an earthquake coming" and the 16.3 percent who said, "There might be an earthquake coming" had fairly adequately grasped the view presented in the responsible media. But the 10.1 percent who did not know and the 6.1 percent who said, "The bulge *doesn't* signify that an earthquake is coming" lacked something in awareness of the uplift. Thus, out of the 857 people who had heard of the uplift, only 72.7 percent understood that it might have been an earthquake precursor. This constitutes 43.0 percent of the entire sample, down from the 59.1 percent who had heard of the uplift.

Awareness of the uplift and of its possible significance as an earthquake precursor still does not insure that the earthquake threat has a personal meaning for individuals. Palmdale may seem a long way off and any associated earthquake equally remote. Accordingly, we asked everyone who had heard of the uplift—except for the 88 people who were definite that the uplift did not signify a coming quake—whether they expected damage where they lived in case of an uplift-connected quake. Only 82 people expected a great deal of damage, but 426, or 29.4 percent, of the entire sample expected either some or a great deal of damage where they lived. If we eliminated the people who did not know whether scientists were saying that the uplift might be an earth-quake precursor, we were left with 25.3 percent who had heard, understood, and appreciated the personal relevance of the uplift. This left a balance of 29.7 percent who claimed to have heard of the uplift, but who either did not understand that scientists con-sidered it a possible precursor or did not anticipate much damage where they lived.

These findings are summarized graphically in figure 9. From left to right, the graph identifies groups of people for whom the uplift was decreasingly significant. The small segment for whom earthquake threat is salient[1] is included for comparison, although

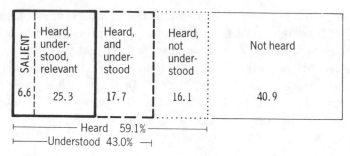

Figure 9. Awareness of the Southern California Uplift

not all of these people expected damage where they lived. We shall use these four main categories of awareness in future analyses of uplift awareness throughout this report.

As another way of exploring *quality of awareness,* we also asked everyone who had heard of the uplift—except for those who denied any connection with a possible earthquake—the following question: "How seriously do you take the Palmdale bulge as a sign of a coming earthquake?" More than half said they took the uplift seriously ("fairly" or "quite" seriously), and of these, more than one in five said they took it quite seriously. However, a substantial 39 percent of persons who had heard of the bulge said they did not take it seriously. As parts of the total sample, 11.4 percent had heard of the uplift and took it quite seriously, and 29.3 percent had heard of it and had taken the uplift either fairly seriously or quite seriously. This figure is quite close to the proportion who saw the uplift as relevant.

Predictions, Forecasts, and Warnings of Many Kinds

While the southern California uplift was the most scientifically credible and timely reason for increased attention to the prospect of a serious earthquake in the near future, the message of impending disaster came from many quarters. Messages from scientists ranged from perennial reminders that a great earthquake is overdue in southern California to the relatively specific near prediction issued by James Whitcomb. From the margins and outside of the scientific establishment, but wearing the mantle of science, were the forecasters of the Jupiter Effect epidemic of great earthquakes in 1982 and Henry Minturn with his December 20, 1976 forecast for Los Angeles. Annual forecasts by an assortment of seers and psychics often included earthquakes. The forecast that much of California would break off and slide into the Pacific Ocean as a result of great earthquakes in 1969, proclaimed in a best-selling work of fiction, has been preserved as an enduring element in California earthquake lore. The original date has generally been forgotten. A television evangelist devoted an hour-long special and a paperback book to the forecast of an earthquake for 1982, claiming converging evidence from the uplift, the Jupiter Effect, and the biblical Revelations. Thus, forebodings of earthquake disaster were in the air in southern California.

How aware are people of these forecasts and forebodings? How accurate is their understanding of the announcements? To what extent do they discriminate among them, or merge them into one multifaceted prediction?

ANNOUNCEMENTS REMEMBERED

Our information on predictive announcements comes from the series of questions beginning with the two queries on "predictions, statements, and warnings" presented earlier in this chapter. After up to five answers were recorded, the interviewer took up each answer in turn, asking a series of questions about the particular announcement.

One or more announcements were remembered by 86.6 percent of southern Californians. However, the majority were only able to give one answer to the follow-up question. Only 29.2 percent were able or willing to identify two or more announcements, and a meager 6 percent could name three or more.

The many forecasts and cautions to which southern Californians have been exposed are not kept separate in memory by most of our respondents. Either people lump them together into a generalized forecast of disaster, or they allow one specific announcement to speak for all.

Interviewers tried to get enough detail from respondents about each of the announcements they mentioned so that we could tell whether they had some specific forecast or forecaster in mind. We did not expect people to remember exact names and details of an announcement, but we looked for clues. For example, if someone mentioned a Caltech professor's prediction or spoke of an earthquake predicted to occur by April 1977, we assumed they were referring to the James Whitcomb announcement. In order to allow for possible confusion between different announcements, we provided for each answer to be coded under from one to three headings. For example, a reference to "the Caltech professor who predicted an earthquake for December" was coded under Whitcomb/Minturn, since the respondent had apparently mixed the two in his mind.

The announcements were grouped under four general headings and under "mixed" types (table 7). For clarity of communication, we shall distinguish between "combined" and "mixed" types. If an answer confused two or more announcements that fall within the same general category, such as scientific announcements, we called it a combined answer. For example, reference to "a Caltech professor who predicted an earthquake by April 1977, based on a bulge in the desert" confuses two announcements. But since both sources are scientific, we placed this under the combined type, "Uplift/Whitcomb." On the other hand, if we were told that "Minturn predicted an earthquake in December on the basis of the Palmdale bulge," the confusion was between a scientific and a pseudoscientific announcement. We classified this response under the mixed type, "Uplift/Minturn."

More than a third of the answers were nonspecific: for example, "I heard on television that an earthquake is overdue" or "Everybody says there will be an earthquake soon." Only slightly more specific were the "general scientific" forecasts, such as "Scientists have predicted an earthquake in southern California." If we combine these types, 42.2 percent of all answers were nonspecific. Another 6 percent either mixed or combined types of announcements, thus achieving specificity at the cost of confusion.

Of those who were specific about an announcement, the great majority referred to the pseudoscientific prediction by Minturn. If we include the combined and mixed references to Minturn's prediction, a total of 34.6 percent of the answers referred to this prediction. The interviewing took place from one to three months after the date when the predicted quake failed to materialize, so recency and intensive media coverage undoubtedly accounted for

TABLE 7

EARTHQUAKE PREDICTIONS, FORECASTS, AND CAUTIONS

Type of announcement	Percent of all answers	
General forecasts	36.9	36.9
Scientific announcements:		15.4
General scientific	5.3	
Uplift	5.0	
Whitcomb	3.9	
General scientific/Uplift	.3	
General scientific/Whitcomb	.2	
Uplift/Whitcomb	.7	
Pseudoscientific announcements:		37.2
Minturn	30.5	
California breakoff	6.0	
Jupiter Effect	.3	
Minturn/California breakoff	.3	
Minturn/Jupiter Effect	.1	
Prophetic announcements:		6.1
Religious prophecies	.8	
Secular prophecies	5.3	
Mixed types:		4.4
General scientific/Minturn	1.3	
Whitcomb/Minturn	1.0	
Minturn/Secular prophecies	1.2	
Other mixed types:	.9	
Total percent	100.0	100.0
Total number of answers	1,788	1,788

much of the salience of Minturn. Without the inflated reference
to Minturn, the general category of pseudoscientific announcements would not have been so prominent in the table. The later
evidence reported in the analysis of change and stability confirms
this assumption (see chapter thirteen). Nevertheless, the second
most frequent specific answer was another pseudoscientific tenet,

that California will someday break off and slide into the ocean in a great earthquake, mentioned by 6.9 percent of the sample.

Other answers were scattered, reflecting the diversity of forecasts to which southern Californians were subjected but indicating no consensus. It is important to remember when interpreting these findings that respondents volunteered their answers without help from the interviewer. Their answers did not detail all of the announcements they had heard, but only those that were sufficiently at the forefront of memory to be recalled immediately when the subject of earthquake predictions was broached. If we had been able to follow up each announcement as we did with the southern California uplift by mentioning the forecast or prediction and asking whether respondents had heard of it, many of the announcements would undoubtedly have been recognized by a large share of the people.

ATTRIBUTED SOURCES

The preceding discussion compares scientific and nonscientific announcements according to *our classification* of the information respondents gave us. For example, if a respondent mentioned the Palmdale bulge or an earthquake that was supposed to happen by April 1977, we classified the statement as referring to a scientific announcement because we recognized the source. But the respondent may have had quite a different idea of the source of the announcement. The question naturally arises whether people generally distinguish correctly between announcements from scientific and nonscientific sources or whether they mix them up, ascribing nonscientific announcements to scientists, and vice versa.

For each announcement they mentioned, respondents were asked the following question:

Do you happen to remember who it was that originally made this prediction?

Interviewers were instructed to write down the name or other identification exactly as the respondent gave it. Then a second question was asked:

Do you know whether this person was a: Scientist, Seer or Psychic, Religious Speaker, Amateur scientist, or Some other type of person (specify)?

In table 8, we have cross-tabulated the source attributions by our respondents with our classification for five of the most significant announcements. Reflecting the media's consistent identification of the uplift and the Whitcomb announcement with science, the great majority of respondents who mentioned them correctly attributed them to scientists. Three-quarters of the people who referred to vague and general predictions and cautions thought they knew the source. Most frequently they attributed the announcements to scientists, but quite frequently they attributed them to prophets. By the time of our survey, the idea that California would some day break off from the North American continent and slide into the Pacific Ocean following a great earthquake was most commonly attributed to seers and psychics, but a small— though substantial—minority attributed this forecast to scientists.

The Minturn prediction is of special interest because it received such extensive media coverage and because so many people remembered it. The confusion over who Minturn was had not been cleared up by the time of our survey. Nearly two out of every five respondents who mentioned this announcement thought that it was issued by a scientist. Although Minturn had publicly claimed to be a scientist, about 23 percent of respondents called him a seer, psychic, or religious speaker. Certain of the mass media were largely at fault for fostering this confusion.

We conclude that people are generally correct in recognizing a scientific announcement as scientific, but they also attribute many nonscientific announcements to scientists. While prophets are credited or blamed for many of the earthquake predictions, forecasts, and cautions, scientists are held responsible for the lion's share.

EXPECTED INTENSITY

When we discussed awareness of the southern California uplift, we concluded that full appreciation required the recognition that an earthquake could do damage where the respon-

TABLE 8

How People Identify the Source of Selected Earthquake Predictions, Forecasts, and Cautions

Attributed source \ Identified source	General predictions and forecasts %	Minturn forecast %	California breakoff %	Whitcomb forecast %	California uplift %
Scientist	37.7	38.0	15.4	79.0	84.6
Amateur scientist	7.6	14.4	3.4	5.8	2.7
Secular or religious prophet	20.9	22.9	49.6	6.6	0
Other	8.5	6.1	6.0	2.0	2.7
No answer or don't know	25.3	18.6	25.6	6.6	10.0
Total	100.0	100.0	100.0	100.0	100.0
Total number	660	619	117	105	110

dent lived. Roughly a quarter of our sample had reached this standard of awareness. In somewhat parallel fashion we asked whether the many and diverse earthquake warning announcements people had heard referred to catastrophic or to benign events. For each of the announcements mentioned, respondents were presented with a card specifying four broad degrees of intensity and were asked the following question:

> Please look at this card and tell me how strong the earthquake is supposed to be. (Destroy many buildings and take many lives; Destroy some buildings and take a few lives; Do some damage, but no widespread destruction; Do little or no damage; or Didn't they say?)

Forty-nine percent of all announcements were identified as presaging earthquakes of the highest intensity. Adding the quakes that were supposed to "destroy some buildings and take a few lives" brings the total to almost two-thirds of all announcements referring to destructive earthquakes. With respondents unable to specify the intensity for 23 percent of the announcements, only 9.8 percent of the announcements were specifically associated with low-intensity earthquakes. In short, the announcements about which people told our interviewers were seldom thought to refer to trivial events. If people have earthquakes on their minds, they are thinking of damaging quakes.

We looked once again at the number of earthquake predictions, forecasts, and cautions that people could name or describe, but this time we included only those that are supposed to destroy some or many buildings and take some or many lives. Sixty-four percent of the respondents had heard at least one announcement concerning an earthquake expected to destroy buildings and take lives, but few could think of more than one such announcement.

Does the expected intensity vary by the type of announcement? We have graphed the relationship in figure 10 so as to convey two distinct items of information. In the square area above the baseline, the graph shows the amount of damage expected for each type of announcement in the usual fashion. The differences are not great, but they are significant by the usual statistical tests. On the average, when people think of scientific announcements, they think of less destructive earthquakes than they do when thinking of prophetic forecasts. There is a steady progression in

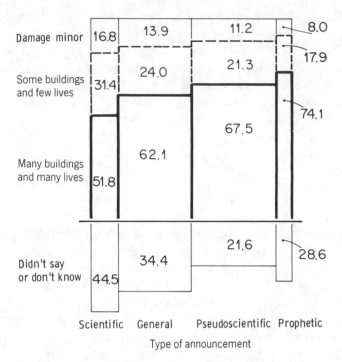

Figure 10. Expected Damage by Type of Announcement

severity from scientific to general, then to pseudoscientific, and finally to prophetic forecasts and near predictions.

The figures above the baseline apply only to announcements for which people were able to choose an intensity. Below the baseline, we have graphed the items to which people were unable to attach an intensity. These are the instances in which people had heard that there either may or will be an earthquake but could not say whether it will be mild or destructive. These figures vary considerably by type of announcement. People were least often definite about the intensity of the quake expected on the basis of a scientific announcement, and they were most often definite in the case of pseudoscientific forecasts.

There may be reason for concern about the relative potency of scientific and nonscientific announcements on the basis of this graph. When people remember scientific near predictions, they are least likely to have a clear idea of how destructive an earthquake to expect. If they do have a definite idea, it is least likely to be a highly destructive earthquake. The earthquakes associated with scientific announcements are vaguer and more benign than those associated with prophetic and pseudoscientific forecasts. These differences may come about because of the cautious and often reassuring manner in which the scientists announce their near predictions, compared to the sensational way in which seers and soothsayers warn of impending doom. Or, the differences may tell us about the perspectives of those people who remember hearing scientific announcements as compared to those who remember prophetic and pseudoscientific announcements. Most of the pseudoscientific references were to the Minturn forecast for December 20, 1976. Minturn himself, in the days shortly before the forecast date, assured the community that the earthquake would not be a very big or destructive one. In spite of his assurances, most people who mentioned his forecast were convinced that a destructive earthquake had been predicted.

Whichever explanation is correct, there is reason for concern that scientific announcements may suffer reduced potency in stirring people to action because they are often remembered as being benign and vague.

Sources of Information

In chapter three, we learned that television news programs, newspapers, and radio were the chief sources of information about earthquakes for the majority of people in our sample. Did people learn about different kinds of predictions, forecasts, and cautions from different media? In order to answer this question, we first grouped the announcements that people mentioned into scientific, general, pseudoscientific, and prophetic types. In addition, we looked separately at the Minturn forecast and the forecast that California will break off and fall into the ocean. These two forecasts merit separate attention because of the wide recognition each received. We recorded the chief source of information for each as given to us by the respondents.

The most general observation from table 9 is that the order of reliance on the media remains largely the same irrespective of the type of prediction. Television is the principal source for all types of announcements, and newspapers come next. There is a reversal, however, between radio, which usually ranks third, and "people,"

TABLE 9

CHIEF SOURCE OF INFORMATION BY TYPE OF EARTHQUAKE
PREDICTION, FORECAST, OR CAUTION

Type of medium	% Inclusive types of announcements				% Specific announcements	
	Scientific	General	Pseudo-scientific	Prophetic	Minturn	California breakoff
Television	47.1	58.3	51.3	43.7	54.9	37.4
Newspapers	27.5	14.1	18.5	23.6	17.9	22.0
Radio	10.1	11.4	13.6	5.6	13.4	11.4
People	6.2	8.8	11.1	7.6	9.7	15.4
Magazines	22.2	1.5	1.3	5.6	1.0	4.1
Books	0	0	.3	.7	.2	.8
Other and don't know	6.9	5.9	3.9	13.2	2.9	8.9
Total	100.0	100.0	100.0	100.0	100.0	100.0
Number of announcements mentioned	276	660	708	144	619	123

which usually ranks fourth, in the case of prophetic announcements. A similar reversal also applies to the folkloristic belief that California will fall into the ocean. Magazines and books fall behind the other media except, again, in the case of prophetic announcements, when they rank even with radio but behind "people."

Bearing in mind that the general order of reliance on the media is more similar than dissimilar and that television and newspapers are the most important media in all cases, we can still observe some *affinities* between particular media and types of announcements. There is some affinity between television and general announcements. Relatively more of the people who mentioned rather vague and general earthquake forecasts credited them to television. Perhaps television commands a low level of attention for detail, or specializes in very brief news items, or perhaps it is just that more people are exposed for longer periods to television. In contrast, there is an affinity between newspapers and scientific announcements. The reporting of scientific announcements is facilitated by the provision for longer items in the newspaper, and people who are interested in science are probably more motivated to make the effort to read newspaper stories. Radio and "people" as sources show affinity with pseudoscientific announcements. These affinities are confirmed separately for both the Minturn and "breakoff" forecasts. It is in accordance with theories of rumor that pseudoscientific beliefs should be spread especially by word of mouth, while the printed word is especially prominent in the spread of scientific information. The special role of radio, however, may be a historical accident relating to the circumstances under which the Minturn forecast was publicized. On the other hand, radio call-in and talk shows may contribute to the spread of rumors by airing them and by being especially responsive to timely public preoccupations, even when the program moderators attempt to discredit the rumors.

Prophetic announcements, while credited principally to the leading media, show a distinct affinity with books and magazines and with "other" and "don't know" as a source. One interpretation for this affinity is that the worlds of secular and religious prophecy have their own networks and media for communicating among those who are interested in prophecy. To a greater extent than is true for the other types of announcements, they supplement the standard media with their own books and magazines and, perhaps, with tracts and meetings.

We also have a separate record of people's chief source of information about the southern California uplift. The record includes people who mentioned the uplift in answer to the open-ended question about predictions, forecasts, and cautions as well as the much larger number of people who remembered hearing about the uplift when asked about "a bulge in the earth near Palmdale in the Mojave Desert." The pattern of information sources is almost identical to that for all scientific announcements, and it is equally different from the patterns for general, pseudoscientific, and prophetic announcements.

Correlates of Earthquake Awareness

It has long been recognized that news spreads unevenly through any population; some groups of people hear and grasp the significance of important information quickly, and others frequently fail to hear the news or to grasp its significance when they hear it. An important task in preparing the community to cope successfully with an earthquake and to respond constructively to an earthquake prediction is to identify those groups of people who are out of the mainstream of public communication. Public officials and leaders in the private sector can then devise ways to see that these people have the same opportunity to protect themselves from danger as others do. Comparing awareness of the uplift among different population segments is one way to identify the groups in need of special attention.

PATH ANALYSIS PROCEDURE

We have approached the question of unequal awareness through the general strategy of multiple regression, employing the specific technique of path analysis to organize our findings. Since we shall use this same procedure in several chapters in Part Three as well as in this chapter, a brief generalized explanation is in order. The dependent variable, or the variable to be explained in the present case, is *awareness of the uplift*. This variable is created by assigning values from zero to three to the four categories of awareness already described. We first record the correlations between the dependent variable (awareness of the uplift) and each of a large battery of items that we think might influence the dependent variable. We further sort the items in the battery according to whether we think that they might affect awareness *directly* or whether we think that their effect might be *indirect* because of their influence on some variable with a direct effect. This sorting process gives us a list of *background variables,* whose effects on awareness of the uplift should be mainly indirect, and a list of *mediating variables,* which act directly on awareness and are, in turn, affected by some of the background variables. For the most part, this sorting process is based on what seems most plausible on a priori grounds rather than on the findings from our investigation. The method will, however, tell us if a background variable has direct as well as indirect effects on the dependent variable.

The path analysis procedure picks up those hypothesized mediating variables that reach a satisfactory level of correlation with the dependent variable and discards the rest. It then selects the background variables that reach the criterion level of correlation with one or more of the retained variables or directly with the dependent variable. The result is graphed as a pattern of causal flow from background variables to mediating variables to the dependent variable, with a magnitude value (path coefficient) assigned to each of the causal links. Throughout this investigation we have set .08 as the minimal path coefficient for inclusion of a relationship in the final pattern. Because of the large number of cases in our sample, this criterion is a few points higher than needed to meet the usual 1 percent confidence limit. Setting the criterion conservatively in this fashion reduces uninterpretable complexity that results from inclusion of statistically significant but trivial relationships.

We begin each path analysis with the same sets of hypothesized mediating and background variables, except as explained in the appropriate text. Four clusters of mediating variables are used. The first cluster, *communication,* includes the following specific measures: number of newspapers read regularly; number of media sources from which earthquake information was drawn; range of earthquake topics discussed with friends, relatives, coworkers, and others; and number of group meetings dealing with earthquakes attended. The second cluster, understanding of and *respect for science* as applied to earthquake prediction, includes the following: index of favorability toward science; belief in the accuracy of scientific prediction at the present time and in the future; attitude toward the public release of earthquake predictions; and having some idea of why earthquakes occur. The third cluster is *attitude toward earthquake danger* and includes two items: salience of the earthquake threat, and fatalism about earthquake danger. The final cluster, *integration into the community,* includes the following: a composite index of community bondedness combining length of residence, subjective identification of the community as one's home, participation in organizational activities in the community, and having friends and relatives nearby; awareness of groups of people who would be especially endangered in case of an earthquake; trust in public officials and scientists as being frank with the public about impending earthquake danger; and positive or negative evaluation of officials' preparedness efforts.

The background variables fall into three clusters. First, *individual and household characteristics* include: age; sex; whether one is Anglo, Black, or Mexican-American; educational attainment; occupational socioeconomic status of breadwinner; household income; marital status; and whether there are schoolchildren in the household. Second, *disaster experience* includes: a composite index of earthquake experience; number of damaging earthquakes experienced; personal experience of injury or loss in an earthquake; having close friends or relatives who experienced injury or loss in an earthquake; experience with natural disasters other than earthquakes. Third, *situational earthquake vulnerability* includes: a composite index of residential earthquake vulnerability; a composite index of workplace earthquake vulnerability; living in a zone of greater than average earthquake vulnerability, including a zone with a high concentration of buildings constructed before the earthquake codes of 1934 took effect, a potential inundation zone beneath a dam, a zone that combined the two hazards, and the zone most affected by the 1971 San Fernando earthquake.[2]

The hypotheses associated with each of these background and intervening variables are too many and in most instances too obvious for elaboration here. We shall discuss the relationships that turn out to be strong enough to be retained by the path analysis as each dependent variable is examined. It is important, however, for the reader to bear in mind the full complement of variables so as to recognize which relationships are not confirmed as well as which ones are.

UNDERSTANDING AWARENESS OF THE UPLIFT

The final explanatory model for awareness of the uplift is diagramed in figure 11. Three of the four significant mediating variables reflect involvement in communication. Being a regular reader of one or more newspapers, learning about earthquakes from several different media sources, and having discussed earthquake topics informally with several partners all make substantial contributions toward being aware, understanding the significance, and appreciating the relevance of the southern California uplift. The other significant mediating variable—that is, having some idea why earthquakes occur—fits in with a general characterization of the *aware* individual as one who makes broad use of communications opportunities and is interested enough to

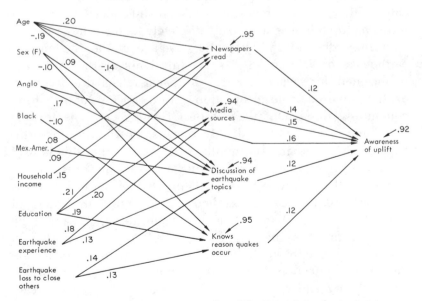

Figure 11. Awareness of Uplift: Causal Analysis

attempt to understand the dynamics of earthquakes. It is striking that attitudes such as fatalism, attitudes toward science and public authorities, and community bondedness do not substantially affect levels of awareness. Awareness is almost strictly a matter of exposure to and use of relevant communication media, insofar as we have been able to uncover the significant correlates.

The analysis was repeated twice, and each time we added a different measure of fear of earthquakes to the hypothesized mediating variables. One analysis used the *index of fear and concern* described in chapter six, which deals with feelings about a prospective earthquake. The other analysis used reported fear experienced during past earthquakes. In neither case was fear a significant determinant of awareness. Awareness of the uplift is primarily a cognitive rather than an affective phenomenon.

In addition to the four mediating variables, being of advanced age and being Anglo both make substantial direct contributions to awareness. It is consistent with a wide range of research into other disasters and public communication that the social "majority" group (Anglos) should be better informed than the minorities. But it is important to observe that ethnicity has a double effect, both indirectly (through differential involvement in relevant communication) and directly (over and above the effects of communication differentials). The principal Spanish-language newspaper in the metropolitan area almost completely ignored the uplift. By featuring extended and dramatic coverage of the Guatemalan earthquake of February 3, 1976, while ignoring the uplift announcement for several months, the paper reflected a diversion of attention from the local situation toward concerns of the Latino community throughout the Western Hemisphere. The leading black newspaper published only one item pertaining to earthquakes during the first six months of 1976. Whether this lack of concern by the ethnic press for the local earthquake threat accounts for the low awareness levels or whether the lack of press coverage and low awareness levels are parallel indicators of minority concerns and values is a question that cannot be answered from our data.

Age, like ethnicity, has both direct and indirect effects on awareness, but its effect on the mediating communication variables is contradictory. Older people are more consistent newspaper readers and engage in a little more informal discussion of earthquakes.

However, they use a narrower range of media sources. Over and beyond these indirect effects, it is young adults rather than the middle-aged and elderly who are most frequently ill informed about the uplift. This observation contradicts findings from some of the earlier research on disasters, which showed that older people are often not in the public communication mainstream and are frequently less interested in matters of public concern than younger people.[3] This relationship is sufficiently important to merit closer examination. Figure 12 shows a strikingly consistent and linear relationship. Simple awareness, understanding, and appreciation of relevance all increase steadily with each increment of age.

In a metropolitan environment with extensive television, radio, and newspaper coverage, the elderly may no longer be at a significant disadvantage. The alienation of a generation or more of young people, many of whom responded by taking no interest in public affairs, may have made *youth* rather than the elderly the communication problem. The preoccupation with schooling, becoming established in a vocation, or maintaining a family may translate such hypothetical future events as a possible earthquake into

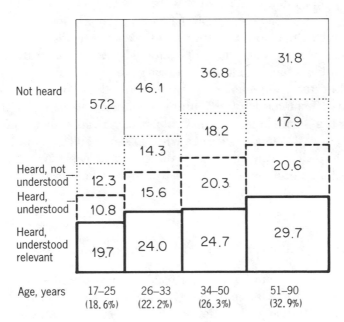

Figure 12. Awareness of Uplift by Age

low-priority concerns. Whatever the correct explanation or combination of explanations, it must be a matter of concern that fully 57 percent of adults under twenty-six years of age do not even remember having heard of the uplift.

Being well educated and living in a household in which the breadwinner's occupation ranks high in socioeconomic status are the background variables next most predictive of high awareness, after being Anglo. Living in a household with a substantial income is also quite predictive.[4] However, the effects are strictly indirect. Each of these characteristics enhances one or more aspects of communication involvement, which in turn foster awareness. Sex has significant but contradictory effects on the mediating variables, so that its total effect on awareness of the uplift is trivial.

Earthquake experience is the fourth strongest background predictor of awareness. Having relatives or close friends who suffered earthquake injury or loss is also important, but, again, the effects are strictly indirect.[5] There may be an interesting qualitative difference in the effects of these two kinds of experience. The less emotional fact of having been through several severe earthquakes without having suffered personal damage fosters both the more impersonal attention to media treatments and informal discussion with friends. The more emotional and personally meaningful fact of close association with an earthquake victim fosters informal discussion and some thought about why we have earthquakes, suggesting a more profound interest in the topic.

While the complete causal model is moderately successful by the usual standards in explaining awareness of the uplift ($R^2 = .15$), the great bulk of the variance in awareness is left unexplained. Practical work done with these variables in mind could lead to a significant increase in the general level of uplift awareness, but individual differences would still be a fact to contend with.

UNDERSTANDING PREDICTION AWARENESS

A similar analysis was completed with the number of predictions heard (and reported) as the variable to be explained (fig. 13). Although "predictions heard" and "awareness of the uplift" have much in common as measures of a general awareness

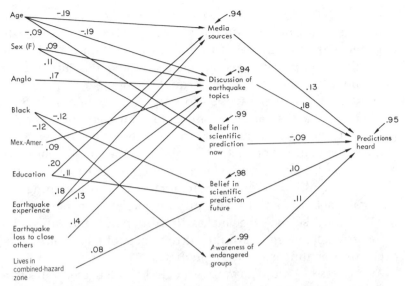

Figure 13. Predictions Heard: Causal Analysis

of the earthquake warnings disseminated in southern California, they differ in emphasis. Awareness of the uplift concerns a specific scientific set of announcements and includes a sense of personal relevance as its strongest condition. Predictions heard takes simply the number of announcements remembered, whether they are scientific, nonscientific, or too amorphous to categorize, and omits the question of personal relevance.

Very likely because of its heterogeneity, the index of predictions heard was less adequately accounted for than awareness of the uplift ($R^2 = .10$). As before, neither prospective nor past earthquake fear was significantly related to the dependent variable. The two strongest mediating causes were the major communication variables: number of media sources relied on for earthquake information, and range of informal earthquake discussion partners. Predictions heard and awareness of the uplift are similar in the importance of media usage and informal discussion. However, disciplined newspaper reading and having ideas about earthquake dynamics drop out.

Attitudes toward science play a part in this model, but in a strangely contradictory fashion. Believing in the future potential for earthquake prediction is a positive correlate of predictions heard, while believing that scientists can already predict earth-

quakes rather accurately is negatively correlated. As our subsequent examination of attitudes toward science will indicate
(chapter ten), a strong belief in current prediction capability is
unjustified and reflects misunderstanding and possibly even a
magical view of science. The same qualities of misperception and
misunderstanding that have led to an overestimation of current
prediction capability seem to contribute to an inability to specify
particular announcements heard or to specify more than one.
Thus, belief in future prediction capability is the sounder measure
of a reasonable appreciation of science and contributes to the
ability to identify one or more distinct earthquake-warning announcements. It is not the generally favorable or unfavorable attitude toward science that makes the difference, but rather the
more specific conception of the current state of and future prospects for, scientific earthquake prediction.

Awareness of groups that are especially endangered reflects a
socially conscious attention to the earthquake threat. Like the
strong faith in future rather than in current earthquake prediction,
this also means a discriminating rather than an undifferentiated
perception of earthquake danger. To an important extent, the
measure of predictions heard seems to distinguish those who have
retained a moderately complex view of the situation from those
whose perceptions are simplistic and global.

The same list of background variables applies to predictions
heard as to awareness of the uplift, with two exceptions. Household income, which was only significant as a correlate of newspaper readership, drops out as newspaper readership falls out of
the list of mediating variables. And living in one of the zones
subject to both old-building and inundation vulnerability is added
for its contribution to belief in future scientific prediction capability. But none of the background variables affects predictions heard
directly, and the simple (zero-order) correlations between background variables and the dependent variable are generally of
lesser magnitude. Educational level continues to be a leading
predictor of predictions heard, through its effects on wide use of
the media and faith in eventual scientific prediction. Earthquake
loss experienced by close friends and relatives is the strongest
predictor among the background variables, and general earthquake
experience ranks third, both through their effects on communication variables.[6] In contrast to the finding for awareness of the

uplift, the substantial effects of age on mediating variables have a canceling effect, so that the overall correlation between age and predictions heard is statistically nonsignificant. As before, sex effects also cancel out.

In summary, sensitization and exposure to both media and informal discussion are crucial in explaining awareness of the earthquake prospect. Education, experience with earthquakes, and Anglo ethnic identity make important indirect contributions to awareness in both of our analyses. But the two measures of awareness are different in significant respects. Our variables provide a fuller explanation for awareness of the uplift than for predictions heard. Ethnicity and age are important for uplift awareness, through both direct and indirect effects, but age is unimportant, and ethnicity less important, in explaining predictions heard. Awareness of the uplift may be a more intellectual matter, fostered by high income and socioeconomic status and by majority ethnic status, while remembering distinct predictive and warning announcements of various kinds is more related to conceptions of prediction and a social awareness about earthquakes. Both types of awareness are fostered by earthquake experience, chiefly through its effects in sensitizing people to both formal and informal communication about earthquakes. Relatively speaking, however, the mere fact of having extensive earthquake experience contributes more to awareness of the uplift, while the more emotional experience of having close friends and relatives who have experienced earthquake loss or injury is more important for remembering a range of distinguishable earthquake-warning announcements.

Understanding Earthquakes

Our analysis of earthquake awareness can be rounded out by looking at some indications of how much people understand about earthquakes. We had neither the desire nor the time to administer a sophisticated test of knowledge and understanding about earthquakes to our sample of southern Californians. While it is neither to be expected nor is it necessary for the general public to have textbook understandings of geology or seismology, we thought it worthwhile to try out a short test that included representative items of information as part of the first follow-up wave of interviewing. In figure 14, we report the answers to six questions as given by 551 new respondents in August 1977.

The items are arranged for convenience, in reverse order according to the size of the "don't know" response. Thus, nearly everyone was confident about saying whether a doorway is a safe place to be during an earthquake. At the opposite extreme, more than half freely admitted that they did not understand the technical meaning of the steps on the Richter scale. The following observations are suggested: (1) The most widespread sense of understanding, coupled with the nearest approximation to consensus in giving the correct answer, applies to the immediately practical question of where one should be during an earthquake. The least widespread sense of understanding applies to strictly scientific aspects of earthquake understanding. Still, it is surprising that such large fractions of the lay public did claim to understand something about tectonic plates and the Richter scale. (2) Except in the mistaken supposition that widespread panic follows an earthquake—a belief fostered by the mass media—large majorities of the people answering each question chose the right answer. This observation indicates that some minimal degree of earthquake understanding is indeed widespread in this corner of "earthquake country." (3) Nevertheless, the fact that a fifth or more of the population mistakenly believe that aftershocks are not to be feared and that southern California could suddenly fall into the ocean illustrates the tenacious character of some popular fallacies. The number of people in the entire county of Los Angeles who might respond inappropriately in an emergency because of these misunderstandings could easily run into the hundreds of thousands.

Summary of Part Two

Part Two began with the response of organizations and the media to a series of earthquake forecasts and near predictions. It has carried us through public involvement in earthquake communication to the resulting state of public awareness.

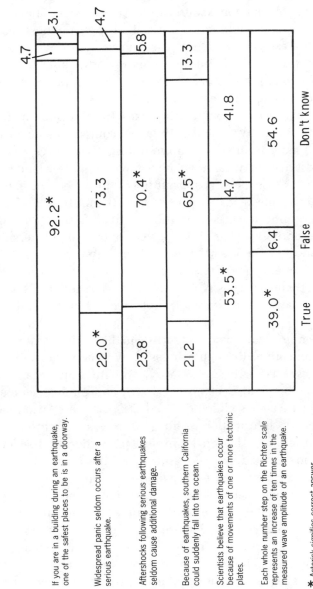

Figure 14. Understanding Earthquakes

Although media attention to the earthquake threat was extensive and varied in the year of the bulge, the media were initially slow in responding, and it was alternating feast and famine for the public. The organizational source of most news material meant that advice on household and individual preparedness was skimpy until late in the year. But through various devices, the threatening uplift became increasingly newsworthy after the initial month or two of perfunctory treatment and retained its newsworthiness throughout the year.

Most people learned about earthquakes from several media sources, but television was rated as the chief source. The majority relied on the media as an authoritative information source, while extensively discussing what they heard with family members, friends, and work associates. A substantial minority learned about earthquakes from the media but kept it to themselves, while a much smaller minority accepted the word of friends and associates as authoritative. The usual pattern of opinion leadership is impaired in the case of earthquakes, because very few people know anyone whom they consider to be even modestly expert. Nevertheless, there is suggestive evidence of an earthquake *social circle* that mediates the relationship between the media and the public.

At times, people went beyond attending to the media and sifting media communications through discussion with family members, friends, and associates. In April, May, and June and again in October, November, and December, Caltech and public agencies such as the Los Angeles Office of Civil Defense were swamped with requests for information. And two waves of affirmative rumoring, to the effect that an imminent prediction of a severe earthquake had been suppressed, inundated the community in October and November. The early wave of information seeking accompanied gradual recognition of the potential seriousness of the situation, combined with *authentication* through intensified media coverage, a second and more concrete forecast, and an official declaration by the California Seismic Safety Commission. The second period of information seeking was associated with affirmative rumoring at a time when media attention to the earthquake threat had declined drastically after a period of accelerating expectations, coupled with the authentication of threat implied by the inclusion of leaflets on individual and household earthquake preparedness in telephone bill mailings and the airing of earthquake-preparedness spots on local television.

Following that year of exceptional attention to the earthquake threat, most people could remember some warning they had heard, although they were often vague about details and frequently merged the variety of predictions and forecasts into a single amorphous warning. Pseudoscientific and prophetic forecasts were remembered as having been more specific and threatening than were the scientific announcements, which often seemed vague and benign. Only three-fifths of the people remembered having heard about the Palmdale bulge, while only a quarter of the people appreciated the possibility that the uplift could presage an earthquake that would create damage where they lived. Awareness of the uplift and of other warning announcements seemed to be almost entirely a cognitive matter of involvement in earthquake communication through exposure to the media and through participation in informal discussion. Most affective considerations, such as fear of earthquakes, had no effect on the level of awareness. The one significant affective element was prior experience of personal injury or loss in an earthquake or similar experience by a close friend or relative.

We now turn our attention to the translation of awareness into action, which is the subject of Part Three.

Part Three

From Hearing to Heeding

CHAPTER SIX

Are the People Really Concerned?

Government and private organizations moved slowly. The media seldom ventured beyond what agencies offered them and what they found in their own slim archives, except in one dramatic episode of television folly. But a message that the familiar earthquake threat had taken on extraordinary proportions spread widely during the year of the Palmdale bulge. Most people heard and remembered the message, though what they remembered and in what detail varied greatly. People often tried to close information gaps by actively pursuing more information. A period marked by public reminders of the threat without much clarifying news evoked massive rumoring and probably fostered unparalleled attention to a pseudoscientific forecast in late November and December.

But awareness and action are different. Floodplain dwellers often remain in their homes while flood waters are visibly rising about them. In the case of the much less visible earthquake threat, how often is awareness translated into action? In Part Three we shall attempt to answer this question.

One way of doing something about earthquake danger is to have individuals and households take stock and make their own preparations. Another way is to support government action. Still another course is to organize people at the grass roots to work together as neighbors and work groups. We examine these three kinds of action in chapters seven, eight, and nine, respectively. But first we ask a more general question about the relationship between awareness and action.

According to one viewpoint, the way to get people to do something or to support government action is to keep hammering away at the theme of the earthquake threat until awareness is high enough to trigger action. The assumption is that a high level of awareness is in itself sufficient to stimulate action. Inaction can be explained entirely on the basis of insufficient awareness.

According to an alternative viewpoint, the causes for action are qualitatively as well as quantitatively different from the causes of awareness. While the level of awareness is important, a high level of awareness alone will not trigger action. In chapters six and seven, we will explore some prime candidates for inclusion in a list of "other conditions" necessary for action. Fear and concern over earthquakes and a *quality* of awareness are subjects of the present chapter. People's ideas about whether anything can be done and whether people are disposed toward collaborative or individualistic action provide the opening themes for chapter seven. After laying the groundwork in these first two chapters, we can then address the more general question of how awareness is translated into action; in chapters eight and nine, we will look at household preparedness, support for government programs, and grass-roots organization.

Fear and Concern over Earthquakes

Harry Moore described an attitude of bravado as being part of the indigenous disaster culture in hurricane-afflicted Gulf Coast regions of the United States. Instead of fear, Moore often found "an added element of pride in the ability to face danger and pleasure in observing the awe-inspiring spectacle of natural forces rampaging."[1] Popular writers prefer to depict Californians' attitudes toward earthquakes as apathetic, with occasional contrasting references to panic. While feelings are not always admitted or accurately expressed in words, we have tried through direct questioning to secure preliminary evidence on whether bravado, apathy, or terror prevails.

We measured fear and concern with a set of three questions. Respondents were first asked:

Which of the following best describes your own feelings about the possibility of experiencing a damaging earthquake? Would you say you are very frightened, somewhat frightened, not very frightened, or not at all frightened?

As indicated in figure 15, over 60 percent acknowledged being substantially frightened. Twenty-seven percent admitted being very frightened, and 35 percent said they were somewhat frightened. Only 14 percent said they were not frightened. Since the word "frightened" is stronger than words such as "fear," these figures represent an impressive admission.

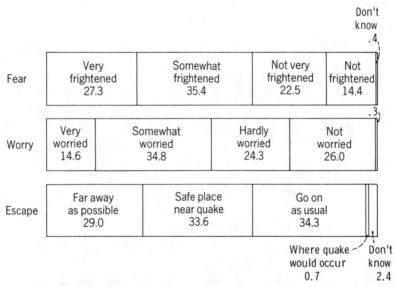

Figure 15. Three Measures of Concern over Earthquake Threat

In a second question, respondents were asked,

How worried are you about the possibility of a damaging earthquake striking southern California?

Respondents chose from the usual four answers, from "not worried" to "very worried." If we accept the answers at face value, being worried is less prevalent than being frightened. While 63 percent admitted being substantially frightened, only 49 percent said they were substantially worried. These worriers include 15 percent who were very worried, compared with the 27 percent who were very frightened. Worry has a greater connotation of persisting concern than does fright, which can be momentary. Nevertheless, about half of our respondents admitted that they were substantially worried over the prospect of an earthquake.

Another way to find out how people feel about earthquakes is to ask what they would do in case of a quake. The following question was posed:

> If you were certain that a damaging earthquake was going to occur at a specific time in a place where you live or work, would you: try to be where the earthquake would occur, try to get as far away as possible, try to find a safe place near the earthquake, or go on as usual and be wherever you are at the time?

Only eleven people expressed bravado by choosing the first answer, with the bulk of the people dividing fairly evenly among the three remaining answers. A substantial 34 percent said they would go on as usual. These may be the people who are often labeled apathetic or fatalistic. Another 34 percent accepted the course most often proposed in disaster mitigation plans and followed in the People's Republic of China, and that is to find a relatively safe location without trying to leave the immediate earthquake area. Fully 29 percent said they would try to get as far away as possible; this figure represents a larger number of people than the number who said either that they were very frightened or that they were very worried.

We should not assume from these answers that 29 percent would actually try to get out of Los Angeles on the freeways, or that a third of the people would actually go on as if nothing out of the ordinary were happening. What people actually do in a crisis situation probably depends much more on the kind of leadership and instructions they receive, the amount of advance warning they have had, the practical opportunities available to them, and other contingencies. But these answers confirm our impression from the two preceding questions: the majority of people are actively concerned about the earthquake danger, and they not only admit fear and even worry but also say that they would interrupt their normal routines to some extent in order to minimize personal danger if they were confident an earthquake was imminent.

Without taking answers to the third question literally, we can still treat them as behavior indicators, giving us our first opportunity to compare the impact of awareness and fear on the disposition to act. We have tested the relationships between the stated disposition to escape from an earthquake and both the number of predictive announcements remembered and the level of fright over the earthquake prospect. The relationship of flight to fear is clear and consistent, but flight disposition is not meaningfully related to awareness of earthquake warnings. In further analysis, a Pearson correlation coefficient of .27 between disposition toward flight and the combined fright and concern questions is not increased by the addition of either number of warnings remembered or awareness of the uplift to the regression equation.

PAST AND PROSPECTIVE FEAR

Our measures of fear and concern are at least partially measures of *prospective* fear—that is, concern and anticipated feelings about a future earthquake. Such prospective fear might reflect a belief in the imminent occurrence of a disastrous quake as well as a fear of earthquakes, and it thus might confound feeling with awareness. A measure of fear experienced in past earthquakes would be immune to this criticism.

The first question in our basic interview which mentioned the word earthquake asked whether respondents had ever experienced various kinds of natural disaster, including earthquakes. Respondents who had experienced an earthquake were then asked:

> Thinking back to your experience(s), which of the following best describes your overall feelings during the earthquake? Would you say you were: Very frightened and upset, Somewhat frightened and upset, Not very frightened and upset, Not at all frightened and upset, or Did you enjoy the experience?

Without distinguishing between respondents who had been through disastrous earthquakes and the majority whose experiences were strictly benign, we report the answers in figure 16 for the 1,323 who had ever felt an earthquake. More than half admitted having been frightened and upset. Thirty-two percent said they were very frightened; this is an even larger number than the

Figure 16. Fright During Previous Earthquakes

27 percent who said they were frightened over the *prospect* of an earthquake.

In order to relate fear during previous earthquakes to the more prospective fear, we grouped the three questions described earlier into an index. Answers to each question were given scores from one to four, with four signifying the highest degree of concern. The scores were then summed to create a simple index of concern for each person. For convenience the summed scores were divided into four categories, identified as "low concern," "low medium concern," "high medium concern," and "high concern."

The relationship between concern over the prospect of a future damaging earthquake and the feelings people report having felt during past earthquakes is one of the few strong ones we encountered in the investigation. The magnitude of this relationship is comparable to that of the relationships among the three prospective fear and concern items.

However, when we search for relationships between the index of concern and the intensity of prior earthquake experience, the awareness of the uplift, or other forecasts and warnings, we find very little. The tabulations (not reproduced here) show only trivial relationships of borderline statistical significance.

The striking difference between the strong relationship of prospective fear and concern with fear in previous earthquakes and the weak relationships of prospective fear and concern with the severity of prior experience and awareness of future danger calls attention to the strong tendency for fear and concern to vary independently of the experiences that seem objectively threatening. For most people, fear of earthquakes may be a more characteristically personal response than a product of the experiences they have had with earthquakes or of their awareness of earthquake hazard. We shall look further into this question later in this chapter.

RECENTLY CHANGED CONCERN

We have no direct way to know whether the fear and concern people admitted was greater than it had been before announcement of the uplift and subsequent public attention to escalated earthquake hazard. In the absence of preannouncement data, we asked people whether their concern had changed. We do not take the results as an accurate indication of the amount of change but rather as a measure of how people feel about the year of the bulge.

Respondents were asked:

> During the past year, would you say your concern about a damaging earthquake striking southern California has increased, decreased, or remained about the same?

The majority (65.0 percent) said their concern had not changed. Slightly fewer than one-third (30.1 percent) acknowledged an increase in concern, while 4.2 percent said their concern had decreased. Most of the people did not think of the first year of the uplift as a period in which they were stirred to greater concern over earthquakes than they had been earlier. Nevertheless, a substantial minority did remember that year as one of increased concern. The people who reported increased concern were disproportionately the same ones who expressed higher degrees of fear and concern over earthquakes in the three questions used in the index of concern.

MOVING AWAY FROM EARTHQUAKE DANGER

The most tangible expression of intense fear stimulated by the increased attention to earthquake danger during the year of the bulge would have been a decision by many people to pack up their belongings and move away from southern California. A cursory review of population estimates and district data on real estate listings as well as the Los Angeles City Attorney's inquiries about San Fernando Valley property values in the wake of Professor Whitcomb's near prediction failed to reveal a net exodus from the area. We also have evidence from our survey that bears on this issue.

In a series of questions (reviewed in chapter three), we asked respondents which of several earthquake topics they had discussed informally with family members, friends, neighbors, and coworkers. One of the topics was listed simply as "moving out." A total of 22.3 percent of the respondents said that they had discussed moving out at some time during the last year. "Moving out" may refer to a permanent move or to only a brief evacuation, and discussions may have been serious or casual. The number who seriously debated the wisdom of moving away from southern California must be smaller.

Evidence of more serious intentions was supplied by the answers to another question. After the main portion of the interview dealing with earthquakes was completed, interviewers announced:

> The following questions are about yourself, your household, and your community. These questions help provide the information necessary to define the types of households we collect our opinions from.

After several questions about the respondent's local community, the interviewer asked:

> Now, thinking ahead to the next *five years*, how likely is it that you will move from (name of the local community) or beyond a three-mile radius from your present home? Would you say you will: Definitely move, Probably move, Probably not move, or Definitely not move?

Respondents who said that they would definitely or probably move were then asked:

> Why do you think you will move?

Our interest was in ascertaining how many people were seriously contemplating moving because of the fear of earthquakes.

Out of the entire sample of 1,450 people, only ten people mentioned earthquakes in answering the follow-up question. Of these ten, seven said they would definitely move, and three said they would probably move. Some of these ten also probably had other reasons besides earthquakes for moving. There is little here to suggest that many people are seriously enough disturbed over the earthquake prospect that they plan to move away.[2]

A skeptic may well retort that the people who feared earthquakes most intensely had already moved before our interviewers arrived and were thus not included in the sample. This is a superficially plausible argument, but one that cannot stand the test of careful examination. Human attitudes are almost universally distributed among populations in continuous series. If there were a great many people who feared earthquakes so intensely that they moved away within the year after announcement of the southern California uplift, there would also have been a great many whose fear had not quite carried them past the threshold for moving but who were still seriously contemplating a move. In the absence of contradictory evidence, the most reasonable interpretation of our data is that only an inconsequential number of people have moved or are likely to move away from the local community because of the earthquake predictions, forecasts, and cautions of 1976. The high levels of fear and awareness reported are not yet translated into escape *behavior*.

Salience of Earthquake Concern

We have drawn a fairly consistent picture in which the majority of people acknowledged fear at the prospect of a severe earthquake and admitted having been frightened during earthquakes they had already experienced. But there are inconsistencies. Levels of fear seem to be personal matters, relatively unrelated to past experience with quakes or to awareness of earthquake danger, yet three out of ten people said their concern increased during the year of the bulge. The people who were most fearful and concerned about earthquakes most often said they would get as far away as possible if they knew a severe quake was coming. But we found no evidence that an appreciable number of people were seriously contemplating a move away from earthquake country after the year of the bulge. One step toward unraveling such apparent contradictions is to distinguish between fear and concern on the one hand and salience on the other.

Salient matters are those that are constantly on our minds, that continually command our attention, that preoccupy us. We are sometimes preoccupied with a minor irritant about which we do not feel deeply, simply because we are constantly reminded of it.

Or, we can be deeply fearful and concerned over some eventuality, yet seldom think of it because we are preoccupied with more immediate concerns. Our question is whether the media attention to earthquake threat and the admitted fear of earthquakes have combined to make earthquakes a salient concern for southern Californians.

When approaching potential interviewees, we initially avoided mentioning our interest in earthquakes. Once the topic of earthquakes was brought up in the interview, we could expect people to become increasingly preoccupied with the topic until the close of the interview. Hence, it was essential to introduce the investigation without mentioning earthquakes and to ask questions from which we could *infer* salience. The respondents were first informed that we were interested in studying people's attitudes and opinions about problems facing their local communities and the greater Los Angeles area. We then asked a short series of open-ended questions that gave respondents ample opportunity to mention earthquakes if earthquakes were at the forefront of their attention.

The interview opened with the following question:

> First, we would like to know what, in your opinion, are the three most important problems facing the residents of southern California today?

Interviewers were instructed to record the first three problems the respondent mentioned. All but 41 of the 1,450 respondents named one or more problems, and most named three problems. Even with three chances, only 35 people—or 2.4 percent—mentioned earthquakes.

Next, respondents were asked,

> If a friend was moving to southern California in the near future, is there any particular problem you might warn him or her of before making the decision to move here?

About 64 percent answered "Yes." These 904 respondents were then asked,

> What particular problem about southern California would you point out?

Interviewers were instructed to record only the first answer to this question. Only 26 people mentioned earthquakes.

Finally, we asked what we thought would be a more pointed question sequence to bring out preoccupation with earthquakes. Respondents were asked,

> Compared to other sections of the United States, do you think southern California is a more or less hazardous place to live in?

The largest number of respondents (42.1 percent) answered that it was about the same as other places. Almost a third (30 percent) said it was less hazardous, and 19.6 percent felt it was more hazardous. If people thought that southern California was either more hazardous or less hazardous, they were asked,

> Why do you think southern California is (more/less) hazardous?

Again, interviewers recorded only the first answer. Of the 287 who thought southern California was a more hazardous place to live, only 21 gave earthquakes as the reason. Of the 433 who found southern California less hazardous, 25 mentioned earthquakes, saying that the earthquake threat is less severe than the threat from such hazards as tornadoes, hurricanes, winter storms, and floods that are common to other areas.

If we look at the answers to all of these questions together, ninety-five people, or 6.6 percent of the entire sample, mentioned earthquakes one or more times. For only one person was the earthquake concern so salient that earthquakes were mentioned in answer to each of the three questions. Only ten people mentioned earthquakes in answer to two of the questions.

Plainly, even after a year of news about the uplift and other earthquake harbingers, very few people living in earthquake country were preoccupied with the threat to their safety. Problems such as crime, cost of living, taxes, unemployment, smog and pollution, transportation, crowding, education, and busing come to people's minds before the problem of earthquake danger. Even those few who find southern California a relatively hazardous place to live more often think of climatic conditions and high population density as the principal hazards.

If people are not moving out of earthquake country in droves in spite of professed fear of earthquakes, it could be because earthquakes do not require daily coping as do the cost of living or fears of mugging. High fear without corresponding salience is insufficient to stir people to action. The most striking difference between our findings and the findings of Japanese investigators using similar questions is the high salience of earthquake concern in Japan. In Japan, the high salience is accompanied by an impressive level of preparedness activity.[3]

Lest we infer too much from the low salience of earthquake concern, our results can be compared with findings for a different problem at a different period in American history. Seeking to shed light on the wave of intolerance against left-wing views that prevailed in the United States during the decade after World War II, Samuel Stouffer conducted a nationwide survey of tolerance for unpopular ideas. In spite of rampant intolerance on the political scene, in 1954 only about 6 percent of Americans mentioned communists when asked the question, "What kinds of things do you worry about most?" and a probing follow-up question stressing "political and world problems."[4] The purpose for making this comparison with our own findings is to point out that low salience is not incompatible with widespread popular support for drastic courses of action. High fear and concern combined with low salience *could* mean a high potential for action in any situation that made the earthquake threat seem imminent, critical, and personal.

Who Are the Fearful?

As we try to ascertain whether high levels of awareness are sufficient to wake people to action or whether something else, such as a fear of earthquakes, must be added to awareness, we first ask whether awareness of earthquake threat and fear are interrelated. Simple cross-tabulations reveal no statistically significant relationship with the number of predictive announcements heard and remembered, and only a very weak curvilinear relationship with awareness of the uplift is shown. Because the latter relationship is trivial, there is little to be gained by trying to explain why fear is slightly higher at the two extremes of awareness. For practical purposes, fear and level of awareness are independent.

But when we relate people's *reported change* in level of concern during the previous year to the two measures of awareness, the findings are quite different (fig. 17 and fig. 18). Relationships in both cases meet the .001 criterion of significance and are linear, except for a trivial reversal in the case of people who have not heard of the uplift. Broader or more comprehending awareness increases the likelihood that people will say that their concern about earthquakes increased during the past year.

If we take both the index of concern and the reported change in concern literally, we are faced with contradictory findings. If greater awareness means increased concern during the past year, levels of awareness and concern should be positively correlated. But they are not. A plausible way to overcome this contradiction is to reinterpret the reports of recently increased concern. Greater awareness of the earthquake warnings issued during the previous year tends to make people *think* that their fear and concern have

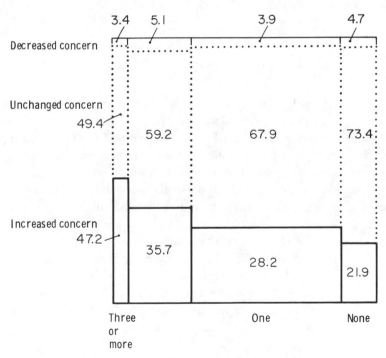

Figure 17. Changed Concern over Earthquakes by Number of Announcements Heard

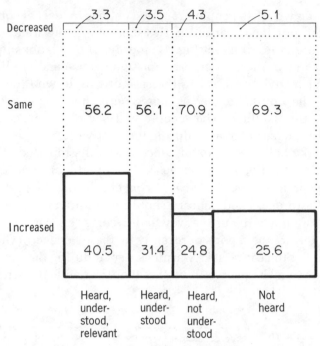

Figure 18. Changed Concern over Earthquakes by
Awareness of Uplift

increased, even though "before and after" measures would have
shown little, if any, change. In retrospect, people explain their
fears on the basis of recent striking events, unjustifiedly assuming
that they were less fearful before these events occurred. People
envelop significant, benchmark events in emotional meanings. It
is the emotional meaning attached to the succession of warnings
during the year of the bulge that is reflected in the reports of
recently increased concern.

Examination of changed concern based on data gathered at different intervals of time (Part Five) may require us to reconsider
this interpretation. But for the present, the evidence is most
convincingly interpreted as indicating little, if any, connection
between levels of fear and concern and levels of awareness of
announcements concerning future earthquake threats.

THE CORRELATES OF FEAR AND CONCERN

The procedure introduced in chapter five has been
followed again in our attempt to "explain" individual variations

in levels of fear and concern on a comprehensive basis. To ensure comparability, we conducted a path analysis, using the standard list of background and intervening variables and treating the index of fear and concern as the dependent variable (or effect). The basic model is summarized in figure 19. All relationships involving statistically significant path coefficients of .08 or greater are reported.

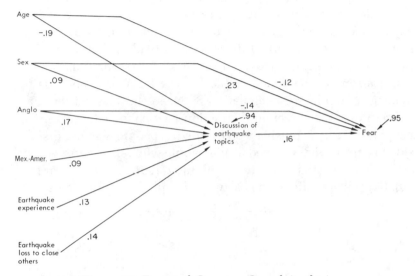

Figure 19. Fear and Concern: Causal Analysis

The causal model for earthquake fear and concern is simpler than either of the models for awareness, and more of the explanation comes directly from the background variables of sex, ethnicity, and age. Sex stands out above all the other variables, with women reporting higher levels of fear than men. Non-Anglos (Blacks, Mexican-Americans, and other minorities) are more fearful than are white Anglos, and young adults are more fearful than older people. Only one mediating variable—discussion of earthquake topics—makes an important contribution to earthquake fear. Level of fear and concern appears to be a relatively stable variable, more characteristic of the person and less affected by exposure to the media and to other aspects of earthquake experience than are awareness levels.

Because discussion makes a substantial contribution to fear, the indirect effects of being young and being female augment the total contributions of these variables to fear. The effects of ethnicity, on the other hand, are muted, because the direct and indirect effects of being a white Anglo on level of fear lead in opposite directions. Both general experience with earthquakes and more personal experience with the calamitous effects of earthquakes contribute indirectly (but not directly) to fear through fostering discussion.

We anticipated that people who rely more on interpersonal discussion rather than the media for their information would experience greater fear because rumors abound in informal discussion and because informal discussion is likely to be more emotional and undisciplined than are media presentations. Some clarification can be added to the finding from path analysis by making a simple cross-tabulation between the level of fear and concern and the threefold distinction (see chapter three) among people who rely exclusively on the media, people who use discussion to supplement the media, and people who rely disproportionately on discussion. As anticipated, the relationship is linear (fig. 20). But the big difference is between people who rely exclusively

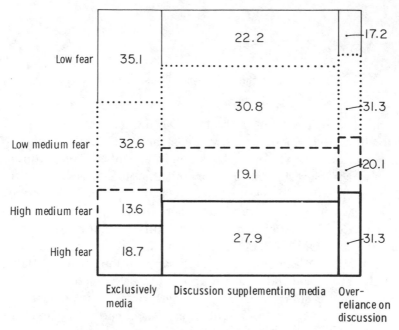

Figure 20. Extent of Concern over Earthquakes by Patterns of Communication Use

on the media and exhibit less fear and concern and people who engage in discussion—whether to filter media exposure or as a primary source of information—and exhibit higher levels of fear. If it is the nature of discussion to heighten fear, carrying on that discussion against the background of principal reliance on the media does little to moderate its effect.

Comparing the correlates of fear with the correlates of awareness will clarify further the distinctiveness of cognitive and emotional responses to the earthquake threat. In chapter five, we referred back to the analyses of the number of predictive and warning announcements people remember and their awareness and appreciation of the uplift.

Culture and status variables relate to awareness and to fear in opposite directions. Thus, women, young adults, and the non-Anglo population tend to have low earthquake awareness but high levels of fear and concern. On the other hand, some kinds of experience with earthquakes may enhance both awareness and fear indirectly but not directly. Engaging in discussion contributes to both awareness and fear, but widely ranging use of the media contributes only to awareness. In certain respects, awareness seems to reflect sophistication in the use of communication sources and in earthquake understanding, while higher levels of fear and concern often accompany a less discriminating use of communication sources.

We conclude that the independent variation we first observed between levels of earthquake awareness and levels of fear and concern results from the summing of positive and negative relationships. Underlying cultural and status variables and patterns of communication use predispose people in opposite directions— that is, either toward high awareness and low fear or toward low awareness and high fear. However, high general levels of involvement in informal communication about earthquakes enhance both awareness and fear, as experience with earthquakes may do indirectly.

The most obvious practical implication of this finding is that the same experiences have very different effects on different populations, and we must design our earthquake preparedness programs so that they are sensitive to these differences. Further practical recommendations must wait until later chapters, when we will have better grounds for deciding whether it is more productive to stimulate awareness without enhancing fear, to intensify fear without increasing awareness, or to raise the levels of both simultaneously.

The Quality of Awareness

Besides the affect—fear—associated with earthquakes, the *quality of cognition* of earthquake warnings may influence their conversion into action. Is the babel of earthquake forebodings a matter of potential concern to those who hear it, or is it merely an amusing diversion from more serious preoccupations? We could approach this question by asking people whether they *believed* the predictions they remembered. But earthquake forecasts are intrinsically probabilistic rather than factual, and thus they are not strictly subject to belief and disbelief. Instead, they can be taken seriously or dismissed lightly, and *in toto* they may lead people to expect a serious earthquake soon or to retain serious doubts.

In the course of the questioning about each of the respondents' answers, interviewers asked:

> How seriously do or did you take this prediction? Quite seriously, Fairly seriously, Not very seriously, or Not seriously at all?

As figure 21 indicates, most of the announcements were not taken seriously. Just under a third were taken fairly seriously or quite seriously.

In order to refine our understanding of public awareness of earthquake predictions, forecasts, and cautions, we have tabulated separately the number of announcements that people both heard *and* took seriously (table 10). To facilitate comparison, we have repeated the percentages from the earlier table. While 87 percent had heard one or more announcements, only 32 percent had heard and taken seriously two or more. Over half of the people (55 percent) had heard one or more announcements but did not take any of them seriously.

Perhaps people fail to take an earthquake forecast seriously not because they do not believe it is likely to come true, but because they do not expect the earthquake to be unusually severe. How-

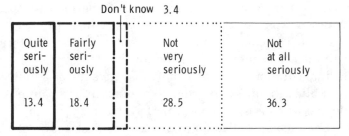

Figure 21. How Seriously Earthquake Announcements
Are Taken

TABLE 10

NUMBER OF EARTHQUAKE PREDICTIONS, FORECASTS, AND CAUTIONS
HEARD, TAKEN SERIOUSLY, AND INVOLVING CASUALTIES

Number of announcements	Heard %	Taken seriously %	Involving casualties %	Taken seriously and casualties %
None heard	13.4	13.4	13.4	13.4
None	—	54.7	23.0	56.9
One	57.4	26.1	47.0	24.5
Two	23.2	4.8	14.5	4.4
Three or more	6.0	1.0	2.1	0.8
Total	100.0	100.0	100.0	100.0
Total number	1,450	1,450	1,450	1,450
Cumulative Percent				
One or more	86.6	31.9	63.6	29.7
Two or more	29.2	5.8	16.6	5.2
Three or more	6.0	1.0	2.1	0.8

ever, we saw in chapter five that most of the forecasts people remembered were for destructive quakes, which rules out this explanation. The comparison between columns two and three in table 10 further documents this conclusion.

The final column in the same table may give the best indication of the public awareness of earthquake forecasts and cautions that people see as causes for concern. Here we have included only those announcements that both forecast the destruction of buildings and loss of life *and* are taken seriously by the respondents. About 30 percent of the people in our sample could identify one or more such announcements, and only about 5 percent could identify more than one.

After starting with an amazing array of earthquake forebodings, we have arrived at the conclusion that less than a third of the people can identify even one forecast or caution that they see as a cause for serious concern, and only one in twenty can identify more than one. If forebodings of earthquakes are in the air, they remain ethereal for the majority and are simplified to a single forecast for most of the remaining minority.

WHO TAKES EARTHQUAKE WARNINGS SERIOUSLY?

By comparing the direct path coefficients between our standard set of background and intervening variables and the number of announcements taken seriously with the path coefficients to the number of announcements remembered, we can see how awareness of something differs from taking something seriously. Of course, these cannot be entirely different: one cannot take seriously what one is unaware of! When number of predictions remembered was added to the battery of variables in one trial set of calculations, the path coefficient of .42 far exceeded any other measure of relationship. But in trying to find out whether other things besides awareness are necessary for action to occur, we focus now on the differences (figs. 22, 11, and 13).

The chief difference lies in the significance of fear. How frightened and concerned people were over earthquakes made no difference in how many earthquake announcements they remembered or in their awareness and appreciation of the uplift, but people who were fearful of earthquakes were more likely to take

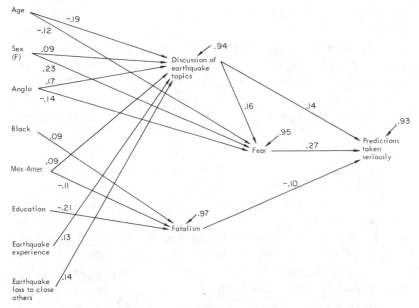

Figure 22. Predictions Taken Seriously: Causal Analysis

forecasts and warnings seriously. The *quality* of awareness, as distinct from the *fact* of awareness, is strikingly influenced by affect.

A second important difference has to do with fatalism. Anticipating our discussion in the next chapter, we used a simple index of four items contrasting the attitude that there is really nothing one can do to lessen personal risk from earthquakes with the opposite view that one *can* take steps that will measurably lessen earthquake risk. The hypothesis that people who are fatalistic about the effects of earthquakes are disinclined to take forecasts and warnings seriously is supported, although the relationship is only a modest one.

Neither of these findings is simple or obvious. Plausible cases could be made for two general principles: (1) that fear sensitizes people to perceive and attend to stimuli that they might ignore in the absence of fear, and (2) that people are more inclined to attend to stimuli that have implications for their own course of action than to attend to stimuli without action implications. But these two general principles are refuted by the absence of correlations with the number of announcements remembered. The significance of fear and action implications applies to the quality of awareness rather than to the fact of awareness. Other factors influence attention and remembering, while fear on the one hand and a sense of being in control of one's own destiny on the other make the difference between taking announcements seriously or dismissing them lightly.

A cluster of differences may convey a third general contrast. Relying on a wide range of media sources, reading newspapers regularly, and having faith in the future of scientific earthquake prediction are all related to remembering announcements but not to taking them seriously. Together, they suggest the well-informed person. It is not surprising that people who are generally better informed also remember more earthquake announcements. But it is only the indirect contribution of education to taking announcements seriously by way of its effect in undermining fatalistic attitudes that contradicts the conclusion that being informed has nothing to do with whether announcements are taken seriously. Making wide use of media sources of information, however, is related only to announcements remembered. And the correlations with faith in current and future scientific prediction capability drop out when we consider announcements taken seriously. While we cannot go so far as to say that taking the recent earthquake warnings and forecasts seriously necessarily reflects a certain naïveté, there does appear to be less sophistication involved in taking announcements seriously than in hearing and remembering them.

The differences between merely being aware of earthquake forecasts and taking them seriously are generally similar to those found between awareness and fear. People who fear earthquakes or are predisposed to fear by their social status and experience are the ones who take earthquake forecasts most seriously. The important addition is the impact of fatalistic attitudes, which often deter people from taking announcements seriously in spite of their fears.

CREDIBILITY OF DIFFERENT ANNOUNCEMENTS

Not all announcements are taken equally seriously. The presumed scientific or nonscientific character of the announcement and the communication source are the most important variables we uncovered in explaining these differences. We shall defer a detailed comparison of reactions to scientific and nonscientific announcements until we discuss people's respect for science comprehensively, exploring how it affects their approach to earthquake hazard (chapter ten). In general, scientific announcements are more often taken seriously than are prophetic and pseudoscientific announcements, although the relationship is more complex than this. Scientific announcements are taken more seriously even though they are usually thought to refer to earthquakes of lower intensities than are prophetic and pseudoscientific announcements. For each type of announcement, the anticipated intensity of the quake makes only a slight difference in how seriously it is taken.

Where people learn about an announcement also makes a difference. We classified all the announcements people remembered by the chief source of information and by how seriously the announcement was taken. The most striking finding is that magazines and books are much more credible than are other sources (fig. 23). From the infrequency with which magazines and

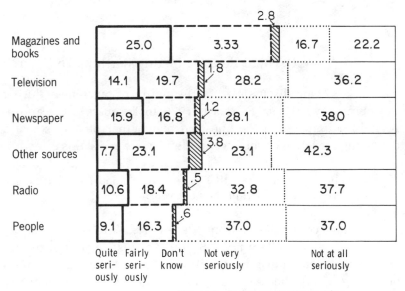

Figure 23. How Seriously Predictions, Forecasts, and Cautions
Are Taken by Chief Source of Information

books were identified as the chief sources of announcements re-membered, we might have prematurely discounted their impor-tance in earthquake-preparedness communication. But infrequent sources can sometimes be quite powerful, and perhaps prophetic announcements would have been taken less seriously if they had not been disproportionately reported in books and magazines.

The differences among the other sources are not striking. Tele-vision and newspapers are about equally credible, coming next after magazines and books. Radio falls below television and news-papers, having about half the credibility of magazines and books. The variable mixture of "other sources" falls between radio and the leading media in average credibility. "People" have the least credibility as sources of information. The low level of credibility suggests that many people recognize the difference between rumor and more carefully substantiated information. This finding also underlines the power of the mass media. Although discussion with family, friends, and coworkers undoubtedly contributes to the interpretation of earthquake announcements, attention by the media is a little more effective than word-of-mouth dissemination in leading people to take an earthquake forecast or prediction seriously.

Will There Be a Damaging Earthquake Soon?

Our discussion of the quality of awareness during the bumper year from February 1976 to February 1977 appro-priately culminates in the question of whether people expect a damaging earthquake soon. Respondents were asked this directly:

How likely do you think it is that there will be a damaging earthquake in southern California *within the next year?*

Respondents could choose from "definitely," "probably," "proba-bly not," and "definitely not." By only a small majority, the re-spondents voted against the likelihood of a damaging earthquake's occurring within the next year (fig. 24). In light of the relatively short lead time of one year, which few scientists would have endorsed, the size of the positive vote is striking. Since the ques-

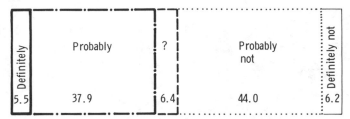

Figure 24. Probability of a Damaging Earthquake Within
the Next Year

tion specifically asked about a "damaging" earthquake, the positive expectation is all the more notable.

Perhaps the most striking point is made by comparing the
number of people who said there will probably or definitely be a
damaging earthquake within a year to the number who were able
to identify one or more forecasts of a destructive earthquake which
they took seriously. The 43.4 percent who expected an earthquake
included many more than the 29.7 percent who remembered a
prediction, forecast, or caution meriting serious concern. Whatever the source of people's convictions about a coming earthquake, the convictions persist when the source can no longer be
recalled easily.

At the time of this writing, the 43.4 percent who answered
positively have been shown wrong by events. There may be some
basis for concern here: If confidence in the ability of scientists to
predict earthquakes has led some of the public to take the warnings from scientists more seriously than scientists do themselves
and the result is that the expectations of this sector of the public
have not been confirmed, will their confidence in future warnings
be diminished?

The number of earthquake announcements taken seriously and
the level of fear and concern explain most of the difference
that we were able to account for between people who did and
did not expect an imminent severe earthquake (fig. 25). In a separate analysis, we found that expecting an earthquake soon is
partly a matter of having heard and remembered earthquake announcements. However, the stronger relationship with the
number of announcements taken seriously subsumes the modest
relationship. Level of fear and concern, while making a sub-

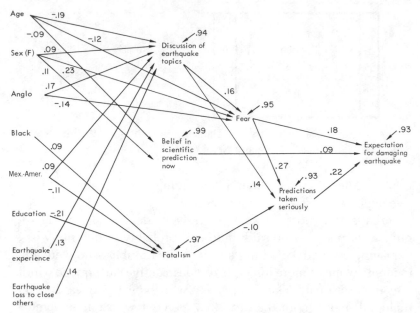

Figure 25. Expectation of a Damaging Earthquake: Causal Analysis

stantial contribution to explaining the number of announcements taken seriously, also makes a substantial independent contribution toward explaining the conviction that a severe earthquake is imminent.

A third mediating variable, belief in current scientific prediction capability, appears in this path model. Since women and younger adults are especially disposed to believe that scientists can already predict earthquakes accurately, the indirect effects of sex and age through levels of fear and concern are bolstered by the addition of this third variable.

Insofar as we could explain earthquake fear and concern, it was found to be distinctively characteristic of women, young adults, and non-Anglo ethnic and racial minorities and of people who engaged in widely ranging informal discussion of the earthquake threat. Taking predictive and warning announcements seriously appears to be a product of earthquake fear and concern. This is enhanced directly by the same widely ranging discussion that augmented fear and concern, with the additional consideration that fatalistic attitudes militate against taking announcements seriously, regardless of fear and discussion. In parallel fashion, expecting an earthquake imminently is a consequence of taking predictive and warning announcements seriously, augmented by the same fear and concern that fostered taking announcements seriously, and with still a further qualification: the greater one's faith in current scientific prediction capability, the greater the likelihood of one's expecting an earthquake soon. Although the contribution of this variable is less than the contributions of fear and of taking announcements seriously, its appearance as we move from vague feelings to actionable expectation is important.

Conclusion

In this chapter we have attempted to take the next step beyond looking at awareness of earthquake threat. We have examined the prevalence of fear and concern about earthquakes and have found that it varied independently of awareness. A high level of fear disposed people to take seriously the forecasts and warnings they heard. Thus, fear and the range of awareness together go the furthest to explain why some people remember and take seriously more such announcements than others do. In spite of a fairly high level of fear and concern about earthquakes, about seven out of ten people do not remember any announcement that they took seriously. But a further step in the investigation shows that many people have formed the conviction that a damaging earthquake is imminent, even though they no longer remember any specific announcements that they took seriously. While less than a majority expect the damaging earthquake within a year, there is a more widespread sense of imminence than would likely have been found among earthquake scientists or than was confirmed by subsequent events. Together, fear and taking announcements seriously supply most of our explanation for this sense that a damaging earthquake is imminent.

As we consider the *quality* of awareness of the earthquake threat, we find that cognitive awareness makes a small contribution (indirectly, through number of announcements taken seriously) to a general sense of imminent expectation. But the larger contribution is made both directly and indirectly by level of fear. It is a plausible hypothesis that this cluster of variables will help to explain the translation of awareness into action.

CHAPTER SEVEN

Are They Looking Out
for Themselves?

In chapter six, our answer to the question, "Are the people really concerned?" was enigmatic. The majority of the people admitted that earthquakes frighten them, and nearly half said they expected a damaging earthquake within a year. But they did not take seriously most of the earthquake warnings they remembered, and earthquake hazard could not compete successfully with crime, cost of living, taxes, unemployment, smog and pollution, transportation, crowding, education, and school busing for people's attention. Perhaps the most significant finding was that the emotional variable of earthquake fear has a stronger effect than the cognitive variable of earthquake awareness in determining who takes earthquake warnings seriously and who expects a damaging earthquake in the immediate future.

Earthquake awareness, fear of earthquakes, and the quality of earthquake awareness are three obvious candidates for explaining whether people do anything to prepare for a future earthquake. A fatalistic attitude about the disastrous effects of earthquakes is a plausible fourth candidate, working to impede rather than foster preparedness. Hence, we begin this chapter by asking whether people believe that anything *can* be done to mitigate the earthquake hazard. We shall follow this discussion by examining what people have actually done to prepare themselves and their households for potential disaster.

Fatalism

People living on the brink of disaster, like soldiers in combat and residents of hurricane country, often develop fatalistic attitudes: If the course of an enemy bullet or the impact of a hurricane or earthquake is beyond the potential victim's control, there is no point in worrying or in wasting time and energy on protective measures. If fatalistic attitudes toward earthquakes are prevalent, we should expect very little support for hazard-reduction programs by governments and little interest in individual- and family-preparedness measures.

Four questions were used to measure fatalistic attitudes about earthquakes. The most frequently endorsed expression of fatalistic attitudes was the statement:

> I believe earthquakes are going to cause widespread loss of life and property whether we prepare for them or not.

Sixty-one percent of the respondents agreed with this statement, including 11 percent who agreed strongly.

Respondents divided about equally in agreeing or disagreeing with a second statement:

> If I make preparations for an earthquake, I am almost certain they will work.

Two percent did not answer or could not make up their minds, whereas 49 percent agreed and 49 percent disagreed. Very few felt sure enough to agree or disagree strongly.

More strongly worded statements of fatalism provoked more disagreement than agreement, although a large minority of respondents still clung to fatalistic views. When asked about the statement,

> There is nothing I can do about earthquakes, so I don't try to prepare for that kind of emergency,

41 percent agreed, including 7 percent who agreed strongly. And even the expression of almost total helplessness,

The way I look at it, nothing is going to help if there were an earthquake

was endorsed by 32 percent.

If we compare these statements (fig. 26), three out of five people were fatalistic about the general impact of an earthquake, but fewer were fatalistic when it came to the possibility of taking steps to protect themselves. Between the most fatalistic and most hopeful were those people who said that earthquakes will inevitably kill and destroy but that individuals can still take timely steps to improve their own survival chances. The majority were not hopeless about enhancing their own survival chances, but there appeared to be widespread lack of confidence in the effectiveness of the protective measures that were currently known to respondents.

It is encouraging that more than a third of the people rejected fatalism in even its most acceptable garb. However, the large minorities who endorsed the two statements justifying hopelessness and inaction may pose a serious impediment to achieving earthquake preparedness throughout the community. When we add to the "hopeless" those who lacked confidence in the effectiveness of the measures they might take, the foundation for concerted community action appears to be shaky.

In order to examine possible relationships, we have assigned values ranging from one to four for answers to each of the four questions and summed them to produce an index of earthquake fatalism. On the basis of the index scores, respondents were divided into three approximately equal groups, labeled "high fatalists," "medium fatalists," and "low fatalists." As expected, fatalists were slightly less likely than others to have heard of the uplift. However, fatalists who had heard of the uplift were no less likely than others to understand its significance and appreciate its relevance. Fatalists also expressed a little less fear and concern over the earthquake danger than did nonfatalists, presumably because there was nothing they could do anyway. More important than these weak relationships are the findings already reported in chapter six. Fatalism substantially disposes people not to take earthquake-warning announcements seriously and substantially disposes them against expecting a damaging earthquake soon.

One other item expresses an attitude often associated with fatalism. In situations of continuing threat and uncertainty, there

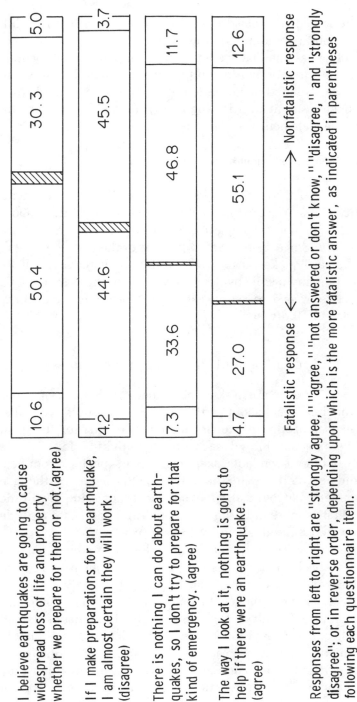

I believe earthquakes are going to cause widespread loss of life and property whether we prepare for them or not.(agree)	10.6	50.4	30.3	5.0
If I make preparations for an earthquake, I am almost certain they will work. (disagree)	4.2	44.6	45.5	3.7
There is nothing I can do about earth-quakes, so I don't try to prepare for that kind of emergency. (agree)	7.3	33.6	46.8	11.7
The way I look at it, nothing is going to help if there were an earthquake. (agree)	4.7	27.0	55.1	12.6

Fatalistic response ← → Nonfatalistic response

Responses from left to right are "strongly agree," "agree," "not answered or don't know," "disagree," and "strongly disagree"; or in reverse order, depending upon which is the more fatalistic answer, as indicated in parentheses following each questionnaire item.

Figure 26. Extent of Earthquake Fatalism

are often people who develop feelings of personal invulnerability. Automobile commuters, aware of accidents involving other people, often assume that accidents *only* happen to other people. Although attitudes of invulnerability are more often implicit than explicit, we included one question to find out how many people would openly admit to a feeling of invulnerability from earthquakes. The statement was worded,

> I don't believe an earthquake could really harm me.

Only 8.5 percent of the respondents agreed to this claim of invulnerability. Thus, we conclude that the widespread fatalism about earthquakes is not accompanied by a conscious sense of invulnerability. Since more than 90 percent of the people feel vulnerable to earthquakes, it may be possible to overcome fatalistic attitudes in many people by demonstrating that there are realistic and effective ways of lessening earthquake hazard to the community and to the individual.

Individual and Household Preparedness

With so much skepticism about earthquake warnings and so much fatalism about earthquake damage, could we realistically expect people to prepare their households for the great quake? Perhaps not. But we have already found that for a sizable minority of our respondents, skepticism about specific announcements did not interfere with the conviction that a great earthquake was imminent. We found also that fatalism is not a simple attitude but one that is more often held in the abstract and that attitude changes when individual survival is at stake.

In order to assess individual household preparedness, we developed a checklist of suggestions that are frequently made to individuals and householders. The list is not exhaustive—we had to keep it at a manageable length and to limit it to steps that could be communicated easily in the interview. Still, the list of sixteen measures is diverse and representative enough to indicate reliably the extent of personal preparedness. In addition, people were given opportunities to name any emergency supplies that they had on hand and any preparations they had made that were not on the list. The number of respondents who had anything to add was small and the steps were varied, so these replies have been disregarded in the ensuing analysis.

Even with a checklist, there is no simple way to classify people as prepared or unprepared for an earthquake. One difficulty is that most of the suggested measures for earthquake preparedness are steps that people often take for other reasons. For example, the normally resourceful and prudent person would probably have a battery-operated radio and a flashlight in working condition, regardless of the earthquake threat. We have tried to deal with this problem by asking people whether each suggested action was taken because of a future earthquake or for other reasons. Even this solution is not altogether satisfactory, since people often cannot discriminate precisely among the reasons for a given action. Furthermore, we have evidence to suggest that the phrase "because of a future earthquake" was sometimes interpreted too narrowly. The amount of action stimulated by the earthquake threat may have been slightly underestimated in our data.

Another difficulty in assessing preparation for an earthquake is the respondent's desire to appear admirable in the interviewer's eyes, so that respondents may claim to have made preparations that they have not actually made. It is principally the responsibility of the interviewer to counter this tendency through the relationship he or she establishes with the respondent. But we also employed one device to make it easier for respondents to admit they had not taken particular steps. Besides telling us what steps they had taken, respondents were also invited to tell us what steps they *planned* to take. We do not accept literally the respondents' declarations of measures they planned to take. However, we felt it would sometimes be easier for respondents to admit the many preparations they had not taken if they were given the opportunity to say at the same time that they still planned to take them.

The list of answers was printed on a card that the interviewer handed to the respondent. The actual wording of the leading question was as follows:

I am going to read you a list of preparation suggestions that have been made by various agencies and groups that are concerned with earthquake preparedness. (HAND CARD) As I read each of the following, please tell me if you *have done* any of these things either because of a future earthquake or for some other reasons, whether you plan to do any of these things because of a future earthquake or for some other reasons, or whether you *don't plan to do any of these.*

One general observation is that most of the people readily admitted not having taken most of the suggested steps. Thus, whatever ingratiation effect there was could not have been overly distorting.

We look first at ten basic steps that anyone could have taken, regardless of family status and home ownership. The items have been grouped into closely related clusters, as verified by the statistical procedure of factor analysis (fig. 27).

The majority of the people said that they have working flashlights, battery-operated radios, and first-aid kits. Most people have these items irrespective of the earthquake threat, though about one person in ten attributed their possession of these items to the prospect of an earthquake. Although the majority have made these simple preparations, more than 25 percent of the respondents would be without emergency light and 45 percent

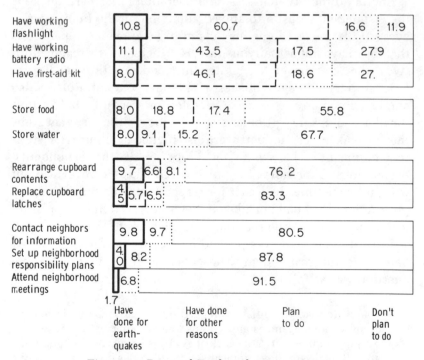

Figure 27. Personal Earthquake Preparations

would have no way to follow emergency broadcasts in case electric service was disrupted in an earthquake. Similarly, 46 percent would be without first-aid supplies.

Since water supply and the local distribution of food items are likely to be interrupted in a severe earthquake, people are often encouraged to maintain emergency supplies of water and of canned and dehydrated food. Many fewer people have taken these two steps, but if they have done so, the prospect of an earthquake is more likely to have been the reason. An uninterrupted water supply seems to be more generally taken for granted than is continued food distribution: twice as many people have stored food in anticipation of an earthquake as have stored water.

The danger that objects might fall from shelves and either break or injure people is of concern in an earthquake, but the frequent suggestions to rearrange the contents of cupboards and to install or replace secure latches on cupboard doors have been even less widely followed than the suggestions to store food and water.

Finally, neighborhood cooperation has been proposed as an aid to individual families in preparing for an earthquake. The simple step of soliciting information and ideas from neighbors and friends is acknowledged by less than one in ten of our respondents. Only one in twenty-five has participated in setting up neighborhood or block meetings about earthquakes.

From this review we are forced to conclude that most households are unprepared for an earthquake and that the prospect of an earthquake has stimulated relatively little preparatory action.

Three more items on the list presented to respondents applied primarily to homeowner-occupied dwellings rather than to rented homes. Out of our total sample, 689 (47.5 percent) lived in owner-occupied households. In just under 25 percent of these households, inquiries have been made about earthquake insurance (fig. 28). Only about half of these inquiries have led to the purchase of earthquake insurance, and this figure, 12.8 percent of the total respondents, probably exaggerates the number of homes covered by earthquake insurance. Respondents in some instances may not have known what type of householder's insurance coverage was in effect for their homes and may not have distinguished between earthquake insurance and other forms of insurance. A few people said that their homes had been structurally reinforced in some way for earthquake reasons.

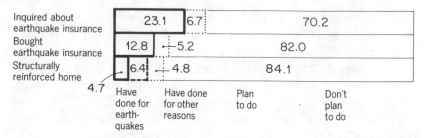

Figure 28. Homeowners' Earthquake Preparations

Since the ratio of benefit to cost for earthquake insurance varies for different homes and different locations and since many buildings do not require structural reinforcement, the failure to take these two steps does not necessarily mean that the homeowner is unprepared or is lacking in forethought. However, without at least making inquiries about earthquake insurance, the householder could hardly weigh the possible benefits against the costs in order to make an intelligent decision on whether to purchase insurance. In three out of every four households, as far as the respondent knew, these inquiries had not been made.

A final three items were especially applicable to households in which there were children. We did not include all families with children but only those families in which one or more children were living at home at the time of the interview. Six hundred (41.4 percent) of the households had minor children living at home. Three steps have been widely recommended for parents in such households. In figure 29 we find the first substantial indication of precautions taken specifically in preparation for an earthquake. Nearly half of the 600 respondents reported that they have instructed the children in what to do in case of an earthquake. More

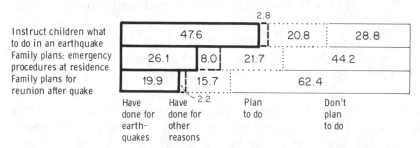

Figure 29. Earthquake Preparations of Households with Children

than a quarter have developed family plans to be followed in an emergency, such as shutting off gas. And about one family in five has some plan for getting the family members together again after an earthquake. Compared to the general disregard of most other earthquake preparations, this evidence of families with children planning to maintain the supportive family unit in an emergency is encouraging. Nevertheless, these minimal parental responsibilities for the welfare of the children have still been ignored in a large share of homes.

The household containing children and the owner-occupied household have responsibilities in preparing for earthquake disaster that are not applicable to other households. Do people in these households also take more seriously the complete range of personal preparedness measures? Based on the ten generally applicable preparedness items discussed first, both households with children and owner-occupied households have slightly higher rates of preparedness than do other households. However, the effect of owner occupancy is stronger and more consistent than is the effect of having children in the home. Owner occupancy makes an especially noticeable difference in possession of the household emergency staples (flashlight, battery-operated radio, and first-aid kit), while having children makes little or no difference.

Who Is Prepared?

The general evidence of unpreparedness signals important work to be done, at least in the event of a true earthquake prediction and warning. In attempting to correct the underpreparedness it should be helpful to know which segments of the public are more and less well prepared. We have already seen that having minor children in the home makes little difference in the level of preparedness, while owner-occupied households are noticeably better prepared than are renter-occupied households. In order to simplify comparisons of preparedness, we computed an *individual preparedness* index. The index simply states the number of measures taken (whether for earthquake or for other reasons) as a proportion of all the measures that could have been taken. The latter number is different for owner-occupied, adult-child, and other households. The resulting index scores were then simplified to identify four sets of respondents, from the most prepared to the least prepared.

A path analysis similar to those reported in earlier chapters was used to identify the pattern of significant influences affecting levels of individual and household preparedness (fig. 30). Four variables turned out to affect preparedness levels directly. As we had anticipated, fatalists are distinctly less likely to be prepared than nonfatalists. Surprisingly, however, the path-analytic procedure eliminated level of earthquake fear, how seriously earthquake warnings are taken, and whether people expect a damaging earthquake imminently in favor of more powerful variables. As we shall see, this finding does not necessarily signify that the three disappearing variables are unrelated to personal and household preparedness, but it does show us that any such relationships are subsumed under the more direct and powerful relationships between preparedness and the four key variables in figure 30.

The three crucial variables besides fatalism all have an important feature in common. Discussion of earthquake topics, community bondedness, and attending earthquake meetings all indicate

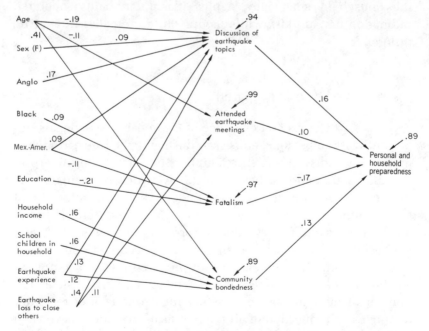

Figure 30. Personal and Household Preparedness: Causal Analysis

the presence of social ties and exposure to interaction in the neighborhood and the community. Discussion of neighborhood topics and attending earthquake meetings reflect involvement in the filtering process described in chapter three by which media communications are made relevant to people's daily lives. Participation in both informal discussions and in more formal and active meetings enhances people's disposition to respond actively rather than passively to the earthquake threat. As we found earlier, increased and diversified exposure to earthquake discussion in the mass media raises levels of earthquake awareness but does not help to overcome the passivity with which people receive most warnings. Active involvement in the filtering process does help to stir people to action.

Regardless of direct involvement in the social filtering of earthquake information, bondedness in the community makes an independent contribution to active preparedness. There is no obviously rational reason why people who feel strong ties to the local community should be any more concerned about their personal ability to survive a destructive earthquake and its aftermath than people who are less involved locally. Instead, the difference is the familiar one between the attitudes of participant and spectator. The spectator attitude makes it difficult for one to overcome the sort of detachment from the passing scene which impedes the shift from a passive to an active mode of response, even when personal comfort and survival are at stake.

The distinctive part played by these three community-involvement variables in the translation of awareness into action suggests the theory advanced by Emile Durkheim.[1] According to Durkheim, social solidarity invests life with meaning, and social isolation divests it of meaning. The meaningfulness imparted to events when the individual sees them through the eyes of a community of like-minded or similarly concerned persons enables that individual to address the situation and act on it. Isolation within the community leads to passivity and an inability to size up and address problems actively.

But what of the disappearing variables? Do fear of earthquakes, taking warning announcements seriously, and expecting a damaging earthquake imminently do nothing to stir people to self-protective action? Looked at separately, the number of warning announcements remembered and taken seriously (or quality of awareness) and the expectation of a damaging earthquake are not significantly related to individual and household preparedness. The oft-noted discrepancy between words and deeds,[2] between understandings and actions, is accented once again by these findings. While there is a distinctive difference between qualities of awareness, it has little if anything to do with the disposition to take self-protective action.

Awareness of the uplift and earthquake fear, however, show interesting patterns that complicate the picture somewhat. Being aware of the uplift and, especially, appreciating its relevance are clearly related to preparedness level (fig. 31). Appreciating that the uplift could mean an earthquake that would probably do damage where the respondent lives indicates a more vital quality of awareness than does simply taking warnings seriously. Thus, it is more likely to stimulate action.

If feeling personally at risk from an uplift-related earthquake fosters preparedness, do other ways of being at risk have the same effect? Is this finding an instance of a more general relationship

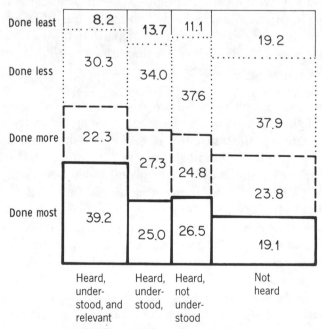

Figure 31. Earthquake Preparedness by Awareness of the Uplift

between feeling at risk and taking precautionary action? In our July 1978 survey, we included two items that were designed to help us answer this question:

In the event of a damaging earthquake, how safe do you think you will be in your *home*? Do you think you will be very safe, somewhat safe, somewhat unsafe, or very unsafe?

Do you consider the *location* of your residence, that is, the area where you live, hazardous if a damaging earthquake strikes the Los Angeles area?

Of the 536 respondents in this sample, about 18 percent felt that their residences would be unsafe to some degree, and almost 25 percent believed that their locations were hazardous. We note in passing the unrealistic sense of security expressed in the answers given by most of the respondents. But regardless of the distribution of answers, neither item was correlated with level of individual and household preparedness. Follow-up questioning dealing with the specific nature of hazards, such as living in a multistory building or near an earthquake fault, also failed to reveal any relationships with preparedness. Thus, we must conclude that even the sense of being at risk does not in itself move people to action.

Figure 32 shows that while there is indeed a relationship between fear and preparedness, it is of a curvilinear nature to which the path-analytic procedure using linear correlation is insensitive. The graph gives support to a widely held hypothesis about the relationship between fear and action, which is that fear motivates action, but only up to a point. When the amount of fear exceeds a critical threshold, the effect is a sort of paralysis. From the graph we see that actions increase as fear and concern increase until the highest level of concern is reached, and then the level of preparedness falls drastically.

If we turn back to figure 25 in the preceding chapter for comparison with figure 30, we may be able to round out our understanding of the difference between expecting an earthquake imminently and doing something to prepare for the quake. In both cases, discussion of earthquake topics and rejection of fatalism are prime variables. Discussion contributes to fear and to taking warnings

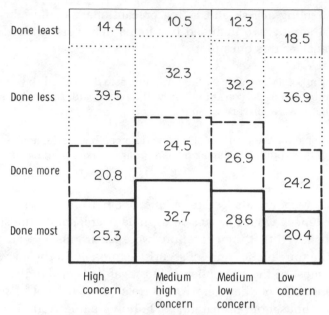

Figure 32. Earthquake Preparedness by Extent of
Concern over Earthquakes

seriously, both of which foster imminent expectation of a damaging earthquake. But this causal chain has little, if anything, to do with getting people to do something about the earthquake threat. Informal discussion of earthquake topics among family, friends, and coworkers has two rather independent effects. Those features of discussion that intensify fear and encourage people to take warnings more seriously are generally unproductive as far as promoting action is concerned, and those aspects of discussion that promote action do not necessarily heighten fear and make people take warnings more seriously. If we can judge from the nature of the two key variables that turn up for the first time in the path diagram for preparedness, it is the socially bonding aspect of discussion rather than the alarm-raising feature which fosters action.

Feeling that events can be controlled (the opposite of fatalism) also has two independent lines of effect. It contributes directly toward taking warnings seriously and indirectly toward believing that a destructive earthquake is imminent, but in a separate effect it fosters preparedness. We have no special insight into why these effects should be distinct.

The practical implication of these findings is that heightening awareness and stimulating fear of the earthquake hazard can make only limited contributions in any program to motivate people to take a few simple precautionary steps to ward off some of the possible effects of a severe earthquake. It is much more important to show people that something can be done that will credibly enhance survival chances and to involve them in the community and in social exchange about the earthquake threat.

Indirect Effects

In spite of a weak tendency for women to report more discussion of earthquake topics than men, the sexes do not differ in preparedness. Preparedness does increase fairly decisively with age until the over-fifty category is reached, when the drop is striking (fig. 33). Earlier, we found that the elderly were the most likely to appreciate the meaning and relevance of the uplift, but now we find that they are poorly prepared for the quake. This anomaly seems to result from reliance on the mass media without the benefit of the integrating effects of discussion and of participation in meetings. The strong identification of the elderly with the community is not complemented by the more active involvement necessary to stimulate action.

Household income, education, and ethnicity are all related to preparedness. Preparedness goes up steadily with income; this becomes plausible because of the connection with community bondedness (fig. 30). Education combats fatalism and thereby fosters preparedness, but only up to the level of entering college. Anglos are better prepared than are either blacks or Mexican-Americans. The contrast between Anglos, who engage in more discussion of earthquake topics, and blacks, who are more fatalistic, is clear. However, our analysis cannot explain the anomaly that Mexican-Americans, who engage in considerable earthquake discussion and are less fatalistic than either blacks or Anglos, should nevertheless be no better prepared than are Blacks.

Having children (especially schoolchildren) in the household

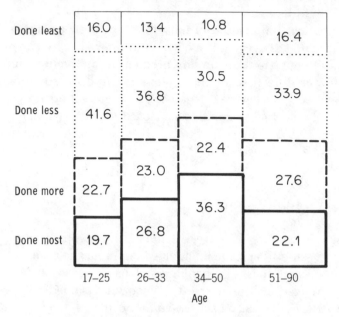

Figure 33. Earthquake Preparedness by Age

does foster preparedness. Stressing once again the hiatus between awareness and action, we found earlier that awareness of the uplift was lower in households with children.

Having experienced several severe earthquakes, having close friends or family members who have suffered loss or injury in an earthquake, and having had past experience with disaster agents other than earthquakes all contributed significantly to personal and household preparedness. The relationship with the breadth of earthquake experience may be partly spurious, because people who have lived longer in southern California will have experienced more earthquakes than have people from other regions of the United States, and they will also probably be more firmly bonded to the local community. Hence, the breadth of earthquake experience may not be a causally effective variable. The case for earthquake loss or injury to close friends and family members is more credible, since people affected in this way are more likely than others to attend earthquake meetings and to engage in formal earthquake discussions, both of which foster preparedness.

Knowing What to Do in an Earthquake

If the picture of household preparedness is dismal, there may yet be a brighter side. Knowing what to do in an emergency is a more passive kind of preparedness, but it is nonetheless important. Have people listened to the advice that is frequently given through the mass media and sometimes dispersed by word of mouth on what to do when an earthquake strikes? Have they stored this advice in memory for future use, or has it faded into a morass of vague earthquake awareness, like so many of the forecasts and warning announcements?

The following question was included in the third wave of follow-up interviews, administered in July 1978:

> Now we'd like to get your opinion on what you should do if you are indoors in a home when a severe earthquake strikes. Should you . . . ?

The seven question completions are given in figure 34. To each completion the respondent could answer "yes," "no," or "don't know." We have starred the correct responses in the graph, based on widely accepted expert judgment.

Compared with the record for household preparedness, these results are encouraging. Nearly everyone knows better than to approach a window or to use an elevator in a high-rise building, and most people appreciate the relative security afforded by doorways and halls. Only in getting outdoors as quickly as possible and in calling the police or the fire department for instructions are sizable minorities on the wrong track.

Much of this wisdom is not new and was disseminated before the year of the bulge, and some of it is equally applicable to any mass emergency. But most people have paid sufficient attention to the prospect of a severe earthquake to learn some simple rules for survival at the moment of crisis. Although the rules are simple, the diffusion of knowledge of such rules throughout the population is much wider than for any other kind of knowledge or awareness in our investigation. It is also striking that the prevalence of fatalistic attitudes has not deterred people from learning simple rules for survival in an earthquake.

When people address a situation involving personal risk, their

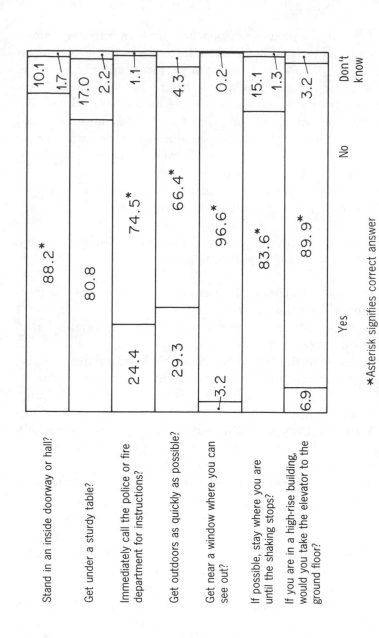

Figure 34. What You Should Do if Indoors in a Home When a Severe Earthquake Strikes

attention probably focuses most sharply on the dramatic moment of impact. It is easier to visualize in imagination the probable consequences of alternative courses of action at the moment when the quake strikes than during the vague and indeterminate pre-earthquake period. The consequences of correct and incorrect action are more obvious, and the drama of the moment heightens the sense that real consequences will ensue. Furthermore, learning simple rules for survival means only that one is ready to act, not that one has taken the next step of translating that readiness into action.

But will people act according to this knowledge when an earthquake actually occurs? Self-reports of response to the magnitude 5.0 earthquake on New Year's Day, 1979, do not indicate gross disregard of these rules (chapter fourteen). Nevertheless, many people who have not stored food and water or kept fresh batteries in their radios and flashlights know that they should do so. Only the next severe earthquake will tell us whether this unparalleled display of knowledge will be converted into equally appropriate behavior.

CHAPTER EIGHT

Let Government Do It

We are beginning to see clearly that promoting awareness of earthquake hazard is not enough to move people from contemplation to action. Fear of earthquakes must be added to hazard awareness in explaining how seriously people take the warnings they have heard and whether they expect a damaging earthquake soon. But how seriously people take warnings and whether they foresee imminent disaster have very little to do with whether they take a few simple steps to prepare their households for an earthquake. Fear makes some difference, but moderate fear is more effective than high levels of fear in motivating preparedness. A fatalistic attitude about earthquake danger is the greatest obstacle to personal and household preparedness, while informal discussion of earthquake topics and attendance at earthquake meetings, coupled with strong bonds to the local community, contribute most to preparedness.

We have also witnessed declining levels of accomplishment as we move from general awareness to quality of awareness and finally to action within the home and family. Most people have heard some warnings, fewer take them seriously or expect a damaging earthquake soon, and far fewer have taken any of the simple precautionary measures recommended by civil defense agents and other authorities.

But preparedness is not strictly an individual matter. At the very least, individual preparedness is facilitated both by general and specific community involvement. But the more significant measures to protect the community in the event of an earthquake require collaborative action, with government agencies often playing key roles. In this chapter we shall ask whether people support collaborative action and government leadership in earthquake preparedness.

Community and Individual Orientations to the Earthquake Prospect

Some problems divide communities into individuals and households, each seeking a private solution without cooperation with or compassion for others. Other problems unite communities, breaking down barriers and evoking compassion and altruism. Much research has shown that a widely shared natural disaster usually has the latter effect. A disastrous tornado, hurricane, flood, or earthquake unifies the community for the duration of the emergency period.[1] This orientation toward community welfare and collaborative solutions to problems makes an indispensable contribution toward dealing effectively with the crisis brought on by a disaster agent.

The National Research Council Panel on Public Policy Implications of Earthquake Prediction asked whether people would respond to prediction with comparable altruism and community orientation or whether the attitude would be one of every individual and household for themselves.[2] Without a credible prediction of crisis proportions, we cannot answer that question conclusively. But much of the groundwork for altruism will have been laid if (a) people already know about groups of people who are in greater danger than most; (b) they view these groups and their problems in personal rather than impersonal terms; (c) they believe that something can be done for them; and (d) they feel that something ought to be done for them by persons outside of their immediate circle of family and friends. A prediction could hardly elicit a spontaneous outpouring of *cooperative altruism* if these conditions did not prevail.[3]

Being aware of groups in special need is the first prerequisite for cooperative altruism. Respondents were asked:

If a damaging earthquake were expected in southern California, do you think any particular groups of people would be in *greater* danger than others, or do you feel the risk is about the same for everyone?

The great majority of survey respondents (62.2 percent) replied that there were some groups in greater danger, about a third (34.6 percent) said the danger was the same for everyone, and 2.5 percent didn't know. The 912 *socially aware* respondents were then asked an open-ended follow-up question:

> Which groups of people do you feel would be in *greater* danger from a damaging earthquake?

In order to eliminate self-serving responses, we then asked respondents if they considered themselves to be in any of these specially endangered groups. The 2,007 responses (names of groups in special danger) were only reduced to 1,830 when self-memberships were removed, and 82 percent of the socially aware did not include themselves in any of the groups they mentioned.

A further comparison between respondents who did and did not say they belonged to one of the endangered groups showed that if one claims membership in an endangered group, one is likely to mention significantly ($p < .01$) more nonmembership endangered groups than if one does not claim membership in an endangered group. This finding casts new light on membership in an endangered group. Rather than being a harbinger of self-interest, self-inclusion in an endangered group may sensitize people to the existence of other groups who share this condition of high risk and thus may contribute to altruism in the community.

What kinds of groups were identified as especially endangered? As revealed in table 11, over 60 percent of references were to relatively impersonal categories of people living in unsafe structures or in hazardous locations. Only about half as many references were to people who were endangered because of more personal characteristics such as age, disability, or confinement. Our respondents thought more spontaneously of dangerous *environments* than they did of *personal attributes* that diminish an individual's ability to prepare for or respond to the earthquake threat.

As we interpret these findings, we must remember that answers were volunteered in response to an open-ended question. If presented with a checklist of group names, many more of our respondents would undoubtedly have recognized the endangered status of the elderly, the disabled, and children in schools. But our unprompted answers should supply better clues to the likelihood

TABLE 11
GROUPS IDENTIFIED AS BEING IN SPECIAL DANGER

Type of endangered group	All groups mentioned %		Groups in which respondent is not a member %	
Unsafe structures	36.0		35.5	
Old/unsafe/pre-1934 buildings	19.1		18.4	
Apartments/high-rise	16.9		17.1	
Unsafe locations	24.9		24.7	
Proximity to disaster agent (by fault, near epicenter)	8.6		7.9	
Flooding (below dams, near water)	6.8		6.9	
High-density areas	4.8		4.9	
Hillside homes	4.7		5.0	
Personally and socially impaired	18.7		19.1	
Elderly	9.9		10.0	
Disabled	7.3		7.5	
Poor	1.5		1.6	
Institutional settings	12.3		13.1	
Children in schools	6.5		6.9	
People in hospitals/ prisons/group residential facilities	5.8		6.2	
Other	8.1	8.1	7.6	7.6
Total	100.0	100.0	100.0	100.0
Total number of responses	2,007		1,830	

of cooperative altruism in the event of an earthquake prediction crisis.

The evidence we have reviewed lends force to the conjecture that while most people are sensitive to unequal risk from earthquakes, their concern is more impersonal than personal. They are not thinking so much of individuals who are bedridden at home or in hospitals and need help in getting to safety as they are of buildings collapsing. Since altruism implies a rather personal concern, the prevalence of impersonal concern suggests that the foundation for a genuinely altruistic outpouring in case of a credible earthquake prediction may not yet have been securely laid.

Whether the concern for those at greatest risk from an earthquake is personal or impersonal, we must determine whether our respondents believe that anything can be done for the endangered. If the widespread fatalism described in chapter six colors public attitudes toward people who are especially endangered, altruism can be no more than a passive feeling of sympathy.

After each respondent had named the groups considered to be in special danger, the interviewer asked:

> If a damaging earthquake were expected, is there anything that should be done ahead of time for the (. . .)?

In asking the question, the interviewer named the first group mentioned by the respondent and then repeated the question for each of the other groups the respondent had named.

Overwhelmingly, our respondents indicated a belief in the meliorability of earthquake-related hazards for endangered groups; at least 75 percent of all respondents who mentioned endangered groups believed that something could be done. Respondents were particularly optimistic about those who live in older buildings (90.9 percent) and in areas of possible inundation (91.2 percent), for children in schools (92.3 percent), and for residents of hospitals, prisons, and other group-care facilities (92.2 percent). They were slightly less optimistic about the possibility of taking remedial actions on behalf of apartment and high-rise dwellers (79.9 percent) and of people in close proximity to a fault or to the quake's epicenter (75.6 percent).

The striking contrast between the optimism expressed here and the more generalized attitude of fatalism as shown in chapter seven commands our special attention. Are the two measures of fatalism related? Scores on the fatalism index were cross-tabulated with meliorability for each of the especially endangered groups. All relationships confirmed a connection between the two manifestations of fatalism, and seven of the eleven were statistically significant. Does membership in an endangered group affect belief in meliorability? Membership in most environmentally endangered groups is significantly related to belief in meliorability, but negatively so. Membership in more personally endangered groups (the elderly, the disabled, poor people, children in schools, and institutional residents) seems unrelated to meliorability attitudes.

Positive correlations between the two manifestations of fatalism encourage us to take the findings seriously and to speculate about why there should be such a difference. Three plausible explanations come to mind. First, questions used in the fatalism index could be read as asking about the *elimination* of risk, while questions about especially endangered groups implied only the *reduction* of risk. There may be more realism than fatalism in recognizing that risk can be reduced but not eliminated. This interpretation is consistent with differing endorsement rates for separate items in the fatalism index. Second, the best way to overcome fatalistic attitudes may be to deal in specifics. When attention is turned away from the awe-inspiring total earthquake experience toward specific groups and concrete actions, the possibilities for dealing with problems of more manageable proportions may blunt the disposition toward fatalism. Third, the social conscience that we acquire as members of society may keep us from being as fatalistic about the prospective misfortunes of others as we are about our own. The fact that nonmembers of environmentally endangered groups were more sanguine about doing something for these groups than were members themselves lends some credibility to this speculation. (The lack of a similar correlation for personally endangered groups does not undermine this conclusion, because cell frequencies were small and because there was near-consensus that their conditions were meliorable.)

Our findings up to this point indicate that widespread awareness of especially endangered groups and confidence that something can be done for them augur well for altruistic response to an earthquake warning, while the preponderant attention to environmentally endangered rather than personally endangered groups could inhibit altruistic responses. The question remains of who should look out for the especially endangered. Is their need a community responsibility? Or should they and their families assume this responsibility?

We asked each respondent who had said that something could be done for an endangered group before the next earthquake the question of who was responsible for doing it. The question was open-ended, with no suggested response categories. The most consistent and impressive finding is the reliance on government (table 12). For every especially endangered group, the majority of the respondents placed responsibility on local, state, or federal government or on some combination of government entities. About four out of five respondents held government responsible for helping the impaired, while just over two-thirds expected government to assume responsibility for each of the other categories. The tendency to hold government responsible is greatest in the case of the elderly, the poor, people who dwell in old, unsafe buildings, and the disabled. Government is least often held responsible—though still by more than half of the respondents—for people living in hillside homes and in apartments and high-rise buildings or near faults and other impact areas. The rate of government responsibility is also relatively low for people in institutional settings. This observation is deceptive, however, since the agents and managers who are held responsible by 16 percent of the respondents will, in most instances, be acting as agents of some government entity.

It is hardly surprising that as many as a third of our respondents hold residents or property owners of hillside homes, apartments, and high-rise buildings responsible. When severe rainstorms threatened the homes of Malibu residents, several writers of letters to the editor in the *Los Angeles Times* on March 10, 1978, objected to spending taxpayer dollars to shore up the homes of people who themselves had chosen to live in precarious cliffside dwellings or directly on beach sand. Nevertheless, close to 60 percent of the respondents in each case held government responsible. Transfer of more responsibility to government for people living in old and seismically unsafe buildings undoubtedly reflects the public attention focused on the plight of such residents by political debate and media coverage. Again, it is not surprising that few held the elderly, the disabled, and children in school responsible for their own safety. But how seldom we turn to primary groups—family and friends—is underlined by the small percentages here.

The last step in our analysis has added one positive and one negative weight to our estimate of the potential for collective altruism in case of a serious earthquake warning. Positive signs now include widespread awareness of especially endangered groups, belief that something can be done for these groups, and assignment of responsibility for ameliorating their situations to the community rather than to the potential victims and their families. Since the placement of responsibility was unrelated to whether respondents included themselves in the endangered groups, this sense of community responsibility is not contaminated by self-interest. But the prospect for a spontaneous outpouring of help is dimmed by the impersonality of the categories of the endangered that people thought of first and by the overwhelming tendency to look to government rather than to neighbors, friends, and fellow citizens. There is indeed a strong sense of community responsibility to help those who are most at risk, but that responsibility is laid squarely on government.

Will ordinary citizens rise to the occasion in spontaneous collective support for those around them who are most at risk in case of a severe earthquake warning? Our evidence raises serious doubts. But a well-conceived program to sensitize people to the potential plight of the elderly, the disabled, children in schools, and institutionalized populations and to show people what informal groups of friends and neighbors could do to help might tip the scales toward a predisaster therapeutic community, like that so often found after the event.[4]

What Should Government Be Doing?

People look to government at all levels to deal with earthquake hazard, but have they thought about what public officials should be doing? Sometimes, having no idea of what can be done, people nevertheless clamor for officials to figure something out and then do it. While a demanding but uninformed public leaves officials free to select the programs they consider most prudent, it also places a burden of unaided decision making on their shoulders. Still, if people have reasonably concrete ideas

TABLE 12
AGENTS RESPONSIBLE FOR ENDANGERED GROUPS
(in percentages)

General category	Responsible Agent								
	Own responsibility	Family, friends	Local government	Local, state, and federal	Individual and government	Property owners	Admin., mgrs.	Other	Total
Unsafe structures	15.7	0	36.4	32.9	2.5	6.9	1.0	4.6	100.0
Unsafe locations	23.7	0	30.5	36.2	2.5	1.0	1.2	4.9	100.0
Personally and socially impaired	4.9	5.2	30.1	48.9	2.4	.3	3.0	5.2	100.0
Institutional settings	5.4	2.7	25.6	42.6	1.3	.4	15.7	6.3	100.0
Unsafe structures									
Old/unsafe/pre-1934 buildings	10.8	0	40.5	37.9	2.9	4.7	0	3.2	100.0
Apartments/high-rise	22.1	0	31.1	26.6	1.9	9.7	2.2	6.4	100.0
Unsafe locations									
Proximity to disaster agent (by fault, near epicenter)	23.1	0	27.7	37.7	1.5	.8	.8	8.4	100.0
Flooding (below dam, near water)	24.2	0	25.8	44.4	1.6	0	1.6	2.4	100.0

TABLE 12 Continued

Unsafe locations								
High density areas	11.8	0	46.1	27.6	5.3	4.0	2.6	2.6	100.0
Hillside homes	35.5	0	27.6	29.0	2.6	0	0	5.4	100.0
Personally and socially impaired								
Elderly	3.4	6.9	31.6	49.5	2.9	.6	1.7	3.4	100.0
Disabled	5.4	3.9	26.3	49.6	1.6	0	5.4	7.8	100.0
Poor	11.6	0	38.5	42.3	3.8	0	0	3.8	100.0
Institutional settings								
Children in schools	8.4	3.4	33.6	36.1	1.7	.8	10.1	5.9	100.0
People in hospitals/prisons/ group residential facilities	1.9	1.9	16.3	50.0	.9	0	22.1	6.0	100.0

about what government could be doing, we can justifiably infer that there is genuine public interest and concern. The prospect for public involvement in shaping and executing government policies and programs is much brighter. Interviewers asked the following questions of all the people in our sample:

> Given the fact that earthquakes do occur in southern California, what do you think are the most important things *government agencies* should be doing *now* to prepare for future earthquakes?

Answers were recorded verbatim, with up to five answers per interview. Figure 35 indicates the number of suggestions people were able to make.

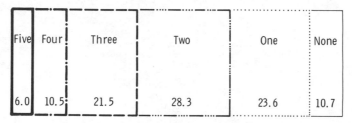

Five	Four	Three	Two	One	None
6.0	10.5	21.5	28.3	23.6	10.7

Figure 35. Suggestions for Government Action

Apparently, most people are concerned and have given some thought to what government agencies should be doing. Only one in every ten had nothing to suggest. Two-thirds of the respondents had two or more suggestions to offer, and more than a third had at least three suggestions. This distribution of suggested governmental actions did not subsequently change when the question was repeated for a new sample of respondents six months later, in July 1977.

No effort was made to evaluate the merits of specific suggestions. Some of them were relatively impractical and many were vague or general, but very few were unreasonable or irrelevant. Only five persons suggested shifting responsibility through prayer. We can safely conclude that most of the respondents have some ideas about the steps that might be taken by the government or about the general directions for government action.

Most of the suggestions can be grouped under three headings (table 13). The most frequent references were to structural improvements (upgrading and enforcing building codes, reinforcing or destroying unsafe buildings, making dams and freeways safer), and these made up a third of all specific suggestions. References to the need for educating the public about earthquake safety and predictions and conducting earthquake drills in public buildings followed closely (26.2 percent). "Educating people" was by far the most frequently suggested (22.9 percent) specific preparedness item. The third major category of response (25.7 percent) was achieving a state of emergency preparedness and readiness to handle problems after the disaster strikes—for example, insuring the adequacy and availability of shelters and supplies, medical care, evacuation plans, and good communication systems.

The detailed list of suggestions reveals a prevailing emphasis on immediately and obviously practical steps. Steps that are only indirectly practical were less popular. For example, increased support for scientific research on earthquakes made up only 4.8 percent of the responses, and the improvement of earthquake prediction only 3.5 percent. In light of continuing study of the desirability and feasibility of government-subsidized earthquake insurance, it is also striking that only seven people suggested that government agencies should make earthquake insurance available.

HAZARD REDUCTION AND EMERGENCY PREPAREDNESS

A recurring issue in disaster preparedness is the distribution of effort and resources between hazard reduction and emergency response. The distinction is between preparations to minimize disruption, damage, and casualties when an earthquake strikes and preparations that enable us to deal promptly and effectively with disruption, damage, and casualties after the earthquake. Emergency planning includes such steps as preparing a community emergency plan, storing food and medical supplies, and establishing emergency communication systems to be used in case regular communications are disrupted by the quake. Hazard reduction includes such steps as stricter enforcement of building safety codes and educational programs to teach people how to make their homes safer in the event of an earthquake.

Emergency response is more dramatic, and its effects more ob-

TABLE 13

SUGGESTIONS FOR GOVERNMENT ACTION

Measures suggested	Percent of all suggestions
Structural Safety	35.8
Make safer buildings, earthquake-proof buildings	9.0
Enforce building codes	6.7
Improve building codes	5.7
Upgrade old buildings	5.6
Provide loans to upgrade or rebuild	3.2
Destroy old or unsafe buildings	2.2
Prohibit building on faults	.9
Other suggestions concerning buildings	1.1
Upgrade dam safety	1.0
Improve safety of highway construction	.4
Education	26.2
General reference to public education	22.9
Conduct drills in public buildings	2.3
Other specific educational measures	.6
Other educational suggestions	.4
Plan for Emergency Care and Relief	25.7
Establish more emergency shelters	6.0
Establish centers with emergency supplies	5.5
Develop an effective civil defense program	3.6
Improve the general emergency plan	3.3
Provide for emergency medical care	3.1
Develop an evacuation plan	2.8
Develop emergency communication systems	1.0
Other emergency care and relief	.4
Improve Scientific Research and Technology, including Prediction	7.6
More scientific research needed (unspecified)	3.1
Refine prediction techniques	2.7
Subsidize groups to improve scientific research or prediction	1.7
Control earthquakes scientifically	.1
Upgrade Utilities	2.0

TABLE 13 (Continued)

Measures suggested	Percent of all suggestions	
Collective and Voluntary Action		.8
Organize people, work as a community	.5	
Organize care for groups in special need	.3	
Regulate Announcement of Earthquake Predictions		.7
Monitor or control release of predictions	.3	
Announce all predictions	.2	
Reduce sensationalism concerning predictions	.2	
Other Suggestions		1.2
Make earthquake insurance available and affordable	.2	
Other financial suggestions	.2	
Pray	.1	
Other	.7	
Total	100.0	100.0
Total number of suggestions	3,146	

vious and immediate, than is the case with hazard reduction. Saving the lives of the injured, putting out fires, getting snarled traffic moving, and reuniting families after an earthquake are more exciting and heroic than inspecting buildings for safety, ordering unsafe dams drained, and helping householders to locate and remove objects that might fall and injure them in a quake. Consequently, there has been fear in some quarters that the public may not appreciate the need for hazard-reduction programs as fully as they do the importance of emergency preparedness. Coupled with the fact that police and fire officials often play a more significant role than planning and building safety officials in local disaster preparedness planning, this fear leads many to hold out little hope for developing the hazard reduction component in a balanced community response to earthquake prediction.

A careful effort has been made to classify each of the suggestions made by our respondents into hazard reduction and emergency modes of response. If the benefits of the proposed action will be realized in lessened disruption and damage and fewer casualties when the quake strikes, the action is classified under the hazard-reduction mode of response. If the benefits are to be realized after the quake has struck through dealing more effectively with the resulting disruption, damage, and casualties, the suggested action is classified as emergency-response mode. A goodly proportion of the suggestions could not be confidently classified in one more or the other, so they are placed in an "undetermined" category (21.2 percent).

Contrary to the fear just mentioned, considerably *more* of the suggestions fall into the hazard-reduction mode (49.4 percent) than into the emergency mode (29.4 percent). While we cannot be certain how much support will be forthcoming in actual situations, we can draw two important conclusions from this finding. First, there is widespread public understanding of the need to prepare for earthquakes through programs aimed at reducing the hazard of earthquakes as well as through improving emergency-response capability. Second, when people think of earthquake planning, they think of reducing the earthquake hazard more often than they do of upgrading an emergency response capability.

Investment for Hazard Reduction

One of the difficulties in converting public support for hazard-reduction activities in principle into support for specific programs is cost. Although there is clear public sentiment for the government to take action to reduce hazards, the support could be meaningless unless people are also committed to spending money for these actions. In an effort to subject the public attitude to a more severe test, we asked a set of four questions in which the cost of selected hazard-reduction activities was emphasized. Respondents were asked the following general questions:

Please look at the card below and tell me how important you think it is for the government to *reduce* the *possible* hazards of earthquakes by investing *large* amounts of money into:

The question was asked four times, with the following completions:

A. Prediction studies?
B. Enforcement of building safety codes and building repairs?
C. Establishing new systems for issuing scientific earthquake predic-
tions?
D. Loans to rebuild or reinforce unsafe structures before an earth-
quake?

Respondents could choose among the answers: "Very important,"
"Important," "Somewhat Important," "Not Very Important," and
"Not Important At All." The results are summarized in figure 36.

The respondents answered overwhelmingly in the affirmative
for all four of the investment areas. For each proposal, 80 percent
or more said that substantial investment was at least "somewhat
important." Even for the least popular item, more than a quarter
of the respondents thought investing large amounts of money was
very important.

A closer look at figure 36 indicates that we may have tapped
two qualitatively different areas of hazard-reduction planning.
Investment in areas of structural safety were considered particularly important by the respondents, with 65 percent and 48

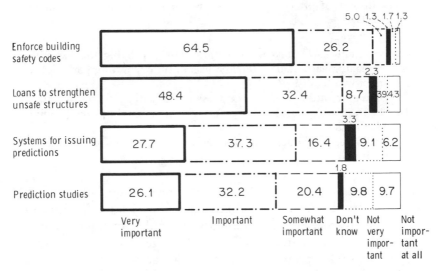

Figure 36. Importance of Investing Large Amounts of Money

percent, respectively, giving evaluations of "very important"; investment in prediction studies and earthquake-warning systems received fewer "very important" replies, with 28 percent and 26 percent, respectively.

This widespread support for investment in pre-earthquake hazard-reduction planning is surprising when compared with pronouncements by most disaster-planning agency officials, who contend that the public is only interested in disaster or hazard-reduction planning right after a major catastrophe. Government agencies responsible for public welfare and safety often cite a lack of public interest as the reason they are unable to marshal sufficient local backing for costly hazard-reduction preparations.

Perhaps the discrepancy between our encouraging findings and the pessimism of many public officials lies in the realm of public priorities. Although southern California residents believe that too little is spent on earthquake planning, they may be unwilling to see other programs and services cut to provide this additional funding. In order to compare the ranking of earthquake preparedness with other funding alternatives, we included the following question on priorities in the November and December survey of 1978:

> Suppose local government officials had additional funds to spend on some important project. Would you rather see the additional money spent on:
>
> A. Improving earthquake preparedness or on improving flood control?
> B. Increasing earthquake preparedness or on expanding park and recreational facilities?
> C. On better earthquake preparedness or on better police protection?
> D. On improving earthquake preparedness or on improving public education?
> E. On better earthquake preparedness or on better public hospital facilities?

As demonstrated in figure 37, funding for earthquake preparedness is a strongly favored alternative in comparison to funding for parks and recreation and is slightly favored over flood control. But earthquake preparedness is ranked far below expenditures for improving police protection and hospital services and especially far below expenditures for better public education.

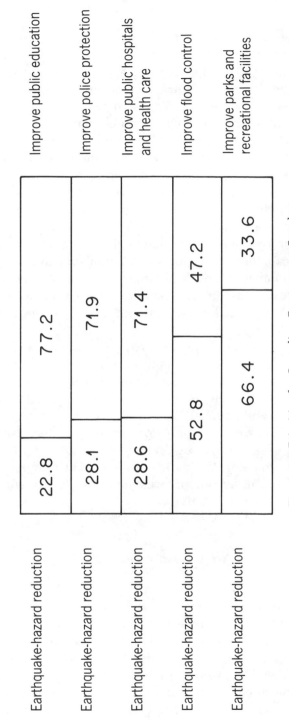

Improve public education

Earthquake-hazard reduction 22.8 | 77.2

Improve police protection

Earthquake-hazard reduction 28.1 | 71.9

Improve public hospitals and health care

Earthquake-hazard reduction 28.6 | 71.4

Improve flood control

Earthquake-hazard reduction 52.8 | 47.2

Improve parks and recreational facilities

Earthquake-hazard reduction 66.4 | 33.6

Figure 37. Priorities for Spending Government Surplus

How is general concern for financing earthquake preparedness related to the ranking of earthquake priority areas for funding? Is there a segment of the population that would support increased funding, and, if so, how substantial is this group? In order to answer these questions, we computed two indexes. The *earthquake priority index* is simply the number of times (from one to five) that a respondent selected earthquake preparedness over the alternative. In computing the *composite government investment index,* values from three for "very important" to one for "not important at all" were assigned to each of the four items on the importance of investing large amounts of money, giving a range of total scores from zero to twelve. The relationship between the two indexes is moderately strong (*gamma* = .258) and significant (*tau* = .203, p < .001), indicating that people who believe it is important to spend large amounts of money on earthquake preparedness are also inclined to assign higher priorities to earthquake preparedness in competition with other government programs.

The correlation between the two measures reassures us that there is a substantial core of support in the community for public expenditure for earthquake-hazard reduction, but the problem of priorities seems to explain why this support is difficult to mobilize. While support for earthquake-preparedness expenditures is massive, especially for enforcing safety codes and reinforcing unsafe structures, few people assigned top priority to earthquake programs. Only 4 percent favored earthquake-hazard reduction over all five alternatives, and only 13 percent favored it over four or five alternatives.

Who Are the Activists?

Once again we search for clues that might suggest how to facilitate action in support of earthquake preparedness. The procedure is to compare activists with inactivists, using correlational techniques that are summarized as a path analysis. In chapter seven, we reviewed action taken individually and by households, and in chapter nine, we shall look for evidence of participation in collective action. In this chapter, we have been examining *support* for community action rather than the action taken by our respondents. Since most of our respondents look to government more than to themselves in earthquake preparedness, it is important to understand support for public action as well as to understand direct action. The reader should not forget the distinction between the two when comparing findings from this chapter with the findings in earlier chapters.

The distinguishing theme of this chapter is *community* rather than individual or household action. We approached support for community action in two rather different but nevertheless complementary ways. One way was to ask whether people were able to suggest things that government agencies should be doing. The ability to offer suggestions during the interview situation would demonstrate that the respondent both endorsed government action and had thought about what can be done. The other way was to ask about willingness to have the government spend large amounts of money in support of hazard reduction. This question would test willingness to make some financial sacrifice for earthquake preparedness.

The *suggestions* index is simply the number of suggestions, from none to five, that the respondent offered with suitable probing. The summary measure of *support for government spending* is not very sensitive, because the level of support on two of the four items is so high. Consequently, we have chosen an index based only on support for the two less popular items, which had to do with systems for issuing predictions and with prediction studies. Index scores range from zero to six, with the maximum score identifying people who said it is very important for government to spend large amounts of money on both warning systems and prediction research.

The two path analyses are summarized in figures 38 and 39, for comparison. First, what features are common to both diagrams? Participation in discussion of earthquake topics is important in both, as it was in the earlier analyses of individual preparedness and of the quality of awareness. Our evidence continues to document the need to stimulate informal discussion among family members, friends, neighbors, and coworkers if we are to involve people in concerted preparedness activity. Belief in the eventual success of scientific earthquake prediction also plays a part in both measures of support for government preparedness. Younger people make more suggestions and are more enthusiastic about

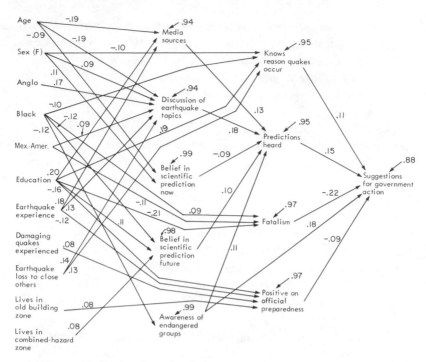

Figure 38. Suggestions for Government Action: Causal Analysis

government expenditure than are older people. And higher levels of education mean both more suggestions and more support for public expenditures.

If these findings are not unanticipated, the evidence on earthquake experience is more baffling. We were not surprised to find that having experienced several earthquakes and having had close friends or family members who suffered injury or loss in an earthquake contributed to support for government action. But we found that people who have experienced one or more *damaging* earthquakes have fewer suggestions to offer and assign less importance to government expenditure on earthquake-warning systems and prediction research. Closer examination of the diagrams reveals that both earthquake experience and earthquake loss to close others foster informal discussion of earthquake topics and thus indirectly contribute to support for government action. Since most people who experienced the San Fernando earthquake of 1971 or other damaging quakes did not themselves suffer loss, that experience may add little or nothing to the impact of earthquake experi-

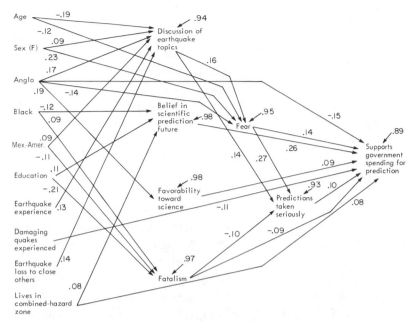

Figure 39. Support of Government Spending for Prediction:
Causal Analysis

ence of all kinds. But why there should be a weak negative effect on support for government action is unclear.

Mexican-Americans are disposed to support government preparedness according to both measures, because they engage in discussion of earthquake topics (though not as much as Anglos) and because they are not fatalistic about earthquakes. Blacks, however, have fewer suggestions to offer and are less convinced of the importance of government expenditures. In both cases, their disbelief in the eventual success of scientific earthquake prediction and their fatalism about earthquake survival have negative effects. In the case of suggestions for government action, the negative effects are enhanced by their limited awareness of predictions and forecasts and their dearth of ideas about earthquake causes. Anglos are disposed somewhat differently toward the two kinds of support for government preparedness, so we shall return to them later.

While the similarities, especially in the effects of earthquake experience, are interesting and sometimes challenging, there are substantial differences in the two measures of support for government action. Offering several suggestions for government action is distinctively associated with three communications and awareness variables. In addition to the common variable of informal discussion, other variables that dispose people toward having ideas for government action are using several media sources, being aware of specially endangered groups (that is, being socially aware), and having some idea about why earthquakes occur. These last three variables suggest a sophisticated kind of awareness. Respondents who had several suggestions for government action rely less disproportionately on word-of-mouth information and have thought about the causes and social consequences of earthquakes.

Two other variables also suggest the discriminating observer of the earthquake scene. Disbelief rather than belief in present scientific prediction capability is associated with offering suggestions for government action. Such disbelief can have either of two quite different meanings. If disbelief in present prediction capability is coupled with similar disbelief in future scientific prediction capability, it is likely to signal an antiscientific or skeptical view. But scientific prediction capability at the time of the investigation was more a hope than a reality. Hence, disbelief in current prediction capability coupled with belief in eventual scientific prediction could signify a discriminating understanding of the state of progress in earthquake prediction. Since we found that disbelief in present prediction capability and belief in future scientific prediction capability both contributed to the offering of suggestions for government action, it is plausible to interpret this finding as further confirmation of the sophisticated-observer hypothesis.[5]

In the same vein, the number of predictions someone had heard contributed to that person's having suggestions for government action, while the number of predictions taken seriously contributed to supporting large government expenditures for warning systems and prediction research. Again, having a broad awareness of the earthquake scene without necessarily taking everything seriously is associated with offering suggestions for government action.

The modest relationship between being critical of official preparedness and having suggestions for government action may serve as still another sign of discriminating awareness, as we shall suggest later in the chapter.

In chapter seven, we found that having fatalistic attitudes about earthquake survival was the greatest impediment to taking recommended individual and household precautions and also was the most highly correlated variable. Similarly, earthquake fatalism again shows the highest correlation and is the greatest impediment to offering suggestions for government action.

Finally, being Anglo—especially as compared with black—and being male, in a resolution of conflicting tendencies, contributed to a person's having more suggestions.

If not being fatalistic and exhibiting discriminating awareness and communication are critical for having ideas on government action, fear of earthquakes and taking predictions seriously are central in the explanation of support for government spending on warning and prediction. Fatalism is still an obstacle, but a much weaker one. In chapter six, we offered the hypothesis that fear may be the additional element necessary to move people from passive awareness to action. The crucial part played by fear in explaining quality of awareness was encouraging, but the hypothesis was not confirmed for personal and household preparedness or for supporting government action by offering several suggestions. But now we find some confirmation for the importance of adding fear to awareness in explaining support for spending government funds on warning systems and prediction research.

A generalized positive attitude toward science contributes understandably toward willingness to spend money for warning systems and earthquake research. And women, chiefly because they experience more earthquake fear, are stronger supporters of government expenditure than are men.

While Anglos have more suggestions to offer because they participate in more discussion and have heard more predictions and forecasts, they show more conflict over support for government spending on warning systems and prediction research. Their participation in discussion and their favorable attitude toward science dispose them toward supporting expenditures. But their less intense fear of earthquakes and a negative correlation that is not attributable to intervening causes included in our model diminish support for public expenditures. We can only speculate about the direct line from Anglo identity to muted support for government spending, but it may reflect the growing movement for economy in government and for tax reduction that culminated in 1978 in passage of California's Proposition 13, restricting property tax levies.

How Well Is the Community Prepared?

We have established that there is widespread public support for government action and that most people have some idea about what government should be doing, understand the need for hazard reduction as well as for emergency response planning, and are willing to have government funds spent for hazard reduction—but only after public schools, health services, and police protection are improved. We found that participation in informal discussion of earthquake topics, confidence in the eventual success of scientific earthquake prediction, experience with earthquakes, and increments of education all reinforce the disposition to support government preparedness activity. But, like being prepared individually and in the household, having ideas about what government should be doing depends on one's being free of fatalistic attitudes and having a sophisticated and discriminating earthquake awareness. Supporting government expenditure for warning systems and prediction research depends distinctively on fear of earthquakes and on the quality of earthquake awareness.

As a coda to this discussion, we asked how satisfied people were with what government officials had done. Respondents were asked:

> In dealing with earthquake preparedness problems, would you say public officials are doing a: Good job, Average job, or Poor job?

The largest number—41.1 percent—gave the noncommittal answer, "doing an average job." A sizable 10.5 percent were unable to answer. But 29.0 percent said that officials were doing a poor job, compared to 19.4 percent who said they were doing a good job.

We have already called attention to the association between giving a poor evaluation of government performance and having ideas about what government can do. On the other hand, there is no such association with supporting government expenditure. Thus, we are led to suspect that the people who think less well of government accomplishments are not so much those who merely want government officials to do more as they are those who have thought about and have some understanding of the earthquake problem. A significant correlation between awareness of the uplift and a negative view of government accomplishments tends to confirm this interpretation, as the critics of government preparedness were drawn disproportionately from those who were the best informed and most thoughtful about the earthquake threat.

Since the more alert and informed citizens had the least favorable view of government progress, there is reason to be concerned about the generally lukewarm appraisal of official action for earthquake preparedness. We cannot be sure that the same attitudes prevail at the present time. For example, some of the more informed citizens may have been reassured by delivery of the task force's *Report on Earthquake Prediction* to the mayor of Los Angeles.[6] But this report is more a promise than a plan, and other public actions are equally lacking in dramatic impact. The status of government response in relation to popular expectations should be a matter of continuing concern.

Although this evaluation of the government's handling of earthquake planning is not especially positive, it should be placed in perspective. One way of doing this is to find out how respondents evaluated preparedness efforts taken by themselves and the rest of the community as well as by officials and agencies. To investigate these comparative evaluations, respondents in the early 1978 survey were asked:

> How well prepared do you feel *you* are to deal with a future damaging earthquake? Are you very well prepared, somewhat prepared, fairly unprepared, or totally unprepared?

Two similarly worded questions were also asked about the preparedness of the *general public* and *of public officials and government agencies.*

Table 14 shows that while respondents felt they were much better prepared than the general public, an even larger percentage believed that the government was better prepared.[7] Two out of

TABLE 14

PERCEPTIONS OF PREPAREDNESS: SELF, PUBLIC, AND GOVERNMENT

	Percentage		
Degree of preparedness	Public	Self	Officials and agencies
Very well prepared	0.5	6.6	9.7
Somewhat prepared	17.4	36.9	46.0
Fairly unprepared	45.7	28.5	26.3
Totally unprepared	34.1	27.6	13.4
Don't know or no answer	2.3	.4	4.6
Total	100.0	100.0	100.0
Total number	1,367	1,367	1,367

five people still thought that the government was not especially well prepared. But three times as many respondents thought government officials and agencies were either somewhat prepared or well prepared as thought this of the general public. And the respondents rated government preparedness above their own.

Summary and Conclusions

Do people support collaborative action and government leadership in earthquake preparedness? Can we anticipate a surge of altruistic concern in case of an earthquake prediction? Most people recognize that risk from earthquakes is distributed unevenly in the community and believe that something can and should be done for those most at risk. However, they identify high-risk groups in mostly impersonal terms and place the responsibility for helping them squarely on government rather than on altruistically disposed citizens.

Most people have thought enough about what government should be doing to volunteer suggestions, the majority of which deal with hazard reduction rather than with emergency response.

A large majority of the respondents went so far as to agree that it is very important for government to spend large amounts of money upgrading the structural safety of buildings and that it is important or very important to spend large amounts to refine earthquake prediction and to improve warning systems. But the bubble of support seemed to burst when people were asked about priorities in spending surplus government funds, as they overwhelmingly chose public education, police protection, and hospital services ahead of earthquake preparedness.

Support for government earthquake-preparedness activity, as measured by both the number of suggestions volunteered and endorsement of substantial government expenditure, is enhanced by participation in informal discussion of earthquake topics with family members, friends, and associates; by confidence in the ultimate success of scientific efforts to predict earthquakes; by higher educational attainment; and by youth. Experience with earthquakes *seems* to enchance support for government activity, although the findings are ambiguous. Mexican-Americans are most supportive, and blacks are least supportive, with Anglos in between. Not being fatalistic is the strongest correlate of volunteering several suggestions for government action and is a weaker correlate of support for spending government funds.

People who are more discriminating in their awareness of the earthquake threat and understanding of earthquake prediction offer more suggestions for government action but are not disproportionately supportive of government expenditure for earthquake safety. On the other hand, fear of earthquakes, taking predictions seriously, and viewing science positively foster support for government expenditure, although these factors are not necessarily associated with volunteering more suggestions.

On the whole, people are not greatly impressed with the job of earthquake preparedness that government is now doing. But by comparison with what they think of the preparedness of their fellow citizens, government looks good. In general, the better informed have a less sanguine view of government accomplishments than do poorly informed citizens.

The ambivalence among Anglos over support for government programs to mitigate the earthquake hazard may best capture the problem we face. Their participation in discussion of earthquake topics, their respect for science, and the many ideas they have about what government could be doing all foster support for government programs. But their only moderate fear of earthquakes and, probably, a lack of confidence in the effectiveness of government initiatives and a desire for economy in government counterbalance the positive influences. Thus, verbal enthusiasm is not matched by effective support for strong government initiatives in earthquake preparedness.

CHAPTER NINE

Support and Obstruction
from the Grass Roots

In earlier chapters, we have shown that there were both substantial desire for more information on personal and household preparedness and popular sentiment favoring increased government action to prepare for an earthquake. But neither fear nor expectation of a damaging earthquake were directly important in explaining why some people were more actively concerned about preparedness than were others. Rather, we found that interaction within one's social network provided a much better explanation of when a person would actually take steps to prepare for a potentially damaging event than did prediction awareness and earthquake fear.

In this chapter, then, we will shift our focus from individuals to groups, both formal and informal, in order to investigate further both what attracted the attention of groups to the earthquake threat and what conditions lead to various types of action by groups. If individual concerns are transformed into action through group participation, some key questions about the collective experience should be addressed. What conditions mobilize group interest in earthquake topics? What resources are available to satisfy their information needs? When do groups become active, and what types of activities do they undertake? When do people form spontaneous groups in order to seek information and to act collectively?

Methodology and Group Descriptions

Our unit of analysis will be the "group." A group can be either an informal collectivity or a formal organization that, in either case, has held at least one meeting or discussion on an earthquake-related topic.[1] Several groups responsible for the general safety and welfare of Los Angeles residents (e.g., the sheriff's department, local police stations, Red Cross chapters, and official emergency-preparedness agencies) have held organizational meetings in order to improve their ability to respond to an earthquake-created emergency situation, legally fulfilling their institutional role obligations. Such organizational meetings were *not* included in this study, because institutional requirements make them responsible for involvement in earthquake-created emergencies.

The process of drawing a sample of groups and collectivities proceeded in two stages. In the first stage, possible groups were located from three primary sources and one supplemental source.[2] The first primary source was our surveys. In each of the five waves of interviews with randomly sampled Los Angeles County residents, respondents were asked:

> Within the last year, have you heard any lectures, speakers, or special presentations about earthquake, earthquake predictions, or earthquake preparedness at club meetings, school programs, church groups, work groups, neighborhood or block meetings, or anywhere else?

If the respondent answered affirmatively to any part of this question, a follow-up question was asked to identify the group more specifically. Respondents who said that they had attended a group meeting were then contacted by phone for additional information about the meeting and about the group that sponsored it.

The second primary source was organizations within the Los Angeles area that furnished speakers on earthquake topics. These organizations were contacted, and lists of groups for whom presentations had been given were compiled. These organizations included two emergency preparedness agencies (civil defense and the Red Cross), a locally prominent earthquake-research institution (Caltech), and a group that offers earthquake-preparedness programs for a fee. These are the only organizations that routinely provide speakers on earthquake topics to community groups on request.

If any meetings or programs were mentioned in the six newspapers being monitored, attempts were made to contact informants from the sponsoring groups to identify the meetings' organizers. This was the third primary source.

In order to identify as many of these groups as possible, "snowball" sampling techniques were used as a supplemental source. Attempts were made to follow up any references made by previously identified informants (or from any other source) about groups that had held earthquake meetings. Frequently, informants or organizers had knowledge of other group meetings that had preceded or followed the one they attended. When sufficient information was available, organizers of these informant-identified meetings were also interviewed.[3]

The second stage of the sampling process involved in-depth interviews with all the meeting organizers who could be located.[4] The orienting question was either why earthquakes were deemed important enough to be given time in an already existing group or organization or why the topic of earthquakes had brought new groups or previously existing informal groups together at least long enough to hold a meeting. The follow-up interview had three major objectives: (1) to discover why a meeting was held at a particular time, especially in relation to significant predictions or other events; (2) to determine whether the focus of the meeting was on preparedness measures for individual and family units or on actions by citizens' groups for the larger community; and (3) to determine whether the one organizational meeting was followed by others dealing with earthquake topics and whether groups that were newly formed to deal with earthquake concerns survived past an initial meeting.

The final sample (N = 135) upon which this analysis is based contains all groups for which sufficient information was available.

Work-related organizations were by far the most numerous settings in which earthquake information was disseminated (table 15). Social, civic, or service clubs and schools were also popular sponsors. Attendance at these meetings was largely mandatory (81 percent) in occupational groups, and audience size was frequently over 200 (36 percent). Formal organizations with stable memberships and routinized procedures were more frequent sponsors of earthquake meetings than were the less well-defined collectivities, with their more fluid membership boundaries.

TABLE 15

GROUPS THAT HELD FORMAL MEETINGS ON EARTHQUAKE TOPICS
FROM JANUARY 1, 1976 TO JUNE 30, 1977

Type of group	Number	Percent
Occupational, professional	57[a]	42.2
Civic, social, service	29	21.5
Schools	20	14.8
Community, open meetings	13	9.7
Churches	8	5.9
Neighborhood, residential	8	5.9
Total	135	100.0

[a]Meetings that took place at schools but that were for the faculty only (that is, for employees of the school district) were included in the occupational category.

Most programs (86 percent) were presented for general adult audiences. Senior citizens and schoolchildren, groups that were earlier identified as especially endangered, were the only examples of special audiences (7 percent each). For senior citizens, all presentations were sponsored by senior centers that had lunch programs. Programs for children were sponsored either by youth-oriented service clubs (e.g., scouting programs) or parochial schools.

With the exception of occupational groups, most meetings attracted fewer than forty-five participants. Residential groups, either neighborhood or condominium owners' associations, attracted the smallest attendance (usually less than fifteen), with this drawn from groups that were generally smaller to begin with.

Occupational groups were also the least likely to use preprogram announcements, probably because attendance of employees at periodic safety meetings was mandatory. For all other types of group meetings, organizational newsletters were the most common method of announcing an earthquake program. Schools and churches made the most frequent use of newsletters. The mass media were infrequently used, except for community-wide meetings that were open to the general public.

Earthquake preparedness was by far the most frequent topic of discussion at these group meetings (table 16). In only 10 percent of the meetings were scientific matters or predictions discussed exclusively, and in another 15 percent they were included along with preparedness topics. The meetings were mainly concentrated in scientifically oriented clubs and occupational groups (e.g., engineering clubs). In a few instances, scientifically oriented meetings were open to the public, sponsored through a university's lecture series. Meetings that combined both scientific and preparedness information usually had two speakers on the program, with one presenting geophysical information on earthquakes and the other discussing how to protect and prepare yourself.

The preponderance of meetings emphasizing preparedness paralleled the overwhelming public concern for information on individual and organizational preparedness. Although media attention to earthquake predictions initially stimulated about a quarter of these groups to hold meetings and resulted in some discussion of predictions in about 40 percent of them, the primary importance of the media's prediction focus was to sensitize people and groups to the need for more adequate preparedness information and planning.

There were three primary purposes for having earthquake meetings: to provide members with information (43 percent); to pro-

TABLE 16

TYPE OF EARTHQUAKE INFORMATION PRESENTED AT GROUP MEETING

Type of information	Number	Percent	Adjusted percent
Preparedness	99	73.3	74.5
Scientific and/or prediction	14	10.4	10.5
Both	20	14.8	15.0
Unknown	2	1.5	—
Total	135	100.0	100.0

vide the organization with information that could be used to update its earthquake planning or to improve its training for an earthquake event (47 percent); and to exploit earthquake concerns to serve other group purposes (10 percent).

Organizational Lag

Since the timing of individual information seeking was so closely related to significant earthquake events and to the media's attention to earthquake topics, we anticipated that group meetings on earthquake-related topics would follow similar patterns. However, no such patterns were found. The timing of earthquake meetings did not correspond with the occurrence of significant earthquake events either for all groups or for just those groups that held meetings because of members' concerns about earthquake threat. Separating group sessions into information-seeking meetings and information-disseminating meetings likewise revealed no relationship to events (fig. 40). Meetings in which scientific or prediction information was presented were not correlated in time with peaks in media attention to these topics. And meetings devoted to preparedness did not systematically follow peaks in media attention to preparedness.

In spite of the absence of apparent relationships between the occurrence of group meetings and significant events or peaks in media attention, earthquake predictions were cited as the reason for sponsoring a meeting in about 45 percent of the sampled groups, and earthquake predictions were discussed in almost 62 percent of the groups. Furthermore, one of the most popular sources of earthquake speakers, the civil defense office, received no requests for speakers on earthquake topics until March 1976, and there had been no requests to any agency during the preceding eight months. Also prior to March, groups and organizations had requested only very modest levels of earthquake information materials from the civil defense office. Clearly, earthquake events that took place from February to April 1976 must have had some impact in arousing group interest after a period of quiescence.

Prediction events were, then, important both in the motivation for groups' attention and as discussion topics during meetings. The problem is to explain what factors were muting or modifying

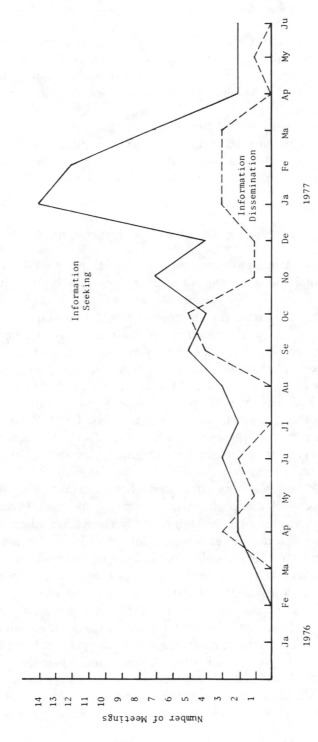

Figure 40. Monthly Distributions: Information-Seeking and Information-Dissemination Meetings

the effects of these events, making the mobilization of formal collectivities appear to be unrelated to significant events. For purposes of analysis, we shall assume that groups do respond to events but with a variable *organizational lag* that obscures the relationship.

Three nonmutually exclusive factors that promote organizational lag have been identified, namely, the diffusion of earthquake meeting ideas, resource scarcity, and the primacy of the organizational planning.

DIFFUSION OF EARTHQUAKE-MEETING IDEAS

Although information was missing for some groups in the sample, at least one out of every four meeting organizers had attended an earlier earthquake meeting that had motivated him or her to set up a similar presentation for another group in which he or she was a member. In many of these instances, a group member was the link between the occurrence of an earthquake meeting in two different types of groups. For example, one woman working for the state of California attended a mandatory lecture for employees on disaster preparedness which included an earthquake component. She was so impressed with the suggestions on earthquake preparedness that she had the homeowners' association in her condominium complex set up an evening presentation on the topic.

In other instances, the structures of the organizations themselves promoted the proliferation of earthquake meetings. For example, four presentations stemmed from a nutritional-program director's concern about earthquake danger for senior citizens. In November 1976, this program director became aware of the earthquake threat and its possible effects on "her seniors" by overhearing conversations about predictions at the center she managed. Although the seniors who used the center did not seem overly anxious about the media reports that earthquakes were anticipated in the near future, the manager began to worry about how these people would react if an earthquake occurred when they were alone. She scheduled a luncheon presentation to help the seniors prepare both their homes and themselves for such an event. Because she was pleased with the presentation, she suggested that other site managers of nutritional programs in the San Fernando Valley, who were under her direction, sponsor similar presentations. Subsequently, three additional meetings were held, one each in January, February, and March 1977.

The diffusion of earthquake information and meeting ideas through members' group affiliations was important in determining when such meetings might occur. For example, the initial senior citizens' meeting described above took place during the height of the rumoring episodes and was specifically related to members' concerns as perceived by the site manager. But the follow-up meetings occurred during the first quarter of the next year and thus were seemingly unrelated to any major prediction or earthquake events. As ideas were diffused through extended groups or among groups, they seemed to become dissociated from the initial stimulus for having an earthquake meeting.

In many cases, the initial meeting triggered some members' concern about friends, acquaintances, or coworkers in other parts of their networks who might also find such information useful. Frequently, these disseminators reported that they themselves were worried about a coming quake and thought that everybody should know more about earthquake preparedness. The only type of meeting resulting from this method of dissemination was on earthquake preparedness and planning. Whatever the reasons for disseminating the idea to have an earthquake meeting, these subsequent meetings frequently resulted from earlier meetings that were closely related to significant events.

RESOURCE SCARCITY

Resource scarcity refers to the dearth of agencies or organizations in the community that could or would provide speakers on earthquake topics to civilian groups. Information-seeking attempts by groups were often tied to the success of the seeker in finding an acceptable avenue through which to locate a speaker. For most groups that had to use external resources, this search was especially frustrating. Few avenues were available to civilian groups, and none of the resource groups advertised their speakers' services.

The major resource for *preparedness* in Los Angeles County

was the civil defense office. Because city-related emergency planning took priority, providing speakers for groups that requested them had to be fitted into the staff members' schedules. For this reason, groups that called to request a speaker would often have to wait until the meeting could coincide with free time in a staff member's schedule. Also, emergencies requiring the presence of the Civil Defense officer occasionally delayed meetings at the last minute. Such unavoidable delays often irritated the requesting group's members, sometimes to the point of not rescheduling an earthquake meeting. In this way, meeting dates sometimes followed the requesting date by a month or more, and sometimes the meetings were postponed indefinitely. Organizational lag, then, did not result solely from the diffusion of meeting ideas among groups but also from the need to use and coordinate with already overworked public resources.

The major source of scientific or prediction speakers in southern California was Caltech. When the Caltech Speakers' Bureau was contacted, calls were closely screened to determine the type of group requesting a speaker and the size of the anticipated audience. Since Caltech did not consider a service orientation to be one of its fundamental purposes, the Speakers' Bureau frequently denied requests from civilian groups and organizations that could not guarantee attendance of at least fifty to a hundred persons. This criterion excluded such groups as a local board of Realtors, a community library, a group of mental-health workers, and several teachers trying to get speakers for their classes. If the requesting group did meet the attendance criterion, their meeting still had to take place at a time convenient for the scientists with respect to their teaching and research schedules.

Again, the scarcity of sources for scientific information for groups also resulted in a lag phenomenon. An overworked, voluntary resource provided speakers only when the organization's primary goals and tasks were not interrupted. In the case of Caltech, an extra filtering process had been incorporated in an attempt not to overload the system while reaching as many people as possible. This filtering process had two consequences. First, it increased the possibility of lag—the group that did not qualify had to continue looking for another scientific resource that could provide a speaker for their meeting. Second, it also increased the likelihood that smaller groups would not be able to hold a meeting that included scientific information. It was these smaller groups, frequently, that did not have the intraorganizational resources to sponsor their own meetings and were reliant on seeking an "expert" from outside the group. This filtering mechanism thus actually diminished the number of group meetings on earthquake topics.

PRIMACY OF ORGANIZATIONAL PLANNING

Organizations frequently plan their event or meeting calendars well in advance to facilitate the group's functioning. This penchant for future planning often resulted in earthquake meetings that were held months after their original inception. For example, the program chairwoman of an elementary school PTA in the San Fernando Valley reported that she laid out her monthly program schedule late in October 1976. At that time, she said, earthquake predictions were in the news, and "valley people were remembering the '71 quake." But because there were "traditional" programs (Thanksgiving plays in November and Christmas pageants in December) and required school events (a back-to-school night and a musical program), she was unable to schedule the earthquake program until early 1977. The program, a well-advertised and well-attended meeting that included a Spanish translator, finally took place in March 1977—five months after the idea for the meeting had initially arisen.

This example points out an important temporal factor that affected the occurrence of earthquake meetings: the Christmas holidays. The total number of meetings declined drastically in December 1976 (although *individual* information seeking reached its highest peak in six months in December, coinciding with the Minturn prediction). In this instance, the holiday season provided a traditional set of organizational activities that took priority over the more recent concern of those organizations about earthquake topics. Although earthquake threat and prediction concerns were still important to the general public at this time, the concerns within formal groups and organizations had been preempted.

Although at first glance the occurrence of group meetings does not appear to be related to significant earthquake events, we have tried to demonstrate that the factors producing organizational lag may have accounted for much of this discrepancy. Because meeting ideas were diffused through organizations and between groups, because the scarcity of resources (i.e., speakers) often resulted in "fitting" meetings into the speakers' already over-crowded schedules, and because organizations were oriented to-ward future planning, earthquake meetings often were delayed and were dissociated from the events that initially had given rise to the motivation for sponsoring meetings on earthquake topics.

Continuity and Extent of Concern

Even if group meetings had occurred in concert with significant earthquake events, the mobilization of more formal collective attention to earthquake concerns would require (1) the continuation of organizational interest in earthquake topics and (2) some organizational mechanism or program to translate this interest into action. Without these aspects of organizational atten-tion, it is doubtful that the individual-level concerns about earth-quake threat could be sustained once the impetus of the prediction events, which focused popular attention on the threat and its consequences, passed.

CONTINUITY OF ATTENTION

While organizational interest in earthquake pre-paredness could result in a widespread information-dissemina-tion mechanism for the general public, there is little indication that such longitudinal attention occurred. Eighty-three percent of these groups held only one earthquake-related meeting. Those groups that are often identified with the grass roots—neighbor-hood and residential associations—were the ones *least* likely to hold more than a single earthquake session.

Only about one in five of the groups exhibited any sustained interest in earthquakes. The interest in earthquakes in about 10 percent of the groups was temporary, covering a few weeks' dura-tion. Service, social, and civic clubs and community-based groups typified this temporary interest, usually in connection with a short program or lecture series on earthquakes which they were sponsoring. Only about 7 percent of the groups sustained their interest in an earthquake topic for several months. Half of these were new groups that had just emerged to take advantage of increased public concern about earthquake threat, and the other half were groups that had previously existing programs concerned with emergency preparedness (Mormon church groups and scouting programs) in which earthquake preparedness was included as part of an ongoing concern. We shall refer to these latter as having a continuing interest in earthquake preparedness. We speak of sustained interest in reference to the duration of interest in both new and continuing interest groups.

STRUCTURAL IMPACT

Fewer than one in ten of the groups made any changes in organizational structure because of the group's attention to earthquake concerns. Ninety percent evinced no noticeable structural change to accommodate earthquake concerns. In most of these groups, the motivation behind the meeting was to satisfy organizational needs—updating emergency plans, holding routine employee safety meetings, having a topical speaker for a club meeting, presenting an interesting classroom lecture—rather than to satisfy members' requests or suggestions.

Five percent of the groups—primarily schools, service organizations, or civic clubs—expanded their structures either to include a new unit or to add new duties to a currently existing functional position within the organization which was to be concerned with earthquake matters. The other 5 percent were the newly emergent, largely entrepreneurial, groups.

EXTENT OF CONCERN

By combining these two indicators of organizational concern into a typology (fig. 41), we find that almost 80 percent of these groups had only the briefest concern with earthquake threat and sponsored only one meeting, which had no further effect on the group (cell A). For these unchanged groups, two patterns led to this limited attention. One of the patterns related

STRUCTURAL IMPACT

	Stability	Expansion	Emergence	
Singular	A (N = 107)	B Public service organizations Residential group (N = 3)	C Neighborhood meetings (N = 2)	(112)
Temporary	D Service clubs Care facilities Information centers (N = 9)	E Palmdale schools Adult class Explorer scouts (N = 4)	F	(13)
Continuing	G Mormon groups Service (N = 5)	H	I Enterpreneurial Groups Grass-roots group (N = 5)	(10)
	(121)	(7)	(7)	

Duration of involvement (vertical axis label)

Figure 41. Typology of Group Involvement in Earthquake Concerns

to the organization's needs, and the other related to the informal influences exerted on organizers which temporarily aroused and activated their interests.

The unchanged and largely unresponsive groups were those by far the most likely to have held meetings to fulfill some organizational need not related to earthquakes at all. These organizational needs included being required to provide safety instructions to employees, having earthquake drills to fulfill legal obligations, finding entertaining speakers on topical subjects, or providing information to a small group or special committee within a larger group which would aid in developing an emergency plan. Such meetings did not occur in response to any specific significant earthquake events; rather, their timing reflected only intraorganizational dynamics.

However, a few of these groups did respond to earthquake predictions. Not only were many of these meetings motivated by prediction concerns but some attention was also directed toward prediction discussions during meetings (although a substantial proportion had no such discussions).

For these groups, some degree of concern about earthquake threat was obviously needed to get the organizations to respond even in this limited way. Because organizers often claimed responsibility for initiating these meetings, the manner in which they became concerned is of great importance. When organizers got the idea to have these meetings from others, they were likely to have had earthquake discussions with *many* different discussion partners; in fact, their discussions were more broadly located than were those of the more involved groups' organizers. Perhaps it was the multiple informal channels through which earthquake ideas were received by the organizers that led to the belief that some minimal attention to earthquake matters (usually preparedness) should be undertaken. Perhaps, also, it was this arousal of organizers' interest through informal discussions that accounts for the occurrence of these meetings in response to significant prediction events. As extensions of their agitated or aroused networks, organizers might be more motivated to arrange such meetings as quickly as possible in comparison with those arranging such meetings merely to meet a biannual requirement to have a safety meeting.

Only 20 percent of the groups attended to the earthquake threat in a more vigorous fashion. The expanded groups and the groups with a continuing interest in earthquake matters were usually those whose organizational goals were compatible with some sort of earthquake-preparedness planning. The already existing groups that demonstrated a greater involvement in earthquake topics (cells D, E, and G in fig. 41) frequently were oriented toward providing public services, either in institutional settings (hospitals, schools, and libraries) or on a voluntary basis (scouting and community-oriented clubs).

Of the groups that displayed an increase in involvement, the expansion groups (cell E) experienced a salience of earthquake concerns that the unchanged groups (i.e., the stability groups, cells D and G) did not. Because of certain situational factors (e.g., nearness to the uplift and the presence of especially interested members), earthquake topics became particularly salient for a short period of time for the expansion-temporary groups, causing them to develop new units to deal with earthquake-related concerns. The unchanged groups did not experience the agitated arousal of interest that would have necessitated innovative group responses to their earthquake concerns. Instead, they incorporated their interests into their ongoing structural frameworks.

For the more activated groups, earthquake-prediction concerns were not an important factor in the initial motivation to sponsor a meeting. It is certain, however, that members of these groups were aware of earthquake predictions, because the majority of them discussed predictions during their meetings, although prediction and threat were not their major concerns. If the predictions actually indicated a coming quake, these groups wanted to be able to make their services available or to be prepared to handle emergency situations. They were functioning within an emergency-preparedness rather than a hazard-mitigation mode of planning.

Few new groups came into being at this time (cells C and I, fig. 41). They ranged from neighbors coming together for a single meeting about earthquake safety to a fully organized community group that brought legal action against a state agency trying to implement seismic-safety legislation. The emergent groups were of three types.

1. *Mutual assistance, or self-help,* groups emerged to assist participants in planning cooperatively for a coming quake. The purpose of such groups was to reduce the hazards affecting their members by providing information on earthquakes, predictions, or preparedness and by coordinating group planning. Mutual assistance groups are examples of classic grass-roots groups—that is, similarly disposed people acting together to solve a common problem. Action in these groups was more likely to take place through already established, informal networks than through new associations.

Only two self-help groups emerged during the study period (cell C). Both were neighborhood groups, and both were singular in their duration. The first group was simply a collection of neighbors and friends who came together to get more information on earthquake preparedness; the second group actually formulated neighborhood-responsibility plans.

2. *Entrepreneurial groups* were the most numerous groups to emerge during the study period. Earthquake concerns were *not* primary concerns for the organizers of these groups, which served more enduring interests of the organizers by offering merchandized services for potentially endangered and concerned clients for whom earthquake concerns might be primary.

Clubs were the most frequent of the groups employing earthquake topics strategically. Three of the continuing-emergent groups (cell I) that used this strategy were also clubs: Youth for Earthquake Safety, Quake Watchers, and Earthquake Forecasters. Quake Watchers was the most formally structured organization; it included a leadership hierarchy, a newsletter, and an emergency hot line for reporting anomalous phenomena, although the group never held any meetings. Both Youth for Earthquake Safety and Earthquake Forecasters were less formal groups with ambiguous memberships. Although both held meetings, these were not well attended.

The fourth emergent group in this category was a small group of women who used their teaching and professional skills in home economics to put together a very appealing presentation on earthquake preparedness aimed at individual households. This was the only group that was exclusively entrepreneurial, not soliciting outsiders to become members.

The organizers of these groups were capitalizing on the topicality of earthquake matters while furthering their own, previously existing interests.

For all of these groups, the popularity of their appeal was closely tied to the arousal of incipient earthquake interests in the greater community. Service was being offered to lessen people's fears and to prepare them for coming quakes. Once these diffused concerns declined (as evidenced by the information-seeking attempts and the extent of media coverage) in early 1977, the appeal of such groups also declined. Their audience and pool of potential members had turned to other, more topical matters.

3. *Issue-oriented groups* actively promoted or opposed some anticipated legislative or policy change. Two types of issue-

oriented groups *could* have emerged with respect to earthquake concerns: those that supported prosafety legislation (proponent groups) and those that opposed such measures (oppositional groups).

Proponent groups would share with the mutual-assistance groups a primary concern about the effects of a damaging earthquake on their members. But unlike the mutual-assistance groups, proponent groups would turn to some external agent (such as the local government) to mitigate the hazardous conditions, rather than depending on their own actions. The actions of these groups would be oriented toward solving major community problems. During the course of our study, no proponent groups emerged.

Oppositional collectivities, however, did emerge, and these were some of the most fully mobilized groups identified in this study. Only one of these collectivities, however, could be called an emergent group, namely, the Citizens' Committee to Save the Littlerock Dam (CCSLD). In two other instances where oppositional sentiment was mobilized, no identifiable group came into existence.

For this group, like the entrepreneurial groups, earthquake effects were, at best, secondary concerns. The primary concern was the effect of legislation intended to reduce earthquake dangers. Group members believed both that the proposed legislation would affect them adversely and that they could do something to mitigate those effects through collective action.

Obstruction from the Grass Roots

During this study, three issues emerged in and near Los Angeles County, each involving a major earthquake-mitigation concern: building safety, dam safety, and land-use limitations. In each of these instances, the proposed implementation of seismic-safety legislation was met with overwhelming organized resistance from the communities involved. Conflict emerged when major government agencies attempted to implement seismic-safety legislation aimed at reducing the loss of life and property in the event of an earthquake of destructive magnitude. In each instance, conflict resulted in dramatic polarization, making compromise or negotiation difficult. Because of the sustained conflict, the hazard-mitigation intent of the legislation was stalled.

One of the features that makes this type of conflict unique is that the resisters were among the intended beneficiaries of the legislation. Potential victims joined in collective action to block implementation of measures that would have reduced their exposure to risk of injury and death in case of a severe earthquake.

CASE STUDIES

Data for these case studies were collected through extensive interviews with officials of the implementing agencies, local government representatives, and involved citizens. Several public and organizational meetings in each community were attended, and an extensive written history was compiled for each community using media accounts, government communiqués, organizational minutes, and court and public-hearing transcripts.

Instances of this type of community conflict were found in three southern California cities: Ventura, Los Angeles, and Littlerock.

Ventura. In June, 1977, city officials of Ventura, California, received formal notification from the California State Geologist identifying part of their city as a potentially hazardous earthquake fault zone. This identification was part of the implementation of the Alquist-Priolo Geological Hazard Zone Act requiring delineation of potential damage areas along known active surface faults throughout California. (Once such a zone is established, local governments are required to withhold building permits until investigation has determined that the site is not threatened by surface displacement from future faulting.) Upon receipt of the preliminary review maps, city officials discovered that the area identified as the proposed Ventura Fault Zone bisected two city projects. The city hired a local geological consulting firm to complete additional trenching at the two sites in order to comply with the law. The firm, however, could find no evidence of surface faulting at either site. This began a lengthy and sometimes hostile attempt on the part of city officials and citizens to prevent the establishment of the Special Study Zone and to provide additional evidence to refute the State's allegation that an active fault did exist in the area.

Los Angeles. In October, 1974, the Los Angeles City Council began to develop a Seismic Safety Ordinance requiring all pre-1934 unreinforced masonry buildings (built before the disastrous Long Beach, California, earthquake) used as theaters to be brought up to current structural, plumbing, and electrical codes. Over the next two years this ordinance was changed several times in response to the protests of several special-interest groups such as representatives of the movie theater industry. The final ordinance stated that all pre-1934 buildings must be brought up to structural codes and that these would be posted before they were repaired to warn occupants of the hazard. Building owners would have until 1987 to make all repairs before demolition. This final version resulted in several hostile and emotionally charged city council meetings. One councilperson charged that the ordinance would cause the loss of nearly 50,000 jobs in his district alone because of loss of business and cancellations of building insurance policies. He gathered nearly 400 constituents to protest the ordinance. In light of the overwhelming opposition, the council deferred voting on the matter. Later, after several similar meetings, the council adopted a compromise bill setting up a two-year program to survey and identify the pre-1934 buildings but not to post the warning signs.

Littlerock. The California State Department of Water Resources (DWR) notified the Littlerock Creek Irrigation District (LCID, owners of the Littlerock Dam, located in the Antelope Valley in southern California) that a meeting would be held in June, 1976, regarding the revocation of LCID's permit to store water behind the dam. DWR had determined that the dam would be unsafe during either a maximum design earthquake (of about 8.3 magnitude) or a maximum design flood (of two to three feet overtopping of the spillway). The dam is very close to the San Andreas fault and directly upstream from the town of Littlerock. While officials of DWR saw this action as a culmination of a ten-year effort to get LCID to rehabilitate the dam, the latter group felt it had already taken appropriate steps, making the issue a low priority one. The heavily attended revocation hearing was the catalyst which produced widespread community discussion about the state's action. It was also the beginning of a community-based attempt to halt DWR's actions, resulting in a temporary court injunction prohibiting DWR from draining the dam.

Issue Publics

In each of these instances, the "issue" of seismic safety was being debated by two principal factions, each attempting to influence policy decisions relating to the implementation of seismic-safety legislation.

The faction *supporting* seismic safety was led by some type of government body (the state Department of Water Resources, the state Department of Mines and Geology, or the Los Angeles City Council's Building and Safety Committee). The government agents were trying to fulfill their role as "protector of the public good." The agencies saw themselves as taking positive steps to protect lives and property from a possible catastrophic earthquake that scientists were saying was inevitable within the next ten years or so.

The *anti-seismic-safety* faction combined vested interest groups and people whom the proposed actions were intended to protect from earthquake hazards. The latter and some of the former were people who inhabited and used pre-1934 buildings, who lived beneath an "unsafe" dam, or who lived on top of a surface fault. These anti-seismic-safety factions will be referred to as the "opposition collectivities."

The opposition collectivities, while not necessarily rejecting the public-safety intentions underlying the legislation, focused on the *certain* negative effects that implementation would have on their way of life. In Ventura, for example, extensive revenue from the sale of an oceanfront redevelopment project was jeopardized by the proposed fault zone, since the Ventura Fault allegedly bisected the site. Also, the fault reportedly ran under schools, a hospital, the sheriff's office, and a proposed reservoir. Local residents were concerned about property values within the zone and about their ability to decide freely what to do with that property.

In each of these instances, the negative effects of the legislation were seen as far outweighing any possible benefits. Opposition collectivities did not consider the risk of an earthquake as damaging to their way of life as the effects of the "protective" legislation would be. Their contention was that the consequences of the government's actions were a substantially greater threat to the local community than was the threat of a possible destructive earthquake.

DEFINING THE SITUATION

We have no difficulty in understanding the response of vested interests, such as those of apartment owners willing to risk their tenants' lives for the sake of a few more years' rental income or of developers willing to gamble that the great quake won't come until they have built and disposed of their property at a profit. The problem is in understanding the mobilization of popular opposition among people for whom the risk far outweighed the tangible gain by any rational calculus.

In order to understand the differential assessment of acceptable risk, it is necessary to look at the process by which people define a situation as threatening or risky under conditions of extreme uncertainty. Researchers have suggested that the process of developing contradictory definitions of the same situation is primarily based on two components: personal factors, such as past experience and present perceptions of the environment, and social factors, such as perceptions of how others are responding and comparisons of one's information and perceptions with those of significant others.

Considering the personal factors in the risk-assessment process, it has been suggested that individuals are not easily able to conceptualize disasters that have not occurred or that they have not experienced before. People appear to need direct experience with misfortune to stimulate action. Kates[5] and Burton and Kates[6] have pointed out that elaborate adjustments to cope with natural hazards often evolve only after repeated experience with the hazard. However, unlike many other natural disasters, major earthquakes occur very infrequently in any specific locality, and thus most residents are unable to draw upon personal experience in evaluating the threat or risk.

Assessment of risk also involves individual perceptions of the environment. Several researchers[7] have pointed to the fact that individuals tend to assess and interpret threat by referring to physical cues. One well-established finding is that people often need to observe changes in the local community's environment for a threat of an impending disaster to be taken seriously and for precautions to be initiated.[8] However, there are no observable external signs by which people can verify the threat of a coming quake, as there are for other natural hazards such as floods, tornadoes, and hurricanes.

Although individual factors are important, social factors in the risk-assessment process may be more influential. Since individual decision making does not take place in a vacuum, an individual's perceptions and subsequent action choices may be largely shaped or limited by interaction with others in his or her social circle. For example, Charles Fogelman and Vernon Parenton[9] have pointed out that as Hurricane Audrey (1957, Louisiana) got worse, "congregating behavior"—that is, discussion of what to do, where to go, and so on—increased, expanding from family members to neighbors to city officials. Moore et al.'s study[10] confirmed the hypothesis that those who evacuate during the predisaster period are much more likely to have discussed the potential danger with others than are those who do not evacuate. Similarly, Drabek[11] found that the majority of his sample attempted to confirm evacuation requests, with nearly 45 percent appealing to peers for such confirmation.

Thus, both personal and social factors affect the way in which individuals discriminate between dangerous or threatening conditions and benign ones. However, Williams,[12] in discussing response to warnings of disasters, has pointed out that most people would rather believe they are safe than that they are in danger. If incoming information is not clear or is accompanied by contradictory information, the subsequent definition of the situation is likely to lead to a delay in action or to an assessment that action is not necessary. In the case of earthquakes, defining the situation as threatening or determining an acceptable level of risk is especially problematic. Since there are no observable precursors in the local environment and the science of prediction is still new, the situation facing the public can be characterized by a lack of explanatory definitions, cues, and expectations with which to guide behavior. Individuals, then, tend to organize their experiences and perceptions concerning the risk situation within overarching frameworks of knowledge as they are interpreted through their social networks.

For our communities, risk was not limited to an assessment of earthquake danger or imminence. More important to the local residents was discrimination between the *certain* effects of the agency's proposed actions and the *possible* effects of inaction. The locals focused on the certain effects that implementation would have on their way of life. For example, Littlerock residents claimed that most local growers would be forced to cease farming and abandon their farms entirely because they could not afford to pay irrigation costs for water from the state's water project. They maintained that revocation actions would bring to an end a small-town agricultural way of life by undermining the local economy and eroding the tax base for local schools. These effects, then, related to some kind of tangible damage to the community and its way of life.

More important, however, were the anticipated effects of implementation on community values and principles commonly held by the majority of local residents. By focusing on this anticipated *symbolic* damage, the community defined the issue as one of moral principles rather than of expediency (e.g., economic considerations).

Three kinds of symbolic damage to the communities become salient, providing a much broader base upon which conflict developed. First was damage to the community's image or sense of autonomy or pride—the idea of what the community stands for. For example, the spirit of independence and self-sufficiency became apparent in this explanation of why the citizens of Littlerock decided to fight the state's proposed actions:

> At the time that the State Department of Water Resources, through their safety of dams division, decided that this dam should be drained, causing anguish and privation to the community, certain citizens decided perhaps to test the idea that Americans are not responsive to government, but that government is supposed to be responsive to its citizens.

This populist sentiment certainly reflected the locals' belief in autonomy over their own affairs, defining the water district's responsibility for the dam's safety as a local matter. Littlerock residents felt that their small-town way of life was being threatened by "big government's intervention."

Residents in all three communities felt they were being denied self-determination with respect to both individual and community use of property. This was an especially important issue in Los Angeles and Littlerock, since historic structures and architecture styles were threatened. These concerns brought new groups into conflict and provided new strategies for the resisters to use. For example, Littlerock residents began working to have the dam proclaimed a historic landmark.

Second, charges of discriminatory treatment were made. Both Ventura and Littlerock residents felt that their communities had been singled out because they were small municipalities rather than powerful metropolitan cities. Ventura residents, for instance, continually questioned why their community had been singled out, especially when there were other communities (i.e., Los Angeles) with histories of greater earthquake activity. In Littlerock, allegations were frequently voiced by members of the Citizens' Committee to Save the Littlerock Dam concerning the seismically "unsafe" dams in metropolitan Los Angeles (Bouquet Canyon Dam was one frequently mentioned) whose owners were not being forced to spend large amounts of money for rehabilitation. Often this "unfair, discriminatory" treatment was laid at the feet of agencies attempting to establish new programs. If officials of the Department of Water Resources (DWR) could make "an example" of Littlerock, they would then be able to force other dam owners to comply with department requirements to upgrade their dams. The decision to start with Littlerock was, according to the locals, a strategic move on the part of DWR officials.

However, the Los Angeles residents who would be most affected by the proposed seismic ordinance felt they were being discriminated against on the basis of economic and racial characteristics, since the pre-1934 buildings were in the older, predominantly ethnic-minority areas of the central city.

Third, the predictability of life and the perpetuation of normal life patterns came into question. For example, for Littlerock residents to admit that their dam was unsafe would have been to acknowledge their inability to carry on life as usual and to concede that they had not planned or ordered their lives in the best possible way. This definition also applies to Ventura residents' acceptance of the Special Study Zone and Los Angeles residents' acceptance of the vulnerability of their older buildings. Along with this idea goes acknowledgment of the inability to control events. People feared that once standards were accepted and complied with, DWR might initiate new standards, the Los Angeles building codes might be revised, or the state geologist might change the criteria used to establish the Special Study Zones, requiring the communities to comply with these new standards at a later date.

These symbolic issues not only provided the needed motivation to attract additional resisters but also helped to create a bond among the resisters and to solidify in-group opinion. This solidarity was based primarily on a shared assessment of the risk to the community from a damaging earthquake and the effect the proposed implementation would have on the community's way of life. Local communities weighed the intent of the legislation against what they believed would be the certain effects, both tangible and symbolic, of implementation on their communities. In all three instances, the negative effects were seen as far outweighing any possible benefit. The general contention of the local residents was that the consequences of implementation posed a substantially greater threat to the local community than did the threat of a destructive earthquake. They were therefore more willing than were the implementing agencies to accept a greater degree of risk from a possible earthquake.

Conclusions

When formal organizations and groups serve as a conduit for preparedness information for their members or for their own organizational needs, they must take advantage of increased threat awareness among the general public. Although threat awareness of earthquake-related concerns is raised in conjunction with prediction announcements, earthquake events, and media programs on seismic hazards, resource scarcity and other conditions result in the organizational-lag phenomenon. The impetus for organizational attention is therefore frequently dissociated temporally from the heightened general concern, and the crucial opportunity is lost for the organization or group to become more active with respect to earthquake activities.

Sustained grass-roots collective action—either for self-help in earthquake preparedness or to support public earthquake hazard-mitigation programs—failed to develop, despite widespread anticipation of a damaging earthquake. Although not conclusive, our data indicate that in the absence of an obvious, imminent, and severe threat, sustained collective action will not take place, especially without organizational leadership and resources.

With respect to self-help activities, two other explanations are also possible. First, in the United States, unlike in Japan and China, little consideration has been given to the possibility of citizens' mutual-assistance collectivities in emergency-preparedness activities. Most preparedness materials are directed either toward measures that individual households can take or toward enhancing the safety of employees in the workplace. Without some model of what this type of group could do to protect its members, it is unlikely that mutual-assistance groups will emerge. Second, the pervasive responsibility attributed by the general public to the government for ameliorating the threat to especially endangered groups and the media's positive emphasis on governmental preparedness may lead to a belief that grass-roots self-help groups are unnecessary.

With respect to the lack of public support for hazard-mitigation efforts, further questions are raised by our study. Under what conditions would the "possible" effects of a destructive earthquake be sufficient to mobilize a proponent collectivity? Is the specification of time, place, and magnitude sufficient, and must the source (the predictor) be credible? Is a formal endorsement by civil authorities necessary? While it may be desirable to have all of these components present whenever a prediction becomes known to the public, indications from the scientific community are that this is unlikely in the near future. Because predictions will continue to be issued, however, it is important to identify the conditions that will lead to the emergence of both proponent and oppositional collectivities.

Another question is raised concerning collective response to environmental threats: Why have proponent groups been the most common type of grass-roots group to emerge in response to technological hazard, while only oppositional groups were mobilized in response to the earthquake hazard in southern California? The answer may lie in how acceptable levels of risk are determined. Again, the conditions and processes that affect the determination of what constitutes a significant threat with respect to various hazards need further investigation.

PART FOUR

Odds and Ends

CHAPTER TEN

Understanding and Respect
for Science

In the preceding chapters we have examined, first, what the people of southern California have heard and remember about the earthquake threat, and second, what they want done about it or have done for themselves. Appreciation of the earthquake threat is pervasive but vague, and it is low on the hierarchy of immediate concerns for the average citizen. People are convinced that government has the responsibility to meet the earthquake challenge. But public support is acquiescent rather than assertive, while organized opposition to certain government actions is voluble and potent. Few people have taken even the most elementary steps to prepare their household for an impending earthquake.

Before we start to examine the effects on awareness and action of a long period of waiting we shall explore in greater depth two questions on which we have already touched. First is the prevailing attitude toward science, as it is revealed through the acceptance and understanding of scientific communications about the earthquake threat. The second is the effect of living in a zone where the risk in case of an earthquake is appreciably greater than it is in the larger metropolitan region or where the memory of the last destructive earthquake should be especially acute. The first question will be examined in this chapter, the second in chapter eleven.

Constructive response to an earthquake warning depends crucially on public appreciation of science. When meterologists issue tornado or hurricane forecasts, people often decide whether to take the forecasts seriously by looking for telltale cloud formations and wind changes and by feeling for sudden temperature drops. But there are no generally accepted signs that enable people to confirm earthquake forecasts through the testimony of their own senses. The scientific finding will be the only information which people will have available in deciding whether to take protective action or to go on with life as usual.

In chapter six, we noted that people more often take earthquake forecasts and warnings seriously if these are attributed to scientists than to other sources. Nevertheless, the majority of scientific announcements are not taken seriously, and the public respect for science will be explored in this chapter. A more fundamental question is whether people think about earthquakes in terms that are compatible with scientific thought. We shall ask whether people use *naturalistic* or *physical* frames of reference, in contrast to mystical and teleological perspectives. Since we know that both scientific and nonscientific attitudes abound in American society, a further question of great importance is whether people are polarized into proscience and antiscience blocs. Do people who look toward mystical sources of authority actively reject science and view scientists as enemies? And finally, are people prepared to accept forecasts by scientists and seers strictly on the forecasters' authority, or do they seek personal understanding and confirmation for the views of authorities?

Respect for Science and Scientists

We asked the 1,450 respondents in our basic field survey directly about scientific prediction in the present and in the future:

How accurately do you believe scientists can predict earthquakes at the *present* time? Would you say: Quite accurately, Somewhat accurately, Not too accurately, or Not at all?

Everyone who did not answer "quite accurately" to the first question was asked the second question:

In the future, how accurately do you think scientists will be able to predict earthquakes? Would you say: Quite accurately, Somewhat accurately, Not too accurately, or Not at all?

A striking 84 percent said they believe that scientists either can or will be able to predict earthquakes fairly accurately (table 17). About half of these people believe that prediction either is or will be *quite* accurate. Only one person in fourteen was either completely skeptical or was unwilling to make a judgment. Fully 42 percent believe that scientists can already predict earthquakes "somewhat accurately" or better. Compared with scientists' claims, these findings indicate widespread overconfidence in current scientific capabilities (faith in science may include elements of magical belief!).

TABLE 17

HOW ACCURATELY SCIENTISTS CAN PREDICT EARTHQUAKES

Degree of accuracy	Now %	Future %
Quite accurately	5.4	42.1[a]
Somewhat accurately	36.4	41.5
Not too accurately	38.3	9.1
Not at all accurately	18.1	4.2
Don't know or no answer	1.7	3.1
Total	100.0	100.0
Total number	1,450	1,450

[a]Includes the 5.4% who answered "quite accurately" now.

A more general assessment of attitudes toward science and scientists is provided by reaction to six statements, reproduced in figure 42. In order to counteract "acquiescence bias," we worded items so that in three instances *agreement* expressed a positive attitude and in three instances *disagreement* expressed a positive

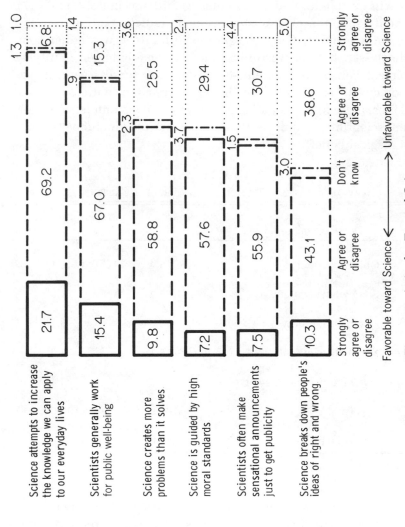

Figure 42. Attitudes Toward Science

attitude. For ease of interpretation, we arranged the answers on the graph so that replies favorable to science always appear to the left. As a result, half of the answers on the extreme left are "strongly agree" and half are "strongly disagree," depending on the specific statement.

The responses were overwhelmingly favorable toward science. None of the six items drew less than a 53 percent favorable response, and one item drew a 90 percent favorable response. Nevertheless, the range of endorsement is interesting and reveals something about where the ambivalence toward science is felt. The two items commanding the most positive responses affirm that science is constructively oriented toward human use. At the other extreme, 44 percent agreed that science breaks down people's ideas of right and wrong. Reflecting a similar concern about the moral implications of science, sizable minorities accused scientists of occasional publicity-seeking sensationalism and questioned whether science is guided by high moral standards. Nearly three out of ten people said they fear that science creates more problems than it solves.

The generalized ambivalence that asks whether the moral and social costs are worth the utilitarian accomplishments of science may be widely applied to earthquake prediction. Balancing the prevalent faith in current or future prediction capability is the specter of personal anxiety, self-centered survivalism, social disruption, and economic recession in the wake of a prediction.

The image of publicity-hungry scientists must be compared with another view sometimes expressed—that scientists know a great deal more than they are willing to tell the public. We sometimes hear after a major disaster that scientists knew the disaster was imminent but were afraid to tell the public for fear of creating an even worse disaster. And sometimes there are dark hints that scientists withhold information to serve their own ends. We tapped this sentiment by asking:

> Do you think scientists and public officials are giving us all the information they have on earthquake predictions, or are they holding back information?

Respondents who believed information was being withheld were then asked:

> Do you think they are holding information back: Because of their con-
> cern for the people's welfare, or to protect their own interests?

People were evenly divided over whether scientists are telling all
or are holding back information (table 18). But more of the people
who think that scientists are holding back information attributed
this to concern for the public interest than to self-interest.
Nevertheless, nearly one person in five suspects scientists of holding back information about earthquake predictions at least partly
out of self-interest. The difference in attitude toward scientists
and public officials is not striking, although scientists are trusted
a little more than are public officials.

The view of a *paternalistic* government-and-science establishment protecting the public from potentially unsettling news and
the alternative concept of a *self-serving* government-and-science
establishment controlling the flow of information command about
equal support. Together, these views insure a widespread disposition to believe in a reservoir of secret information to which the

TABLE 18
ARE SCIENTISTS AND PUBLIC OFFICIALS
WITHHOLDING INFORMATION?

Action and reason	Scientists %	Public officials %
Giving all information	45.2	42.6
Holding back information	46.1	48.6
For people's welfare	21.5	22.4
For their own interests	11.2	12.5
For both people's welfare and their own interests	8.7	9.0
Other and don't know	4.7	4.7
Don't know or no answer	8.7	8.8
Total	100.0	100.0
Total number	1,450	1,450

public is not privy. According to generally accepted theories, beliefs of this sort constitute fertile ground for the rapid growth and spread of rumor. They also contribute to credibility problems when scientists and government officials attempt to reassure the public in times of crisis.

Frames of Reference

A more difficult question to explore than whether people believe in science and have favorable attitudes toward scientific enterprise is whether people think about earthquakes in a manner that is compatible with science. We do not expect the public to be masters of scientific thought; even well-trained scientists often lapse into unscientific ways of thinking about events outside their scientific specialties. We also do not expect the ordinary citizen to have a deep and correct understanding of tectonic-plate theory and of other advanced earth-science theories. But we *are* concerned over whether people think of earthquakes as physical events, manifesting physical processes and having physical causes. If people employ a physical *frame of reference* when they think about earthquakes, communication between scientists and the public should be facilitated. In contrast, people might apply a mystical or magical frame of reference, with earthquakes occurring because of the ideas in someone's head or because of the work of a sorcerer. Or they might apply a teleological or religious frame of reference, with earthquakes being part of some grand design for the world, a punishment for the sins of mankind, or harbingers of the millennium. People who think of earthquakes in these terms are unlikely to interpret a scientifically based earthquake warning as it is intended.

We asked the following question and open-ended probe:

> People have various ideas about why there are earthquakes. Do you have *any* ideas *why* earthquakes occur? (Yes or No) What are they?

Spaces were provided for as many as five separate answers. Of the 1,450 respondents, 75 percent responded affirmatively. When their replies to the follow-up question were classified, 93 percent of the answers were found to refer to physical causes (table 19).

TABLE 19
CAUSES OF EARTHQUAKES

Earthquake cause	Percent	
Physical: naturally occurring		81.4
Fault movement	23.1	
Earth movement	25.0	
Earth's heat	10.0	
Sea, tidal waves	1.8	
Moon, planets	3.2	
Other	18.3	
Physical: human action		11.8
Drilling, digging	6.3	
Underground explosions	4.2	
Dam filling	.3	
Scientific research	.2	
Other	.8	
Nonphysical: naturally occurring	3.8	3.8
Nonphysical: human action		3.0
Divine retribution, evil forces	.9	
Unreasonable physical link	2.1	
Total	100.0	100.0
Total responses	1,816	1,816

Causes classified as physical are not necessarily scientifically valid. All that is required is that there be a plausible physical connection between the cause and the occurrence of an earthquake. For example, "launching satellites that pollute the atmosphere" was classified as magical or mystical because we could think of no plausible physical connection between atmospheric pollution and the occurrence of an earthquake. The nonphysical explanations referred principally to a divine plan of punishment for the sins of mankind and to a secular theme of interfering with nature.

There is a further distinction of importance. Whether causes are physical or nonphysical, they may lie outside of human control or may involve some kind of human action to trigger the physical causes. For example, if an earthquake is precipitated by the weight of the water newly impounded behind a dam, the immediate cause is physical (increased pressure because of the weight of the water), but it was human action that put the water there. Similarly in cases of nonphysical explanations, an earthquake that was foreordained as part of an ancient divine plan is different from an earthquake that is visited on a sinful nation as punishment. In the latter example, the sins of the people would serve as the trigger.

Some people volunteered references to human action in answer to the leading question on why earthquakes occur. But whether they did so or not, they were asked a second leading query, followed again by an open-ended probe:

> Do you think there are things that *people do* that make earthquakes *more* likely to occur? (Yes or No) What are some of these things?

We used the answers to both open questions in searching for answers that involved human triggering actions.

When the two classifications were combined, as in table 19, 81 percent of the explanations identified naturally occurring physical causes and another 12 percent identified physical causes triggered by human action. The small group of nonphysical causes divided fairly equally between naturally occurring causes and causes triggered by human action.

The category of physical causes triggered by human action deserves special attention. Most of the responses did not refer to scientifically accepted mechanisms such as impounding water behind dams. Instead, they seemed to imply that the triggering human action interfered too deeply with nature or was socially reprehensible. The fear that drilling and digging in the earth is likely to set off an earthquake implies magic more than it does physical causation. The second most frequent answer in this category, underground bomb testing, undoubtedly reflected the abhorrence of atomic warfare. Hence, a great many if not all of these answers melded a physical framework with either a magical or a moralistic framework.

We have been discussing physical and nonphysical frames of reference strictly according to numbers of answers falling into each category and not according to how many people employ each perspective. The crucial question is how many people employ a *strictly* physical frame of reference and how many understand earthquakes as *strictly* naturally occurring events. Approximately a third of our respondents discussed earthquakes exclusively in terms of naturally occurring physical causes. Another third gave only physical causes but included some involving human triggering actions. Most of this group have probably blurred the distinction between physical causation and an implied theory of value coherency as a vital force in the natural world. Another 3 percent cited one or more nonphysical causes but saw earthquakes as strictly naturally occurring events. And 4 percent employed nonphysical causes and human triggering actions.

Just as we found overwhelming respect and support for science coupled with significant realms of ambivalence, so we have found overwhelming use of physical models in explaining earthquakes compromised by the blurring of lines between physical and nonphysical causation.

Public Coexistence of Science and Nonscience

The last observations underline a point: scientific and nonscientific ways of viewing the world coexist widely in our society. Accepting an explanation for earthquakes that is compatible with science does not necessarily mean rejecting all explanations that are incompatible with science. Earlier, we were impressed with the overwhelming faith in the capacity of science to predict earthquakes. Now we must look back at whether this acceptance of scientific claims means an equal rejection of claims by the competitors of science.

Directly after answering the question on how accurately scientists will be able to predict earthquakes, respondents were asked:

Are there any other people besides scientists who can sometimes tell when an earthquake is coming? (Yes or No) Who are these people?

A total of 31.2 percent of our sample answered "yes," and most of these people (20.8 percent of the total sample) identified the forecasters as psychics, mystics, occultists, and the like. Another 3.4 percent ascribed this capacity to religious figures. A few thought that farmers could foretell earthquakes. Other answers were scattered or were too vague to classify.

The question was followed by another, designed to identify belief in a sort of folk wisdom that ordinary people can apply.

As I read each of the following, please tell me if you think people can use any of the following signs in their daily life to tell when an earthquake might be coming: Unusual animal behavior? Unusual weather? Premonitions, instinct, or ESP? Unusual aches or pains? Any other signs (specify).

Answers were entered as simply "yes" or "no." Three of the folk signs are widely accepted (table 20). Two-thirds of the respondents said they believe in animal behavior, more than two-fifths in earthquake weather, and more than a third in premonition.

Two significant observations are derived from these data. First, the widespread endorsement of folk signs shows that people believe nature can be apprehended directly and personally, without appeal to authority or to technical knowledge. Second, the substantial support for scientific and nonscientific modes of predic-

TABLE 20
SIGNS IN DAILY LIFE USED TO PREDICT EARTHQUAKES

Signs in daily life	Percent of total sample[a]
Unusual animal behavior	67.5
Unusual weather	43.5
Premonition, instinct, ESP	38.5
Unusual aches, pains	7.9
Small tremors	1.0
Water levels	.8
Other	3.3

[a]Total sample = 1,450 cases.

tion means that many people accept both. Apparently, faith in the capability of scientists to predict earthquakes coexists comfortably with faith in folk prediction and mysticism.

While these observations seem almost obvious, the fact that they were secured by comparing answers to questions formulated in three different ways renders the evidence inconclusive. In order to overcome this methodological deficiency, we devised a battery of comparably worded questions for inclusion in the interviews conducted in June and July 1978, with a sample of 536 adult residents of Los Angeles County. The questions were as follows:

Now I'd like to ask you a few questions about earthquake predictions. I am going to read a series of statements to you about predictions of a future destructive earthquake. As I read each statement, try to imagine how *seriously* you would take that prediction, that is, whether you would take it *very* seriously, *somewhat* seriously, *not very* seriously, or *not seriously* at all. REPEAT RESPONSE CATEGORIES AND STEM AS OFTEN AS NECESSARY. First,

Suppose a well-known *religious leader* said that a destructive earthquake would strike your community within a week. How seriously would you take this prediction?

If a well-known *scientist* made such a prediction?

If a *self-educated* person who had *spent a lot of time studying earthquakes* made such a prediction?

If a well-known *psychic* or *astrologer* made such a prediction?

If the *mayor* of your city or the *governor* of California issued such a prediction?

Now, suppose *you* had a strong *premonition* or *feeling* that a destructive earthquake would strike your community within a week. How seriously would you take your premonition or feeling?

Suppose there were a great many reports of *unusual animal* behavior, so that people were saying a destructive earthquake would strike within a week?

Suppose many longtime residents of California agreed that we were having *earthquake weather*, so that people were saying a destructive earthquake would strike within a week?

If we look first at the "very seriously" and "somewhat seriously" responses together as indicating how many people assign credibility to each prediction source, the sources fall into five groups (fig. 43). About three-quarters of the respondents would take seriously either a prediction issued by a well-known scientist or a prediction based on a great many reports of unusual animal behavior. The proportions are almost identical, although the core of "true believers" is larger for animal behavior than for the scientist. About half of the respondents would take seriously either their own strong premonition or feeling or the prediction issued by an informed amateur. Again, a much larger core of respondents would take their own premonitions very seriously, second only to those who would take a prediction based on animal behavior very seriously. Just over three-eighths would take seriously a prediction issued by the mayor or governor. About one-quarter of the respondents would take seriously a forecast by a well-known psychic or astrologer or a forecast based on earthquake weather. Finally, just under one in five would take seriously the forecast issued by a well-known religious leader.

The general pattern of responses to these questions is similar to that secured in the basic field survey using a different question format. In addition, the high credibility assigned to the self-educated expert in the 1978 survey shows that widespread interest in Henry Minturn's earthquake forecast for December 20, 1976, was not an idiosyncratic response but instead reflected a populist element in American thinking. We shall defer discussion about the implications of this finding and about the associated observation concerning high endorsement of folk signs to the next section.

We can now address the question of polarization versus mixing of scientific and nonscientific beliefs. With 73 percent of the respondents willing to take a scientific prediction seriously and 49 percent willing to take their own premonitions seriously, there must be at least 22 percent and probably more who accept both. One way to approach this question is to test for the opposite of polarization, namely, a single underlying dimension of belief in the predictability of earthquakes. Scientific prediction and animal behavior are so easy to believe that anyone who thinks earthquakes are predictable at all should accept them. Religious forecasts, however, are so hard to believe that only people who believe

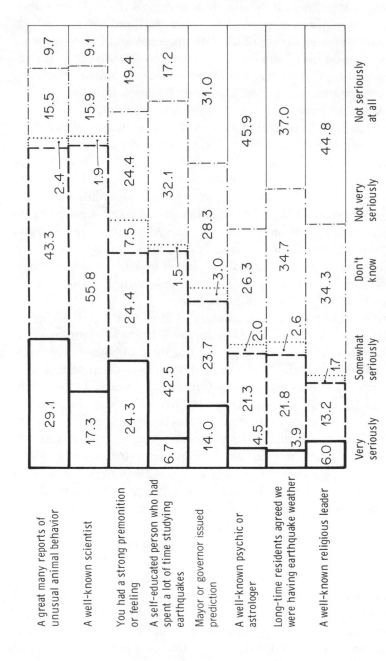

Figure 43. How Seriously a Prediction of a Destructive Earthquake
Within a Week Would Be Taken According to Source

in all of the other grounds for prediction should take a religious forecast seriously. Guttman scale analysis provides a statistical test for the unidimensional model. The result does not quite reach the standards accepted for a true scale. The model goes far enough, however, in explaining the data to provide some justification for thinking that what modes of prediction people endorse are better explained by how predictable people think earthquakes are than by whether people fall into proscience or antiscience camps.[1]

Factor analysis is another technique for assessing polarization. In the case of polarization, analysis should either produce a single factor on which scientific and nonscientific modes of prediction showed opposite signs or a scientific and a nonscientific factor with key items having opposite loadings on the two factors. The analysis, using the method of principal components with iterated communalities, produces one principal factor (85 percent of explained variance) and a second minor factor (15 percent of explained variance). The principal factor is loaded the most heavily with faith in psychics and personal premonitions and less heavily with faith in earthquake weather, religious leaders, and animal behavior, in that order. The minor factor is loaded most heavily with the scientist and the amateur scientist and less heavily with the mayor or governor. The most important observation is the extent of overlap between the two factors. All the prediction sources load positively on both factors. While there is a modest degree of "specialization" between the scientifically and non-scientifically disposed, there is no polarization.

Our finding, therefore, is that science and nonscience do coexist in the realm of earthquake prediction in the sense that belief in one type of prediction does not imply disbelief in the other. But they do more than coexist: they also exhibit considerable *integration*. On the whole, disbelief in prediction means skepticism about both scientific and unscientific sources.

In order to see the extent to which faith in scientific and nonscientific forecasting coexist in individuals, we have classified individuals into four types. The *prediction belief typology* uses the original question format in the basic field survey. People who believe that scientists will be able to predict earthquakes somewhat or quite accurately in the future or can do so quite accurately now but who reject all other predictors and folk signs except animal behavior are called *strictly scientific*. Since many scientists are taking seriously the possibility of using animal behavior as an earthquake sign, we felt that one could believe in animal behavior as an earthquake sign and still be strictly scientific. People who express faith in scientific prediction but also believe in one or more other ways of predicting have been called *believers*. These are people who combine faith in science with faith in nonscience in their view of earthquake prediction. Antiscientific people do not believe in the future of scientific prediction but instead accept some other kind of predictor. And the *skeptics* reject both scientific and nonscientific prediction capabilities.

More than half of the people in our sample were classified as believers, indicating that they have faith in the prospect for scientific prediction but also accept some nonscientific form of prediction (fig. 44). About half as many were classified as strictly scientific. About one person in nine was classified as antiscientific, accepting some nonscientific basis for anticipating an earthquake but lacking confidence in the eventual prediction of earthquakes by scientists. Skeptics made up the smallest group, with only about one person in twenty disbelieving altogether in the forecasting of earthquakes.

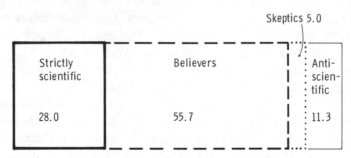

Figure 44. Types of Prediction Belief

Since the most highly publicized direct attacks on science have come from fundamentalist religious groups, as in the creationist attack on teaching evolution in public schools, our exploration of polarization is incomplete unless we bring some measure of religiosity into the analysis.[2] As a measure of religiosity, we have only answers to the question, "How important is religion to you?" Since most people said it was important, the most meaningful separation was between those who said "very important" and all others. There is no significant relationship, positive or negative, between the importance of religion and the favorability toward science. There are significant affinities between the assigning of great importance to religion, the use of a nonphysical frame of reference, and an antiscientific prediction belief. At the same time, 44 percent of the people who offered exclusively naturally occurring physical causes for earthquakes and 46 percent of the people who believed only in scientific earthquake prediction said that religion is very important in their lives.

This pattern suggests that there is a segment of the very religious who see the world through a frame of reference that is incompatible with science and who are skeptical of scientific claims and aspirations. But they are not in active confrontation with science, and they may not even realize the incompatibility of their perspectives. If these people were in confrontation with science, the clearest relationship would have been with the index of favorability toward science; in fact, there is no relationship. Furthermore, the incompatibility does not apply to many, if not most, of those who said religion is very important to them. Thus, the evidence on religiosity bears out the general conclusion that coexistence rather than polarization is the prevailing relationship between science and nonscience.

Personal Understanding

Science can have opposite connotations in one important respect. At times it brings to mind the scientific establishment, with the paraphernalia of sophisticated laboratories and equipment and discourse that is conducted in technical jargon incomprehensible to outsiders. When this view prevails, scientific findings must be accepted on the scientists' *authority*, since the lay person can neither understand nor personally corroborate the scientists' evidence and reasoning. At other times, science brings to mind the independent-minded and often lone investigator who rethinks received ideas and then devises an ingenious but simple test to confirm a new set of ideas. When this view prevails, every individual can play at being a scientist by acquiring a *personal understanding* of prevailing scientific theories and making one's own evaluation of their credibility. The two meanings have clear application to earthquake prediction. The individual may see the scientific pronouncement as something to be accepted on scientific authority, or he or she may seek to understand the grounds for a scientific prediction and may make a personal judgment concerning its credibility. The important practical implication is that in the latter case, scientific pronouncements are most likely to be taken seriously when they are accompanied by comprehensible explanations of the relevant physical mechanisms and prediction techniques.

The issue of authority and personal understanding is not limited to scientific prediction; it applies equally to nonscientific forecasts. As a general issue, it may be affected by the theme of populism often noted by observers of American culture. A strong element of populism would lend support to the demand for personal understanding as opposed to the uncritical acceptance of either scientific or nonscientific authority. Two sets of evidence have already indicated a strong tendency toward personal understanding rather than toward uncritical acceptance of authority. First, three-fourths of our respondents claimed to have some idea of why earthquakes occur, and they were able to back this up with some kind of personalized explanation. The majority of the reasons given were clearly recognizable devolutions from physical mechanisms described by scientists.

Second, the widespread belief in folk signs shows that people feel that nature can be apprehended directly and personally, without appeal to authority or to technical knowledge. Even among believers in mystical forecasting, we were initially surprised to find that many more people respected the validity of personal premonitions than were willing to take mystics and similar people seriously as earthquake forecasters. Although the respected scientist commands more serious attention than the amateur scientists, it is striking that half of our respondents indicated that they would take the amateur's forecast seriously. In the factor analysis we reported earlier in this chapter, respect for the scientist and for the self-educated amateur fell into the same factor, indicating a close affinity between the two in the public mind.

A third set of evidence bearing on this question comes from the reasons that people gave for expecting a damaging earthquake. The 630 respondents who said there definitely or probably would be a damaging earthquake within a year (chapter six) were then asked,

What makes you believe that a damaging earthquake will occur within the next year?

Most gave reasons for their belief, with some giving as many as three.

Half of the answers fell into the category of scientific and physical causes (table 21). The largest number of these (39 percent) made reference to *mechanisms or principles* having some basis in science. They included references to the idea that we are over-due for a quake (10.1 percent), the increased frequency or severity of quakes (7.9 percent), the history of earthquakes in southern California (7.2 percent), the idea that earthquakes occur in cycles

TABLE 21

WHY AN EARTHQUAKE IS EXPECTED

Reason earthquake is expected	Number		Percent	
Scientific and physical		470		50.6
Scientific authority	111		12.0	
Physical mechanisms and				
principles	359		38.6	
General		279		30.0
Vague references	106		11.4	
Media coverage	173		18.6	
Pseudoscientific	(54)	54	(5.8)	5.8
Prophetic		112		12.1
Secular and religious	29		3.1	
Personal	83		9.0	
Other	(14)	14	(1.5)	1.5
Total[a]	929	929	100.0	100.0

[a]Includes multiple answers.

or patterns (3.7 percent), and references to changes in the physical character of the earth (3.1 percent). A smaller group, 111 (12.0 percent) of the respondents, mentioned a scientific prediction or a scientist who had made such a prediction. These answers included references to the southern California uplift (2.9 percent), to Whitcomb or the Caltech announcement (.9 percent), and to general unspecified scientific predictions (8.1 percent). Although few of these respondents can be assumed to have sophisticated scientific understanding of the mechanisms, the majority can be seen as making an effort to assimilate scientific ideas into their own experience. A more generous classification would have added most of the *pseudoscientific* reasons to the category of "physical mechanisms and principles," since these reasons include climatic changes and earthquake weather, the Jupiter Effect (alignment of the planets), and California's breaking off at the San Andreas Fault line.

The same preponderance of personal understanding over appeal to authority applies to prophetic reasons. Of the 12.1 percent of reasons in this category, 9.0 percent cited personal feelings or experience, compared with 3.1 percent which cited a recognized mystic or religious figure.

While it is the preponderant attitude, personal understanding is not characteristic of everyone. Besides the 12 percent citation of scientific authority and the 3 percent of prophetic authority, 30 percent made references so vague as to be uncodable, and 19 percent mentioned extensive media coverage. But in light of the vast accumulation of evidence concerning the impact of media coverage and authority on public opinion, it is surprising that these categories are not much larger.[3]

Conclusions

Announcement of the uplift and subsequent developments created occasions for popular discourse over scientific ideas. We have used this discourse as an opportunity to explore the accommodation between scientific and folk thinking. We could not disagree with Perlman's observation that "only a small fraction of the public understands science as scientists or science reporters might hope they would," nor should we expect anything different.[4] But we are concerned, for both theoretical and practical reasons, about understanding whether there is a proscience and antiscience polarization that might embroil the community in nonconstructive controversy just when the need for concerted action is greatest, and whether a natural disaster such as an earthquake is interpreted through frames of reference that are incompatible with scientific thought.

Our principal conclusion is that coexistence rather than polarization is the rule as far as science and nonscience and naturalistic and nonnaturalistic frames of reference are concerned. Our findings confirm Morison's assertion that "the progress of science undoubtedly has some effect in reducing the grosser forms of superstition. . . . But it is doubtful that the scientific way of the world has ever completely displaced older, more magical approaches to deep questions."[5] We find both secular and religious mysticism important at certain phases of the encounter between scientific and popular thought, and we see a naturalistic frame of reference diluted by *moralistic* and *sacred-nature* perspectives. But the coexistence for most people does not seriously undermine faith in science, primacy of physical frames of reference in interpreting physical events such as earthquakes, and optimism over the prospects for scientific prediction of earthquakes.

These findings also have practical implications for the communication of scientific information about earthquakes. Scientists must be prepared to deal constructively with a public that puts its faith overwhelmingly in science but that is not ready to pledge exclusive allegiance to science. They must expect most of the believers in science to turn occasionally to other realms for whatever help they can get in foretelling earthquakes.

It is revealing in this connection to compare the relationship of prediction-belief patterns with earthquake awareness and action. Figure 45 shows the kind of linear relationship one might expect, with awareness and appreciation of the uplift highest for those people who believe in scientific prediction but who reject nonscientific forecasting. Fewer of the *believers*—that is, the great majority who credit both scientific and nonscientific forecasting— exhibit comparable appreciation of the uplift. And awareness is much lower among those who doubt that scientists will be able to predict earthquakes at all. But the relationship with personal and household preparedness is different (fig. 46). When we move

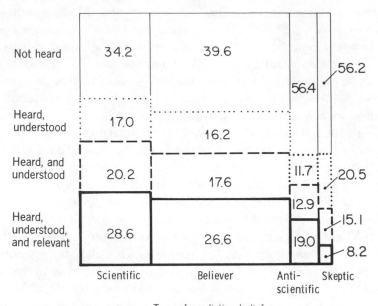

Type of prediction belief

Figure 45. Awareness of Uplift by Type of Prediction Belief

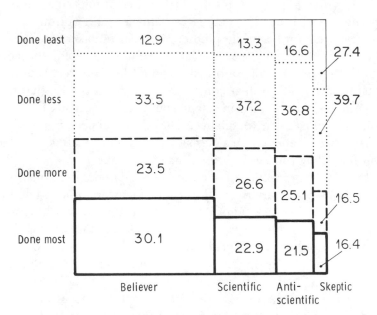

Type of Prediction Belief

Figure 46. Personal Earthquake Preparedness by
Type of Prediction Belief

from cognition to action, it is the believers who are best prepared for an earthquake. Although scientists may discourse more compatibly with the intellectually disposed *strictly scientifics*, public officials may find those who believe more indiscriminately in the predictability of earthquakes to be most cooperative in achieving community preparedness. If believing in personal premonition, earthquake weather, and prophecy is more indicative of informal integration into the neighborhood than it is of intellect, we are reminded of earlier findings that earthquake awareness without social integration makes little if any contribution to preparedness action (chapter seven).

Scientists must also learn to deal effectively with the public's prevalent unwillingness to accept either scientific or nonscientific forecasts and warnings purely on authority. A substantial portion of the public—perhaps even a majority—place their greatest reliance on a sense of *personal understanding*. Some of the misconceptions, the pseudoscientific perspectives, and the unjustified faith in folk signs are the products of poorly guided efforts to translate the earthquake threat into personal understandings. The patient explanation of physical mechanisms in popularly comprehensible terms should pay dividends in public receptiveness to warnings based on scientific analysis.

A brief concluding note on science and religion may be in order. Although the great majority of our respondents said that religion is important in their lives, very few of them suppose that religious leaders can forecast earthquakes and few tried to explain earthquakes in religious terms. It is the secular mystics rather than the religious mystics who today offer an alternative to scientific prediction of earthquakes. Similarly, those to whom religion is most important are no less favorable toward science and no less confident in the prospect for scientific earthquake prediction than are the less religiously inclined. In short, there is no evidence here to suggest that religion plays a part in whatever resistance we have found to the acceptance of scientific earthquake prediction.

CHAPTER ELEVEN

The Neighborhood Makes
a Difference

Sociological theories and common sense lead us to suppose that awareness, interest, and action are heightened when many of the residents in a compact neighborhood have shared similar disaster experiences or find themselves subjected to a common hazard. The shared experience and common hazard become mutually relevant topics for conversation; more information is circulated and people think more about what to do. Recognizing the existence of a concerned constituency, organizational leaders and locally based public officials incorporate these concerns into organizational and governmental life. If this entire process is sufficiently advanced, a *disaster subculture* develops, as described by Moore, Wenger, and Weller.[1] In this chapter, we test the applicability of this scenario to earthquake-hazard response in Los Angeles County.

Living in Special Zones

The most widely publicized source of special vulnerability in southern California is the danger that certain kinds of buildings constructed before 1934 will collapse in an earthquake. Prior to that year, masonry structures were built without reinforcement, and wood-frame and stucco homes were often not bolted to their foundations. Zones with unusually high concentrations of buildings constructed before 1934 should be recognized by their residents as areas of special risk in an earthquake. Hence, we sought to identify the census tracks in which the largest proportions of structures were built before 1934; these would constitute the first zone of special vulnerability. We call this the *old-building zone*.

During the San Fernando earthquake of 1971, the Van Norman Dam was on the verge of collapsing for several days. While the water level behind the dam was being lowered, thousands of residents were evacuated from the zone of potential inundation. Subsequently, the owners of all dams in California were required by state law to prepare inundation maps, identifying the zones of potential flooding in case of dam collapse. These maps were to be delivered to authorities in the respective counties so that appropriate evacuation plans could be incorporated into local emergency plans. A sample of residents living in these potential *inundation zones* constitutes our second zone of specialvulnerability.

When we began to locate census tracts for inclusion in these zones of special vulnerability, we discovered that a surprisingly large share of Los Angeles County residents live in potential inundation zones and that there is considerable overlapping between the two kinds of zones. We eventually grouped the relevant census tracts into the following three zones: an *inundation zone*, an *old-building zone*, and a *combined-hazard zone*, which included tracts that were hazardous by both criteria.

Research dealing with other kinds of natural disaster has often identified prior experience with a disaster agent as a relatively powerful predictor of response to disaster warnings. Although most residents of Los Angeles County have experienced earthquakes, few of them have experienced a disastrous earthquake from within the zone of major damage or threat. Only people living within the main impact area for the San Fernando-Sylmar earthquake of 1971 would have had such an experience in Los Angeles County during the past four decades. The main impact zone consists of those neighborhoods within which structures were destroyed or heavily damaged and those neighborhoods in which residents were evacuated until authorities could be certain that the Van Norman Dam would not collapse. Residents of the *San Fernando earthquake impact zone* constitute our fourth special sample.

Potential overlap between the vulnerability areas and the San

Fernando earthquake impact area could be a source of unclearness in the analysis. The decision was thus made to constitute the three vulnerability zones exclusively of census tracts falling outside of the San Fernando earthquake impact zone. Because a large portion of that zone could also be subject to inundation, it was not practicable to constitute the San Fernando earthquake impact zone exclusively of tracts that were not vulnerable by our criteria. Hence, the San Fernando impact zone includes some neighborhoods potentially subject to inundation.

The object of our analysis was to compare each of these zones with a representative sample of Los Angeles County residents living in neighborhoods that were free from special vulnerability or earthquake experience. A single *control sample* was designed for use in all comparisons.

Before drawing the sample for our basic survey—the source for most of the analyses reported in Parts Two and Three—we attempted to estimate how many individuals would turn up in the countywide sample from each of the four zones and from the control neighborhoods. On the basis of these estimates, we drew additional cases in three of the zones in order to make the samples sufficiently large for confident analysis. This "oversampling" procedure, in turn, required some refinements in our techniques for statistical analysis; these refinements are explained elsewhere. The sample size for each of the zones and for the control group is presented in table 22.[2]

The general procedure followed is to compare each special sample with the control sample for most of the measures of awareness and action already introduced in Parts Two and Three. If there are no differences or only a trivial number of differences, the analysis need not be carried further. The conclusion is that living in the zone in question has no special effect on awareness and response to the current earthquake threat. If there are more than a trivial number of statistically significant differences, the next step is to determine whether these differences might have been the result of differences between the special sample and the control sample with respect to age, educational attainment, occupational socioeconomic status, household income, or ethnicity. *Analysis of covariance* is the statistical technique employed to neutralize the effects of the first four of these covariates. Because ethnicity is not a continuous and quantifiable variable,

TABLE 22

SAMPLE SIZE BY SPECIAL ZONES

Zone	Number of tracts	Nonover-sampled respondents	Over-sampled respondents	Total
Control	38	503	—	503
Inundation	7	95	30	125
Combined-hazard	12	155	44	199
Old-building	41	542	—	542
San Fernando earth-quake impact	7	90	110	200
Total		1,385	184	1,569

we shall either use it as a set of three "dummy variables" in the analysis of covariance or employ other techniques for analysis as appropriate.

If a special sample does not differ significantly from the control sample with respect to the four covariates or to ethnicity, it will not be necessary to proceed through all of the steps in the analysis. Consequently, we will begin by reporting the differences between each special sample and the control sample with respect to the four covariates of age and social stratification and with respect to ethnicity (table 23).

The inundation zone and the San Fernando earthquake impact zone do not differ significantly from the control sample on any of the four age and social stratification covariates. Differences in age and social stratification are therefore not available as alternative explanations for any differences we find between these two samples and the control sample. But residents in tracts with heavy concentrations of old buildings and residents in tracts that combine inundation hazard with an abundance of old buildings are significantly older than the members of the control group, and their household incomes are significantly lower. Household incomes are especially low for residents of the old-building zone, and the concentration of older people is especially striking in the combined-hazard zone. The two zones are at the opposite poles

TABLE 23

AGE, SOCIAL STRATUM, AND ETHNICITY BY SPECIAL SAMPLES

Variable compared	Control	Inundation	Old-building	Combined-hazard	San Fernando impact
		Mean			
Age (years)	40.7	40.0	42.8*	47.1*	41.6
Educational attainment	12.5	12.6	11.9*	13.4*	12.8
Occupational status	42.7	38.6	40.6	47.5	46.3
Household income ($)	18,124	16,462	12,364*	14,470*	18,465
Income adequacy	2.76	2.70	2.24*	2.74	2.93
		Percent			
Black	10.7	1.6*	19.9*	10.6	1.0*
Mexican-American	13.1	18.4	14.8	10.6	3.5*
White Anglo	69.2	65.6	54.6*	73.8	91.0*
Other	7.0	14.4*	10.7	5.0	4.5
Total	100.0	100.0	100.0	100.0	100.0
Number of persons	503	125	542	199	200

* Asterisk signifies that the mean or percentage is significantly different from the corresponding value for the control sample at or beyond the 1 percent confidence level. Other values listed are not significantly different at the 5 percent level.

of the educational distribution. Residents in the combined-hazard zone reported higher average educational attainment than did residents in any other zone. Residents in the old-building zone reported the lowest educational attainment of any sample. It is clear that we must supplement uncontrolled comparisons between each of these special samples and the control sample with analysis of covariance to determine what differences are artifacts of the age and social-stratification differences.

Differences in ethnicity are pervasive. Only the combined-hazard zone is ethnically representative of the less hazardous areas of the county. The inundation sample is quite similar to the control sample in the proportion of white Anglos, but Mexican-Americans are heavily overrepresented and blacks correspondingly underrepresented. The old-building zone has its share of Mexican-Americans, but blacks are overrepresented and white Anglos underrepresented. The San Fernando earthquake impact zone stands out as disproportionately populated by white Anglos, with only two blacks and seven Mexican-Americans in the sample. Except in the case of the inundation zone, it was necessary to test for the possibility that observed differences from the control sample are artifacts of ethnic or racial imbalance in the population.

As a prelude to examining each of the special samples separately, we have summarized in one extended table all the simple comparisons made between each special sample and the control sample (table 24). Means or percentages are reported for comparison with control sample means or percentages, along with the level of significance of the differences. In order to simplify the reading of an otherwise complex table, we have reported means or percentages for special samples only when they are significantly different from the respective means or percentages for the control sample.

Inundation Zone

Out of a large number of variables, only three significantly distinguish the inundation-zone population from the control-area population. One of these differences reaches the 1 percent level, and the other two reach only the 5 percent level.

TABLE 24

COMPARISONS BETWEEN SPECIAL SAMPLES AND CONTROL SAMPLES

Variable compared	Control	Inundation	Old-building	Combined-hazard	San Fernando impact
Personal characteristics and earthquake experience					
Owner-occupied household	59%	—	37%	34%	—
Relatives nearby	—	—	—	—	—
Groups, organizations nearby	1.24	—	.95*	—	.86*
Reads newspaper regularly	—	—	—	—	—
Earthquake experience index	2.02	—	—	—	2.24*
No damaging quakes	—	—	—	—	—
Damage to self or friends	.73	—	.86	—	1.75*
Other disasters experienced	—	—	—	—	—
Significant orientations					
Earthquake fatalism index	—	—	—	—	—
Earthquake invulnerability	1.79	—	1.69*	—	1.66
Favorability toward science	11.75	—	—	12.29*	—
Accuracy of scientific prediction now	2.77	3.08	—	—	—
Accuracy of scientific prediction future	4.09	—	—	4.28	—

TABLE 24 Continued

Idea about earthquake cause?	—	—	—	—	—
Nature of earthquake cause	—	—	—	—	—
Folk signs for earthquakes:					
Animal behavior	66%	—	—	75%	33%
Unusual weather	42%	—	—	—	—
Premonitions	—	—	10%	—	—
Aches and pains	6%	9%	—	—	—
Prediction belief: skeptic	4%	—	—	—	—
Scientists and officials with-holding information	—	—	—	—	—
Communication					
Media-discussion balance	—	—	—	—	—
Number of media sources	3.64	—	—	—	4.01
Discussed earthquake	—	—	—	—	—
Range of topics discussed	—	—	—	—	—
Range of discussion partners	—	—	—	—	—
Topics discussed:					
Predictions	—	—	—	—	—
Family preparations	—	—	—	—	—
Why earthquakes happen	25.92	—	—	35.40*	—
Quakes around the world	16.21	—	—	22.71*	—
Old unsafe buildings	11.80	—	—	—	—
Dams, flooding	—	—	—	—	17.09

TABLE 24 Continued

Variable compared	Control	Inundation	Old-building	Combined-hazard	San Fernando impact
Moving out	8.62	—	—	13.68*	—
Other topics	—	—	—	—	—
Earthquake hazard awareness					
Number of announcements heard	—	—	—	—	—
Types of announcements heard	—	—	—	—	—
Number taken seriously	—	—	—	—	—
Types taken seriously	—	—	—	—	—
Awareness of uplift	1.23	—	—	—	1.62*
Awareness of groups at risk	1.40	—	—	1.86*	—
Breadth of awareness	—	—	—	—	—
Meliorability of group risk	3.25	—	—	—	2.95
Self in group at risk	.06	—	.15*	.24*	.13
Know whether fault nearby?	63%	—	53%	48%	—
Is fault nearby?	2.00	—	2.31*	—	2.24
Fear index	—	—	—	—	—
Changed concern	—	—	—	—	—
Earthquake next year?	—	—	—	—	—
Release uncertain prediction?	—	—	—	—	—

TABLE 24 Continued

When release 50/50 prediction	—	—	—	—	—
When release 90/100	1.57	—	1.74*	—	—
Hazard-reducing action					
Personal-preparedness index	—	—	—	—	—
Neighborhood cooperation	—	—	—	—	—
Measures taken and planned	17.25	—	20.66*	—	23.16*
Taken for future earthquake	9.16	—	11.19	—	14.46*
Government expenditure for hazard reduction (inclusive)	12.78	—	—	13.56*	13.38
Expend. for building safety	—	—	—	—	—
Expend. for prediction and warning systems	6.12	—	—	6.76*	6.57
Number of suggestions for government action	2.05	—	—	2.54*	2.38*
Type of suggestions:					
Structural safety	38%	—	31%	27%	—
Education	—	—	—	—	—
Emergency preparedness	23%	—	28%	36%	30%
Scientific research	18%	—	13%	—	—
Evaluation of government preparedness	1.81	2.01*	2.00*	—	—

*Asterisk signifies that the mean or percentage is significantly different from the corresponding value for the control sample at or beyond the 1 percent confidence level. Other values listed are significantly different at the 5 percent level. Values that are not significantly different are omitted.

The most reasonable interpretation is that the three "significant" differences are actually products of chance. In any series of comparisons, occasional differences large enough to be considered significant when viewed singly are to be expected on the basis of chance.

Elsewhere in this report we have observed that there seems to be little awareness of hazard from the potential collapse of dams in case of an earthquake. When asked about earthquake hazard, people think most often of unsafe buildings and of proximity to earthquake faults and much less frequently of dam failure. The earlier findings gain support from the observation that residents of potential inundation areas exhibit no greater earthquake awareness, concern, preparedness, or concern for government action than do people in safer areas of the county. One might anticipate some defensive denial of risk, but a total absence of differences unexplainable by chance cannot be credibly attributed to such a mechanism.

Even in the absence of greater concern and preparedness, we might have expected that knowing they lived below a dam would have sensitized people to earthquake topics. There was, however, no trace of heightened sensitivity. We looked especially at answers to the question, "If a damaging earthquake were expected in southern California, do you think any particular groups of people would be in greater danger than others . . .?" to see whether respondents would spontaneously mention people who live below dams. Residents of inundation zones were no more likely than other respondents to think of people living below dams as being in greater danger, nor were they more likely than others to think of themselves as being in special danger because they lived below dams. We must conclude that residents living below dams are either unaware that they live in potential inundation zones or fail to recognize their situation as calling for special thought and safety preparations.

Zone of Old Buildings

Residents in the zone with unusual concentrations of old buildings differ from the control sample in several respects. The number of statistically significant differences is sufficient to justify a search for patterns. For convenience, we have abstracted from table 24 into table 25 only those items on which old-building-zone respondents differed significantly from the control sample. Items in table 25 cannot be interpreted, however, without reference to the many items in table 24 for which there are no significant differences.

We recall that blacks are overrepresented and white Anglos are underrepresented in this zone and that residents are a little older and are lower in both education and income than the control sample. Fewer of the residents belong to groups and organizations in the local community, fewer live in owner-occupied homes, and a few more reported that they have experienced damage in an earthquake or that they have close friends or relatives with such experience. This last difference probably results from the inclusion of a few tracts from the impact zone of the Long Beach-Compton earthquake of 1933. Otherwise, this group does not differ from the others in earthquake experience, newspaper readership, or the presence of relatives nearby.

There are few differences in significant orientations that might shape earthquake-prediction response. Residents in the old-building zone are even less prone to claim invulnerability to earthquakes than are those in the general populace. They do not differ in their faith in various kinds of earthquake forecasting, except for a possible slightly more frequent acceptance of personal aches and pains as earthquake-premonitory signs. There are no differences in communication patterns concerning earthquakes and earthquake danger.

Residents living in neighborhoods where old buildings abound were no more or less aware of the various near predictions, forecasts, and cautions that were publicly discussed in 1976 and no more or less aware of the uplift than are residents in control neighborhoods. Fewer of them believed they knew whether there was a fault near their residence, but more of those who thought they knew believed that there was a fault nearby. More residents in this zone mentioned groups in special danger in case of an earthquake and included themselves. This difference is explained by references to people who live in old or seismically unsafe structures. Residents were no more likely than respondents in the control sample to mention people who live in old and unsafe structures as being in special danger, but they were more likely

TABLE 25

SIGNIFICANCE LEVELS OF DIFFERENCES BETWEEN
OLD-BUILDING AND CONTROL SAMPLES

Variable compared	Analysis of variance	Analysis of covariance
Personal characteristics and earthquake experience		
Owner-occupied household	(−).01	(−).01
Groups, organizations nearby	(−).01	(−).05
Damage to self or friends	.05	.001
Significant orientations		
Earthquake invulnerability	(−).01	(−).01
Folk signs: aches and pains	.05	—
Communication		
—— none ——		
Earthquake-hazard awareness		
Know whether fault nearby?	(−).05	—
Is fault nearby	.01	.001
Self in group at risk	.01	—
When release 90/100 prediction?	(−).01	—
Hazard-reducing action		
Measures taken and planned	.01	.05
Taken for future earthquake	.05	.01
Type of suggestions for government action:		
Structural safety	(−).05	(−).01
Emergency preparedness	.05	.01
Scientific research	(−).05	(−).01
Evaluation of government preparedness	.01	.01

Significance equals or exceeds indicated levels. When the .05 level is not reached, differences are treated as nonsignificant and identified by the symbol —. The direction of all relationships is positive, except when identified by the symbol (−).

to mention this group while having themselves in mind. Although they were no less favorable toward the eventual release of earthquake predictions, they were more disposed to delaying issuance of a relatively certain prediction than were respondents in the control sample.

Old-building-zone residents were found to be no more and no less prepared for an earthquake according to our battery of personal and household measures than were residents in the control area. However, they attributed more of their preparedness to the prospect of a future earthquake. And if they actually do go ahead with what they said they plan to do but have not yet done, they will be better prepared than those in the control sample. They offered no more and no fewer suggestions for government action than did members of the control sample, but their emphasis was a little different. They more often proposed emergency-preparedness measures and less often proposed government action to increase the structural safety of buildings or funds for scientific research. In their evaluation of government preparedness, they were more favorable than those in the control sample.

When the variables that distinguished between the old-building zone sample and the control sample are reexamined, reducing the effects of the four age and social-stratification variables and ethnicity simultaneously, there are only a few changes (see right-hand column in table 25). A disposition to delay the release of a relatively certain prediction is more characteristic of older respondents; controlling age statistically eliminates the difference in this variable. Similarly, including oneself in an especially endangered group disappears as a distinguishing characteristic. Differences persist on items that suggest a slightly augmented sense that the earthquake prospect ought not to be treated with an attitude of strict normalcy.

Combined-Hazard Zone

The residents of the combined-hazard zone live in neighborhoods where there are both a concentration of old buildings and the possibility of flooding in case a dam should collapse in an earthquake. In light of our finding that residents in simple inundation zones showed no awareness of the special hazard to which they are subjected, we might expect the combined hazard sample to be indistinguishable from the old-building sample. Insofar as there are differences, we must look for other explanations before prematurely attributing them to the existence of doubly hazardous conditions.

The combined-hazard sample differs strikingly from the old-building sample in the higher level of education and ethnic representation (tables 23 and 26). Although both samples are low on household income, incomes are more adequate in the combined-hazard sample than in the old-building sample when household composition is taken into account, using standards published by the Bureau of Labor Statistics in the U.S. Department of Labor. The combined-hazard sample is also distinctly older than any of the other samples. This configuration suggests that the sample may be drawn disproportionately from some of the neighborhoods favored by an earlier generation as desirable places in which to make a permanent home. Some of the sample tracts that fall in the combined-hazard zone, such as those in Hollywood and Pasadena, contain a mixture of longtime residents with ties of sentiment and culture to the local community and recent immigrants to the United States who are of moderately high socioeconomic status. However, samples from the two zones are alike in the low proportion of owner-occupied households. The possible significance of these zones as *natural areas* is discussed later in this chapter.

The two samples from old-building zones are alike in their distinctiveness from the control sample in only two respects: (1) In offering suggestions for government action, they are a little less likely to mention steps to enhance the structural safety of buildings and a little more likely to mention preparedness for emergency, and (2) they are less likely to claim that they know whether there is a fault near their residence.

The heightened sense of being especially at risk because of living in old buildings that was strictly an artifact of the racial composition of the old-building-zone sample withstands the controls and appears to be a distinctive feature of combined-hazard-zone residents. But, like the inundation sample, these residents did not see themselves as being at risk because of living below dams.

TABLE 26

SIGNIFICANCE LEVELS OF DIFFERENCES BETWEEN
COMBINED-HAZARD AND CONTROL SAMPLES

Variable compared	Analysis of variance	Analysis of covariance
Personal characteristics and earthquake experience		
Owner-occupied household	(–).01	(–).01
Significant orientations		
Favorability toward science	.01	.05
Accuracy of scientific prediction in future	.05	.05
Folk signs: animal behavior	.05	—
Communication		
Topic discussed:		
Quakes around the world	.01	.001
Old unsafe buildings	.01	.05
Moving out	.01	.01
Earthquake hazard awareness		
Awareness of groups at risk	.01	.01
Self in group at risk	.01	.001
Know whether fault nearby?	(–).05	.01
Hazard-reducing action		
Number of suggestions for government action	.01	.01
Government expenditure for hazard reduction (inclusive)	.01	.01
Expenditure for prediction and warning systems	.01	.01
Type of suggestions for government action:		
Structural safety	(–).05	(–).01
Emergency preparedness	(–).05	.01

Significance equals or exceeds indicated levels. When the .05 level is not reached, differences are treated as nonsignificant and identified by the symbol —. The direction of all relationships is positive, except when identified by the symbol (–).

Residents in the combined-hazard zone were more favorable toward science and had faith in the eventual prediction of earthquakes by scientists. The latter observation is complemented by greater support for government spending to improve earthquake-prediction and warning systems. They also believed more strongly in animal behavior as an earthquake sign. More of them have discussed earthquakes around the world, the problem of old buildings, and the possibility of moving out. Besides recognizing their own vulnerability in old buildings, they showed awareness of a wider range of groups in special danger. There were no differences in personal preparedness or in ascription or intention, as there were for the sample from the old-building zone. But combined-hazard residents did have more suggestions for government action, and they expressed more support for government expenditure for earthquake-hazard reduction.

Controlling statistically for age and social stratification covariates has little effect on the findings. Even after introducing controls, this sample appears to be somewhat more sophisticated than the single-hazard old-building sample because of the more favorable orientation toward science and scientific prediction and the lower disposition to compensate for lack of special preparedness through statements of intention and doubtful ascription of their own preparedness to the earthquake prospect.

Perhaps living where old buildings are concentrated leads people to find less hope for the success of government action to facilitate reinforcement or reconstruction of unsafe buildings and to be more aware of the need for readiness to deal with catastrophe when it occurs. But awareness is not translated into the completion of concrete self-protective measures or into greater attention to near predictions, forecasts, and cautions concerning future earthquakes.

Nevertheless, in different ways, the two samples may share an augmented attitude of preparedness that has not yet reached the threshold for conversion into action. By engaging disproportionately in the discussion of earthquake happenings, the problem of old buildings, and the possibility of moving out, the combined-hazard sample may have developed a sensitization and some preliminary understanding that could facilitate action if the need became clearer. Similarly, old-building-zone residents who insisted that they still plan to make earthquake preparations and who attributed general-preparedness measures (such as having a flashlight and a first-aid kit) to the earthquake prospect may have been expressing a heightened sense of obligation to be prepared. Feeling that they ought to be more prepared than they are may render them more responsive to public leadership in a recognized time of urgency.

San Fernando Earthquake Impact Zone

Except for a small corner of the old-building zone affected by the 1933 earthquake, our vulnerability zones have not suffered severe earthquake damage within the lifetime of even the oldest residents. Vulnerability is thus hypothetical and is not based on collectively remembered experience. A contrast is provided by our *San Fernando earthquake impact zone*, consisting of tracts where the greatest damage occurred in the 1971 earthquake and of tracts where the entire population was evacuated for several days until danger that the Van Norman Dam would collapse had been alleviated. Although the earthquake was strongly felt and minor damage occurred throughout the county, severe damage, loss of life, and evacuation affected only a restricted area.

Table 27 lists the variables on which the San Fernando zone sample differs significantly from the control sample and indicates which of these differences remain significant when only Anglos are included in the comparison.[3] As we expected, the San Fernando sample reported significantly more intense experience with earthquakes, and a significantly larger proportion have personally experienced earthquake damage or injury or have friends or relatives who have had such experience. They did not differ on home ownership, regular reading of a newspaper, or having relatives nearby. But they were less likely to belong to organizations in the immediate vicinity, and in this respect they displayed an oft-noted characteristic of suburbanites. These three background differences are unaffected by controlling ethnicity.

Only two weak differences in significant attitudes emerged, and both of these disappear when ethnicity is controlled. On such matters as fatalistic attitude toward earthquake damage, appreciation of science, confidence in scientific prediction and nonscientific forecasting, and trust in scientists and officials, San Fernando

TABLE 27

SIGNIFICANCE LEVELS OF DIFFERENCES BETWEEN SAN FERNANDO
EARTHQUAKE DAMAGE ZONE AND CONTROL SAMPLES

Variable compared	All ethnic groups	White Anglos only
Personal characteristics and earthquake experience		
Groups, organizations nearby	(−).01	(−).01
Earthquake experience index	.01	.01
Damage to self or friends	.01	.01
Significant orientations		
Earthquake invulnerability	(−).05	—
Folk signs: earthquake weather	(−).05	—
Communication		
Number of media sources	.05	.05
Topics discussed: Dams, flooding	.05	—
Earthquake hazard awareness		
Awareness of uplift	.01	—
Meliorability of group risk	(−).05	—
Self in group at risk	.05	.05
Is fault nearby	.05	—
Hazard-reducing action		
Buy insurance	.01	—
Measures taken and planned	.01	.01
Taken for future earthquake	.01	.01
Government expenditure for hazard reduction (inclusive)	.05	.01
Expenditure for prediction and warning systems	.05	.01
Number of suggestions for government action	.01	.01
Type of suggestions: emergency preparedness	.01	.01

Significance equals or exceeds indicated levels. When the .05 level is not reached, differences are treated as nonsignificant and identified by the symbol —. The direction of all relationships is positive, except when identified by the symbol (−).

zone residents were representative of white Anglos in the control sample.

Again, only two weak differences in earthquake communication patterns appeared, and only one of these survives the ethnic control. One might have expected the memory of the Van Norman Dam threat and the more recent discussion of rebuilding a safer dam to have made dams and flooding a salient topic for discussion. But even this difference ceases to be significant when only Anglos in the two samples are compared.

The weak tendency for San Fernando zone residents to glean earthquake information from a wider range of media sources, suggesting greater interest and sensitization to earthquake matters, withstands the control for ethnicity. But the interest and sensitization were not translated into active discussion of earthquake topics.

Differences in hazard awareness and a slight skepticism about the ameliorability of hazard are not statistically significant when only white Anglos are compared. However, the more frequent identification of self as a member of a group that is disproportionately at risk is not explained away by ethnic differences.

Several differences in support for hazard-reducing action apply whether or not ethnicity is controlled. The differences, however, are in support for action rather than in actual steps taken. San Fernando zone residents were no better prepared for an earthquake as individuals and households than were residents of the old-building zone, but they more frequently said that they still plan to take additional steps, and they more often attributed their preparedness to the prospect of an earthquake.

San Fernando zone residents had more ideas for government action and supported expenditure for earthquake prediction and improved warning systems more strongly than did the control sample. Excluding blacks and Mexican-Americans from the comparison brings out the latter difference even more strongly. And, like residents of both vulnerability zones, San Fernando zone residents were disposed more toward emergency preparedness than toward hazard mitigation.

In summary, living in neighborhoods that were damaged or evacuated in the 1971 earthquake has surprisingly few effects on attitudes and actions. The observed effects are passive rather than active, suggesting sensitization to earthquake concerns plus normative pressure and support for individual and governmental action.

A Localized Disaster Subculture?

With the San Fernando earthquake zone sample, we can answer a further question that helps to deal more precisely with the concept of earthquake subculture. Do San Fernando residents hold distinctive attitudes because they individually remember the personal trauma of the 1971 earthquake? Or has the earthquake memory been kept alive through institutionalization and as neighborhood lore, equally affecting newcomers to the zone and those who experienced the trauma personally? This issue is an application of the more general question of whether persons in a category share attitudes because they are all affected similarly by a common *life situation* or because the attitudes are transmitted as part of a *subculture*.[4] If only the residents who lived in the earthquake damage and evacuation zones in 1971 held these distinctive attitudes, we would hardly be justified in speaking of a subculture or of subcultural themes. However, attitudes generated by the earthquake experience in individuals may have been diffused and communicated to newcomers to the zone and kept vital by emergent symbols and discussion.

From his investigations of hurricanes along the United States coast on the Gulf of Mexico, Harry Moore concluded that a region subjected frequently to the same disaster agent develops a *disaster culture,* which "serves to define situations and thereby to determine to a large degree the sorts of actions persons and institutions and communities will take when they find themselves in the stressful situation." The disaster culture includes "those adjustments, actual and potential, social, psychological and physical, which are used by residents of such areas in their efforts to cope with disasters which have struck or which tradition indicates may strike in the future." Paradoxically, the disaster subculture (or more correctly, subcultural themes) served both to foster an often self-destructive pride in one's ability to face the danger and to supply rational elements that facilitated survival.[5] Similarly, anthropologists have pointed out that cultural myths are often the repository for disaster-survival lore. In a comprehensive and systematic elaboration of the disaster-subculture concept, Dennis E. Wenger and Jack M. Weller stress both organizational and subjective subculture components as well as both adaptive and maladaptive aspects.[6]

Wenger and Weller have suggested three conditions that are crucial for development of disaster-subculture themes. Southern California earthquakes fit one of these conditions in producing "salient consequential damage" that cuts "across class and status lines in the community." While earthquake impact is repetitive, which is another of the proposed crucial conditions, disastrous quakes are relatively infrequent. And the seasonal periodicity that facilitates development of tornado, hurricane, and flood subculture themes is altogether lacking. But more frequent small tremors serve as reminders.

The third condition, that "subcultures appear more likely to develop if the focal agent allows for some period of forewarning," is definitely not met, except in preparations for aftershocks.[7] For two reasons, the absence of forewarning may not have impeded subculture development. First, we have already found that survival knowledge for use during and immediately after a quake is widely diffused. For example, 90 percent of our metropolis sample knew that they should avoid elevators in tall buildings, and 88 percent knew that an inside doorway or hall is a relatively safe place. Second, prevalent belief in folk signs by which one can tell that an earthquake is coming was already well documented at the time of the 1933 Long Beach earthquake, and it is confirmed by our evidence of confidence in unusual animal behavior, personal premonition, and earthquake weather.[8] Thus, folklore may incorporate belief in a period of forewarning when objective evidence provides no such assurance.

The reasoning can be carried one step further. We hypothesize that subcultural themes should be developed most sharply in clusters of neighborhoods where the destructive impact of an earthquake has been acutely experienced in recent years. If this is indeed the case, the attitudes that we found most characteristic of people living in the San Fernando earthquake zone should apply to newcomers as well as to people who lived there during the quake. Subcultural effects should override life-situation effects.

To sort out subcultural from life-situation effects required that we combine intrazonal with interzonal comparisons in a single analysis. In order to keep cell frequencies sufficiently large, we created a simplified fourfold table that could be subjected to a two-way analysis of variance. On one dimension we separated residents in the two zones (for subculture effects). On the other dimension we separated respondents who had experienced property damage or injury in an earthquake personally or through close friends or relatives from respondents who reported no such experience (for life-situation effects). Analysis and interpretation were simplified by the finding that there were no important interaction effects. Findings are summarized in table 28.

The fact that the independent measure of intensity of earthquake experience distinguishes between people with personal experience of earthquake trauma and people who have not had such experience, while failing to distinguish between residents and nonresidents, provides validation for the analytic separation we are making. The suburban nature of the San Fernando zone is emphasized by the difference in organizational ties.

Gleaning information about earthquake matters from a wider range of media sources, being more aware of the uplift (the Palmdale bulge) and its potential significance, and being able to offer more suggestions for government action all follow the pattern that suggests the effects of having personally experienced earthquake trauma rather than the effects of subculture. Although three variables supply a scant basis for generalizing, they do suggest a common manifestation of sensitization to the earthquake hazard or of special interest in the topic.

Another four variables fit the subculture-effects pattern. Stating the intention to make additional earthquake preparations, supporting government expenditure for prediction research and improving warning systems, and perceiving oneself as belonging to a group especially at risk distinguish San Fernando earthquake-zone residents, irrespective of whether they have personally experienced earthquake loss. These items convey a more normative orientation, that the government *should* act and that individuals *ought* to be prepared, while being in a special risk group provides some of the justification for the normative element.

One item, the tendency to ascribe personal-preparedness measures already taken to a concern over future earthquakes, shows significant effects of both personal experience and subculture. On a strictly post hoc basis, it is plausible to interpret this response as combining the element of sensitization to earthquake concerns with the normative element of an obligation to prepare for an earthquake.

We do not find evidence in these data of a comprehensive or potent disaster subculture localized in the zones of 1971 earthquake damage and evacuation. We are left with few differences between the people in these zones and elsewhere. Nevertheless, some plausible evidence for a modest but noticeable subculture effect has been adduced. The absence of heightened levels of interpersonal discussion seems to rule out the most effective mechanism for establishment and maintenance of disaster subculture themes. The fact that items providing ultimate support for the subculture hypothesis seem to incorporate a normative orientation toward earthquake preparedness lends plausibility to the conclusion that truly subcultural elements have been uncovered.

VULNERABILITY-ZONE SUBCULTURES?

While we usually think of a subculture as being rooted in a shared history, as in the institutionalized memory of the San Fernando earthquake, we must not overlook the possibility that public preoccupation with the hazard of old buildings could have produced comparable subcultural themes in neighborhoods with high concentrations of old buildings. Accordingly, an effort has been made to separate subcultural from life-situational effects in the two relevant vulnerability zones. In both instances, living in a building constructed before 1934 has been the criterion for distinguishing between more and less vulnerable life situations.

The analysis, as summarized in table 29, is complicated by the necessary inclusion of ethnicity (black versus white Anglo) in the old-building zone and by the presence of several interaction effects. Nevertheless, the overall conclusion is simpler than it was for the San Fernando zone. Whether people actually live in old buildings or not has few if any effects on awareness and attitudes; most of the zonal differences qualify as subcultural effects.

TABLE 28

Significance Levels for Various Effects of Location and Personal Experience with Earthquake Damage: Two-Way Analysis of Variance

"Effect" variable	Significance of F-ratio		
	San Fernando versus control zone	Personal experience with earthquake damage	Two-way interaction
Groups, organizations nearby	(−).001	—	—
Earthquake experience index	—	.001	—
Number of media sources	—	.01	—
Awareness of the uplift	—	.05	—
Self in group at risk	.05	—	—
Know whether fault nearby?	—	—	—
Measures taken and planned	.01	—	—
Taken for future earthquake	.01	.01	—

TABLE 28 Continued

Government expenditure for hazard reduction (inclusive)	—	—	—
Government expenditure for prediction and warning systems	.01	—	—
Number of suggestions for government action	—	.01	—
Suggest emergency preparedness	.01	—	.05

Significance equals or exceeds indicated levels. When the .05 level is not reached, differences are treated as nonsignificant and identified by the symbol —. The direction of all relationships is positive, except when identified by the symbol (–).

TABLE 29

SIGNIFICANCE LEVELS FOR VARIOUS EFFECTS OF LOCATION
AND EARTHQUAKE VULNERABILITY: TWO-WAY ANALYSIS OF VARIANCE

"Effect" variable	Zone	Vulnerability	Two-way	Ethnic	Ethnic plus zone	Ethnic plus vulnerability	Three-way
		Old-building zone					
Owner-occupied household	(−).001	(−).05	.05	—	.001	—	.01
Groups, organizations nearby	.01	—	—	—	.05	—	—
Damage to self or friends	.01	.05	—	—	—	—	—
Sense of earthquake invulnerability	.001	—	—	.01	—	—	—
Know whether fault nearby?	.001	—	—	—	—	—	—
Measures taken and planned	.05	—	—	.001	.001	—	—
Taken for future earthquake	.05	—	—	—	.001	—	—
Suggest structural safety	(−).001	—	—	.001	.05	—	—
Suggest emergency preparedness	—	.05	.01	.01	—	—	—
Suggest scientific research	—	.05	—	.01	—	—	—
Evaluation of government preparedness	.001	—	—	—	—	—	—

TABLE 29 Continued

		Combined-hazard zone	
Owner-occupied household	(−).001	(−).05	—
Favorability toward science	.05	—	—
Accuracy of scientific prediction: future	.05	—	—
Discussed quakes around the world	—	—	—
Discussed old unsafe buildings	—	—	—
Discussed moving out	.05	—	—
Awareness of groups at risk	.05	.05	.05
Self in group at risk	.001	.001	.01
Know whether fault nearby?	.001	—	—
Gov't expend. for hazard reduction	.001	—	.01
Gov't expend. for prediction/warning system	.001	—	.05
Number of suggestions for government action	.001	—	—

TABLE 29 (Continued)

"Effect" variable	Zone	Vulnerability	Two-way	Ethnic	Ethnic plus zone	Ethnic plus vulnerability	Three-way
		Combined-hazard zone					
Suggest structural safety	(–).001	—	—				
Suggest emergency preparedness	.001	.001	—				

Significance equals or exceeds indicated levels. When the .05 level is not reached, differences are treated as nonsignificant and are identified by the symbol —. All relationships with membership in the indicated categories of persons are positive, except when identified by the symbol (–).

Either there are zonal disaster-subculture themes, or more general natural-area subcultures find expression in earthquake attitudes.

Conclusion

The aim of this chapter has been to shed further light on the effects of earthquake vulnerability and earthquake experience on awareness and response to recent near predictions of a destructive earthquake. We introduced a critically different theoretical element by looking at respondents according to the characteristics of the zones in which they live rather than according to their individual and household characteristics. This approach makes insights from ecological theory in sociology applicable to our materials. The theory holds that, apart from human intention, the urban community becomes subdivided into natural areas that create distinctive environments for their habitués. It also accentuates the relevance of cultural theory, since the development of distinctive subcultures is facilitated when people who share common life situations dwell in mutual proximity.

Four very general observations can be made from the observed differences between zonal and control samples. First, there is an impressive array of important variables on which zonal and control samples do not differ after the effects of age, education, occupational status, household income, and ethnicity have been removed. The key awareness variables, namely, awareness of the uplift, predictive announcements remembered, and predictive announcements taken seriously, are missing. Neither fear and concern over earthquakes nor the sense of increased concern during the past year is included. And the zonal subsamples do not differ in the extent of personal and household earthquake preparedness. Living in a zone of heightened earthquake vulnerability or a zone of recent destructive earthquake experience has not affected the extent to which people are informed about recent predictive announcements, the amount of concern people feel over the earthquake threat, or the actions they have taken to improve their own survival chances.

The second general observation is that there is almost no awareness of the potential danger of inundation. Los Angeles County is dotted with dams that are used for water storage and flood control.

The safety of many of these dams in case of a major earthquake is an unknown quantity. Extrapolating from our sample to the total county population, between two and two-and-a-half million people live in the zones of potential inundation. Yet, living below a dam has no apparent effect on earthquake attitude and response.

The issue of dams has received less public attention than the issue of old buildings, although it is probable that more people are at risk from dam failure than from building collapse. Inundation maps have only just been prepared, and they have not been publicized. Appropriate evacuation zones and routes and other emergency procedures in case of dam failure have not been published. Also, there is no organized interest group whose special concern is dam safety, as there is for building code maintenance.

The third general observation is that there is little consistency of effect among the three zones of old buildings, combined hazard, and the San Fernando earthquake. Only a disproportionate tendency to suggest improving search-and-rescue and other post-disaster response capabilities characterizes all three zones. But some minimal signs of social sensitization could be inferred for each of the zones. Combined-hazard-zone residents are more aware of groups at risk and engage in more discussion of earthquake topics. People living in the other two zones seem to be responding to disproportionate social pressures toward preparedness when they insist that they still intend to become better prepared and when they attribute a larger-than-usual share of the measures they have already taken to the earthquake threat. These tendencies could mean a latent readiness to respond in case of a credible warning or an emergency. In two of the zones there is greater support for spending money on improving earthquake prediction and earthquake-warning systems, which again suggests that a higher priority is placed on earthquake-hazard reduction as a government responsibility.

Fourth, there is little evidence to suggest that the patterns we have discerned came as responses to announcements of the uplift and other near predictions and forecasts in 1976. None of the subsamples exhibited disproportionate awareness of the uplift or of other predictions and forecasts. If there were offsetting positive evidence, this observation might be discounted on the ground that people can be sensitized without remembering specific announcements and details. But it is more difficult to discount the finding that people who live in the special zones were no more likely than members of the control sample to say that their concern about earthquakes increased during the preceding year.

NATURAL-AREA SUBCULTURES?

We must not overlook the alternative hypothesis that some of the differences we found are simply manifestations of natural-area subcultures rather than chiefly reflections of the kind of earthquake vulnerability or experience prevalent in the area. If we have tapped three distinctive natural areas, in each of which the world is viewed through a distinctive set of tinted lenses, the approach to earthquake hazard could be no more than a by-product of a comprehensive worldview.[9]

The combined-hazard zone includes several neighborhoods best labeled as *transitional elite*. Portions of Hollywood, Pasadena, Silver Lake, and similar districts occupy foothill areas; a generation or two ago, when the Los Angeles metropolitan region was beginning to fill up with people, these were considered most desirable places to live. Today, because of the location on or near foothills and the accessibility to the central city, land values in these areas are often high. But the homes, though often handsome by earlier standards, are old, and they may be less desirable than the land. During their periods of ascendance, several of these communities were prestigious places to live and hosted local developments in literary and artistic culture. Ties of sentiment and culture have kept many older couples there and have attracted younger residents who are more interested in a cultural tradition than in current neighborhood prestige. At the same time, the old homes have undergone attrition, with some having been divided into rental units or replaced by apartment structures, attracting a different kind of population. The cultural and intellectual traditions of these natural areas may account for the more prevalent discussion of earthquake topics and the greater awareness of vulnerable groups.

The San Fernando earthquake zone is suburbia *par excellence*. The sense of history here is less likely to extend back much before the San Fernando earthquake, and it certainly does not extend back before the 1950s, when the valley's expansion took place.

Neighborhood linkages exist primarily through children, and people look to the media more than to knowledgeable neighbors for information. There is no tradition of serious culture as a setting for discussing earthquakes. For many, this region of the San Fernando Valley is the neighborhood they moved up to after starting out in preponderantly working-class neighborhoods. Preoccupied with their own upward mobility and material well-being, residents can be sensitive to risks in their own situations without becoming alert to the special vulnerability of others.

The old-building zone is harder to characterize, except that it is disproportionately weighted with *central city* neighborhoods. The neighborhoods are often of the same vintage as the combined-hazard zone neighborhoods, but the homes were often less elegantly built originally and the neighborhoods have less in the way of distinctive reputations and desirable foothill locations to slow down the ecological processes of deterioration and succession. They may be more anomic, except as they are broken down into solidary ethnic and racial communities. Thus, blacks in these neighborhoods have been sensitized to the problem of old buildings through ethnicly pitched political discourse, but others in the zone show no distinctive sense of earthquake vulnerability in spite of the concentration of old buildings. Nevertheless, without feeling that their situation is exceptional, they do feel vulnerable to earthquakes, as indicated by the sense that they ought to be better prepared than they are.

A ZONAL EARTHQUAKE SUBCULTURE?

More discriminating analyses of the possible effects of individual experience and neighborhood subculture were conducted, though with only the few relevant variables. In the San Fernando zone, intimate experience with the disastrous effects of an earthquake explains heightened attention to the media information on earthquakes, greater awareness of the uplift, and the offering of more suggestions for government action, without the diffusion of these responses to other residents as part of an earthquake subculture. However, a tendency to view oneself as being more vulnerable to earthquakes than most people, a tendency to claim that one plans to take more earthquake-preparedness measures than one already has, support for government expenditure to improve prediction and warning systems, and a bias toward emergency preparedness rather than hazard mitigation are responses characteristic of residents in the zone, regardless of whether they have had intimate experience with earthquake damage and injury. A tendency to ascribe measures already taken to the earthquake threat seems to be both a zonal and an individual experience effect.

In the old-building and combined-hazard zones, the evidence for subcultural effects is more pervasive. Most of the differences between zonal and control samples apply irrespective of whether people themselves live in old buildings.

To what extent, then, are we justified in thinking of localized earthquake subcultures in residential zones where the risk from old buildings is unusually prevalent and where the memory of earthquake destruction and casualty persists? Because of the limited number of applicable variables and the limited intensity of responses it is clearly inappropriate to speak of earthquake subcultures. At most, we can speak of an earthquake theme in a culture or subculture and of the differential incidence and elaboration of that theme.

But if the theme is a cultural phenomenon, there must be evidence that it is socially transmitted within some identifiable community. There are three kinds of evidence we can use in judging whether shared characteristics are cultural characteristics. First, the sense that one ought to be doing more than one is and the tendency to ascribe commonplace prudence to the earthquake threat are plausible symptoms of weak but nevertheless real *social pressures*. Second, *interpersonal discussion* among family, friends, neighbors, and coworkers should be a crucial medium for the diffusion of cultural elements. The disproportionate incidence of such discussion in only one of the groups tends to undermine the credibility of the cultural explanation. Nevertheless, the fact that each of the three groups satisfies either the first or second criterion lends some encouragement to the cultural interpretation.

Evidence that a special earthquake awareness is disseminated through the mass media could be a third clue to the existence of zonal subcultures. Although we did not locate media that were distinctively attuned to the earthquake hazard in the vulnerability zones, a comparison of earthquake coverage in the San Fernando

Valley News with coverage in the other papers reviewed in chapter two revealed a pervasive practice of relating earthquake events and issues to the memory of the 1971 quake and to the need to prepare for a future quake. The *Valley News* also placed proportionately more emphasis on organizational and governmental earthquake preparedness than did comparable papers elsewhere. Thus, differential news coverage supports the heightened sense of vulnerability and the enthusiasm for government action. Perhaps the observed failure of the *Valley News* to pay special attention to individual and household preparedness explains why area residents are no better prepared than are people in other parts of Los Angeles County. Obviously, the constant reminders of past and future vulnerability contribute to the sense that one *should* be preparing for the inevitable disaster. There is, then, some correspondence between patterns of newspaper coverage and the attitudes characteristic of area residents, irrespective of their earthquake experience. Circumstantial evidence supports the conclusion that elements of a distinctive earthquake subculture are present in the San Fernando earthquake impact zone and perhaps also in the two vulnerability zones.

A REGIONAL CULTURAL MAP?

There is an alternative to the zonal-subculture hypothesis which could explain some of our findings more plausibly. A culture is a mixture of exemplary patterns and prescriptions, resources, and a map. Customs, values, and mores are familiar examples of exemplary patterns and prescriptions. Resources are the tools, strategies, and techniques that are available for coping with situations. As a map, the culture highlights figure from ground in the world of experience and identifies the special significance of objects, places, and experiences. The important feature of a map is that it alerts the reader to respond differently in different places and situations.

The concept of culture as a map is important because it allows us to explore the possibility that the responses we find in different zones are the manifestations of a common *regional* culture whose carriers are responding to the various ways in which the zones are identified on the master map. We may have been on a false course in thinking of distinctive zonal subcultures. The all-encompassing regional map would enable us to deal with the anomaly that residents in two zones seem to be under normative pressure to prepare their households for an earthquake but report only average levels of discussion of earthquake topics with their families, friends, and coworkers. The social pressure might arise from the fact that something about their local situation is singled out on the map supplied by the larger culture. It would also enable us to deal with the fact that feeling oneself to be a member of an especially vulnerable group does not imply any disproportionate awareness of especially vulnerable groups—even of the group in which significant numbers include themselves.

From this point of view there may be an *earthquake awareness* theme in the regional subculture of southern California. Awareness of the vulnerability of old buildings is prevalent throughout Los Angeles County, but it is no more prevalent in neighborhoods where such buildings are clustered than it is in the county at large. The memory of the San Fernando earthquake is similarly stamped in the cultural tradition of the county and is not restricted to the damage zone. Old brick buildings and the San Fernando damage zone are starred on the cultural map, so that people who frequent the appropriate areas feel that they are in special danger and feel that they ought to be doing something to protect themselves from the earthquake threat.

This conception provides a more plausible explanation for some of our findings than does the concept of zonal subcultures or subculture themes. Combined with the idea of natural-area subcultures and ethnic or racial subcultures through which the earthquake threat is given a distinctive slant, it may explain most of our findings. However, institutional mechanisms such as the *Valley News* and the preponderance of zonal over life-situational effects in the two vulnerability zones lend continued plausibility to the idea of zonal disaster-subculture themes. Pending research to sort out the three components definitively, we are disposed to see the regional disaster-subculture map as the foundation on which natural-area subcultures and zonal disaster-subculture processes build further variations in awareness and response to earthquake threat.

PART FIVE

Stability and Change

CHAPTER TWELVE

Waiting and Looking for Omens

Most of the analyses in the preceding chapters have dealt with the public state of mind about a year after the first announcement of the southern California uplift. This initial year of waiting for the big earthquake was also a period of unusual earthquake and forecast activity. In Part Five we shall look at events and responses over the next two years (1977–1978), as the period of waiting lengthened. When months passed without a significant quake, did people lose interest? Did they become skeptical? Did they treat the 1976 warning as a false alarm? Or did they become increasingly anxious and even angry with scientists and public officials? Did they lose whatever enthusiasm they had for earthquake preparedness, or did they profit from the waiting period to enlarge their understanding and enhance their preparedness?

Undoubtedly, the mere passage of time would affect the public state of mind, but the waiting period could either be empty of significant new events or punctuated by incidents that reinforced or undermined prevailing attitudes. And the media might ignore the earthquake hazard for long intervals of time or else subject the public to constant reminders. In chapter twelve we shall look at patterns of communication and the response to potentially important events during the two years of extended waiting.

In chapter thirteen we shall compare key measures of public awareness and response at five moments in time, from early 1977 to late 1978, thus describing the prevailing trends during the second and third years of waiting.

A moderate earthquake struck Los Angeles County without

warning on New Year's Day of 1979. Because we had prepared for such an event, we were able to field a survey within a few days to ascertain the public interpretation of this quake, which came after thirty-four months of waiting for a disastrous event. We could also see how the quake altered trends that had been established during the two years of quiescence. Chapter fourteen deals with the response to the New Year's Day quake.

The analysis of extended waiting is completed in chapter fifteen with a theoretical overview and a search for patterns of change and stability.

The data presented in chapters twelve and thirteen are drawn from the basic field survey and four subsequent surveys, conducted at five- and six-month intervals. The data were gathered according to a *hybrid panel* design that was a compromise between *complete follow-up* and *simple overlap* designs.[1] As summarized in table 30, the design provides a fresh sample of more than 500 subjects, untainted by the effects of prior interviewing, for each wave of interviews. We relied exclusively on these fresh samples to establish the trends reported in chapter thirteen. The design also provides two opportunities to compare the same individual's responses at five- or six-month intervals. And it saves a substantial segment from the basic survey for use in comparing the same individual's responses over the longer period of waiting while minimizing potential distortion from repeated reinterviewing. Whenever the responses by the fresh and reinterviewed samples from a single wave are statistically indistinguishable, they have been combined to maximize the number of cases used in the chapter twelve analyses.

Changing Levels of Communication

The first question to be asked is whether the level, the medium, and the content of communication about earthquake topics changed from early 1977 to late 1978. We are concerned with both media and informal communication and with their interrelationships. Figure 47 provides a bird's-eye view of newspaper coverage for the three years from 1976 through 1978. The high peaks of interest in prediction and warning in 1976 that we discussed in chapter two had no parallels in the next two years.

TABLE 30

HYBRID PANEL DESIGN AND ACTUAL SAMPLE SIZES

Sample designation*	Field survey	Wave one	Wave two	Wave three	Wave four
a	350				
b	600		462		348
c	500	426			
d		551	390		
e			516		
f				536	
g					550
Total	1,450	977	1,368	536	898

*To facilitate time-series analysis, the initial field survey was divided randomly into three samples. The 350 subjects who were not reinterviewed were identified as *sample a*. The 600 subjects of whom 462 were reinterviewed in wave two and 348 reinterviewed in wave four were designated as *sample b*. The 500 subjects of whom 426 were reinterviewed in wave one were designated as *sample c*. Similarly, the 551 subjects who were interviewed for the first time in wave one, of whom 390 could be reinterviewed in wave two, were designated as *sample d*. The remaining samples (e, f, g) were interviewed only once. These arbitrary designations helped us to keep track of separate sets of subjects as they were reinterviewed and to aggregate or decompose each wave appropriately for different analytic purposes.

Attention to current earthquakes was similarly reduced, although interest was rekindled in late March and early April, when disastrous quakes hit Iran and Turkey, and again when nearby Santa Barbara suffered a damaging quake on August 13, 1978. Only earthquake preparedness and safety continued to peak in 1977 and 1978. When this is broken into elements, however, individual and household preparedness quickly dropped back to the low level that prevailed before the Fil Druckey series was featured at the start of 1977. Recurrent surfacing of the Los Angeles City Council debate on how to deal with existing seismically unsafe structures along with politicized controversy over proposed construction of the Auburn Dam and siting of a liquid natural-gas terminal at Point Conception, both in northern California, account

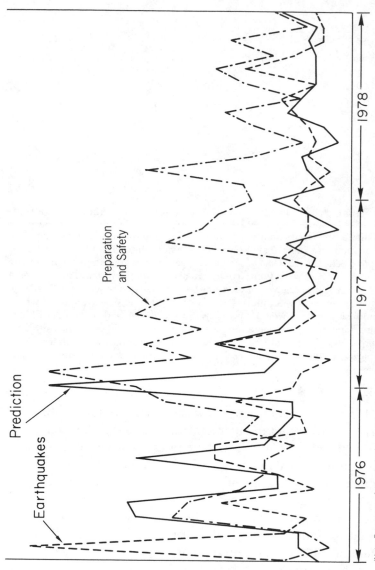

Figure 47. Newspaper Coverage of Earthquake Topics: January 1976 to December 1978

(Note: Frequency of items is by four-week periods. Vertical scales for the three series are different; hence the graph compares trends but not absolute frequencies among the three types of newspaper items.)

for the peaks in the graph. But items on these topics probably do less to bring the earthquake threat home to most southern Californians than do the less frequent items dealing with earthquake forecast and warning and advice on personal and household preparedness.

Does the reduced attention to personally relevant aspects of the earthquake threat apply to all the media? In February 1977 and again in June and November-December 1978, we presented a checklist of media sources and asked respondents if they had "heard about earthquakes or earthquake predictions or earthquake preparedness" from each source. There were substantial declines until June 1978 for all nine sources, with only partial recovery until year's end. The recovery was principally in response to discussion of the recent Santa Barbara earthquake.

Our indicator of *informal* communication is the set of queries about topics dicussed "with people you know." In 1978 significantly fewer people than in early 1977 reported discussions on why earthquakes occur, on predictions, on "moving out," and on family preparedness (table 31). These changes document a general decrease in attention to the prospect of a future earthquake and to its personal relevance, although discussion of earthquakes around the world and the media-featured topic of unsafe old buildings remained steady. A highly significant increase occurred in discussion of only one topic, namely, dams and flooding. The northern California Auburn Dam controversy and the November 6, 1977, collapse of the earth-filled Toccoa Falls Dam in Georgia, with a loss of thirty-nine lives, may have contributed to this increase. A change in local weather, however, from the two-year drought condition at the time of our basic survey to the record rains and flooding at the beginning of 1978 was probably more important. Respondents may have thought more of "flooding" than of "dams" in answering the question, and some may even have forgotten that the governing topic was earthquakes.

The objective measure of newspaper coverage and the subjective reports agree in portraying declining rates of communication about personally relevant earthquake topics during the second and third years of waiting. To what extent were people aware of the decline? Two items that were intended to answer this question were included in the final interview wave in November and December, 1978:

TABLE 31
EARTHQUAKE DISCUSSION TOPICS AT THREE PERIODS OF TIME

Discussion topic	February 1977	June 1978	Nov./Dec. 1978
Predictions[a]	83.0	42.7	48.6
Family preparedness[b]	48.7	42.7	41.9
Why earthquakes occur[a]	50.3	36.4	44.0
Quakes around the world	65.4	61.0	67.7
Old, unsafe, or pre-1933 buildings	43.0	47.8	48.3
Dams/flooding[b]	32.7	54.9	52.6
Moving out[b]	28.3	16.2	19.8
Total number	1,450	536	898

[a]Differences significant at the .01 level.
[b]Differences significant at the .05 level.

Now, let me ask you a question about topics of conversation among you, your family, friends, or coworkers. Compared to a year or two ago, has there been more, less, or about the same amount of discussion (among you, your family, friends, or coworkers) concerning the possibility of a damaging earthquake striking southern California?

Now a question about television, radio, and newspaper coverage. Compared to a year or two ago, do you think there has been more, less, or about the same amount of coverage on the possibility of a damaging earthquake striking southern California?

A plurality of respondents reported that media coverage was unchanged, and a slight majority said that discussion levels are about the same. But nearly twice as many said there was "less" media coverage than said there was "more," and over three times as many felt that discussion of earthquake danger in their circles had declined as believed it had increased. Thus, a substantial awareness of lessened preoccupation with earthquake danger complemented the objective and subjective evidence.

There is one remaining question of considerable importance. If there are parallel declines in the media and in informal discussion, which is cause and which is effect? Did the media reduce their coverage of earthquake matters in response to declining public interest? Or did informal discussion decline because the media provided less for people to talk about? Expressions of satisfaction or dissatisfaction with the current extent of media coverage could supply a clue to the correct answer.

In chapter four we reported the prevailing desire for more media attention to earthquake matters, in response to a five-part question:

> Would you say there has been too little coverage, just about the right coverage, or too much coverage for each of the following: What government officials are doing to prepare for an earthquake; how to prepare for an earthquake; what to do when an earthquake strikes; the Palmdale bulge and scientific earthquake predictions; earthquake predictions by people who are not scientists?

Although this question was not asked in 1977, it was included in the January, June, and November-December waves in 1978. Answers to the first four parts remained unchanged throughout the year, ranging from 61 to 79 percent stating that there was too little coverage. The proportion who wanted more information about predictions by nonscientists increased significantly, from 20.9 percent in January to 27.8 percent in June and to 30.6 percent by year's end.[2] Interest in personally relevant earthquake news continued to exceed actual coverage and showed no sign of waning as the period of waiting approached three years. Whether there were simply fewer newsworthy events to report or whether editors misperceived public interest, declining media coverage rather than lessening public interest seems to have been the key to less frequent informal discussion of the earthquake threat.

The Changing Uplift

As early as May 28, 1976, Los Angeles-area newspapers reported that the uplift was higher and wider than had previously been thought, with the inference that it was still rising. Little more was said about changes in the uplift during the rest of 1976, until December. In that month, newspapers again featured the report of a rising and expanding uplift, but with a new kind of change. In the San Gabriel foothills north of Pasadena, within the circumference of the uplifted region, a subsidence of as much as six inches had occurred. In February 1977 came reports of tilting and of subsidence over a much wider area of the southern California uplift. Subsidence to the north, including in the vicinity of Palmdale, and uplifting farther south led to a suggestion that the uplift might be migrating southward. In March there was an isolated report that the uplift extended much farther east than had formerly been supposed.

After an extended period of relative quiet concerning the uplift, October and November television specials on earthquake hazard featured histories of the uplift, including the changes subsequent to discovery. As December came around again, so did reports on papers presented at the annual meeting of the American Geophysical Union, some of which dealt with the uplift. These were followed later in the same month with reports of a projected resurvey of the uplift by the U.S. Geological Survey. Among the papers summarized was the USGS's historical review of the uplift, reminding readers of its steady rise and expansion for several years and its more recent subsidence, especially around Palmdale.

After December 1977, media attention to the changing character of the uplift faded. For about a year and a half there had been occasional media accounts of changes in the uplift, beginning with an emphasis on the continuing rise and expansion of the uplift and ending with reports of subsidence, especially in the northern portions.

In January 1978 and again in June, we included a question in the telephone interview to assess awareness and interpretation of reports concerning changes in the uplift. The series of questions about changes was asked of all respondents who mentioned the uplift spontaneously in reply to the general question about predictions, forecasts, and other announcements, as well as of all respondents who answered affirmatively when asked if they remembered "hearing about a bulge in the earth near Palmdale in the Mojave Desert" *and* who acknowledged that scientists were saying that it might signify a coming earthquake.

Respondents were first asked, "Have you recently heard of any changes in the bulge?" Regardless of whether they answered "Yes" or "No" to the opening question, respondents in January were then asked specifically about the report that parts of the bulge were sinking. An almost identical 12.9 percent of the January and

June samples had heard of some changes. In January the respondents were divided about equally between those who thought the uplift was rising and those who thought it was sinking. By June, after a notable hiatus in media coverage, perceptions had shifted significantly toward rising and away from sinking, with a notable increase in the number who recognized that it might be doing both. By this time there was little justification in newspaper reports for the increased perception of a rising uplift. We may have been recording either delayed comprehension or a tendency to favor images that gave substance to the prevalent conviction that a great earthquake was on the way.

The January questions about changes in the uplift were followed with a directive query:

> One recent report has been that parts of the bulge are sinking. Do you remember hearing anything about this?

This item was followed by a pattern of questions that was designed to uncover some of the meanings attached to the sinking. The same pattern was applied to the microquake swarm and to the Santa Barbara earthquake, events reviewed later in the chapter. The 220 respondents who had heard that parts of the uplift were sinking were asked,

> Have you heard anyone say that this sinking is a sign that an earthquake *will* happen soon?

A few questions later, they were asked,

> Have you heard anyone say that the bulge sinking means that we are *less* likely to have an earthquake soon?

After each of these questions we asked about credibility:

> What do you think of this statement—that the bulge sinking is a sign an earthquake will happen soon? (—that the bulge sinking means we are *less* likely to have an earthquake soon?) Do you think: It is *definitely* true, It is *probably* true, It is *probably* false, or It is *definitely* false?

A majority (55.9 percent) answered "No" to both questions. The changing configuration of the uplift remained a curiosity, devoid of relevant meaning to most of even those few who had heard of it. A very few people had heard both interpretations, and the remainder were fairly evenly divided between the two interpretations.

Using only the ninety-seven individuals who had heard one or both interpretations, we may hazard a few cautious summary observations. First, there was very little disposition to go out on a limb by "definitely" endorsing or rejecting either interpretation. Second, the disposition to believe was stronger than the disposition to disbelieve. Whether people had heard that the sinking of the uplift was a positive or a negative sign concerning the likelihood of an earthquake in the near future, they were more likely to believe than to disbelieve what they had heard. Among the fourteen people who had heard both interpretations, only one was inclined to disbelieve both. Third, the sinking of the uplift was viewed as more credible as a sign that an earthquake would happen soon than as a sign that an earthquake would be less likely to happen soon. None of the people who heard both interpretations favored the view that an earthquake was less likely, while respondents who had heard only one interpretation were more likely to believe what they had heard if they had heard that the sinking signified the approach of an earthquake. Finally—and here we must be very tentative because of the small number of cases—hearing contradictory interpretations does not foster disbelief, as is often feared. Of the fourteen people who had heard both interpretations, five concluded that either might be true and another five favored the positive interpretation, while only one took the skeptical position and three said they didn't know about either interpretation.

The recognized impact of the reported sinking of parts of the uplift on public estimation of the prospects of an earthquake occurring soon was not great. Only 7.1 percent of the total sample had heard about the sinking *and* heard one of the two interpretations. While a majority of these were inclined to believe one or both interpretations, they constituted only 4.2 percent of the entire sample.

The Microquake Swarm

The report that scientists at Caltech had been studying a swarm of several hundred very small quakes near Palmdale drew front-page attention in major newspapers and was announced on all major network television news programs on September 9, 1977. The implied portent was conveyed by the question included in every news item of whether the small earthquakes presaged a large one. As usual, the media answered by citing examples in which quake flurries had preceded large earthquakes while indicating that there were also contrary examples. The quake swarm study was featured again in December, in reports about the American Geophysical Union meeting in San Francisco. From the nature of the news coverage and from our experience in the community, we believe that word of the quake swarm was generally received as more meaningful than were the reports of changes in the uplift. The young female scientist who was conducting the study, Karen McNally, also seemed to capture public fancy, which may have contributed to interest in the reports.

Although the quake swarm occurred in the uplift area, it seemed to have acquired the status of an independent phenomenon in media treatment. Consequently, we asked everyone about the quake swarm regardless of whether they remembered hearing about the uplift. The pattern of questioning was similar to that followed in the case of the sinking of parts of the uplift. Following are the questions asked in January 1978:

In October, a Caltech scientist announced that there had been hundreds of very small earthquakes within an eight-month period in the Palmdale bulge area. A. Do you remember hearing anything about this?
(If "yes,")

B. Have you heard anyone say that these small earthquakes are a sign that a damaging earthquake is coming?
(If "yes,")

a. Do you remember any particular people who were saying this?
b. What do *you* think about this statement—that these small earthquakes are a sign a damaging earthquake is coming? Do you think: It is *definitely* true, It is *probably* true, It is *probably* false, or It is *definitely* false?
c. Have you heard anyone say that these small quakes are relieving pressure so that a damaging earthquake will *not* occur?
(If "yes,")

a. Do you remember any particular people who were saying this?
b. What do you think about this statement—that these small quakes are relieving pressure so that a damaging earthquake will not occur? Do you think: It is definitely true, etc?

The earthquake swarm was more widely recognized than the sinking of parts of the uplift (table 32). More than three out of every eight people in our sample remembered hearing something about the swarm. Not only did significantly (p < .001) more people remember hearing about the swarms but significantly (p < .001) more of those who had heard of the swarm had also heard one or both of the interpretations of the swarm. A total of 391 people, or 28.6 percent of the entire sample, had heard of the swarm and of some interpretation relating it to the future earthquake prospect. The earthquake swarm was seen by the public as less a curiosity and more a relevant sign for the future. In addition, people who had heard an interpretation were more likely to have heard both interpretations.

TABLE 32

AWARENESS OF THE EARTHQUAKE SWARM

Awareness	Number	Percent of sample	Percent of heard
Heard of earthquake swarm	529	38.7	
Not heard of earthquake swarm	837	61.3	
Total	1,366	100.0	
Interpretations heard:			
Damaging earthquake is coming	142	10.4	26.8
Relieving pressure, no earthquake	117	8.6	22.1
Both	132	9.6	25.0
Neither	138	10.1	26.1
Total	529	38.7	100.0

With more cases at hand, we can report the credibility findings more confidently (table 33). As before, people generally said "probably" rather than "definitely." The tendency to believe rather than to disbelieve applies here also. Seventy-six percent of those who had heard that the small quakes were a sign of a large earth-

TABLE 33

BELIEF IN INTERPRETATIONS OF THE EARTHQUAKE SWARM

Extent of belief	Number	Percent of sample	Percent of heard
Heard sign damaging earthquake coming:			
Definitely true	9	0.6	6.3
Probably true	99	7.3	69.7
Don't know	19	1.4	13.4
Probably false	14	1.0	9.9
Definitely false	1	0.1	0.7
Total	142	10.4	100.0
Heard relieving pressure, no earthquake:			
Definitely true	22	1.6	18.8
Probably true	80	5.9	68.4
Don't know	7	0.5	6.0
Probably false	8	0.6	6.8
Definitely false	0	0	0
Total	117	8.6	100.0
Heard both:[a]			
Both are true	47	3.4	35.6
Earthquake coming is true	39	2.9	29.5
Relieving pressure is true	32	2.3	24.2
Neither is true	1	0.1	0.8
Don't know about either	13	0.9	9.9
Total	132	9.6	100.0

[a]Because of small numbers when both interpretations were heard, replies have been combined into positive and negative.

quake coming believed it was probably or definitely true, and 87.2 percent of those who had heard that the small quakes were relieving pressure believed this. The evidence that being exposed to contradictory explanations does *not* lead to rejection of both is clear. Only 1 of the 132 respondents who had heard the two interpretations rejected them both, while over a third felt that either could be true. Only the disposition to see events as harbingers of disaster—reported for the uplift sinking—was not confirmed for the quake swarms.

In summary, the swarm was more widely known and more generally understood as relevant to the prospect of a future earthquake than was the report of sinking in parts of the uplift. An even 24 percent of the entire sample accepted the swarm as a credible sign concerning the likelihood of a future earthquake, compared with only 4.2 percent who accepted sinking of the uplift as a credible sign.

The Soviet Prediction

On April 22 and 23 of 1978, a few of the local newspapers and some television and radio news programs featured an unusual and sensational announcement. Andrei Nikonov, an earth scientist in the Soviet Union, issued a forecast for an earthquake of magnitude 7.5 to occur in the vicinity of the southern California uplift before the end of the year. The information department of the Soviet Embassy in Washington, D.C., distributed the announcement through a press release sent directly to the *Los Angeles Times* and other media. The prediction was criticized by leading California seismologists. The *Los Angeles Times*, the *San Gabriel Valley Tribune,* and the *Antelope Valley Press* featured the announcement prominently, each with a single story, after which the subject received no further significant media attention.

In the June 1978 panel survey, we added the Soviet announcement to our code for the open-ended question on "predictions, statements, and warnings" heard. Then, after the standard questions had been asked about all announcements mentioned, respondents who had not referred to the Soviet prediction were asked:

Did you happen to hear about a Soviet scientist predicting an earthquake for southern California?

Respondents who answered "Yes" were then asked an abbreviated set of detail questions, covering anticipated date of the quake, intensity, how seriously the respondent took the prediction, the chief source of the respondent's information about the prediction, and anything else important about it.

Despite its recency and ominousness, the Soviet prediction was volunteered by only eighteen people, or 3.3 percent of the sample. Another 21.3 percent acknowledged having heard about it when they were asked directly, making about one-quarter of our sample aware of the forecast. Just over half of the latter group correctly identified the anticipated intensity by endorsing the answer, "destroy *many* buildings and take *many* lives." In response to direct questioning, only two persons correctly identified the predicted time of occurrence as some time before the year's end. Just over a quarter of those who had heard of the forecast said that they took it "fairly seriously" or "quite seriously," while more than two-thirds said that they took it "not very seriously" or "not seriously at all." This is about half as many as the 58 percent who took the uplift seriously; it is fairly comparable with the 29.2 percent who took pseudoscientific announcements seriously and with the 28.5 percent who took prophetic announcements seriously. Since only six and one-half percent of the total sample remembered having heard the Soviet forecast and said that they took it seriously, the acknowledged impact of the announcement was thus quite small.

In this case the limited media attention was probably based on a correct assessment of little public interest. According to a well-established principle, confirmed elsewhere in this investigation, media blackouts on matters of great public concern provoke massive rumoring. Only 5 of the 132 people aware of the Soviet forecast gave family, friends, coworkers, and other people as their chief source of information. Had there been extensive rumoring, this figure would have been much higher. About three-quarters gave the conventional newspapers, television, and radio as their chief sources, and most of the rest said they didn't know what their source had been.

By November-December 1978, less than 1 percent of 898 respondents in the fourth wave made *apparent* reference to the Soviet forecast, including only three people who *specifically* mentioned the Soviet forecast. Before the predicted time window had expired, salience had already dropped to an inconsequential level.

The Santa Barbara Earthquake

The only damaging earthquake in southern California during our study period occurred in nearby Santa Barbara, ninety-five automobile miles from central Los Angeles. Although the magnitude registered only 5.1 and no deaths were reported, there were injuries to people as well as considerable damage to property, and the quake was felt over a wide area, including parts of Los Angeles County. The main quake came at 3:45 P.M. on August 13, 1978, and was followed by the usual spate of aftershocks. Damage, injury, and disruption of normal automobile, rail, and air traffic were sufficient to create the impression of a much greater earthquake. The governor of California officially declared a state of emergency, and the state Seismic Safety Commission scheduled a fact-finding hearing to look into ways of stabilizing buildings such as mobile homes, many of which were shaken off their foundations in the quake. The earthquake was the occasion for discussions of earthquake prediction and earthquake preparedness in Los Angeles County newspapers and on television and radio. The quake had not been predicted, and it was not on the San Andreas Fault or near the uplifted zone.

A battery of questions was included in the November-December interviews covering awareness of the Santa Barbara quake, interpretation of its significance for future quakes in Los Angeles, and preparedness measures that might have been stimulated by reports of such a damaging quake nearby. The opening question was as follows:

> In August, an earthquake measuring 5.1 on the Richter scale hit Santa Barbara and caused widespread damage. Do you remember hearing about this quake?

A total of 747 of the 898 respondents, or 83.2 percent, had heard of the Santa Barbara earthquake. Fresh and reinterviewed samples did not differ significantly, so they have been combined. It is still surprising that more than one in every six Los Angeles County residents did not even remember that there had been a damaging earthquake centered less than one hundred miles from Los Angeles. This observation underlines the existence of a hard core of uninformed residents who seem to be insulated against awareness of significant current happenings.

The questions asked about interpretations of the Santa Barbara quake were similar to those asked in earlier surveys about the sinking of parts of the uplift and the earthquake swarm.

> Have you heard anyone say that the Santa Barbara earthquake is a sign that a damaging earthquake will occur in the Los Angeles area in the future? (If "yes,")
> What do you think about this statement—that the Santa Barbara quake means a damaging quake will strike Los Angeles? Do you think it is: *Definitely* true, *Probably* true, *Probably* false, or *Definitely* false?

> Have you heard anyone say that the Santa Barbara quake relieved pressure along the fault and that a damaging earthquake will *not* strike Los Angeles in the near future? (If "yes,")
> What do you think about this statement—that the Santa Barbara quake has reduced the possibility of an earthquake striking the Los Angeles area? Do you think it is: (etc.)

Unlike the interpretations of the earthquake swarm and the changed configuration of the uplift, these interpretations of the Santa Barbara quake would probably find no support among earth scientists. Nevertheless, 28.1 percent had heard that the tremor in Santa Barbara signaled that an earthquake was coming for Los Angeles, and 15.8 percent had heard that it relieved pressure and reduced the possibility of an earthquake striking Los Angeles. Both interpretations had been heard by 6.4 percent of the respondents (table 34).

As in the case of the earthquake swarm, more people had heard that the quake in Santa Barbara signified a large quake coming for Los Angeles than had heard that the observed quake defused a future quake. However, these interpretations did not circulate as widely as those concerning the quake swarm closer by. The tendency to avoid taking "definite" stands, which we had observed in both previous instances, continued to be manifest. There was little disposition to assign greater credibility to either interpretation, and the previously observed tendency to believe that whichever interpretation one had heard was probably true applied here also. Most people who had heard the contradictory interpretations believed at least one of them, and fully a third believed that both were probably true. Among respondents who had heard both interpretations, the proportion who rejected both was larger in this instance than in the two previous instances, although it

TABLE 34

BELIEF IN INTERPRETATIONS OF THE SANTA BARBARA EARTHQUAKE

Extent of belief	Number	Percent of sample	Percent of heard
Heard sign damaging earthquake coming:			
Definitely true	10	1.1	6.2
Probably true	88	9.8	54.3
Don't know	19	2.1	11.7
Probably false	33	3.7	20.4
Definitely false	12	1.3	7.4
Total	162	18.0	100.0
Heard relieved pressure, earthquake less likely:			
Definitely true	4	0.5	5.7
Probably true	37	4.1	52.8
Don't know	10	1.1	14.3
Probably false	16	1.8	22.9
Definitely false	3	0.3	4.3
Total	70	7.8	100.0
Heard both:[a]			
Both are true	16	1.8	33.3
Earthquake coming is true	8	0.9	16.7
Relieving pressure is true	13	1.4	27.1
Neither is true	11	1.2	22.9
Total	48	5.3	100.0

[a]Because of small numbers when both interpretations were heard, replies have been combined into positive and negative.

was still less than one-fourth. Because of the lesser plausibility of these interpretations of the Santa Barbara earthquake as compared with interpretations of sinking and of the quake swarms in the southern California uplift, it is surprising that more people had not heard and rejected one or both.

Whether people took the Santa Barbara earthquake as a sign for their own futures or not, they might have been reminded by the nearby disaster to prepare for an earthquake in Los Angeles. We asked about six kinds of response that could have been stimulated by hearing and seeing accounts of the Santa Barbara quake. The stem question was:

Since hearing about the Santa Barbara earthquake, have you. . . ?

The specific responses are given in table 35. The responses have been listed in descending order of endorsement for ease of comprehension; this was not the order in which they were presented in the interview.

The endorsement rates for all items were low. Even with the relatively passive items we suggested, including thinking, watching, and worrying, no item was endorsed by even as many as one-fourth of the respondents. Only 7 percent responded in three or more of the ways suggested. However, more than one-third of the subjects responded in some way that related the Santa Barbara earthquake to their own situation.

Some generalizations are justified from the data. First, the items that involve action were least frequently reported, while thinking, watching, and worrying were most common. Second, the response was usually to think about official preparation rather than about one's own preparation or safety at work. This finding is consistent with our earlier observation that people look to government officials to prepare the community for an earthquake. Third, the second-ranked response of watching for signs of a coming earthquake underlined the preeminent desire for a predictable future, which seemed to be more important than preparing concretely for an unpredictable future. This finding is consistent with Slovic, Kunreuther, and White's (1974) model of decision making, in which serious attention is not paid to the probable consequences of a future natural disaster until the individual is convinced that the probability of the event's occurrence is very high.[3]

The fact that only 10.4 percent said that they had less confidence in earthquake prediction is important in questioning the common assumption that faith in scientific prediction cannot withstand the occurrence of unpredicted quakes and false alarms. There may be sufficient popular understanding of the limits of current earthquake-prediction capability to nullify any such effects.

TABLE 35

RESPONSE TO THE SANTA BARBARA EARTHQUAKE

Response to Santa Barbara quake	Number	Percent
Thought about how public officials in Los Angeles have been dealing with earthquake-preparedness problems	182	24.4
Watched more carefully for signs that an earthquake might be coming soon	133	17.8
Worried more about the safety of own home and workplace than before	112	15.0
Less confidence now in the ability of scientists to predict earthquakes than before	78	10.4
Taken any new earthquake preparations or rechecked measures taken earlier	59	7.9
Contacted any agency or group for information about earthquake preparedness	15	2.0
Number of responses to quake:		
None	568	63.2
One	181	20.2
Two	86	9.6
Three	34	3.8
Four	21	2.3
Five	8	0.9
Six	0	0
Total	898	100.0

Proposition 13

In the statewide primary election on June 6, 1978, the California Constitution was amended by an overwhelming popular vote. The specific aim of Proposition 13 was to reduce taxes on real property and to limit their growth in the future. Its effect was to reduce property tax revenues to local governments and schools from residential and business property by half and sometimes by more. Passage came after a campaign in which government waste was widely advertised, and the affirmative vote was generally interpreted as a dramatic mandate for economy in government. Many economies were instituted immediately. The need for drastic economies without delay took on crisis proportions because Proposition 13 applied to the budget year that began on July 1, 1978.

As far as we know, there was no public discussion of earthquake-mitigation programs either as expendable or as having high priority. Police and fire services were often mentioned as activities to be maintained at full strength, while recreational facilities, museums, and welfare were often mentioned as low-priority enterprises. Nevertheless, it seemed unlikely that the high level of popular support for earthquake hazard-reduction expenditures recorded in the February 1977 survey would be impervious to this atmosphere of economy. Coincidentally, Howard Jarvis, who was the coauthor and leading sponsor of Proposition 13, had played a major role during 1977 in preventing passage of an ordinance by the Los Angeles City Council to require posting and rehabilitation or abandonment of seismically unsafe structures in the city.

About six months after the election, in our survey of November and December 1978, we included a series of questions to gauge whether the economy fever had turned the public against expenditure for earthquake hazard mitigation. Before mentioning Proposition 13, we asked:

> Do you think that the government *is* spending too much, too little, or just about the right amount of money on earthquake preparedness?

This question was followed by a pair of questions:

> Have Proposition 13 and the recent discussions about government spending changed your views on how much the government should spend to reduce earthquake hazards?
> (If "yes,")
> Do you now think that the government should spend more or less on earthquake hazard reduction programs?

On the initial question the new and reinterview samples answered significantly differently,[4] so we have reported them separately.

More of the fresh sample said they didn't know, and more of the reinterviewed said government was spending too little. The samples were not significantly different on the other two questions, so their answers have been combined. In both samples, most of the people who had opinions said government was spending too little on earthquake preparedness (table 36). There was thus little disposition seen to nominate earthquake preparedness for inclusion in the "fat" that Proposition 13 was supposed to eliminate from government.

Three-quarters of the respondents denied that Proposition 13 had changed their views. When the 109 respondents who said their views had changed were asked *how* they had changed, the results were even more surprising. Only 15.6 percent said they now thought government should spend less. But nearly three out of four said they now thought government should spend *more* on earthquake hazard-reduction programs!

It is difficult to find a convincing explanation for this claimed reverse effect of Proposition 13. Perhaps six months of public discussion on what to slash and what to preserve in local government had led many citizens to make their own, more careful distinctions between what government should and should not be doing. Or perhaps the view that there was actually a great deal of fat that could be cut from government while leaving enough for essential services, advanced in advocacy of Proposition 13, had led some citizens to believe that more *could* be spent on earthquake hazard reduction without cutting back other valued services. But the major conclusion, that the Proposition 13 "economy fever" did not turn people against government spending for earthquake preparedness, stands firmly on the data.

Clinching evidence could come from comparing responses to the same question given by fresh samples in February 1977, and November-December 1978. In chapter eight, we reported the high rate of support for government spending on behalf of four kinds of earthquake hazard-mitigation activity. Answers to questions about enforcing building-safety codes and establishing systems for issuing earthquake predictions in the final wave are almost identical to those given twenty-one months earlier. But small reductions may have occurred in support for prediction studies (from 58 to 49 percent) and in loans to rebuild or reinforce unsafe structures (from 81 to 72 percent). Thus, the government economy crisis may have had a modest but selective effect on support for

TABLE 36

GOVERNMENT SPENDING ON EARTHQUAKE PREPAREDNESS
AND PROPOSITION 13

Attitude toward spending	Number	Percent
Amount government is spending on earthquake preparedness:		
(New sample)		
Too much	29	5.3
About right	115	20.9
Too little	188	34.2
Don't know	218	39.6
Total	550	100.0
(Reinterviewed sample)		
Too much	15	4.3
About right	73	21.0
Too little	162	46.5
Don't know	98	28.2
Total	348	100.0
Has Proposition 13 changed your views on how much government should spend on earthquake preparedness?		
Yes	109	12.1
No	675	75.2
Don't know	114	12.7
Total	898	100.0
Do you now think government should spend more or less on earthquake hazard-reduction programs?		
More	81	74.3
Less	17	15.6
Don't know and other	11	10.1
Total	109	100.0

earthquake expenditure. Or perhaps extended waiting caused some people to reassess the value of earthquake prediction research—but not of prompt communication of predictions! And perhaps increased exposure to the old-building debate had brought the public closer to those living among the old buildings (see chapter eleven) in their skepticism about the usefulness of programs to renovate unsafe structures.

Continuing Significance of Critical Events

In this chapter we have dealt largely with the awareness and interpretation of the events that took place after our first survey and that might have changed the public view of the earthquake threat. But there are at least three critical events that happened before the first survey whose recognition or evaluation may have changed. These events are the issuance and subsequent withdrawal of James Whitcomb's "hypothesis test," the issuance and disconfirmation of Henry Minturn's forecast, and the announcement of the uplift. We shall consider the first two together.

A major concern of scientists and officials who deal with earthquake prediction and warning is the risk of issuing a false alarm. While the probable consequences of a false alarm are not known, there is a widespread conviction that they would be quite disruptive and would undermine confidence in future predictions and warnings. Both Whitcomb's and Minturn's announcements qualify as false alarms. Whitcomb issued his forecast for a moderate earthquake in the Los Angeles area, to occur anytime within a year of the date of issuance, April 1976. Although he carefully qualified his forecast by calling it a hypothesis test, it was generally interpreted as a prediction and was reviewed by the California Earthquake Prediction Evaluation Council as though it had been a prediction. Then, in December, before the one-year time window had passed, Whitcomb withdrew the forecast.

Did the issuance of such a forecast by a reputable scientist and its subsequent withdrawal disillusion people about future scientific predictions and warnings? For the present, we shall ask merely how many people remembered, about two years later, that a scientist had issued a widely publicized "prediction" and had subsequently withdrawn it.

Similarly, in November 1976, Minturn issued his forecast for an earthquake in the Los Angeles region to occur on December 20 of that year. This event was the one most frequently mentioned when people in our basic field sample were asked what predictions and other announcements they remembered hearing. December 20 came and went without an earthquake. The Minturn forecast fits the classic conception of a false alarm. Again, learning whether people remembered the Minturn forecast and its disconfirmation is the essential first step to uncovering a false-alarm effect.

We assume that if a false alarm is to affect the credibility of other announcements, the false-alarm event should be salient and not merely subject to recall. Hence, we did not ask about Whitcomb or Minturn either by name or by recounting the specific details of the two events. Instead, we worded the two questions as follows:

> During the past year or two, do you happen to remember hearing about an earthquake prediction for the Los Angeles area which was later withdrawn?
>
> A. What do you remember about that prediction or who made it?
>
> During the past year or two, do you happen to remember hearing about an earthquake prediction in the Los Angeles area that didn't happen?
>
> A. What do you remember about that prediction or about who made it?

The results are summarized in table 37.

Neither "prediction" was remembered by the majority of the respondents. But the fact that 43 percent remembered the disconfirmed prediction and 27 percent remembered a withdrawn prediction could have far-reaching effects on public attitudes toward earthquake prediction. Were these respondents thinking of the Whitcomb and Minturn forecasts? When we classify responses according to the clues they contain, it becomes clear that relatively few of the people who remembered a prediction that was later withdrawn had Whitcomb clearly in mind. A few more people correctly identified Minturn with the disconfirmed prediction, but the number is still small. In both cases, larger numbers of respondents referred to a forecast issued by a psychic and to the forecast that California will break off from the North American continent in an earthquake and fall into the Pacific Ocean. Thus, while substantial minorities of the people remembered that there had been earthquake false alarms, their memories of the events

TABLE 37

MEMORY OF PREDICTION WITHDRAWN OR DISCONFIRMED

Information remembered	Prediction later withdrawn	Prediction that didn't happen
Remember hearing about?		
Yes	27.3	43.0
No	72.7	57.0
Total percent	100.0	100.0
Total number	898	898
What do you remember about prediction or who made it?		
Uplift	1.6	3.1
Whitcomb or Caltech	3.3	2.1
General scientific	7.3	6.0
Minturn	3.3	5.2
Psychic	8.6	12.4
Religious	1.2	2.9
California breakoff	4.1	5.4
Soviet scientist	.4	.5
General statement	10.6	7.5
Unclassifiable details	33.1	37.3
Don't know	26.5	17.6
Total percent	100.0	100.0
Total number	245	386

were generally vague and fragmentary and did not point clearly to scientific failures.

Finally, the announcement of the southern California uplift itself may qualify as a sort of slowly developing false alarm. As indicated in table 37, a few people mentioned the uplift as a prediction that was withdrawn or as the prediction of an earthquake that did not happen. In the next chapter we shall examine the trend of answers to identical questions about the uplift asked in all five surveys. But we also asked about the subjective sense of changed evaluation of the uplift in the final interview wave.

All respondents who said they remembered hearing of a "bulge in the earth near Palmdale" and who realized that scientists were

saying that it might be a sign of a coming earthquake were asked
the following question:

> We've been hearing about a bulge in the earth near Palmdale for quite
> a while now. Compared to when you first heard about the bulge, do
> you take it *more* seriously or *less* seriously now as a sign of a coming
> earthquake?

Significantly more of the respondents who were being reinterviewed than of the fresh respondents had heard of the uplift and
appreciated its potential significance. But those in the two samples who had heard and understood did not differ significantly in
the proportion who took the uplift seriously. In both samples, a
plurality said they took the uplift as a sign of a coming earthquake
with about the same seriousness as when they first heard about
it. Those who took it more seriously and those who took it less
seriously were about evenly balanced. There is, then, no evidence
here of a dominant false-alarm effect.

Conclusions

Varying degrees of awareness of earthquake-related
events have been reported. *On the whole, nothing happened with
sufficient force to make drastic changes in public awareness and
attitude toward earthquake threat.* People were not sufficiently
impressed with false alarms that we should expect any great effect.
They sensed that media coverage of earthquake topics had declined and discussion with it, but there was no net loss in desire
for media coverage and no net downgrading of the significance of
the uplift. There appears to have been increased interest in flooding as a potential consequence of earthquakes and a substantial
increase in the minority of respondents who felt that nonscientific
earthquake forecasts receive insufficient attention in the media.

We are especially interested in any tendency for people to interpret events as signs concerning the imminence of a destructive
earthquake in Los Angeles County. The early reports of changes
in the uplift and the report that parts of the uplift were sinking
had been heard and remembered by only 13 and 16 percent of our
total sample, respectively. The earthquake swarm studied by Cal-

tech scientists was better known, at 39 percent, while 83 percent had heard of the neighboring Santa Barbara earthquake.

Very few people had heard that sinking in parts of the uplift might foreshadow the coming quake or signify that the earthquake potential was being relieved, and even fewer thought that either of these interpretations was probably true. Interpretations of the earthquake swarm in the Palmdale region and the neighboring Santa Barbara earthquake were more widely diffused but still reached only a minority. Approximately one person in every seven in the adult population surveyed thought that the latter events did signify a coming large earthquake for Los Angeles. About the same proportion, including some of the same people, thought the earthquake swarms relieved pressure and lessened the imminent earthquake danger, while a much smaller fraction thought the Santa Barbara earthquake relieved strain in Los Angeles. This chapter was intended to provide a background for the next chapter, in which we shall examine changes indicated by questions that were asked repeatedly during the five surveys.

CHAPTER THIRTEEN

The Test of Time

The preceding chapter has shown that occasional newsworthy events kept the earthquake hazard alive as a topic for media attention during 1977 and 1978. But none of these events—not even the Santa Barbara earthquake—was dramatic enough to alter public attitudes drastically. Both media treatment and informal discussion of earthquake hazard seemed to have declined, although the public interest in hearing more on the subject remained high. In this chapter we shall see what changes took place in public awareness, conceptions of prediction, fear and concern, and action during the same second and third years of waiting for a destructive earthquake.

We shall compare answers to the same question at five moments in time, using the basic field survey and the new-respondent samples from each of the four follow-up interview waves.[1] Because the small number of intervals of time preclude sophisticated time-series analysis, we shall depend principally on the inspection of percentage distributions. *Chi-square* values for the complete series will tell us whether to take seriously any apparent trends. To summarize the trends, we have fitted three simple mathematical curves to the series as appropriate. Simple ascending or descending *linear* trend lines are the first choice whenever either appears applicable; the linear trend describes a fairly steady increase or decrease over the twenty-one months. A declining *exponential* curve is suitable for describing a rapid initial decrease followed by a gradual leveling off as time passes; this curve fits a situation in which some spectacular event has affected people's attitudes strongly. While the crisis effect wears off rather quickly, the memory lingers. In a few instances a *parabola*, or common *U*-shaped curve, is fitted to the series. The possible meanings of a parabolic trend can best be explained in connection with specific applications.

The Significance of Time

DIMENSIONS OF WARNING

Warnings are of many kinds, and the effects of a long period of waiting must depend upon the kind of warning that has been issued. Here we shall stress just three dimensions of a warning, prediction, or forecast. First is *lead time*, which is the period of relatively assured safety before the disaster agent becomes active. Second is the *time window*, the span of time within which the community is at risk. The time window begins when lead time ends and continues until an all-clear signal can be safely sounded. Third is the *closed-* or *open-endedness* of the time window. With flooding from high tides, for example, it is possible to state a time after which people can safely relax if the worst has not already happened, whereas a balanced rock above a community remains a threat until it falls.

Henry Minturn's forecast was issued with a lead time of about four weeks and a brief, closed-ended time window of twenty-four to forty-eight hours. The short lead time, the very brief time window, and the assurance that by December 21 or 22 the danger would be past made this forecast easy to conceptualize and face. James Whitcomb's hypothesis test involved zero lead time and a closed-ended time window of one year. Indications are that many people dealt with the yearlong time window of potentially anxious waiting by translating it into lead time.

The southern California uplift conveyed a warning with zero lead time and an open-ended time window. This, we assume, is the most difficult time schedule to deal with. Long time windows preclude the individual or the community's going onto an emergency basis. In effect, the many people who expected the damaging earthquake within a year had imposed some closure on the open-ended window. The quest for omens which we noted in the previous chapter and will see again in chapter fourteen can be understood as an effort to put boundaries on the time window so that people can decide when to live life on an emergency footing and when to live normally. As we shall see, the uplift became increasingly salient as the period of waiting dragged on. Hence, we can most aptly examine theories and evidence on the effects of waiting against the background of an open-ended and ever-extending time window.

THEORIES OF WAITING

Six different but not always mutually exclusive theoretical assumptions have guided our investigation of the effects of waiting. The most obvious hypothesis is that lengthening experience in an open-ended time window should lead to a declining sense of urgency and correspondingly reduced vigilance and preparedness. The second hypothesis carries the same principle a step farther, positing a false-alarm or "crying wolf," effect. The first hypothesis envisions no loss of conviction that disaster will strike eventually. But under the second hypothesis people conclude that the entire alarm was unjustified in the first place and that scientists or other forecasters really do not know what they are doing.

The third hypothesized effect is that of accumulating anxiety and fear, with their many attendant effects. According to this hypothesis, people should resist and resent new information and should practice defensive denial of danger. Earthquake salience should increase, while expressions of fear would be moderated. The fourth hypothesized effect is the translation of accumulating personal tension into more active and aggressive responses. Anger, resentment, and scapegoating should be directed against scientists, for their disturbance of the peace by issuing unsettling pronouncements, and against public officials, for their implied collaboration. Scientists should be viewed with increasing distrust, and appeals for preparedness should be met by active and hostile noncompliance.

While these four possible negative effects of living through a lengthening disaster time window have been widely advertised, a plausible case can also be made for some effects of a more positive kind. The following are two positive effects.

If the extended time window creates occasions for discussion and exposure to media examination of the earthquake threat, the earthquake prospect could become increasingly real and vital. As a new idea, earthquake prediction is poorly grasped and understood by most people. The fifth hypothesis is that extended exposure to the idea in an alert mode can lead to familiarization, appreciation, and sensitization to the signs and implications of earthquake hazard. Carrying this reasoning one step farther, the sixth hypothesis is that responses to early and repeated warning announcements become rehearsals and drills in preparation for the eventual emergency. Through trial and effort, people discard inappropriate responses and replace them with more suitable ones.

We shall not explore these hypotheses one by one in this chapter but instead will refer to them as we attempt to understand the significance of each observed trend.

Earthquake Hazard Awareness

ANNOUNCEMENTS REMEMBERED

The standard question on "predictions, statements, or warnings about earthquakes" was repeated in each of the surveys, and the results are graphed in figure 48.[2] Remembrance of announcements fell dramatically from February 1977 to January 1978, leveling off thereafter. The proportion of respondents who could not remember any recent announcement tripled from February to August and quadrupled from February to January. An exponential curve fits the trend in mean number of announcements remembered quite well.[3] The trend of awareness confirms the impression that 1976 had been a busy year for earthquake intimations and that 1977 and 1978 were quieter.

Yet there *were* new announcements during the latter years. Seers continued to proclaim their forecasts, there were periodic reports on the status of the uplift, and general reminders were still being issued. Why did they no longer make the same impression as before? Perhaps the new developments were less newsworthy because they were repetitions and revisions of prior announcements or because they lacked the urgency or specificity of some

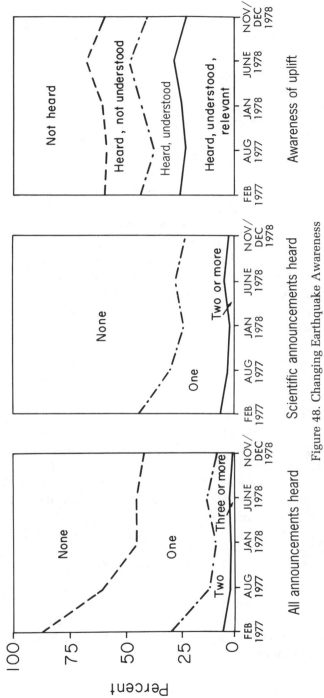

Figure 48. Changing Earthquake Awareness

earlier forecasts, such as Minturn's. Perhaps many people had experienced "saturation" on the basis of the 1976 announcements, or perhaps the threshold for significant experience had been raised. But the fact that people continued to ask for more media attention to earthquake hazard weakens the plausibility of this explanation.

A more tenable explanation may be that experiences are significant when they either create new convictions or undermine old ones. Early announcements caused many people to think seriously about the prospect of an earthquake and conclude that a quake was coming. Once that view was established, and while the conviction remained, new announcements made little distinctive impression. They were more like the familiar sights that remind an automobile driver that he is still on the right road without requiring active attention than like the signs that command attention while one is trying to find the way along an unfamiliar route.

But does this marked exponential decline apply equally to all kinds of earthquake forecasts and cautions? All types of announcements were more salient in February 1977 than later, but the rates and patterns of decline differ. Pseudoscientific announcements declined most dramatically between February and August 1977, closely approximating an exponential curve. A slight decline in prophetic announcements approximated an exponential curve, but more loosely. General or vague announcements also dropped substantially, but mostly between August 1977 and January 1978. The trend of scientific announcements (Figure 48) is a somewhat flattened version of the trend for all announcements.[4]

Because pseudoscientific announcements show the most dramatic exponential decline, we must be wary of the possibility that the fading memory of Minturn's forecast alone accounts fully for the overall trend of awareness. Disconfirmation of Minturn's forecast for December 20, 1976, was less than a month past when our interviewers commenced the basic field survey. Mentions of the Minturn forecast dropped from 37.5 percent in February 1977 to 6.7 percent six months later and to 2.5 percent at the end of 1978. To resolve this question we computed the mean number of earthquake announcements mentioned when references to Minturn are eliminated. Although the decline is now more linear and less concentrated in the first period, there is still substantial decline, with a single interruption of the downward trend between

January and July 1978. The overall relationship is highly significant. The main conclusion is clear. Although the Minturn announcement contributed greatly to the overall trend of awareness, its effect was chiefly to intensify a trend that also characterizes other notices and to exaggerate the loss of awareness between February and August 1977.

While the mention of scientific announcements declined, scientific notices may have increased in prominence relative to other kinds of announcements, especially from February 1977 to January 1978. The Whitcomb announcement—more often identified as coming from Caltech than as associated with Whitcomb's name—was mentioned by only 4.8 percent of our respondents at the beginning of 1977, and this number had dropped to a mere 0.4 percent by the end of 1978. The trend was significant and linear. The uplift, however, increased in salience from August 1977 to July 1978, with the major increase occurring between August 1977 and January 1978. The upward trend appears to have been reversed by a substantial drop in the final period. We shall come back to the uplift later. For the present, while Minturn was being forgotten most rapidly and Whitcomb less rapidly, general warning announcements were being mentioned less often, and other pseudoscientific and prophetic announcements remained fairly constant after an initial drop, the uplift was the one easily identified topic whose salience increased during a substantial portion of the study period. While the increased salience of the uplift contributed to a slight shift toward greater salience of scientific rather than nonscientific announcements, it also signaled a growing tendency for most scientific announcements to be tied to the uplift.

Earlier, in chapter five, we observed that respondents' own source attributions for earthquake notices did not correspond exactly with our classification of sources. Differences were chiefly of two kinds. The vague statements which we classified as *general* announcements were mostly attributed, on further questioning, to either scientific or prophetic sources. And many forecasts that we called *pseudoscientific*—especially Minturn's forecast, the declaration that much of California will break off and fall into the ocean, and the less often mentioned Jupiter Effect—were attributed to scientists.

Trends for source attributions were not substantially different from the trends for types of announcements as we classify them. Attributions to seers and psychics and to religious leaders showed no consistent trends. Attributions to scientists increased more decisively than announcements that *we* could identify as having scientific origins. The reference to *amateur scientist*, applying mostly to Minturn, declined over the entire period according to an exponential pattern. It is interesting to note that although less than half of the people who mentioned Minturn in the first survey, when his forecast was still very salient, correctly identified him as an amateur, larger proportions of those who continued to remember Minturn's forecast correctly identified its author as an amateur.

If we look at the objective classification and subjective source attributions together, we can summarize trends in the following terms: A general decline in remembrance of earthquake predictions, forecasts, and cautions is partly but not entirely explained by the unusual attention focused on Henry Minturn's forecast, which was disconfirmed one to two months before our initial survey. If attention that might have been claimed by another Minturn-type announcement shifted rather than disappeared, it contributed immediately to a relative increase in remembrance of vague general-warning statements. The relative salience of secular and religious prophetic forecasts, whether identified as such by our coders or by the respondents' own attributions, seemed to be a fairly stable component of all notices remembered. Contradicting the general trend, the proportion of all respondents who mentioned the southern California uplift actually increased throughout the period of study. This change contributed to a slight relative increase in the prominence of announcements that were identifiably from scientific sources and to a clearer increase in the extent to which respondents thought of science as the source for whatever predictions, forecasts, and cautions they had heard.

Increases in both relative and absolute salience of the uplift during most of the waiting period might indicate that progressively more people became aware of the uplift and of its significance. Alternatively, the increases might indicate merely that the uplift had become salient to a larger proportion of the people who had heard of it, without any increase in general awareness. In figure 48 we report the four levels of awareness for the five surveys. The reader is reminded that respondents were divided into the following four groups: those who had not heard of the uplift; those who had heard of the uplift but did not realize that it could signify a coming earthquake; those who had heard of the uplift and understood its significance but who did not expect damage where they lived in the case of such an earthquake; and those who had heard and understood and who expected damage where they lived.

None of these types increased or decreased significantly except during an awareness peak in July 1978. Increased salience of the uplift did not signify a spreading awareness and appreciation of the uplift in the population at large. Nevertheless, with declining awareness of other than prophetic announcements, the persisting awareness of the uplift is striking and contradicts any hypothesis of generalized loss of interest and declining awareness during an extended period of waiting for a vaguely but scientifically forecast disaster.

SOURCES OF INFORMATION

We have found that *what* people remembered changed as well as *how much* they remembered during the second and third years of waiting. In parallel fashion, *where* they had heard about earthquakes changed along with *how much* they had heard. In the left-hand portion of figure 49 are graphed the answers to our standard question about "your chief source of information," asked about each of the earthquake announcements people remembered. As reported earlier (chapter three), television was named as the chief source of information more often than all other sources combined for February 1977. But the steady decline in reliance on television thereafter is remarkable. The drop from 52.7 percent to 33.6 percent at the end of 1978 is highly significant and closely approximates a linear trend line.[5] In sharp contrast, principal reliance on newspapers almost doubled (increasing from 18.7 to 36.7 percent) during the same period. This relationship is also highly significant, and the increase is loosely described by a linear trend line.[6] Although television was cited more than two and a half times as often as newspapers at the beginning of the study period, newspapers were cited slightly more often than television by the end of that period.

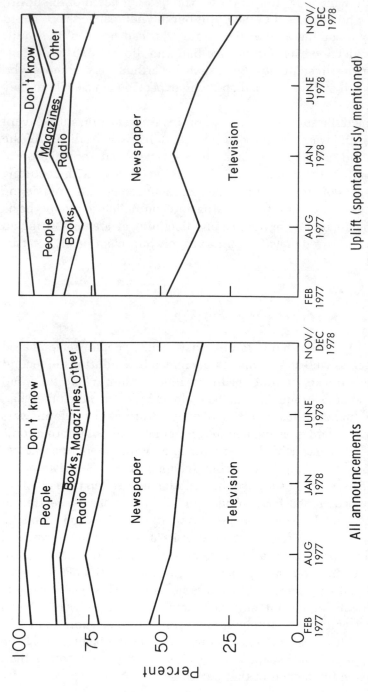

All announcements   Uplift (spontaneously mentioned)

Figure 49. Chief Source of Information on Earthquake Predictions, Forecasts, and Cautions

Although the changes are more erratic and are not statistically significant, the general trend for radio is similar to the trend for television, and the general trend for books and magazines (not graphed separately) is similar to that for newspapers. Hence, the observed changes might be described as a shift away from the airways to the printed word as a prime source of information about future earthquake changes.

One explanation for the shift could be that the credibility of newspapers increased and the credibility of the airways decreased because of the generally skeptical attitude taken by newspapers toward the Minturn prediction. To be defensible, however, this explanation would require an acutely exponential rather than linear change.

Another explanation could be found in elaborating the idea of affinities between particular media and types of content (chapter three). Perhaps the effect of repeated attention to the same topic leads people to seek more detailed and profound information. Having heard repeatedly that a severe earthquake is overdue, people are only attentive to new and elaborated information about the earthquake threat. The printed word can more easily convey such elaborations than can television and radio, with their brief announcements incorporated in daily news broadcasts.

We also noted earlier that scientific announcements are relatively more often ascribed to newspapers, while general announcements are more often ascribed to television. Some of the change in media prominence might have been the consequence of changing types of announcements. Accordingly, we have graphed separately, for comparison, the sources given for information about the uplift (fig. 49) when the uplift was mentioned as one of the "predictions, statements, or warnings about earthquakes" people have heard. The downward trend for television, while less linear, was magnified (from 46.6 percent to 22.2 percent). Starting from a higher level, the use of newspapers is seen to have increased by the same proportion as it did before, from 26 percent to 51.9 percent.

Two observations are suggested by a comparison of the sources for information about the uplift and about all earthquake announcements. First, the shift from television to newspapers cannot be explained primarily by the greater salience of the uplift, since people who remembered the uplift exhibited the same shift to an even greater degree. Second, a disproportionate amount of the shift was made by people who are sufficiently tuned in to the scientific basis for concern about earthquakes to think spontaneously of the uplift when asked about recent earthquake warnings. Thus, the increased relative salience of the uplift and the increased reliance on the print media combine to suggest a pattern of awareness and communication that, while less intense than before, is less frivolous and is better harnessed to reality.

The Predictability of Earthquakes

As months go by without the anticipated earthquake and an unpredicted destructive quake strikes a nearby community, flagging faith in current and future earthquake-prediction capability would not be a surprising side effect. And if anxiety accumulated, there would be another reason to expect weakening confidence in prediction capability. However, earthquake prediction being a new idea, the period of waiting could foster progressive familiarization and education, leading to increased confidence in scientific prediction. The same contrasting lines of reasoning could lead us to expect public support for releasing earthquake predictions to be either undermined or reinforced and public suspicion that scientists and officials are censoring the bad news about a coming earthquake to be magnified or lessened.

Faith in the accuracy with which scientists can predict earthquakes at the present time exhibits a generally upward trend (fig. 50). Belief that scientists can predict *quite accurately* increases dramatically and steadily, but this increase did not begin until after August 1977. Belief that scientists can predict *somewhat accurately* or better increased substantially between February and August 1977, from 41.9 percent to 52.5 percent, with no consistent pattern of change thereafter. The evidence seems to rule out lines of reasoning that posit accumulating doubts as people wait for the long-delayed earthquake. Hypotheses of enhanced familiarity and reinforced conviction from repeated media support for the idea of earthquake prediction are more congenial with these data.

So large a percentage of respondents (from 83 to 87 percent) reported the belief that scientists will eventually predict earth-

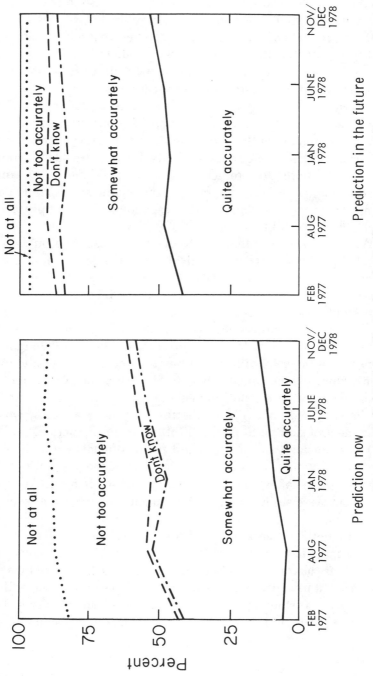

Figure 50. Belief in Scientific Earthquake Prediction

quakes at least "somewhat accurately" that there was very little variability during the study period (fig. 50). Since it is fully explained by inclusion of people who think earthquakes can be predicted quite accurately now, the apparent rise in the number of "quite accurately" responses should be treated as spurious.

If the cumulative familiarization hypothesis has merit, it applies only to the belief that scientists can predict earthquakes *quite accurately* at the present time. This belief is unrealistic, however. At the time of this investigation, most earthquake scientists would not even have agreed that earthquakes could be predicted "somewhat" accurately. We must assume, therefore, that superficial familiarization rather than deepened understanding characterizes this small segment of our respondents. Hearing repeatedly about scientists' efforts to predict earthquakes without fully comprehending the message or grasping the qualifications contained in most newspaper accounts, these respondents have simply taken a perfected capability for granted.

We reported earlier that nearly everyone favors the public release of predictions when scientists are highly confident of accuracy, but there are differences of opinion about the release of predictions for which scientists are less confident of accuracy. A small but significant increase (from 30.4 to 36.5 percent) took place between February and August 1977 in the proportion of respondents who insisted that authorities should be "definitely sure the earthquake will occur" before releasing the prediction. The proportion remained fairly stable thereafter. Thus, doubts and anxieties that are not intense enough to undermine faith in media-validated scientific prediction may have added a small increment of caution to public thinking about prediction.

The suspicion that scientists and public officials are withholding information from the public did not change significantly over the period of extended waiting. Neither anxieties nor disillusionment were strong enough to augment the prevailing level of suspicion.

Nonscientific forecasting must not be overlooked as part of the relevant public experience. We did not see significant changes in the beliefs that other people besides scientists can predict earthquakes, that psychics and mystics can predict earthquakes, or that earthquake weather is a valid premonitory sign. However, between February and August 1977, confidence in unusual animal behavior as an earthquake sign increased from 67.5 to 75.7 percent, and confidence in premonitions and instinct increased from 38.5 to 45.2 percent. Both remained fairly stable at the higher level for the rest of the period. Increased faith in animal behavior could have resulted from continuing media attention and some scientific attention to its possible use in earthquake prediction, but the parallel enhancement of faith in premonitions seems to call for a different explanation for both.

This interval of time is the same as that during which faith in current scientific earthquake-prediction capability increased the most. With faith in three contrasting modes of earthquake forecasting increasing simultaneously, we should look for a common explanation rather than viewing the three separately. Since the majority of our respondents are classified as *believers*—that is, people who accept both scientific and nonscientific methods of earthquake forecasting (chapter ten)—we should not be surprised to see these three popular modes changing together. Whatever cause it was that may have augmented public confidence in the predictability of earthquakes by both scientists and by personal intuition simultaneously was only at work during the first half of 1977. We shall return to this problem with a tentative explanation later.

Earthquake Fear and Concern

We have learned that the awareness of earthquake forecasts and warnings changed both quantitatively and qualitatively over the twenty-two-month study period. But were these changes matched by corresponding changes in concern and expectation? Apart from the memory of any specific earthquake warning, does the earthquake problem weigh heavily on people's minds? Do people fear the prospect of an earthquake? Are the forecasts taken seriously? Do people expect a severe earthquake soon?

SALIENCE

All interviews with new respondents commenced without reference to earthquakes as the topic for investigation.

Interviews opened with three leading questions designed to elicit references to earthquakes if they were very much on the respondents' minds (chapter six). Only after these questions were completed was the respondent told that the balance of the survey would deal with earthquakes. If people mentioned earthquakes once or more in answer to any of the three questions, the topic was said to be *salient* for them. The level of salience was very low; only 6.6 percent of respondents in our basic survey mentioned earthquakes without prompting.

As low as the initial figure was, it was higher than the percentage in any later survey. Salience dropped in August 1977 and again in January 1978 to 50 percent of the initial rate. In July 1978 and again in November-December 1978, salience rebounded, but less than halfway to its original level. The overall relationship, however, is only marginally significant, and none of the trend curves fits within acceptable confidence limits. Salience certainly did not increase during the two years. It is possible—but it has not been demonstrated—that 1977 was a quiet year in which the initial low level of salience dropped even lower and that attention to earthquake news brought a partial recovery of salience in 1978.

FEAR AND CONCERN

Fear of earthquakes could be viewed as a more general attitude than salience, less affected by warnings of moderate to low credibility and specificity. Three questions were used and were weighted equally in establishing an index of fear and concern over earthquakes (chapter six). The index registered a significant drop between February and August 1977 but remained strikingly stable thereafter. The proportion of respondents who expressed high and high-medium fear is loosely described by an exponential curve.[7]

In order to gauge *people's own assessment* of the effect of recent events on their concern about earthquakes, we asked whether their concern had increased, decreased, or remained the same during the preceding year. The majority of respondents in each survey felt that their concern had neither increased nor decreased. However, the number who said their concern had increased dropped significantly (by half) between February and August

1977. An apparent slight rebound in January 1978 was not statistically significant. Otherwise, the proportion who said that their concern had increased did not change appreciably after the drop during the first half of 1977. The overall relationship is highly significant, but because of the irregularity of the trend, none of the curves fits the data within acceptable confidence limits.

Our respondents' own perceptions of change and stability in their concern over the earthquake danger seem to correspond approximately, but not perfectly, with the observed changes in the concern expressed by successive waves of interview respondents. Thus, we can be confident that concern had been raised by events in 1976 but had dropped back to a stable level by late summer in 1977.

The three items that make up the fear index cohere satisfactorily in the basic survey according to the usual standards for index construction. However, their literal meanings are not identical, and it is conceivable that they might respond differently to changing circumstances. Accordingly, we have summarized responses to the three items separately in figure 51. The three items do indeed exhibit different responses.

For all three items, the substantial change occurred between February and August 1977. Each of the changes is significant at the .001 level when we consider only the two adjacent sets of responses. Respondents in August expressed considerably less fright and less worry over the possibility of a damaging earthquake's striking southern California; these two changes are consistent with the change we reported based on the three items together. The third item, however, reveals an equally substantial change in the opposite direction. This item was worded as follows:

If you were certain that a damaging earthquake was going to occur at a specific time in a place where you live or work would you: try to be where the earthquake would occur, try to get as far away as possible, try to find a safe place near the earthquake, or go on as usual and be wherever you are at the time?

The second response was interpreted as indicative of the greatest fear. The proportion of respondents endorsing this response jumped from 29 to 37 percent and remained higher than at first, at least until after July 1978.

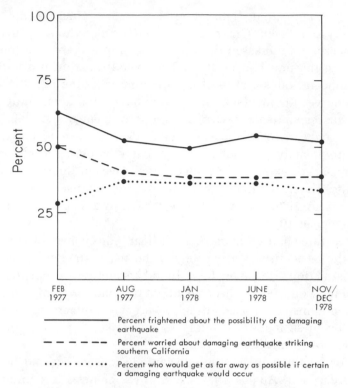

Figure 51. Expressions of Fear and Concern

Apparently, the third item incorporates a critical element separate from simple fear and concern. Perhaps it is the disposition to accept a severe earthquake as a "normal" event, to be dealt with as if nothing out of the ordinary were happening. The observed change would then signify that a growing number of people were no longer viewing a severe earthquake in this *normalized* fashion. While this changed perspective did not cause an increase in fear and concern, it might be reflected in a greater disposition to act in case the threat were made concrete and imminent by a credible short-term earthquake warning.

ANNOUNCEMENTS TAKEN SERIOUSLY

If people remembered fewer earthquake announcements as time passed, did they take them as seriously as they had before? The answer should depend in part on whether respondents attached higher or lower intensities to the forecasted quakes. The number of people who could remember one or more announcements referring to earthquakes that were supposed to destroy buildings and take lives did decline, especially from February 1977 to January 1978. In August 1977 and for the remainder of the study period, fewer than half could recall any recent announcement that referred clearly to a damaging earthquake. However, this trend is fully explained by the declining number of all announcements remembered and an increasing proportion of respondents who were unable to associate intensities with the announcements they had heard. While people became increasingly unclear about the severity of the anticipated earthquake, there was no trend toward remembering more or less severe earthquake forecasts during the period under investigation.

Similarly, the number of people who remembered one or more announcements that they took seriously declined slightly but steadily (fig. 52). But if we pay attention only to respondents who remembered one or more announcements, the proportion who took one or more seriously showed a steady increase from February 1977 to January 1978. This trend is highly significant for the entire study period, and it is loosely described by a convex parabolic curve.[8] More dramatically (but not graphed), of all announcements remembered, the percentage taken seriously rose from 32 to 50 percent by January 1978, remained stable to July, and then dropped partway back, to 42 percent.

Fairly similar curves apply to taking forecasts of destructive earthquakes seriously and to taking scientific earthquake forecasts seriously (fig. 52). The trend toward taking scientific announcements seriously is more dramatic, reaching a peak in January 1978 and declining less steeply until the end of 1978. There have clearly been changes in what we earlier called the quality of awareness (chapter six). As fewer announcements are remembered, scientifically based notices become more salient, and more of these are taken seriously. The composite picture would be simple and encouraging except for the parabolic curves that describe the latter trend. Before attempting to deal with this complexity, we must look for changes in expectation for an early damaging earthquake.

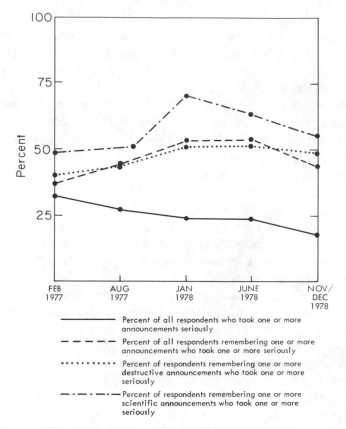

Figure 52. Announcements Taken Seriously

EARTHQUAKE EXPECTATION

Respondents in each survey were asked how likely they thought it was that a damaging earthquake would strike southern California within the next year. The data in figure 53 reveal two different kinds of change. First, the proportion of respondents who said that they "don't know" how likely it is that an earthquake will strike increased between February and August 1977 and again between January and July 1978. Uncertainty was more than three times as frequent in late 1978 (19.5 percent) as in early 1977 (5.5 percent). The overall relationship is highly significant, and the trend is loosely described by an ascending

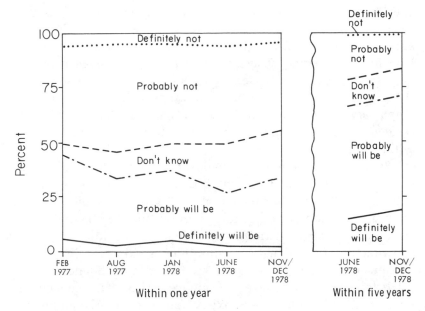

Figure 53. Probability of a Damaging Earthquake

linear trend line.[9] Increasing uncertainty seems an appropriate response during a period of repeated reminders of an undated impending disaster.

Second, there was a significant increase in negative replies and a matching decrease in positive answers between February and August 1977. After this early drop in earthquake expectation, there were only nonsignificant oscillations.

Fear of earthquakes, perceived recent change in concern, and expectation for a damaging earthquake within a year all exhibited the same clear drop between February and August 1977 and were followed by relative stability for the remainder of the study period. This consistency among the three variables makes the changes more obviously interpretable. A substantial segment of the populace are seen to be no longer convinced that disaster is imminent in spite of an earlier conviction to that effect brought on by events in 1976. With disaster less imminent, people are now less fearful than before.

In the absence of more definite credible predictions than had been issued, one year would be an unrealistic period within which to expect a damaging earthquake in southern California. We specified one year in the question, however, in order to assess the sense of imminence about the earthquake threat. In the last two survey waves we added an identically worded question referring to a five-year period. There was no apparent change between August and November-December 1978, and we do not know how the questions would have been answered earlier (fig. 53). The graph serves chiefly to emphasize that most southern California residents expect a damaging quake within a few years, if not within a single year.

If fear and the sense of imminence, but not the conviction that southern California is due for a destructive earthquake, declined substantially during the first half of 1977 and then stabilized, this must have been a period of relaxing tension. If we assume that sustained anxiety undermines confidence and inhibits realistic assessments of the dangerous situation, relaxing tension could explain some of our other findings. Growing confidence in the predictability of earthquakes by science and by folk signs could have resulted from lessened anxiety and urgency. Abandonment of the normalization approach to impending danger by admitting the urge to get as far away as possible from an earthquake could illustrate the ability to face reality as the threat became less imminent. All these developments were most marked during the first half of 1977, immediately after the crisis year of 1976 had passed.

With anxiety and urgency diminished, people might be ready to attend to earthquake notices in a more discriminating fashion, which would account for the rise in the "taking seriously" curve during the next interval of time. Once the lagged effect had worn off, a false-alarm effect concerning new notices might emerge, accounting for the parabolic shape of the relevant curves. These are, of course, post hoc speculations made in an effort to discern a plausible comprehensive pattern in the data rather than demonstrated conclusions from the research.

Action and Action Orientations

We have seen a lessening of media attention and of informal discussion and a corresponding reduction in awareness and in sense of urgency about the earthquake threat. In spite of these changes, we have also seen what may be a less frivolous and more discriminating and realistic pattern of awareness. But are these tendencies translated into action and into those attitudes most closely linked to action? A partial answer was given in chapter twelve. Support for enforcing building codes and for improving the prompt communication of earthquake predictions remained unchanged at a high level, but enthusiasm for government expenditure for loans to reinforce unsafe structures and for prediction studies waned somewhat. Because of this differentiated response, whatever effect the Proposition 13 debates and the extended waiting may have had must have been filtered through special circumstances, such as the well-publicized and seemingly futile effort to overcome political opposition to dealing with old buildings.

There appears to be a continuous but very slight increase in fatalistic attitudes, loosely described by a convex exponential curve. The overall change, however, is not statistically significant. We must therefore limit our conclusion to saying that increased faith in the predictability of earthquakes is not matched by increased confidence that the disastrous effects of earthquakes can be controlled.

INDIVIDUAL AND COLLECTIVE SOLUTIONS

To recapitulate an earlier discussion (chapter seven), we noted the importance of a spontaneous, community-wide surge of altruism in facilitating emergency response in natural-disaster situations. A comparable response might be essential for the community to mobilize effectively to deal with a serious earthquake warning. We asked whether the 1976 warnings had been met with a response pattern conducive to altruism. The appropriate response pattern would be one in which people recognized that some groups were at greater risk than others, could identify some of these groups, thought something could be done to ameliorate their risk, and accepted some collective responsibility for doing this. The relevant set of questions was asked only on the first and last surveys, so we can observe the twenty-two-month change but not the intervening trends.

The social awareness we are measuring could be simply an aspect of general awareness or it might be an emotional matter.

In the former case, it might have declined during extended wait-ing. In the latter case, the anxiety aroused in 1976 could have inhibited altruism, leading to increasing social awareness as the sense of imminence abated.

Recognition that some groups are in greater danger increased significantly, from 62.9 to 69.7 percent. But this finding is counter-balanced by the observation that fewer groups were mentioned as being especially at risk. Most groups were mentioned less often, but residents in old buildings (with a 24 percent drop) and the elderly and disabled (both with 10 percent drops) headed the list. People living near a fault and in high-density areas were men-tioned significantly more often. The one dramatic increase was that 17 percent more of all the socially aware mentioned poor people as being disproportionately at risk. Changes were roughly paralleled by changes in proportions of people who included themselves in the various high-risk categories.

The increase in an abstract awareness that the danger is not the same for everyone without an accompanying concern for specific groups is not encouraging as a sign of growing altruism. Also, increased concern for the poor at the expense of the elderly and the disabled suggests that issues of national politics may be dis-placing a specifically earthquake-focused compassion. With the decrease in urgency and in communication about the earthquake threat, sensitivity to the plight of those who most need to be the beneficiaries of altruistic concern in preparing for an earthquake has also declined.

The optimistic view expressed by most respondents in early 1977 that something could be done to mitigate the risk was not dampened by the end of 1978, and it even increased for some groups. In addition, fewer people were disposed to place the full responsibility for ameliorating their conditions on the potential victims. These two shifts should be favorable for an altruistic response.

Thus, our conclusion must be mixed, although it may parallel the findings for some other variables. The plight of those least able to prepare for and deal with an earthquake became less salient as the period of waiting was extended indefinitely for the disaster that many had thought was imminent. As stagflation intruded dramatically into public awareness, economic distress may have displaced attention from earthquake vulnerability and may have contaminated the sentiment of compassion for the vulnerable. At the same time, a modest qualitative change was taking place within the reduced compass of social awareness. Through noticeable increases in the awareness that something could be done for the vulnerable and that the responsibility to do so ought to be shared, socially aware respondents have taken a small step in the direction of altruism.

PERSONAL AND HOUSEHOLD PREPAREDNESS

The index based on sixteen preparedness measures frequently recommended to the public was computed for all surveys (fig. 54). A slight increase in preparedness scores from the beginning to the close of the study period may be significant ($p < .05$ when only the first and the last surveys are compared). But the striking changes are between February and August 1977 and between August 1977 and January 1978. The proportion of respondents with high and high-medium scores increased by sixteen percentage points during the first interval. During the remainder

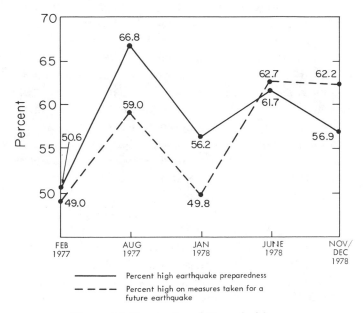

Figure 54. Personal and Household
Earthquake Preparedness

of the first year, scores declined significantly, but not all the way to the original level. Subsequent fluctuation is not statistically significant.

The pattern suggests that some short-lived stimulus triggered a spurt of preparedness, with an inevitable decline as the effect wore off. We have already ruled out fear as the trigger, since the spurt coincided with a decline in fear and in sense of imminence. Increased preparedness could be a manifestation of increasing realism, but so rapid a decline is difficult to explain. In chapter fifteen we shall explore further what the trigger might have been.

To measure the effect of earthquake concern on preparedness more sensitively, we report a companion index including only those measures that people said they took because of the earthquake prospect. When the two indexes change in parallel fashion, we can safely infer that changing concern about earthquakes accounts for changes in preparedness. But when changes in the second index are not accompanied by changes in the first, we must assume that people are simply attributing to the earthquake threat actions that they actually took for other reasons.

Index scores do change according to a similar main pattern, but with a different outcome. The spurt of preparation between February and August 1977 is replicated significantly in the second index. The subsequent deterioration of preparedness until January 1978 is also repeated, but with preparedness dropping back closer to the starting level. Thereafter, however, preparedness rebounds with an even stronger spurt between January and July 1978 and remains at the new high level. Accordingly, the dramatic preparedness spurt and subsequent deterioration during 1977 do seem to be true changes in the state of preparedness caused by changing attention to the earthquake prospect as an extraordinary event. But the subsequent rise and persistence in preparedness levels, attributed to concern over a future earthquake, are not fully paralleled by changes in actual preparedness levels. Hence, during the second half of the study period we see an augmented tendency to explain preparedness actions on the basis of the earthquake threat rather than a true increase in levels of preparedness.

Like many of our other findings, these may be interpreted as encouraging or discouraging. The early peak of preparedness (which was not high in absolute terms) was not sustained, although the overall trend was slightly upward. The discrepancy between the trends of actual preparedness in the second year and preparedness attributed to the earthquake prospect suggests that people are either fooling themselves about their levels of preparedness or are responding to a felt social pressure to be earthquake-prepared by redefining their own motivations rather than by actually taking protective actions.

While these interpretations seem fairly compelling, their acceptance does not preclude a more optimistic assessment of public readiness to act in case of a true emergency, such as a credible warning of imminent earthquake danger. The earlier spurt of preparedness should have familiarized people with some of the twenty-eight steps they might take, making it easier for them to retake them in a more credible emergency. And the greater tendency to attribute the measures actually taken to the earthquake concern may enhance the availability of that motivation as a basis for stimulating further action. Calls to prepare for a damaging earthquake could then be more effective in the event of a credible future emergency.

CHAPTER FOURTEEN

A New Year's Day Surprise

The Earthquake

At 3:14 P.M. on January 1, 1979, an earthquake reported as measuring 4.6 on the Richter scale caused broken windows and minor rock slides in Malibu and Santa Monica. The tremor, described as moderate, was felt from San Diego to Santa Barbara. The quake lasted 40 seconds and was followed by over 100 aftershocks the same day, the largest of which measured 3.4. A Caltech spokesperson said the quake was centered in the ocean floor about four miles south of Malibu and in Santa Monica Bay. The media reported that fire, police, and newspaper switchboards as far inland as Riverside and San Bernardino were swamped with calls "ranging from the curious to the fearful." The quake was felt and commented upon by NBC reporters in the press box at the Rose Bowl in Pasadena, where the USC-Michigan game was in progress.

Damage was minor, and there were no injuries. A plate-glass window at a variety store in Santa Monica shattered, as did store windows in parts of Culver City, and cracked windows were reported as far from the quake's epicenter as Seal Beach and Buena Park. Rock slides were localized in the Malibu Canyon area. Only one minor power outage was reported. Hundreds of spectators watching firemen battle a fire at the Thrifty Drugstore in Santa Monica reportedly panicked and fled when the earthquake struck. Fire officials said that men, women, and children ran screaming in all directions; no one, however, was injured in the flight.

Several reports quoted a police official as saying, "Most people who felt it—and that sure wasn't everybody—pretty much shrugged and remembered they were in southern California and let it go at that." All monitored newspapers carried reports of the quake's occurrence, mostly on the front pages and with photographs of broken store windows. Aftershock activity continued into March.

Various aspects of the New Year's Day quake were discussed in a *Santa Monica Evening Outlook* feature article by Karen Kenney. It would be some time, wrote Kenney, before seismologists could locate the underwater fault slippage responsible for the January 1 quake. Lindley Williamson, a county engineer, was asked by Kenney if such an offshore quake could cause severe slides. He responded that "an earthquake of this size will not cause anything to fall that probably was not on the verge of falling anyway." Earl Schwartz, chief of the Los Angeles City Building and Safety Department's Earthquake Safety Division, assured homeowners that most houses in the Los Angeles area are earthquake resistant, but he warned that chimneys could present a problem: "Chimneys that aren't properly reinforced or anchored can come down. In some cases, it might be advisable to reduce chimney height." Schwartz also recommended installing cabinet latches that will not shake open and securing heavy furniture to the wall. Tips on what to do during a quake were offered by Mike Regan, Los Angeles Civil Defense Coordinator: "Get into a doorway or under a desk if inside; if outside, stay in the car or walk to an open space." Other tips included keeping a flashlight, radio, and family disaster plan in good working order. West Los Angeles Animal Shelter Supervisor George Weissman suggested that residents be aware of altered behavior in their pets. Just before a quake, said Weissman, "a cat might show you more attention than it usually does." An educational psychologist advised parents to explain the quake to children even if only in very simple terms. A brief article that accompanied Kenney's feature announced the renewed availability of the Fil Drukey series on individual preparedness for an earthquake. The guide, entitled "Common Sense and Earthquake Survival," was offered through the *Outlook* for $1.50.

In his column in the *Valley News*, Mike Wyma noted that many Californians were under the care of analysts and therapists for such disorders as phobias about driving, flying, using elevators, sleeping, talking, and even eating. "Given this," he wrote, "it seems odd that so few of us are frightened of earthquakes, at least before they happen." Wyma also wrote that the New Year's Day quake would serve to speed up the pace of work toward "saving as many lives as possible in the event of a killer quake" as well as the pace of scientific work toward accurate earthquake prediction.

The foregoing excerpts describe the earthquake as it was presented to the newspaper-reading public during the days and weeks after it occurred. A briefer account by Waverly J. Person appeared a few months later, with the magnitude upgraded, in the regular bimonthly summary of earthquakes in the U.S. Geological Survey's *Earthquake Information Bulletin*.[1] We present that summary in full.

> The State of California experienced a number of earthquakes during the first 2 months of the year. The first earthquake to cause minor damage occurred on January 1 at 3:15 p.m., PST, alarming some of the fans at the Rose Bowl game in Pasadena. The magnitude 5.0 earthquake was centered about 25 kilometers southwest of Santa Monica in the Santa Monica Bay. Minor damage on the Modified Mercalli Intensity Scale (MM) was reported at Canoga Park, El Segundo, Granada Hills, Hawthorne, Los Angeles, La Verne, La Mirada, Northridge, Studio City, Sherman Oaks and Woodland Hills. The quake was felt strongly over a wide area of the southern part of the State including Kern, Kings, Orange, Riverside, Santa Barbara, San Bernardino, San Diego, and Ventura counties. A number of aftershocks followed; the largest was a magnitude 3.9 at 3:29 p.m., 15 minutes after the main shock. The aftershock was felt strongly in the area, but no additional damage was reported.

The Survey

An essential feature in the design of our research was to be prepared for contingencies that might substantially affect public response to the earthquake threat. Interview schedules were prepared, pretested, and printed in sufficient numbers, and sampling plans were established so that telephone interviewing could begin within a few days after any one of five contingencies occurred. One of the contingencies was the occurrence of a moderate but nondestructive earthquake, strong enough to occasion more than perfunctory reporting in the media and felt throughout Los Angeles County. The New Year's Day earthquake qualified unambiguously under the criteria we had established.

New Year's Day fell on Monday, and was, of course, a holiday. The decision to proceed with the survey was made by telephone among the investigators that afternoon and evening, and the machinery was set in motion Tuesday morning. A few changes were made in the schedule to fit the circumstances, and all copies were corrected by hand within the three days following. Interviewing by telephone began on Monday, January 8, and was completed by January 26; it was essential to complete the interviewing expeditiously, before the memory and effects of the nondisastrous quake faded. A total of 519 interviews were completed, all with people who had not been previously interviewed.

Design of the interview was guided by two broad questions: How was the history of nearly three years of earthquake alerts reflected in reactions to this moderate quake? And how was subsequent attention to the continuing earthquake threat affected by the unpredicted occurrence of the quake?

The Earthquake as Experience

Out of the sample of 509 respondents, 71 percent had felt the earthquake, another 27 percent had heard about it afterward, and 2 percent still did not know there had been an earthquake at the time of the interview. These last ten respondents were dropped from further questioning, except for questions concerning demographic characteristics. Different sequences of questions were addressed to respondents who had felt the quake than were addressed to respondents who had not felt it but who learned about it later. Respondents who felt the quake were asked next:

Thinking back to your experiences in that earthquake, which of the following best describes your first feelings? Would you say you were: Very frightened and upset, Somewhat frightened and upset, Not very frightened and upset, Not at all frightened and upset, or Did you enjoy the experience?

The distribution of responses (table 38) is skewed, with about two-thirds expressing little or no fear at the time of the quake. About one person in twelve acknowledged having been very frightened.

For comparative purposes we have included two other sets of figures. The first is comprised of the responses to a question about feelings during past earthquakes, asked of all respondents in the February 1977 basic field survey who said that they had experienced one or more earthquakes. The second set is the responses of the 509 people in the present sample to the question asked later in the interview:

Which of the following best describes your own feelings about the possibility of experiencing a damaging earthquake—that is, one strong enough to destroy buildings and cost lives—in the near future?

TABLE 38

FEAR OF EARTHQUAKES

Extent of fear[a]	New Year's Day quake[b] %	Previous earth- quakes[c] %	Future damaging quake[d] %
Very frightened	8.7	32.0	28.3
Somewhat frightened	25.3	26.8	35.9
Not very frightened	25.1	19.8	16.9
Not at all frightened	35.4	17.9	18.1
Enjoyed the experience	5.5	2.7	—
Don't know or no answer	0	.8	.8
Total	100.0	100.0	100.0
Total number	367	1,333	509

[a]Answers to the question about the New Year's Day quake included the phrase "and upset."

[b]This column includes respondents who personally felt the quake.

[c]This column includes all respondents in the 1977 basic field survey who had experienced any earthquakes.

[d]This column includes all respondents in the current survey who felt or knew about the New Year's Day earthquake. Enjoyment was not included as an optional response to the prospect of a future damaging earthquake.

The comparison underlines the conclusion that the New Year's Day quake was taken very much in stride and that it did not evoke the fear that the idea of an earthquake as a disastrous event stirs in most people.[2]

To obtain further indications of whether the earthquake was experienced as an extraordinary event or as a minor ripple in the round of life, we asked whether the respondents who had felt the earthquake had attempted to contact anyone personally about the earthquake and whether they had turned on a television or radio or had paid special attention in order to hear news about the quake. Only one person in eight had made an effort to contact someone either for information or because of concern for the other person's welfare. However, nearly half of the respondents who had felt the earthquake had had their curiosity or concern aroused sufficiently to turn on a television or radio or to pay closer attention to news about the earthquake. Even though relatively few people had made special efforts to contact friends, relatives, and associates about the quake, the majority of people who had not personally felt the tremor had first learned about it through personal contact rather than from the media, and they had learned of it within six hours of the event.

One indication of interest is the accuracy with which people identified the magnitude of the tremor. More than half (57.4 percent) of the 509 people correctly identified the magnitude as between 4.0 and 4.9. Of the remainder, 24.3 percent underestimated the magnitude, as compared with 10.2 percent who overestimated it. There was very little tendency to sensationalize the event.

Finally, five people told interviewers their homes had been damaged, and six reported having suffered damage to personal property.

WAS THE EARTHQUAKE PREDICTED?

When asked whether the quake was one that had been predicted, 56 percent denied knowing of any predictions. But twenty-nine people, or 5.7 percent, thought it was "most likely one that was predicted." We shall not burden the reader with the detailed follow-up questions we posed to these twenty-nine. In brief, their ideas were mostly vague, elaborated with the help of folk wisdom and gleaned disproportionately from radio and magazines. They thought the forecast had been issued within the past six months by a scientist or a seer.

Earlier (in chapter ten) we noted a widespread tendency for people to translate scientific communications and prophecies by seers into personal comprehension. Such folk signs as unusual animal behavior and one's own strong premonitions commanded high credibility. We therefore asked the following question:

> Just before this recent quake, did you have any idea that an earthquake was about to happen? (If "yes":)
> What gave you this idea?

About one person in twelve claimed to have had an idea that an earthquake was about to happen. Although this number is small, it is larger than the number who thought the quake had been predicted. No one mentioned scientific announcements as the grounds for their anticipation of the quake. But twenty-two of the forty-two people credited personal intuition—either their own or that of a close friend or relative. Another seven mentioned unusual animal behavior. The very personal nature of these responses is indicated by the fact that only two people gave credit to forecasts by psychics or seers and only four to news media.

Perhaps the most interesting observation comes from further examination of the 102 respondents who said the earthquake "most likely wasn't one that was predicted" and the 93 who were "not sure." They were all asked,

> Why do you think this (may not be) (isn't) the earthquake that was predicted?

Answers were recorded verbatim and were classified into the major categories in table 39. The answers reveal unstated assumptions about the prediction process. Just over one half of our respondents felt that an essential ingredient in the prediction process had been omitted. The largest segment assumed that the medium- to long-term prediction would be followed by a short-term warning when the earthquake was imminent. Another substantial segment assumed that the vague or incomplete near predictions and forecasts would be followed by more precise notices, presumably before the quake occurred. The widespread

TABLE 39

WHY THE NEW YEAR'S DAY EARTHQUAKE WAS NOT
ONE THAT WAS PREDICTED

Reason	Number		Percent: both reasons
	First reason	Second reason	
No advance warning given	68	0	34.9
Magnitude not as predicted	56	3	30.3
Location not as predicted	6	1	3.6
Scientists not specific	33	2	17.9
Other	8	0	4.1
Don't know and no answer	24	0	12.3
Total	195	6	103.1

interpretation of the uplift announcement and other notices as
preliminary alerts would help to explain why few people made
serious preparations for an earthquake and why awareness of the
uplift and predictive announcements in general is so weakly related to both action and concern.

Where did people get this idea? No explicit assurances about
imminent warnings had appeared in the media, and scientists
would not give such assurances. Some of the better informed may
have taken the successful use of short-term warnings in China as
the prototype for American prediction. But we have three more
generally applicable explanations to suggest.

First, we are reminded of the alarm-and-reassurance pattern
practiced by the media (chapter two). People are repeatedly told
that a great disaster will befall southern California but that they
should "sit tight" and not get upset. The message that something
terrible will happen but that there is no need to do anything
drastic right away seems to imply the promise that people will be
told when the time for action is at hand. Second, the long- or
medium-term earthquake warning is quite unsatisfying because it
is not feasible to sustain disruption of normal routines for extended periods of time. If warnings are only meaningful when the

nature of suitable protective responses is clear and those reponses are feasible, they can be made meaningful by assuming that the real warning will be forthcoming later, at a time when action is indicated and feasible. Third, we have found that most people expect government officials to exercise leadership in all aspects of earthquake preparedness and emergency response, including the issuance of predictions and warnings. The predictions and warnings that people remembered had all been seen as the work of scientists or prophets. Many people may assume that when the critical moment approaches, major government officials—line rather than staff—will take charge.

The Earthquake as Omen

In chapter twelve we asked what meanings people gave to the sinking of parts of the southern California uplift, to a wave of microtremors in the uplifted zone, and to a damaging earthquake in nearby Santa Barbara. A substantial minority had heard these events discussed as possible clues to the imminence of a destructive earthquake in Los Angeles. Such discussions seemed even more likely for the New Year's Day quake. We used a similar but elaborated procedure with the following sequence of questions:

> People are saying different things about this recent quake. Have you heard anyone say: "Now that we've had an earthquake recently, there probably *won't* be a big one for quite a while." (Yes or No)
> Do you remember any particular people who were saying this?
> What do *you* think about this statement? Do you think: It is true; It might be true, but you're not sure; or It is false?

> Have you heard anyone say that this recent earthquake *could be* a sign that a bigger one is coming soon? (Yes or No)
> Do you remember any particular people who were saying this?
> What do *you* think about this statement? Do you . . .

> Do you remember anyone saying that the recent earthquake *doesn't* make any difference in whether there will be a big earthquake soon?
> Do you remember any particular people who were saying this?
> What do *you* think about this statement? Do you . . .

Have you heard anyone say that this earthquake was an aftershock of
the 1971 San Fernando earthquake?
Do you remember any particular people who were saying this?
What do *you* think about this statement? Do you . . .

So few people had heard or believed the aftershock interpretation
that we have dropped it from further analysis. About 42 percent
had heard one or more of the other three interpretations, and most
of them had heard only one. With 36 percent exposure, the precursor view was more widely diffused than were all the others combined. The opinion that an interpretation is *definitely* true ranged
from 14 percent for deferral (there won't be a big one soon) to 26
percent for the precursor and no-difference interpretations among
people who had heard the respective versions. Many more people
in each instance acknowledged that the interpretation *might* be
true. Combining answers, about 76 percent each accorded some
credibility to the precursor and no-difference interpretations. The
neutralization view is much less credible. Altogether, 32 percent
of our entire sample had heard and had given at least conditional
credence to one or more of these three interpretations. For 27.5
percent the precursor interpretation had been heard and was seen
as credible, compared to only 5.5 percent for the next most popular version.

Combining "it is true" and "it might be true" answers in table
40 permits us to relate credence to combinations actually heard.
Examining the table against the background of previous analysis
leads us to three general conclusions. First, people are discriminating in what they will and will not believe. Among 171
people who were exposed to just one of the three interpretations,
those who had heard that a large earthquake was coming soon and
those who had heard that the New Year's Day quake made no
difference were disposed to accord conditional credibility to what
they had heard. But those who had heard that the smaller quake
neutralized the threat of a larger one were inclined to disbelieve
what they had heard. Of the 161 people who had heard both that
a big earthquake was coming soon and that there would not be an
earthquake soon, none credited the latter interpretation to the
exclusion of the former.

Second, exposure to contradictory communications does not
lead to increased skepticism about all communications. The ap-

TABLE 40

CREDIBILITY BY EXPOSURE TO INTERPRETATIONS OF THE NEW YEAR'S DAY EARTHQUAKE

Interpretations given credibility	Interpretations heard						
	No big quake soon %	Bigger quake soon %	Makes no difference %	No big/ bigger soon %	No big/ no difference %	Bigger soon/no difference %	All three %
None	68.7	21.7	16.7	12.5	(1)	9.5	(1)
No big quake soon	31.3			0	0		0
Bigger quake soon		78.3		31.3		14.3	0
Makes no difference			83.3		0	28.6	(1)
No big quake soon and bigger quake soon				56.2			0
No big quake soon and makes no difference					0		(1)
Bigger quake soon and makes no difference						47.6	0
All three							(1)
Total	100.0	100.0	100.0	100.0	(1)	100.0	(4)
Total number	16	143	12	16	1	21	4

Only inapplicable cells have been left blank.

parent effect is in the opposite direction, although it is not statistically significant. While 25.7 percent of the 171 people who had heard only one of the interpretations rejected what they had heard, only 14.3 percent of the 42 people who had heard two or more interpretations rejected all of them. This observation has imporant bearing on communication policy. The fear is often expressed by public officials and scientists that if members of the public are exposed to contradictory interpretations of events, many will respond with a skeptical rejection of all interpretations. This fear would plainly not have been justified in this instance.

Third, a very frequent response by people exposed to contradictory interpretations is to conclude that both should be regarded as potentially true. Numbers are too small for comparisons, but it can be observed that viewing two contending interpretations as both potentially true is as frequent, if not more frequent, as accepting one interpretation and rejecting the other, and it is far more frequent than rejecting both. Thus, presenting people with contending interpretations makes a net contribution to open-mindedness rather than to skepticism.

These findings are consistent with those reported in chapter twelve for the sinking of the uplift, the microquake swarm, and the Santa Barbara earthquake.

From 65 to 78 percent of the people who remembered having heard the various interpretations remembered the source of their information. Their answers pointed to another important serendipitous finding. The key question is whether people got the ideas and information they used in trying to make this earthquake experience meaningful from relatively authoritative sources or from rumor. In our interviews with comparable samples of Los Angeles County residents during the preceding two years, the media—television, radio, and newspaper—were consistently given as the principal sources of information about future earthquake prospects. We asked the people in our New Year's Day earthquake sample whether they had heard of the southern California uplift and, if so, what their chief source of information about it had been. True to the pattern in our previous interviews, 88 percent named the media or magazines and books as their chief sources. Only 7.5 percent named friends, relatives, or coworkers. But when we asked the respondents from where they had heard interpretations of the New Year's Day earthquake, the answers were quite different (table 41).

On the average, fewer than 10 percent named the media, books and magazines, or an authoritative source. Even with a sizable group unable to remember the source, over two-thirds named lay people as their source. The most frequent answers were friends and coworkers. The significance of the small quake for the future had been the topic of widespread discussion at work and among friends. Without guidance from authoritative sources relayed through the media, people turned to friends and coworkers for their interpretations.

Consistent with these findings, the investigators personally heard rumors about supposed earthquake forecasts during the month of January. Once again, we find dramatic support for the well-established hypothesis that rumor flourishes when more dependable sources of information ignore public concerns.[3] Though scientists and responsible media editors may have wished to discourage fruitless discussion, their failure to devote sufficient attention to a widespread public concern had the undesired effect

TABLE 41

SOURCE OF INFORMATION ABOUT SOUTHERN CALIFORNIA
UPLIFT AND THE NEW YEAR'S DAY EARTHQUAKE

		Interpretations of the New Year's Day earthquake		
Information source	Chief source concerning uplift %	No bigger quake soon %	Big quake coming soon %	Makes no difference %
Media, publications, authorities	87.7	13.5	5.3	8.2
Laypeople	7.5	62.2	71.0	69.8
Don't know, other	4.8	24.3	23.7	22.0
Total	100.0	100.0	100.0	100.0
Total number	294	37	182	38

of turning people's attention away from authoritative sources and toward unfounded rumor.

Awareness of the Uplift

If the earthquake was followed by a wave of rumor about its significance for the future, interest in the southern California uplift might have been stimulated, and awareness might have been increased. The standard question sequence on awareness of the uplift did not produce answers very different from those recorded in our last regular interview wave, a month and a half earlier. However, when we asked how seriously people took the uplift as an earthquake sign, the results were mildly ambiguous. Leaving out respondents who had not heard of the uplift or who said definitely that scientists do not view the uplift as an earthquake sign, there was a significant decrease, from 26 to 16.7 percent, in the number of respondents who said that they personally take the uplift *quite seriously* as a sign of a coming earthquake.[4] But the number who said that they take it *fairly seriously* did not change.

We then asked the same people two further questions:

Do you think the recent earthquake was the one some people expected on the basis of the Palmdale bulge?

Now that we've had this recent earthquake, would you say that: The danger from the bulge is over, or the bulge will cause more earthquakes?

Only 8.5 percent of all respondents who appreciated the possible significance of the uplift associated it even tentatively with the New Year's Day earthquake. Most respondents categorically rejected any association. Half rejected categorically the conclusion that the danger of earthquakes from the uplift is over as a result of the New Year's Day earthquake, but 40 percent were unwilling to take a position on the second question. Close to 10 percent entertained the possibility that the danger from the uplift had been relieved by the small quake.

In summary, the New Year's Day quake had no apparent effect on awareness of the uplift or on its general credibility as an earthquake sign. However, significantly fewer people are willing

to assign it *high* credibility. The quake was not generally associated in popular thinking with the uplift, but an unusually
large number of people were unwilling to state a position on the
possibility of a connection. With the epicenter placed in Santa
Monica Bay, one might assume that any connection with the
uplift could have been easily dismissed. A trend toward uncertainty is suggested by both the more reserved attitude toward the
uplift as an earthquake precursor and the widespread indecisiveness about the relationship between the uplift and this moderate
earthquake.

The Predictability of Earthquakes

SCIENTIFIC PREDICTION

Confidence in so recent and untested an idea as
earthquake prediction should be easily affected by relevant personal experiences; people might wonder why the New Year's Day
quake was not predicted. In fact, faith in current scientific prediction capability, which had risen since early 1977, did not change
significantly, but faith in eventual prediction changed in a complex fashion. Significantly fewer people (the percentage dropped
from 53.3 to 44.4 percent) said they expected scientists eventually
to predict earthquakes *quite accurately*.[5] But there was no increase
in the 10 percent who doubted that scientists would ever predict
earthquakes accurately. The compensating increase was among
the "don't know" and "somewhat accurately" responses. As with
interpretation of the uplift, the shift was toward uncertainty rather
than disbelief.

If the idea and practice of earthquake prediction were well
institutionalized, one would have expected faith in current predictive capability to drop and faith in eventual prediction to be
more impervious to a single disappointing experience. However,
we remember that faith in eventual prediction was almost consensual before the quake. A consensus view usually promotes acquiescence from many people who have given the subject little
thought and have not made up their minds independently. These
are the people who are most likely to have second thoughts when
events seem to challenge the consensual belief.

IS INFORMATION BEING WITHHELD?

With over half the respondents expressing the belief that scientists can already predict earthquakes either somewhat or quite accurately and holding to that conviction after an unpredicted quake, one might plausibly expect to find widespread suspicion that information was being withheld from the public. The question used in previous surveys was modified to specify the period before the earthquake:

> Before this recent quake, do you think that scientists and public officials were giving all the information they had on earthquake predictions, or were they holding back information?

Again, the evidence is surprising. The proportion of respondents who said they believe that both scientists and officials were telling all that they knew before the earthquake *increased* substantially, from 36 to 46 percent.[6] The decrease in the proportion who believe that either or both scientists and officials were withholding information was even greater, with the balancing change consisting of an increase in the number of "don't know" responses.

A shift in this direction is difficult to understand. Possibly, the grounds for suspicion were aired and found wanting during informal postquake discussion, although how this could have happened is not clear. We cannot rule out the possibility that the increased fear and realism evoked by the quake created enough of a crisis to foster some reduction in divisive mistrust for the sake of crisis unification. Unfortunately, we were not able to include the sequence on altruism in this survey. It would have given us a second set of evidence with which to test the inference that a slight "therapeutic community" effect had taken place.[7]

FOLK SIGNS

The principal rival grounds to science for anticipating an earthquake are the folk signs, of which unusual animal behavior, earthquake weather, and personal premonition are the major examples. If people felt they had personally apprehended the signs that an earthquake was coming when scientists had not done so, the weakened faith in the long-term prospects for scientific earthquake prediction might be part of a shift toward greater reliance on folk signs. If people were convinced, however, that neither folk signs nor science foretold the recent earthquake, the effect might be decreased faith in both grounds for prediction.

We already know that a mere 8 percent of our respondents claimed to have had any advance idea that an earthquake was about to happen and that the majority of these people credited their personal intuitions, while a smaller number credited unusual animal behavior. To complement these open-ended items, we asked the following pair of questions, the first of which is the standard item used in four of the five previous surveys:

> As I read each of the following, please tell me if *you* think people can use any of the following signs in their daily lives to tell when an earthquake might be coming: Unusual animal behavior; unusual weather; premonitions, instincts, or ESP; unusual aches or pains; any other signs?

> Prior to this recent quake, did *you personally* see or feel any of the following signs which could have signified that an earthquake might be coming? (same list as above)

From table 42 we see that the majority of people expressed belief in unusual animal behavior as an earthquake sign and that substantial minorities believe in premonitions and earthquake weather. But relatively few people claimed to have perceived these signs personally. It is clear that belief in folk signs, like faith in scientific capability, does not depend on their successful use in every instance of an earthquake.

Unfortunately, it is very easy for people to "recognize" retrospectively that they had observed crucial folk signs before the earthquake, even though they did not actually anticipate the quake. As a partial check on this practice, we have included in table 42 the frequencies with which premonitions and animal behavior were mentioned by people who told us that they had had an idea that an earthquake was about to happen. One or two people may have mentioned earthquake weather or unusual aches and pains, but the numbers were too few for separate coding. Nearly four-fifths of the unusual animal behavior reports were retrospective, as were nearly all of the references to earthquake weather. However, the number of spontaneous references to pre-

TABLE 42

SIGNS IN DAILY LIFE FOR PREDICTING EARTHQUAKES:
BELIEF AND PERCEPTION

Folk sign	Percent who believe in the sign	Percent who perceived the sign before the earthquake	Percent who gave as reason for anticipating
Unusual animal behavior	68.4	6.5	1.4
Earthquake weather	43.4	7.5	—
Premonition, instinct, ESP	43.8	5.3	4.3
Unusual aches or pains	8.8	1.2	—
Other signs	2.9	.8	—
Base for percentages	509	509	509

monitions is rather close to the number given in answer to direct questioning. A sympathetic interpretation would be that several people did genuinely experience premonitions and therefore did anticipate the earthquake. A skeptical interpretation would be that people have premonitions of foreboding all the time. But premonitions are personal enough that people know whether they have had them or not, whereas it is easier to remember examples of strange animal behavior and unspecified weather conditions after the fact.

Separately, we repeated the questions on generalized belief in folk signs from earlier surveys. Our finding is that belief in the various folk signs was not significantly affected by the earthquake, even though the overwhelming majority of believers failed to observe the folk signs prospectively or retrospectively. In this respect, folk signs and current scientific prediction capability are alike in remaining unaffected by failure to anticipate the earthquake. Only the uncertainty of quite accurate eventual prediction by scientific methods has been brought into question as a consequence of reflection on this unpredicted earthquake.

Fear, Concern, and Expectation

In the preceding chapter we reported that expressed fear and concern over the prospect of an earthquake declined in the first half of 1977 and remained fairly stable thereafter but that the disposition to flee the anticipated site of an earthquake increased. If we compare responses soon after the earthquake with responses just a few weeks earlier, we observe that expressions of fear in answer to each of the three questions increased (table 43). Similarly, the sense of recently increased concern about a damaging earthquake's striking southern California showed a further increase. Each of the shifts is highly significant.[8]

When we compare New Year's Day quake responses with responses given nearly two years earlier, the results are more complicated. The moderate earthquake apparently pushed fear and concern back up to the unusual level that it reached directly after the 1976 bombardment of sensational warnings and accounts of destructive quakes around the world. While awareness of recently increased concern rose also, it remained significantly below 1977 levels. Perhaps because the earthquake was over so quickly and seemed so benign, some people failed to realize its effects on their attitudes.

Disposition to get away from the earthquake site shows still a third pattern. The two-year trend away from viewing a potential damaging earthquake as a routine event was accelerated by the New Year's Day quake. One effect of that quake may have been to intensify the increasingly realistic assessment of earthquakes. The fact that the negative correlation between realism and fear that we observed earlier was not observed here may indicate that the current resurgence of fear was of too short a duration to cause unrealistic denial.

If fear was rearoused by the earthquake, was it because more people now expected an earthquake soon? In fact, the numbers who said there definitely or probably will *not* be a damaging earthquake within the next year appear to have increased, from 44.7 to 52.7 percent.[9] Especially since many more people credited the quake-as-precursor interpretation than credited the opposite interpretation, this observation could readily be seen as evidence of denial.

TABLE 43

EARTHQUAKE FEAR AND CONCERN AT THREE PERIODS OF TIME

Type of fear or concern	February 1977 %	Nov/Dec. 1978 %	January 1978 %
Feelings about experiencing a damaging earthquake:			
Very frightened	27.3	20.6	28.3
Somewhat frightened	35.4	30.7	35.9
Don't know	.4	0	.8
Not very frightened	22.5	25.6	16.9
Not at all frightened	14.4	23.1	18.1
Total	100.0	100.0	100.0
Possibility of damaging earthquake in near future:			
Very worried	14.6	6.4	13.2
Somewhat worried	34.8	32.7	36.9
Don't know	.3	.5	.4
Hardly worried	24.3	27.8	26.1
Not worried at all	26.0	32.6	23.4
Total	100.0	100.0	100.0
If damaging earthquake certain, would try to:			
Get far away as possible	29.0	33.8	44.8
Don't know	2.4	2.7	2.1
Find safe place near earthquake	33.6	33.3	27.9
Go on as usual	34.3	29.5	24.0
Be where earthquake would occur	.7	.7	1.2
Total	100.0	100.0	100.0
In past year, concern about damaging earthquake striking southern California has:			
Increased	30.2	16.2	23.2
Remained about the same	65.6	75.8	72.9
Don't know	0	0	0
Decreased	4.2	8.0	3.9
Total	100.0	100.0	100.0
Total number	1,450	550	509

With the apparent contradictions and unexpected nature of these findings, interpretation is risky. However, we find some support for a judgment we made much earlier in the analysis, that reported levels of fear do not respond to the imminence of the quake but rather to the cognitive and affective image of the quake.[10] Experiencing a quake of near-miss intensity stimulates the imagination and enhances comprehension of the possible dimensions of a really damaging quake. But while *personal* fearfulness makes danger seem just around the corner, *situational* increases in fear need not have this effect.

As one final bit of evidence concerning fear, we included our usual question in the interview's "demographics" section on the likelihood of the respondent's moving away from his or her present community within the next five years. The disposition to move was remarkably stable throughout the study period, and the New Year's Day earthquake did not destabilize it.

Earthquake-Preparedness Action

GOVERNMENT ACTION

The heightened fear induced by the earthquake could have moved people to demand renewed hazard-mitigation efforts from government officials. Or the uncertainties we observed after the quake might have attenuated the prevailing strong confidence in the importance of hazard-mitigating measures. Because of the evidence on fear and realism, it seems less likely that the earthquake as a near miss would have lulled people into thinking preparedness was less important than before.

Between late 1978 and early 1979, there was quite a substantial drop (from 64 percent to 44.6 percent) in the proportion of respondents who said that it is very important to spend large amounts of money on enforcement of building safety codes and building repairs. The reduction from 42.9 to 33.8 percent who said that spending on loans to rebuild or reinforce unsafe structures before an earthquake is very important was less substantial but still significant.[11] It is not clear whether support for the two less popular measures involving prediction also declined.

The finding here resembles the difference between faith in current and in eventual scientific earthquake-prediction capability: as views approach consensus, they are more susceptible to disaffection on the basis of a disruptive event. Those who endorsed prediction studies were already a selected group, and their convictions were not likely to have been shaken by an event of less than crisis proportions. But the bandwagon effect seen in the earlier strong support for building-code enforcement and government loans as earthquake-mitigation measures was undermined in some fashion by the earthquake. Paralleling both faith in eventual scientific prediction and confidence in the significance of the uplift as an earthquake precursor, the shift was toward qualifiedly positive rather than negative answers. Uncertainty again seems to be the key.

Personal and Household Preparedness

Under some conditions the combination of rearoused fear and heightened realism could reinforce tendencies toward vigilance. On January 18, the editors of the *Los Angeles Herald Examiner* reported that they had been flooded with mail from people wanting to know what they should do when an earthquake strikes. The balance of the editorial outlined the steps recommended by the U.S. Geological Survey; these steps are comparable to those included in our standard inventory of preparedness measures. Was this quake indeed the spur to bring personal and household preparedness up to levels more acceptable than those that had prevailed throughout most of our study period?

In order to sharpen the focus on the effect of the New Year's Day earthquake, we revised the wording of the main question and of the responses from which respondents were to choose.

> I'm going to read you a list of preparation suggestions that have been made by various agencies and groups who are concerned with earthquake preparedness. As I read each of the following, please tell me if you *had done* any of these things in preparation before the recent earthquake, or whether you *have done* these things *since* the recent earthquake and in preparation for a future earthquake, or for some other reasons.

Respondents were asked to choose among the following answers: before the earthquake, done in preparation for a future earthquake;

before the earthquake, but done for other reasons; since the earthquake, in preparation for a future earthquake; since the earthquake, but for other reasons; have no idea; have no plan to do so. In order not to complicate the choices unmanageably, we omitted the explicit opportunity to say that measures not taken were still planned.

So few people reported having taken any of the measures since the earthquake that there is little value in presenting detailed figures. The most frequently reported measures taken since the earthquake in preparation for a future earthquake were instructing children what to do in an earthquake (11), making residential family emergency plans (9), and making plans for a family reunion after a quake (8). No one bought earthquake insurance, and only one person was stirred enough to even inquire about it. When measures taken for all reasons are compared with preparedness levels in late 1978, only three show significant changes, and these are not the same measures people told us they were moved to take because of the earthquake. The number of respondents who reported having a working flashlight jumped from 75.2 to 85.9 percent; the number having a working battery radio went from 58.9 to 69.2 percent; and the number having a first-aid kit went from 61.4 to 68.2 percent.[12] Flashlights and radios might have been received as Christmas gifts, but this is hardly likely for first-aid kits, and no comparable increase was reported in January 1978.

Two processes may have contributed to these findings. First, some of the people who instructed their children in survival techniques in the wake of this earthquake may also have done so earlier and thus would not have raised the frequencies for our inventory; the new efforts would still have been a real contribution to earthquake preparedness. Second, items such as flashlights, radios, and first-aid kits may have been "around the house" without all household members' having been aware of them. If the earthquake had stimulated some stocktaking, some people might have rescued flashlights and radios from drawers and cupboards where these had been half forgotten and realized that the Band-Aids and other medical supplies in the bathroom cabinet constituted a minimal first-aid kit. Other items could not be equally susceptible to discovery in the course of stocktaking. If this interpretation is true, it would signal a genuine increment of preparedness triggered by the earthquake. Even though these items had not been newly acquired, by becoming aware of their availability in the household, people were more ready than before to use them in an emergency.

Even if we accept these optimistic interpretations, we are still forced to conclude that the New Year's Day quake had very little effect on personal and household preparedness in general. The quake affected how people felt about a more serious earthquake and changed their feelings about what to do if an earthquake were imminent. While the fear may have been translated into some limited stocktaking concerning preparedness, it did not move people who had not done so before to take hazard-mitigating measures in preparation for an earthquake.

Conclusions

Although the New Year's Day earthquake was taken very much in stride and was not experienced with as much fear as people ascribe to past earthquake experiences or express over the prospect of a future damaging earthquake, it aroused considerable interest. Its possible significance in relation to the anticipation of a more destructive quake in the near future was the topic of much discussion and rumor. Also, it had an unsettling effect on several fairly well-established attitudes about earthquake matters. The quake apparently undermined certainty about the significance of the southern California uplift as an earthquake precursor, about the eventual accuracy with which scientists will be able to predict earthquakes, and about the value of the most popular earthquake hazard-mitigation measures by government agencies. Fear of a future destructive quake was intensified, as was the disposition to see a damaging earthquake as a crisis event, even though confidence that the predicted destructive earthquake would come within a year declined.

Altogether, the evidence fairly comprehensively refutes the *lull* hypothesis, which is that an earthquake of near-miss intensity lulls people into a false sense of security. At most, the effect on personal and household preparedness was limited to some stocktaking, with trivial numbers of people reassessing family plans for coping with an earthquake. An *unsettling* effect rather than either a lulling or heightened-vigilance effect seems to describe most comprehensively the consequences of the New Year's Day earthquake. The unpredicted near miss awakened many people to the realization that a severe earthquake could not be treated as a normal occurrence and that accepted views about earthquake prediction and mitigation were questionable. Since the quake was not a fearsome experience for most people, the increased fear of future quakes was probably an indirect effect, brought on by the reflection and uncertainty provoked by the earthquake.

Although we cannot rule out alternative interpretations, the data suggest the possibility that even the weak crisis atmosphere provoked by this earthquake may have produced some closing of ranks, some subjective movement in the direction of community solidarity. The significant reduction in the suspicion that scientists and officials were withholding predictive information before the earthquake is a surprising finding, susceptible to the above interpretation. Since the quake was overwhelmingly recognized as not having been predicted, and while there was no reduction in the belief in current earthquake-prediction capability, there is justification for treating incipient solidarity as one plausible but unconfirmed interpretation of the data.

In the course of the analysis, at least four other findings emerged, mostly lending confirmation to findings already derived from other evidence in the course of this investigation. First, the tendency to personalize understanding was again noted. Although the total numbers were small, more people claimed to have had a personal idea that the earthquake was coming before it happened than claimed that the quake had been predicted. Second, there was widespread public concern over the meaning of the quake in relation to the prospect of future earthquakes in southern California. In the absence of authoritative attention to this question in the media, people turned to rumor as the prime source for ideas to be used to interpret the earthquake. Third, exposure to contradictory interpretations of the earthquake's meaning did not foster skepticism toward all interpretations and may actually have augmented the disposition to treat alternative interpretations with open-mindedness.

Finally, a new observation of great importance emerged unexpectedly in the course of the analysis. When people explained why they did not feel that this was an earthquake that had been predicted, it became clear that many, if not most, people were implicitly treating the near predictions, forecasts, and cautions they remembered as preliminary announcements. They assumed that these announcements were intended to alert them to listen for short-term warnings that would be forthcoming when the time for action was at hand. This assumption would explain much present inaction. And since scientists and government officials do not generally make any such assumption, this finding exposes an important realm of miscommunication and misunderstanding between authorities and the public.

CHAPTER FIFTEEN

Patterns of Change

The objectives of Part Five are to ascertain the extent and describe the nature of change and stability in response to a sustained near prediction of an earthquake and to explain change and stability on the basis of either specific events and their treatment by the media or the unfolding effects of waiting for disaster. In this chapter we shall review and round out the analysis.

Extent and Nature of Stability and Change

STABILITY

In general, stability rather than change is more characteristic of the responses we have measured. Several crucial types of response have remained without significant change throughout the nearly two years covered by our surveys. For responses that have changed, the change has often not been dramatic. When the evidence of change is unambiguous, the change most often occurred between early and mid-1977, with chiefly random fluctuations thereafter. However, some of the responses that had exhibited greatest stability for twenty-two months suddenly changed in the unsettling aftermath of the moderate and unpredicted earthquake of New Year's Day 1979.

The relative credibility given scientific and nonscientific forecasts and warnings and, after adjustment for the onetime Minturn forecast, the relative awareness of scientific and nonscientific forecasts and near predictions were fairly constant throughout the study period. The level of fatalism about earthquake damage was quite stable. High levels of confidence in the eventual achievement of accurate scientific earthquake prediction and endorsement of government spending to mitigate earthquake hazard changed little during the study period, although both declined under the unsettling impact of the New Year's Day earthquake. The suspicion that scientists and public officials were withholding information concerning predictions also remained at a steady level over the twenty-two months, but it shifted surprisingly toward lessened suspicion after the New Year's Day tremor. Although our information is less complete for these variables, desire for news about earthquake topics remained at a high level, and the tendency to interpret smaller earthquakes and other events as clues to the imminence of the anticipated destructive earthquake was recurrent. Salience of earthquake concern was always low, and, after an initial drop, general fear and concern over future earthquakes was relatively unchanged, even after the New Year's Day quake.

There are several plausible reasons for such relative stability of response. First, some of the variables—for example, earthquake fatalism, scientific versus nonscientific orientation, support for government spending, and the suspicion that important information was being withheld from the public—may be surface expressions of underlying attitudes of greater generality. This highly plausible interpretation is weakened, however, by the observation that such stable responses as support for government spending, confidence in the eventual achievement of accurate scientific earthquake prediction, and suspicion that information is being withheld changed significantly after the New Year's Day quake. The events during the preceding twenty-two months were either too mild by comparison with the New Year's tremor to have had an effect on these responses or they were the wrong kinds of stimuli. In any case, it is difficult to believe that attitudes changed by so mild a stimulus as the New Year's quake are primarily expressions of relatively impervious fundamental attitudes.[1]

A second reason for the observed stability might be that significant changes could have taken place during the interval before our first survey, and our monitoring of individual response began after most responses were already restabilized. This interpretation gains in plausibility from the observation that most of the observed changes took place between our first and second surveys. These changes may have been just the final stages of a much more dramatic and comprehensive set of changes during the initial year of the uplift. The fact that some apparently stable responses were significantly modified by the objectively rather inconsequential earthquake of New Year's Day 1979 lends further plausibility to the speculation that a great deal of change might have taken place before our first survey.

Conversely, examination of the absolute levels for many of the variables impels us to think twice about placing too much weight on this kind of speculation. Support for government spending, faith in the ultimate achievement of scientific earthquake prediction, the desire to hear more about earthquakes, and belief in anomalous animal behavior as an earthquake sign could hardly have been higher. Perhaps salience of earthquake concern could have been higher. Variables that changed during the first interval, such as imminent expectation of an earthquake and expressed fear of earthquakes, were at fairly high levels at the time of the first survey. How plausible is it that more than 43 percent at one time expected a damaging earthquake within a year, or that even more people admitted being frightened at the prospect of an earthquake?

Most likely, awareness and response developed gradually during the months after announcement of the uplift, but little turnabout in general awareness and response had occurred by the time of our first survey.

If we accept the evidence of stability at face value, two further explanations can be offered. The fact that most people took a moderate, qualified, or tentative stance on most questions may have reduced dissonance when the anticipated earthquake failed to materialize. The Chinese have repeatedly insisted that false alarms did not undermine public cooperation in their earthquake prediction program because the people were taught to understand prediction as a science that was still being perfected.[2]

Nevertheless, the level of faith in current earthquake-prediction capability in our sample is unrealistically high. Hence, the realistic appreciation of the tentative nature of earthquake prediction may not be sufficiently widespread to insulate public attitudes from the effects of events such as the unpredicted Santa Barbara quake and the Los Angeles New Year's Day quake.

Finally, stability of response may come from the normal anticipation of earthquakes in southern California. If announcement of the uplift, Whitcomb's near prediction, and Minturn's forecast merely added a sense of imminence to the standing anticipation of an earthquake, only moderate attitude changes should follow disconfirmation. Since the scientific announcements have been vague and qualified and the Minturn forecast was enveloped in controversy, this may be the most generally applicable explanation for response stability.

CHANGE

In spite of the relative stability of response, several significant changes did occur during the study period. People remembered fewer announcements and engaged in less discussion, and the sense of imminence declined. The admission of uncertainty about the likelihood of an early earthquake grew steadily. More people doubted the wisdom of releasing uncertain predictions, and many reconsidered the attitude of treating a severe earthquake as a normal event. The unrealistic assessment of present earthquake prediction capability became more general, and people looked more strongly to government to deal with the problems of especially endangered groups. The earthquake threat may have been assimilated into political issues of more widespread concern, such as the plight of the poor. And the New Year's Day earthquake induced a distinctive pattern of changes that in some instances were the extrapolation of earlier changes and in other instances were a reversal.

Events as Causes of Change

Some changes we recorded were expressions of changing circumstances. People remembered fewer near predictions, forecasts, and cautions, because fewer new announcements were made after 1976. In particular, the prominence of pseudoscientific announcements was shown to have been greatly inflated because of concentrated attention to the Minturn forecast. The popular credibility of the pseudoscientific was probably unaffected, as indicated by the stable rate of mention of the prophecy that much of California would break off and fall into the Pacific Ocean in a great earthquake and by the fact that nineteen months after Minturn's forecast was disconfirmed, half of our respondents said they would take seriously a prediction issued by a self-educated amateur.

Obversely, periodic reports of developments related to the southern California uplift in the absence of other new developments gave the uplift an increasingly focal place in public awareness of the earthquake prospect.

We are tempted to explain the reduced faith in the ultimate accuracy of scientific earthquake prediction following the New Year's Day tremor as just such a simple response to the fact that the quake was not predicted. But this interpretation is difficult to sustain when we remember that faith in *current* prediction capability, which realistically ought to be more responsive to the occurrence of an unpredicted earthquake than faith in eventual capability, remained stable. The fact that a more severe earthquake accompanied by both destruction and casualties in nearby Santa Barbara had no such apparent effect also calls into question the simple correspondence interpretation. Efforts to explain other changes in this simple fashion meet a similar fate. Only changes in levels and kinds of awareness appear to be susceptible to such explanations.

Media Coverage and Earthquake Response

A stronger case can be made for the effects of changing levels of media coverage and informal community discussion of earthquake topics on expectation, concern, and realism. Not only did earthquake expectation, recently aroused concern, and realism about earthquake prediction change consistently with a general change in levels of media coverage and reported discussion, but the changes were more pronounced among respondents who perceived declines in media coverage and informal discussion.[3] The findings here are by no means definitive, but they are sufficiently suggestive to warrant further investigation in later research.

In figure 55 we have graphed the trends in three key variables against the changing newspaper coverage of earthquake events,

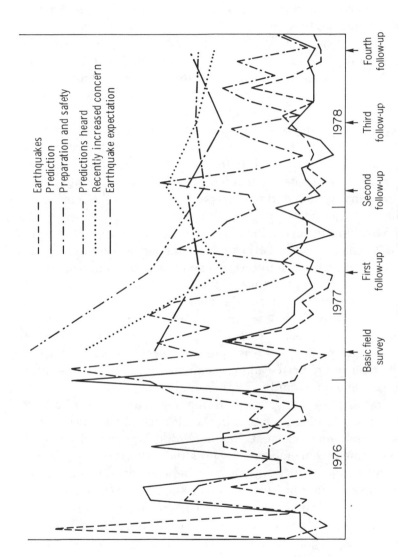

Figure 55. Newspaper Coverage and Earthquake Response

prediction, and preparedness and safety.[4] Both earthquake events and prediction exhibited several peaks in 1976 before our first survey. Both remained relatively low throughout 1977 and 1978, except for correlated peaks just after our first survey, associated with earthquakes in Romania and Iran, and a peak in event coverage without a corresponding peak in attention to prediction a little before our final survey, associated with earthquakes in Santa Barbara and, again, in Iran. While preparedness and safety peaked during the period of concentrated attention to prediction brought on by Whitcomb's near prediction and belated consideration of the uplift and again just before our first survey, with a few weeks' lag behind the Minturn peak, it generally received less attention in 1976 than in 1977 and 1978. Unlike the other two topics, preparedness and safety remained high for several months after the first survey and continued to peak throughout the remainder of the study period.

The declines in predictions heard, recently increased concern, and earthquake expectation can be understood as responses to the drop in media attention to earthquake prediction from just before the first survey until the time of the first follow-up wave, with a lag of a few months. Two smaller peaks in coverage of prediction in the latter half of 1977 might then have accounted for the rebounding level in early 1978 of recently increased earthquake concern and, perhaps, of earthquake expectation. But failure of the number of predictive announcements remembered to exhibit a similar rebound would require special explanation.

We recall from earlier chapters the vagueness of recollection and persistence of expectation in the absence of any specifically remembered announcement. The declining exponential curve of announcements remembered suggests the failure to recognize as new and to assimilate as distinct announcements the continuing flow of information bearing on the earthquake prospect, none of which had the pointedness and weight of the 1976 pronouncements. If the new announcements were insufficiently distinct to be assimilated cognitively, they may nevertheless have stimulated affect. It is not surprising that the sense of recently intensified concern was more sensitive to short-term changes in media coverage than were either cognition or conviction (expectation). If we could extend our observations beyond the five data points, we could test the hypothesis that cognition is most responsive to longer-term trends, leveling out short-term fluctuations; that the sense of momentarily aroused concern is most responsive to short-term changes; and that conviction or expectation is intermediate, responding to short-term fluctuations more than cognition but less than aroused affect and reflecting the longer trend more faithfully than affect but less than cognition.

If our speculations have any merit, discussions related to prediction are critical, and discussions of preparedness and safety are of little or no relevance to the sense of earthquake imminence and aroused concern. It is more difficult to judge the significance of reports of earthquake events because of the correlation with attention to prediction.

The number of predictive announcements remembered is a measure of salience and of cognitive discrimination rather than of simple awareness; it measures recall rather than recognition memory. By contrast, the typology we use to assess awareness of the uplift measures recognition. There is no apparent relationship between awareness of the uplift and media fluctuations. Although media attention to the uplift declined over the total period, awareness of the uplift remained stable and possibly even increased from mid-1977 to mid-1978. Three more specific observations seem justified.

First, once the awareness of the uplift had been fairly widely diffused during periods of more intensive coverage, a continuing lower level of media attention was sufficient to maintain the level of awareness. After an extended period of occasional reminders, the underlying awareness remained steady, although the salience and sense of imminence dropped.

Second, this persistence is impressive, because it applies to recognition of the uplift as personally relevant as well as to the simple recognition that it exists. Having once gotten the message, people retained the awareness of what the uplift could mean to them with the help of a low-key series of media reminders.

Third, awareness of the uplift had apparently come close to a ceiling by the time of our first survey. During our study period and beyond the modest rise from mid-1977 to mid-1978, there was no net increase in the number of people who were aware. The new communications seemed to be reaching only those who had already heard, keeping their awareness alive without augmenting the aware population.

Because of the separations between cognition and conviction and between awareness and action, there may be better ways to work with the hard core of unaware people than by promoting awareness of the uplift.

The foregoing analysis dealt with levels of media attention to broad topics. This type of analysis can only be effective if people respond less to the discrete events as they occur than to the aggregate rates with which events occur or receive public attention through the media. Justification for such an assumption is provided by the poor quality of discrimination between specific announcements and by the number of people who expect an earthquake within a year without being able to name a single supporting announcement. Yet, at the time of our first survey, a large proportion of respondents had separated the Minturn forecast from the background of vague awareness, and the uplift survived as a discrete phenomenon. Hence, we should reexamine our data to see whether plausible connections between changing earthquake response and critical events are suggested.

In chapter twelve, we specifically explored awareness of a few of what we thought might have been critical events. The persistent swarm of small tremors in the uplifted zone, reported in September 1977, and the Santa Barbara earthquake of August 1978 were the two events that attracted considerable attention. Only the former, however, seemed to be widely interpreted as having significance for the earthquake future of Los Angeles County residents. By the end of 1978, in spite of the highly publicized political controversy provoked by Whitcomb's near prediction and the widespread awareness of Minturn's forecast at the time of our first survey, we were surprised at how few respondents remembered a withdrawn or disconfirmed prediction and at how few referred in any credible way to the Whitcomb or Minturn announcements. Nevertheless, the response of significant minorities among our respondents to critical events could have measurably influenced the trends we observed.

In figure 56, we have selected eight events that might plausibly have influenced the earthquake response of substantial numbers

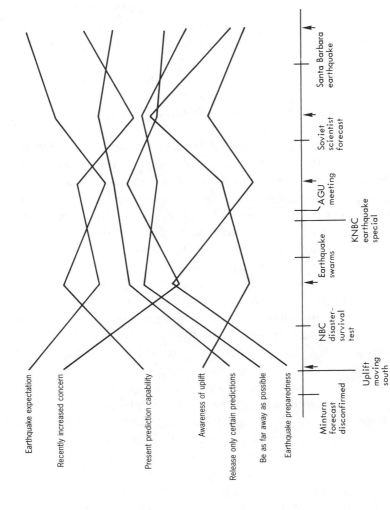

Figure 56. Selected Events and Earthquake Response

of people, and we have used the dates of occurrence of these events to subdivide the horizontal axis of the graph. Thus, in reading from left to right on the graph, one can identify the time when each of the eight events occurred. The date for the median interview in each of the five surveys has also been marked along the horizontal axis for easy comparison. Seven response variables that exhibited change during the study period have been plotted on the graph so that their trends can be related to the eight events. As before, each is plotted using a different scale so that only trends, not absolute levels, can be compared. In addition, and in contrast to the earlier graphs, zero levels for the seven response variables do not correspond with the base of the graph and would all fall at different locations if projected.

The interval from early to mid-1977 was characterized by the greatest range and amount of change. Fewer people expected an earthquake within a year, fewer said that their concern about the earthquake prospect had recently increased, and fewer remembered hearing of the uplift and associating it with earthquake danger. Belief in current scientific earthquake-prediction capability increased, but so did reluctance to release uncertain predictions. More people said that they would try to get as far away as possible if they had advance warning of an earthquake, and the level of individual and household preparedness rose. Except for the modest decline in awareness of the uplift, the changes might constitute a pattern in which the earthquake danger was no longer felt to be as imminent as before, but the prospect was being viewed more realistically rather than being treated as a normal event.

The NBC National Disaster Survival Test, aired to a large nationwide television audience on May 1, 1977, might have contributed to the rise in earthquake preparedness, especially since preparedness declined in the next interval and never reached the same level again and since preparedness ascribed specifically to the earthquake prospect did not increase to the same extent. It is difficult, however, to relate the disaster test to the other changes.

In the absence of any striking event to explain these changes during the recorded interval, we are led to consider whether they might have either been the continuation of a trend begun before our first survey or the delayed effect of earlier events. Either interpretation would be plausible in light of the December disconfirmation of the much-publicized Minturn forecast and the less-publicized withdrawal of Whitcomb's "hypothesis test." If preoccupation with a highly publicized and immediate danger is sometimes handled by denial, the breathing spell that comes when the sense of imminence passes enables people to acknowledge and to begin to deal with the real nature of the threatening event.

When our first round of interviews was conducted, a month or more had already passed since Minturn's forecast had been disconfirmed, and the media clamor had died down. The sense of imminent danger is apparently not dispelled instantly but instead persists for weeks, even months.

The next interval, from mid-1977 to early 1978, saw every variable but one reversing direction. Except for the decline in personal and household preparedness, the lines of ascent and descent are not steep, and they may be better described as a leveling off than as a reversal of direction. Awareness of the uplift and the sense of imminent danger were partially restored, faith in current scientific earthquake-prediction capability was moderated, preparedness deteriorated, and attitudes toward releasing uncertain predictions and toward getting away from the site of an earthquake were little changed. Discovery and frequent discussion of the earthquake swarm, earthquake specials on KNBC and other television networks, and concentrated reporting about the San Francisco meeting of the American Geophysical Union may have restored some of the lost sense of immediacy and contributed to a more realistic assessment of scientific earthquake-prediction capability. But other changes suggest the absence of significant events more than they do positive influences.

During the third interval, the sense of imminence once again declined. Since awareness of the uplift increased slightly, unrealistic faith in current prediction capability decreased, and preparedness rose slightly, realism may have increased. No event stands out during this interval except the Soviet scientist's forecast, which very few people remembered seven to eight months later. This was an interval marked by continuing but unspectacular and infrequent discussion, with greatest attention given to the often highly politicized earthquake-safety issues. We see no obvious coherent pattern here.

The fourth interval was similarly made up of changes that are not obviously interconnected. Most trends are weak, and random variation may account for most of what we see. The Santa Barbara earthquake could have had a significant effect during this interval. But it would be difficult to make a plausible case for the Santa Barbara earthquake as the cause of decreased preparedness, awareness of the uplift, and disposition to be as far away from an expected earthquake as possible, combined with greater earthquake expectation and faith in scientific prediction capability.

In general, a plausible but not necessarily convincing case can be made linking changes during the first two intervals to events during and preceding those intervals. But efforts to find plausible explanations for changes during the second two intervals seem to tax reasonable credulity.

THE NEW YEAR'S DAY EARTHQUAKE

By launching a survey directly after the small New Year's Day earthquake and designing it comprehensively to explore perception, interpretation, and response, we have been able to gain a clear picture of the quake's short-run effects, although we have no way to know how lasting they were.

The New Year's Day earthquake was taken in stride by most respondents. It was not experienced as a very frightening event, although it did raise the level of fear concerning a future earthquake. While a few people claimed personally to have had the idea that an earthquake was about to happen, very few people thought the quake had been predicted. People either had not heard of a prediction, or they had assumed that the relatively vague near predictions in effect would be followed by more specific warning announcements as the time of a predicted quake approached.

Although the quake was not disruptive of normal routines, neither did it as a near miss lull people into a false sense of security. The quake stimulated considerable interest. In the absence of answers from the authorities and the media to their most pressing questions, people sought the meaning of the quake for the future through informal discussion and rumor.

The most general characterization of the earthquake's effects on attitudes and responses is to say that it was unsettling. The established trend toward seeing a destructive earthquake as a crisis event rather than a normal occurrence was intensified. Confidence in the significance of the uplift as an earthquake precursor, faith in the eventual accuracy of scientific earthquake prediction, and support for the most popular government hazard-mitigation measures were shaken. There may have been some stocktaking concerning household preparedness, but there was no general increase in the level of preparedness.

Complementing the unsettling effect was the striking drop in what had been a stable variable: the level of people's suspicion that scientists and public officials were withholding information concerning earthquake predictions. This change may have signaled a modest disposition toward shoring up community solidarity in a situation of potential community crisis.

Response to the New Year's Day earthquake warrants two further observations. First, in spite of the nonlethal nature of the physical event, the moderate earthquake precipitated clearer and more widely ranging changes in relatively stable response patterns than did other specific events during the study period. Compared to a destructive earthquake nearby and such developments on the prediction scene as the miniquake swarm and the Soviet scientist's prediction, occurrence of a nonlethal earthquake of near-miss magnitude at home had more effect in shaking established assumptions and in stimulating reflection, though not action.

Second, the changes triggered by the quake are not understandable except in the context of the prior years' experience with earthquake forecasts, near predictions, and cautions. The stage had been set by the end of 1978, when 36 percent of respondents said there would probably or definitely be a damaging earthquake within a year and 71 percent said the same for within five years. A nonlethal quake occurring against a different background might have had quite different and possibly less significant effects. But the quake took its principal meaning as a reality-reminding step on the inexorable path toward the "big one" that was not far off.

WAITING AS THE CAUSE OF CHANGE

We described the near prediction conveyed by announcements of the uplift as having had zero lead time and an open-ended time window. We hypothesized that people would attempt to give closure to the window, and would often translate time window into lead time. The high percentage initially expecting a damaging earthquake within a year suggests that the closure tendency was at work, and the subsequent reduction suggests a reopening of the time window in the popular view.

Six alternative but not mutually exclusive hypotheses concerning the effect of waiting for disaster were outlined. First, there should be an initial sense of urgency—perhaps translated into action—followed by a period of lessened urgency, as people live through the ever-extending time window. If there is a strong sense of closure, the sense of urgency should be restored as the assumed end of the time window approaches. If the former pattern applies, such variables as imminent expectation of an earthquake and recently intensified concern should decline, either linearly or following a declining exponential curve and approaching a horizontal asymptote. If the latter applies, the trend might be described by a concave parabola. Although five moments are too few for fitting a curve confidently, the exponential curve provides the nearest fit to the largest number of variables, and the parabola fits the fewest. In one instance, that of individual and household preparedness, the spurt of preparedness comes at the second rather than the first moment, which seems best explained as a response to the disaster survival test on NBC television. But the subsequent decline fits the model of lessened urgency, although we cannot specify a curve to fit the foreshortened data.

The second hypothesis is that waiting translates the earthquake warning into a slowly developing false alarm, inclining people toward skepticism and disillusionment about scientific prediction. Since the changes are actually in the opposite direction, we must reject the false alarm, or "cry wolf," hypothesis.

The third hypothesis is that waiting is a period of accumulating anxiety, leading to defensive denial of danger and other pathological responses. Our data provide no evidence to support this hypothesis.

The fourth hypothesis is that accumulating personal tension is translated into active and aggressive responses, expressed as suspicion, resentment, and scapegoating. Again, there is no increased suspicion that information is being withheld, support for government spending continues, and more people have confidence in government preparedness than in their own or the general public's preparedness. Thus, we do not find evidence to support this hypothesis.

The fifth hypothesis assumes that the period of waiting is not one of passivity but instead is one of repeated reminder, clarification, informal discussion, and information seeking. As a result, the period of waiting increases familiarity with the threatening situation and its many aspects and also increases sensitization to the cues that may be relevant at the time of crisis. The most striking evidence bearing on this hypothesis is the increased confidence in current earthquake-prediction capability, with the trend beginning and ending at levels that are unrealistic in relation to actual scientific capability. There is no cumulative growth in awareness of predictive announcements or of the uplift, but there is some change in the quality of announcements remembered, with more focus on the uplift and on scientific announcements. Thus, there is suggestive support for this hypothesis.

The sixth, and final, hypothesis assumes an even stronger positive effect, with waiting and periodic reminders leading to rehearsals and the selection of more effective responses through trial and error. We noted that many people assumed that the crisis event will be preceded by a short-term warning. A relaxed sense of urgency may save people from destructive anxiety. If people had learned more effective responses while waiting, the result could be the existence of a population whose apparent apathy could be overcome rather quickly. We have no real test for this hypothesis, although we have observed that such survival lessons as standing under an inside door frame during an earthquake and not immediately rushing outdoors have been widely learned. And without expressing greater fear, fewer people say they would go on with life as usual if they knew that an earthquake was imminent.

While there has been a declining sense of urgency, there has been no general disillusionment or scapegoating during the waiting period. There has been, however, increased acceptance of scientific earthquake prediction. There has also been some indication that the prospect of a damaging quake is being faced more realistically as the normalcy bias is eroded.

The analytic separation between the effects of waiting and the effects of passing events is artificial. It is undoubtedly important that the period of waiting has been punctuated by a series of unfolding developments and that the media have managed to keep a three-year-old announcement newsworthy. The validity of each of our six hypotheses probably depends in large part on the nature of the events and on the media treatment. The unsettling effect of the New Year's Day earthquake underlines the contingent effects of events on the longer-term waiting effects. No doubt, more combative press and television coverage could have stirred up some of the effects described in hypotheses two, three, and four, but active political leadership to develop a comprehensive community-based program for earthquake preparedness and prediction awareness could undoubtedly have strengthened the effects anticipated under hypotheses five and six.

PART SIX

Some Conclusions

Constructing the Social Meanings of Earthquake Threat

On February 9, 1971, just as its denizens were awaking for their daily assault on the maze of roads and freeways, the Los Angeles metropolis was catastrophically reminded of its vulnerability to earthquakes. The central city was spared by the peripheral location of the quake and by its intermediate magnitude. But for several days the community was held in the grip of an unfolding drama, as authorities successfully drained the broken Van Norman Dam before it could collapse and inundate thousands of homes. At the same time, a relatively new hospital collapsed, and the community was faced with a loss of life. There was also a disruption of transportation and services caused by the destruction of a key portion of the freeway network. The usual flurry of legislative and organizational activity and public preoccupation ensued, with notable advances in seismic safety. But public interest soon lagged; without the spur of an aroused public, many new programs, such as those in the public schools, lapsed into tokenism. By 1975 only the foundering efforts in the Los Angeles City Council to do something about thousands of seismically unsafe old buildings, coupled with occasional promises of an imminent breakthrough in scientific earthquake prediction and reports of incredible Chinese successes, reminded people of the ever-present earthquake threat.

Then, just five years after the San Fernando-Sylmar earthquake, a year of unparalleled attention to earthquake threat began. But this was a wholly new kind of preoccupation: the occasion and the topic were predictions, forecasts, and warnings of earthquakes to come rather than accomplished disaster. Hurricane and flood warnings and notification of tornado and brushfire seasons were familiar experiences for many. Earthquake prediction, however, was a new idea, and there was no fund of common experience from which to draw in understanding, assessing, and responding to the various warnings. Neither the general public nor the established institutions had scripts to guide them. In chapter one we underlined the importance in disaster research of exploring the *social meanings* that are attached to disaster agents. The year of the bulge provides us with a unique case study in the construction of social meanings for a disaster threat that was both inherently ambiguous and socially unprecedented.

There is little evidence of serious individual and household preparation for the earthquake that nearly everyone believed was coming soon, and earthquake safety did not become a cause around which people rallied for collective action. Except for a great deal of informal discussion and attention to media reports and occasional massive rumor waves, life went on as usual. But our evidence confirms that while waiting for disaster, millions of people were engaged in elaborating, revising, and reaffirming the meanings of earthquake prediction and the earthquake threat. In a dialogue with the mass media of communication, the people of southern California engaged collectively in constructing mutually acceptable conceptions of reality. While the crystallization of such understandings may not lead to immediate action of any sort, it serves as a preparation for action or inaction, as signaled by relevant events.

Without implying that our many other findings are unimportant, we shall briefly review those findings that bear most directly on this process of assigning social meanings to the earthquake threat. We will begin with the mass media of communications, which serve as the bridge from ultimate information sources, such as the U.S. Geological Survey, to the general public.

THE MASS MEDIA: BLOWING HOT AND COLD?

Although the mainstream media displayed exemplary journalistic responsibility in most respects, their editors and reporters were unprepared by precedent or understanding for the task of interpreting the ambiguities of earthquake threat to their audiences. Vague and unprecedented disaster warnings are problematic for the media as well as for their audiences, leading to anomalies and irregularities of media coverage. The problems of newsworthiness, sources, affinities between types of coverage and particular media, and ambivalence between expressing alarm and reassurance affected the pattern of communication to the public.

Newsworthiness becomes a problem for the media when warnings persist over an extended period of time or are not especially timely in other respects. Repetition of what is essentially the same warning that has been issued on previous occasions is made newsworthy by new developments that clarify or revise the initial story, such as a wave of small tremors in the uplifted region; by pronouncements from official agencies, such as the Seismic Safety Commission's declaration about the uplift; by discussion on the part of a prestigious group, as in the annual meeting of the Geophysical Union; and by relevance to a socially significant and timely occasion or event, such as the anniversary of a previous great earthquake or the occurrence of a currently devastating earthquake elsewhere. But after an initial peak of interest, items that previously attracted attention lose their newsworthiness. Media editors try to anticipate such declines in public interest, and they often reduce the flow of news more abruptly than public interest would justify. Regardless of timeliness, a warning notice that can be associated with an interesting personality is more newsworthy than one issued by a faceless agency, although such personality interest is ephemeral unless the public figure continues to "perform" for the public. Newsworthiness because of association with political controversies, such as those over nuclear power and environmentalism, is quite ephemeral.

The media depend upon interest groups—both public and private—for their news material when there is no mobilized public controversy or visible dramatic event to be monitored. Therefore, the rise and fall of media coverage and selective emphases in content reflect the work of organizational information sources more than they do media initiative. As a consequence, a warning event that catches the community by surprise receives only modest coverage compared with events that follow. Furthermore, organizations require time to assimilate information and to develop policies and procedures that can be publicly announced. Hence, an event generates a series of news waves, each reflecting the duration of the organizational lag required for a particular agency to assimilate the initial news. Since organizational pronouncements are generally self-interested, themes reflecting the self-interest of the best-organized interest groups receive the most and earliest attention. Themes that are the provinces of no organized interest group, such as the themes of individual and household disaster-preparedness, receive only scant and long-delayed attention.

There are affinities between particular media and particular types of announcements. There is an affinity between television and vague or general announcements and between newspapers and scientific announcements, probably because of the detail and time allowed for items in the respective media. Radio and "people" as information sources show affinity with pseudoscientific announcements, such as the warning that California will break off and fall into the Pacific in a great earthquake. Prophetic announcements, such as earthquake forecasts by clairvoyants and astrologers, show affinity with books and magazines.

The more responsible media are plagued by fears of the opposing evils of public apathy and panic. One consequence of these twin fears is the practice of presenting items according to an alarm-and-reassurance pattern. The typical newspaper, television, or radio item begins with a series of alarming reports, sometimes overstating the threat by blurring the distinction between possible and probable events. The alarming statements are then followed by reassurances or nullifying reports. For example, readers are reassured about the seismic adequacy of most southern California construction, or dissenting opinions are quoted. The reader is then offered little, if any, help in resolving the contradictory message into a reasonable set of conclusions.

Another consequence of media ambivalence is the alternating high and low media coverage as media editors worry about public apathy and panic sequentially. Alarm is less likely to be moderated by reassurance in the announcement of prophetic and pseudoscientific forecasts, since sensationalism is at more of a premium with these stories. As a result, people perceive prophetic and pseudoscientific forecasts more than scientific announce-

ments as identifying earthquakes that are more definitely characterized and of higher intensity.

PUBLIC RECEPTION OF MEDIA REPORTS

How do people receive and sift what the media tell
them about the earthquake threat? Our answers are in terms of
patterns of media use, variable credibility of media sources,
shifting patterns of media use over time, individual variations in
communication styles, and local experts and opinion leaders as
communication links.

Television news and newspaper coverage consistently receive
the widest attention, with television news far outdistancing newspapers and radio in the early stages of disaster warning. But redundancy is the rule, and the fact that people hear the same thing
from several media sources may be crucial.

The evidence on message credibility is anomalous in one important respect. While prophetic announcements are generally less
credible than scientific announcements and prophetic forecasts
are disproportionately attributed to books and magazines, books
and magazines are substantially more credible to the public than
are the other media. Differences in credibility among the other
media are slight. Perhaps prophetic announcements would be
taken less seriously were it not for the stamp of authenticity that
comes from their appearing most often in books and magazines.

A striking shift in the relative importance of the chief media
sources of information took place over the two years between our
first and last surveys. Reliance on television declined steadily and
the importance of newspapers almost doubled, so that newspapers
were cited as principal sources for earthquake information slightly
more often than television three years after the first announcement
of the uplift. This shift is paralleled by increased salience of
scientific as compared with other kinds of awareness. There may
be a general principle that awareness and communication, while
becoming less intense, become less frivolous and better harnessed
to reality during a moderately extended period of waiting. As the
shift occurs, people turn increasingly away from the quick-pitch
media to media that can provide deeper and more extended infor-

mation and analysis. Alternatively, the less serious earthquake watchers may simply have turned their attention to fresh topics, leaving only the more serious to constitute the earthquake-awareness public.

While a combination of media use with discussion in face-to-face groups is the normal communication pattern, individual *communication styles* differ. Two-thirds of our subjects use interpersonal discussion to sift and supplement what they learn about earthquakes from the media of mass communication, confirming the widely documented two-step or multistep flow model. One-fourth of our respondents rely exclusively on the mass media for earthquake information and are therefore not exposed to the important effects of discussion among family, friends, and associates. About one person in eleven accepts interpersonal discussion as a primary source of information about earthquakes. Our evidence suggests that experience with earthquakes reduces willingness to rely primarily on interpersonal talk as an information source. However, having experienced personal loss from earthquakes or having close friends or relatives who have experienced loss motivates people to seek clarification and evaluation of what they hear or read in the media through discussion with friends, family members, and work associates.

Communication style affects response. People who rely on the media as their chief information source but who filter media information through interpersonal discussion show greater awareness of the threat and of its social implications than either those who rely exclusively on the media or those who rely disproportionately on interpersonal discussion. But fear, belief in the probability of a damaging earthquake soon, and steps taken to prepare for an earthquake are all greater for those who have engaged in discussion than for those who rely exclusively on the media. Interpersonal discussion, whether alone or coupled with primary reliance on the media, seems crucial in making the earthquake threat real.

When we looked for evidence of opinion leadership, we found that only 15 percent of our respondents knew someone in their circle of friends and associates who was especially knowledgeable about earthquakes and prediction, while another 2.5 percent identified themselves as experts. If reliance on opinion leaders has been essential to the crystallizing of public opinion on political matters, the dearth of local experts could be a serious impediment to the crystallization of viewpoints concerning the threat of earthquake disaster. Analysis suggests that the local experts and their associates constitute a classic *social circle* within which opinions are sifted, issues are defined, and some consensus is reached. The nonexpert associates may form the crucial bridge between book-reading local experts and the general public, because their discussions encompass a wider range of partners and their social awareness is more acute by comparison with the local experts. The associates may serve as opinion leaders for people outside the informal social circles, even though they neither see themselves nor are seen by others as experts.

HOW REAL IS THE THREAT?

We have observed that informal discussion among family, friends, and work associates contributes an augmented sense of reality to the threat that nearly everyone believes in at least minimally. This observation points up the variation in quality of awareness—the difference between knowing something and really knowing it. Although awareness of earthquake threat is almost universal and earthquakes are viewed with fear when people do think about them, the quality of awareness is low for most people. People are vague about the warnings they have heard, and they readily acknowledge that they do not take most of them seriously.

The ease with which it can be imagined visually allows almost everyone to appreciate the danger of living on a fault, and public controversy has taught most southern Californians the danger of seismically substandard buildings. But even those who are at greatest risk seem blithely unaware of the danger of inundation caused by dam collapse and the danger of rampant brushfires in an arid community with an earthquake-disrupted water supply. Many who grasped the seismologists' fear that the infamous uplift could presage a great earthquake localized the threat so as to exclude the neighborhoods where they lived. Although people overwhelmingly endorsed increased government spending for earthquake safety, they treated it more as a luxury than as a necessity when assigning priorities for government spending. And incredibly few people spontaneously thought of earthquakes when asked about community problems and hazards of living in southern California.

Throughout our study period, the earthquake threat was acknowledged by nearly everyone in spite of failed forecasts, publicly aired disputes among experts, and silence on the part of major political leaders. But it was seldom more than a fascinating sideshow to the main events of daily life.

MAKING THE THREAT MANAGEABLE

It is often said that people cope with the threat of natural disaster by denial. A recurring theme of popular journalism is the head-in-the-sand attitude of Californians toward earthquakes. High rates of endorsement for fatalistic attitudes toward the catastrophic effects of an earthquake, coupled with the low quality of awareness, might appear to support this theme. But more careful examination of the evidence plainly discredits any such interpretation.

In spite of a declining sense of imminence as people waited for the long-delayed earthquake, few people doubted that a damaging quake was in the offing. In spite of unfulfilled forecasts and warnings, most people clung to an often unrealistic faith in scientific earthquake-prediction capability. Although many would discourage early release of uncertain predictions, nearly all asked for more rather than less media coverage of earthquake topics. When unfinished business was met with media silence, great waves of rumor developed as people turned to their peers to find meaning in the situation. Many joined in searching for earthquake harbingers in such events as a flurry of microtremors in the uplifted region and a moderate earthquake in the metropolis. Those who did so found the events more credible as signs that the great quake was coming than as signs that the threat had lessened. And most of those who heard conflicting interpretations kept open minds, eschewing easy denial.

Even the evidence concerning fatalism becomes less clear on closer examination. Fatalism is most widespread toward the prospect of large-scale and impersonal disaster but is less prevalent when the question is personal survival or help for those at greatest risk.

Rather than practicing denial, people appear to be striving for a conception of reality that makes the earthquake threat more manageable. An extended or open-ended time window—the period of time during which the earthquake may occur—is difficult to handle. One might evacuate or stay home or take other protective action for a day or perhaps for a week. But what is one to do when the quake may occur at any time within the span of a year or of several years? The Whitcomb (Caltech) "prediction" of a quake between April 1976 and April 1977 was widely understood as prediction of a quake for April 1977. The difficult concept of probability was often replaced by either-or.

The continuing and even growing faith in scientific earthquake-prediction capability helped to make the threat manageable. But most people were not ready to place all their eggs in one basket; the majority of our respondents paid attention to both scientific and nonscientific forecasts. Again, by refusing to rule out one source of information in favor of another, people retained the ability to confirm reports by comparing information sources.

We have noted several times that earthquakes, as compared with other disaster agents, are especially unmanageable to the public because there are no external signs by which the layperson can tell that a quake is imminent. Nevertheless, we found that a great many of our respondents did not rely simply on authority but instead sought to make the dynamics of earthquakes comprehensible to themselves. Many believed in such visible signs as earthquake weather. And the traditional folklore of unusual animal behavior as an earthquake sign, given legitimacy by Chinese claims and cautious attention from American scientists, was embraced by fully three-quarters of our respondents. In addition, half said they would take seriously their own personal premonition that an earthquake was coming. Clearly, people have been constructing a version of earthquake reality that promises the opportunity to detect for themselves the signs of a coming earthquake.

In absolute terms, the confidence in the preparations that government officials were making for an earthquake was not impressive. But relative to the general public and even to the respondents themselves, government agencies were seen as better prepared. In various ways, people exhibited an implicit confidence that government officials knew what to do and were taking the appropriate steps in preparation for a quake. And, quite serendipitously, we discovered that a great many people took for granted that some kind of short-term warning would be issued before the great quake.

In these several ways, people have transformed the specter of earthquake devastation into something with which individuals and households can cope. And while people are vague and imprecise about many things, they are surprisingly well informed about what to do during the period of impact. Nearly everyone has learned to avoid elevators, to stay away from windows, to rely on the structural stability of inside doorways, and to follow similar measures when an earthquake strikes. In this respect, they are well prepared.

For many people, making a momentous event manageable also means incorporating some teleological or ethical meaning. Surprisingly few people understand earthquakes as simply the wrath of God or as a preface to the Second Coming of Christ. But many who offer a naturalistic account of earthquake causation and dynamics include overtones of moral judgment and higher purpose. Thus, earthquakes are thought to be triggered by underground testing of atomic bombs or by imprudent interference with nature. Bringing a natural event into the social order where human intentions and virtues count for something contributes toward making earthquakes manageable for a substantial population.

EARTHQUAKE PREPAREDNESS AS SOCIALLY NORMATIVE

If there is an element of earthquake preparation in the versions of reality people have constructed during this warning period, how is it to be reconciled with the very minimal salience of earthquake concerns? We are reminded that the communist threat was of equally minimal salience during the 1950s when it was a potent political issue. An issue of low salience can mobilize people to collective action when the issue is perceived as a moral one and other circumstances are appropriate. Is there a moral dimension to earthquake preparedness, as people see it? In sociological terms, is earthquake preparedness normative?

People's frequent expressions of intention to take household-preparedness measures when they had not already done so suggests at least a trace of social pressure. Support for government-preparedness activity acknowledges public responsibility. And a widespread sense of public responsibility to help those who are disproportionately at risk further extends the moral implications of earthquake preparedness.

The normative element in earthquake preparedness is only weakly developed, but the traces are clear. There is at least a modest sense that one ought to prepare for an earthquake and that the responsibility is public as well as private.

The question we cannot truly answer is whether the effects of this period of unusually intensive exposure to discussions of earthquake prediction and seismic safety have been lasting or ephemeral. Through the continuing activities of the California Seismic Safety Commission and the newly formed Southern California Earthquake Preparedness Program, government agencies and private corporations continue to develop and improve the organizational level of earthquake preparedness. But as the Palmdale bulge became little more than dubious ancient history and as reminders that quiescence of the southern San Andreas Fault since 1857 could not last much longer came only on the anniversary of the San Fernando-Sylmar quake, did anything remain of the great collective effort to clarify the social meaning of the earthquake threat? The short duration of improved personal and household preparedness that may have resulted from a nationally televised documentary on disaster preparedness supplies one negative example, and an almost negative example is supplied by the sparse trace of the San Fernando-Sylmar quake that we were able to locate in the collective memory of residents in the zone of impact.

But two examples suggest that key ideas may become so firmly implanted in collective memory that they become resources in the local earthquake culture to be recalled and used when the occasion signals their relevance. One example is the fanciful forecast that much of California would some day break off and fall into the Pacific Ocean in a great earthquake on the San Andreas Fault. This great event was supposed to have taken place in 1969. Today, hardly anyone knows the source of this idea or that it was supposed to have happened a decade and a half ago. Yet nearly everyone in California has heard that it might happen, and many take it as a serious, scientifically based possibility.

A flurry of information seeking in the fall and winter of 1981–82 supplies the second example. Requests for speakers made to the Los Angeles Office of Civil Defense multiplied during 1981, and rumors of an imminent great earthquake flourished in January and February. Although few, if any, of the people who participated in this episode knew the source, the conviction that a great earthquake would strike in February 1982 was widespread. The obvious source was the Jupiter Effect forecast, which was that a rash of earthquakes would occur around the globe when several planets and the sun came into rare alignment with the earth. The Jupiter Effect was often mentioned during our study period, sometimes as a strictly scientific forecast and sometimes through assimilation into either religious or secular prophecies of disaster. Although the forecast had long since been publicly withdrawn by its senior author, few people outside of scientific circles knew this or even remembered why February 1982 was the dreaded month. Stripped of supporting details, the month and year of forecast disaster persisted in the collective memory, reawakening dormant earthquake concerns as the fateful date approached.

In light of these two examples of enduring traces in the collective memory, we should not underestimate the significance of continuing awareness and appreciation of the uplift over the duration of our investigation. We noted that the persisting level of awareness and understanding of the uplift was striking. It contradicted any hypothesis of generalized loss of interest and declining awareness during an extended period of waiting for a vaguely but scientifically forecast disaster. Awareness persisted in spite of lessening media attention and while awareness of nonscientific forecasts was declining markedly. If the two less reputable "pseudoscientific" forecasts remain latent in the collective memory, to be activated dramatically by appropriate cues, there seems little reason to doubt that memory of the uplift persists in the same fashion. Factual detail will have fallen away, as it has for the two pseudoscientific forecasts. And young people and newcomers to the region will not have been directly exposed to this period of learning about earthquakes.

Any substantial renewal of public warnings would surely reawaken in many Angelenos the memory of some of the lessons learned earlier. Many of those who remembered would introduce their recollections into the flurry of interpersonal and media discussion that would quickly ensue. The observation that scientists were approaching an earthquake countdown would now be an idea with precedent. There would be no need for the slow and halting process of realization and appreciation that followed first announcements of the uplift, and much of the experience in thinking about how to respond could be quickly retrieved from shared memories and written records. Hence, while we cannot document the current state of public preparedness for a destructive earthquake, and while it would be unrealistic to suppose that the years of waiting have not taken their toll, we remain optimistic that some net gain in awareness and appreciation remains after the ferment of the year of the bulge.

Notes

1: A Bulge on the San Andreas Fault

1. Linda B. Bourque, Leo G. Reeder, Andrew Cherlin, Bertram Raven, and D. Michael Walton, *The Unpredictable Disaster in a Metropolis* (Los Angeles: Survey Research Center, University of California, 1973).

2. Ad Hoc Interagency Working Group for Earthquake Research, Federal Council for Science and Technology, *Proposal for a Ten-Year National Earthquake Hazards Program: A Partnership of Science and the Community* (Washington, D.C.: Office of Science and Technology and Federal Council for Science and Technology, 1968); Christopher H. Scholz, Lynn R. Sykes, and Yash P. Aggarwal, "Earthquake Prediction: A Physical Basis," *Science* 181 (August 31, 1963): 803–810; Carl Kisslinger, "Earthquake Prediction," *Physics Today,* 27 (March 1974): 36–42; Roger W. Greensfelder, "Progress in Earthquake Prediction," *California Geology* 27 (August 1974): 188–189; Frank Press, "Earthquake Prediction," *Scientific American* 232 (May 1975): 14–23.

3. American Seismology Delegation, "Earthquake Research in China," *EOS* 56 (November 1975): 838–881; Haicheng Earthquake Study Delegation, "Prediction of the Haicheng Earthquake," *EOS: Transactions, American Geophysical Union* 58 (May 1977): 235–272.

4. Peter L. Ward, "Earthquake Prediction," in Geophysics Research Board, Geophysics Study Committee, *Studies in Geophysical Prediction* (Washington, D.C.: National Academy of Sciences, 1978), pp. 37–46; National Research Council, Panel on Earthquake Prediction, *Predicting Earthquakes: A Scientific and Technical Evaluation—with Implications for Society* (Washington, D.C.: National Academy of Sciences, 1976).

5. Garrett Hardin, "Earthquakes: Predictions More Devastating than Events," in *Stalking the Wild Taboo* (Los Altos, Calif.: William Kaufmann, 1974), pp. 123–134. (First published separately in 1967.)

6. J. Eugene Haas and Dennis S. Mileti, "Socioeconomic Impact of Earthquake Prediction on Government, Business, and Community," *California Geology* 30 (July 1977): 147–157.

7. National Research Council, Panel on Public Policy Implications of Earthquake Prediction, *Earthquake Prediction and Public Policy* (Washington, D.C.: National Academy of Science, 1975); National Research Council, Committee on Socioeconomic Effects of Earthquake Predictions, *A Program of Studies on the Socioeconomic Effects of Earthquake Predictions* (Washington, D.C.: National Academy of Sciences, 1978). See also Martin V. Jones and Richard M. Jones, *Scientific Earthquake Prediction: Some First Thoughts on Possible Societal Impacts (A Mini Technology Assessment)* (Bethesda, Md.: Impact Assessment Institute, 1975); Leo W. Weisbecker, Ward C. Stoneman, and the staff of the Stanford Research Institute, *Earthquake Prediction, Uncertainty, and Policies for the Future: A Technology Assessment of Earthquake Prediction* (Menlo Park, Calif.: Stanford Research Institute, 1977).

8. Robert Iacopi, *Earthquake Country* (Menlo Park, Calif.: Lane Books, 1964, 1969, 1971).

9. John Gribbin and Stephen Plagemann, *The Jupiter Effect* (New York: Random House, 1974). But for subsequent recantation see John Gribbin, "Almost a Famous Forecast," *New Scientist* 87 (17 July 1980): 226.

10. Charles E. Fritz, "Disaster," in *Contemporary Social Problems,* ed. Robert Merton and Robert Nisbet (New York: Harcourt, Brace and World, 1961), pp. 651–694; Allen H. Barton, *Communities in Disaster: A Sociological Analysis of Collective Stress Situations* (Garden City, N.Y.: Doubleday, 1969); Dennis S. Mileti, Thomas Drabek, and J. Eugene Haas, *Human Systems in Extreme Environments: A Sociological Perspective* (Boulder, Colo.: University of Colorado, Institute of Behavioral Science, 1975); Enrico L. Quarantelli and Russell R. Dynes, "Response to Social Crisis and Disaster," *Annual Review of Sociology* 3 (1977): 23–49; Douglas C. Nilson, Linda B. Nilson, Richard S. Olson, and Bruce H. McAllister, *Planning Environment Report for the Southern California Earthquake Safety Advisory Board* (Redlands, Calif.: Policy Research Center, University of Redlands, 1981); Gary A. Kreps, "Sociological Inquiry and Disaster Research," *Annual Review of Sociology* 10 (1984): 309–330.

11. When asked what people should do in preparation for the earthquake he had forecast, James Whitcomb paraphrased a friend who had said that experienced Californians take earthquakes in their stride, merely insuring that their best bottles of scotch are safely at the rear of their cupboard shelves.

12. Russell R. Dynes, *Organized Behavior in Disaster* (Lexington, Mass.: D. C. Heath, 1971).

13. Raymond W. Mack and George W. Baker, *The Occasion Instant: The Structure of Social Responses to Unanticipated Air Raid Warnings* (Washington, D.C.: National Academy of Sciences—National Research Council, 1961); Elliott R. Danzig, Paul Thayer, and Lila Galanter, *The Effects of a Threatening Rumor on a Disaster-Stricken Community* (Washington, D.C.: 1958); Stephen Golant, "Human Behavior Before the

Disaster: A Selected Annotated Bibliography," Working Paper no. 9 (Columbus, Ohio: Disaster Research Center, Ohio State University, 1969).

14. Fritz, "Disaster"; Barton, Communities in Disaster; Ralph H. Turner, "Types of Solidarity in the Re-forming of Groups," Pacific Sociological Review 10 (Fall 1967): 60–68.

15. Robert Curvin and Bruce Porter, Blackout Looting: New York City, July 13, 1977 (New York: Gardner Press, 1979).

16. National Research Council, Panel on Public Policy Implications of Earthquake Prediction, Earthquake Prediction and Public Policy.

17. Harry E. Moore, . . . And the Winds Blew (Austin: University of Texas, Hogg Foundation for Mental Health, 1964); Dennis E. Wenger and Jack M. Weller, "Disaster Subcultures: The Cultural Residue of Community Disaster," Preliminary Paper no. 9 (Columbus, Ohio: Disaster Research Center, Ohio State University, 1973).

18. Melvin L. DeFleur and Sandra Ball-Rokeach, Theories of Mass Communication, 4th ed. (New York: David McKay, 1982); Charles R. Wright, Mass Communication: A Sociological Perspective (New York: Random House, 1975); Denis McQuail, Mass Communication Theory: An Introduction (London and Beverly Hills: Sage Publications, 1983).

19. Robert E. Park, "News as a Form of Knowledge: A Chapter in the Sociology of Knowledge," American Journal of Sociology 45 (March 1940): 669–686.

20. Paul F. Lazarsfeld, Bernard Berelson, and Hazel Gaudet, The People's Choice (New York: Duell, Sloan, and Pearce, 1944).

21. Ralph H. Turner and Lewis M. Killian, Collective Behavior, 2d ed. (Englewood Cliffs, N.J.: Prentice-Hall, 1972), pp. 179 ff.

22. Ibid., pp. 20–28; Tamotsu Shibutani, Improvised News: A Sociological Study of Rumor (Indianapolis: Bobbs-Merrill, 1966).

23. Alfred E. Katz, "Self-help Groups," Annual Review of Sociology 7 (1981): 129–155.

24. Mayer N. Zald and John D. McCarthy, The Dynamics of Social Movements (Cambridge, Mass.: Winthrop Publishers, 1979); Ralph H. Turner, "Collective Behavior and Resource Mobilization as Approaches to the Study of Social Movements," in Research in Social Movements, Conflict and Change, ed. Louis Kriesberg (Greenwich, Conn.: JAI Press, 1981), 4:1–24; J. Craig Jenkins, "Resource Mobilization Theory and the Study of Social Movements," Annual Review of Sociology 9 (1983): 527–553.

25. Allan Mazur, The Dynamics of Technical Controversy (Washington, D.C.: Communications Press, 1981).

26. William G. Sumner, Folkways (Boston: Ginn and Co., 1906); John Dewey, Human Nature and Conduct (New York: Henry Holt, 1922); Peter L. Berger and Thomas Luckmann, The Social Construction of Reality (Garden City, N.Y.: Doubleday, 1966); Herbert Blumer, Symbolic Interactionism: Perspective and Method (Englewood Cliffs, N.J.: Prentice-Hall, 1969); Irving L. Janis and Leon Mann, Decision Making: A

Psychological Analysis of Conflict, Choice, and Commitment (New York: Free Press, 1977); Howard Kunreuther, *Disaster Insurance Protection* (New York: John Wiley, 1978).

27. William W. Lowrance, *Of Acceptable Risk: Science and the Determination of Safety* (Los Altos, Calif.: William Kaufmann, 1976).

28. Wilbert Moore, *Man, Time, and Society* (New York: John Wiley, 1963).

29. Irwin Deutscher, "Words and Deeds: Social Science and Social Policy," *Social Problems* 13 (Winter 1966): 235–254.

30. Howard Leventhal, Jean C. Watts, and Francis Pagano, "Effects of Fear and Instructions on How to Cope with Danger," *Journal of Personality and Social Psychology* 6 (1967): 313–321.

2: Crisis or Business as Usual?

1. Leon Festinger, Henry W. Riecken, Jr., and Stanley Schachter, *When Prophecy Fails* (Minneapolis: University of Minnesota Press, 1956).

2. Kathleen Carothers first called this pattern to our attention while using our files for an independent study course at UCLA.

3: People Listen and Talk

1. Ithiel de Sola Pool, "Communication Systems," *Handbook of Communication*, ed. Pool, Wilbur Schramm, Nathan Maccoby, and Edwin S. Parker (Chicago: Rand McNally, 1973), pp. 3–26.

2. Paul F. Lazarsfeld, Bernard Berelson, and Hazel Gaudet, *The People's Choice* (New York: Duell, Sloan, and Pearce, 1944).

3. Raymond W. Mack and George W. Baker, *The Occasion Instant* (Washington, D.C.: National Academy of Sciences–National Research Council, 1961); Allen H. Barton, *Communities in Disaster: A Sociological Analysis of Collective Stress Situations* (Garden City, N.Y.: Doubleday, 1969); Benjamin F. McLuckie, "The Warning System in Disaster Situations: A Selective Analysis," Disaster Research Center Report no. 9 (Columbus, Ohio: Ohio State University, July 1970); Dennis Mileti and E. M. Beck, "Communication in Crisis: Explaining Evacuation Symbolically," *Communication Research* 2 (1975): 24–49.

4. Christopher H. Sterling and Timothy R. Haight, *The Mass Media: Aspen Institute Guide to Communication Industry Trends* (New York: Praeger, 1978).

5. "A Report to Client Newspapers of the Gallup Poll on the Credibility of the Press, Including Higher Circulation Prices, 1974," *News Research Bulletin* 2 (February 1974); Sterling and Haight, *The Mass Media*, p. 273.

6. Serena Wade and Wilbur Schramm, "The Mass Media as Sources

of Public Affairs, Science, and Health Knowledge," *Public Opinion Quarterly* 33 (1969): 197–209.

7. Since only 944 of our respondents lived in households with one or more other adults, we used 944 rather than 1,450 in computing the percentage of people who discussed earthquake topics with "adults in the household." Similar adjustments were made for the 884 who were employed full- or part-time, the 600 with children in the household under the age of eighteen, and the 108 with children eighteen years of age or older in the household. It was assumed that everyone could talk with friends and neighbors and with relatives not in the household, so these percentages are based on the total sample of 1,450 persons.

8. Barton, *Communities in Disaster*.

9. For patterns of communication use in relation to number of earthquakes experienced, *chi-square* = 31.399, 6 *d.f.*, *p* < .001. For patterns of communication use by personal and vicarious loss, *chi-square* = 34.486, 6 *d.f.*, *p* < .001.

10. Lazarsfeld, Berelson, and Gaudet, *The People's Choice*.

11. James S. Coleman, Elihu Katz, and Herbert Menzel, *Medical Innovation: A Diffusion Study* (Indianapolis: Bobbs-Merrill, 1966).

12. The twenty-six variables entered into the analysis were selected on the basis of theoretical interest for disaster research and evidence from prior research on differences between opinion leaders and followers, taking into account the experience in distinguishing promising from unpromising indicators in the current data. Eight demographic background variables were used: age, sex, marital status, presence of school-children in the household, educational attainment, occupational socio-economic status, employment status, and an index of attachment to the local community. Ten measures of mass communication use included the number of newspapers read regularly and whether respondents learned about earthquakes from TV news programs, TV specials, TV commercials, radio, newspapers, magazines, books, pamphlets in the mail, and movies. Two measures of interpersonal communication were range of partners in earthquake discussion and attendance at group meetings on earthquake safety. Three other variables included the number of damaging earthquakes experienced, the number of individual and household earthquake preparedness measures taken (see chapter seven), and an index of favorability toward science (chapter ten). Because local experts are supposed to be "expert," we included three measures of earthquake awareness: awareness of the southern California uplift, number of predictive announcements heard, and awareness of groups in special danger in case of an earthquake warning.

13. Charles R. Wright and Muriel Cantor, "Opinion Seeker and Avoider: Steps Beyond the Opinion Leader Concept," *Pacific Sociological Review* 10 (Spring 1967): 42–43; Charles K. Atkin, "Anticipated Communication and Mass Media Information-Seeking," *Public Opinion Quarterly* 36 (Summer 1972): 188–199.

14. Elihu Katz and Paul F. Lazarsfeld, *Personal Influence* (Glencoe, Ill.: Free Press, 1955).

15. For the relationship with awareness of the uplift, *chi-square* = 28.702, 6 *d.f.* $p < 001$; for number of predictions heard (0, 1, 2 or more), *chi-square* = 19.868, 4 *d.f.*, p < .001.

16. Charles Kadushin, "The Friends and Supporters of Psychotherapy: On Social Circles in Urban Life," *American Sociological Review* 31 (December 1966): 786–802; Robert K. Merton, *Social Theory and Social Structure*, 3d ed. (New York: Free Press, 1968), pp. 441–474.

17. A. W. Van den Ban, "A Revision of the Two-Step Flow of Communication Hypothesis," *Gazette* 10 (Summer 1964): 237–249.

4: But the People Won't Wait

1. Charles Fritz, "Disaster," in *Contemporary Social Problems: An Introduction to the Sociology of Deviant Behavior and Social Organization*, ed. Robert K. Merton and Robert A. Nisbet (New York: Harcourt, Brace and World (1961), pp. 651–694; William A. Anderson, "Disaster Warning and Communication Processes in Two Communities," *Journal of Communication* 19 (1969): 92–104; Thomas Drabek, "Social Processes in Disaster: Family Evacuation," *Social Problems* 16 (1969): 336–349.

2. Herbert Blumer, "Social Problems as Collective Behavior," *Social Problems* 18 (1971): 298–306; Jeffrey Hubbard, Melvin DeFleur, and Lois DeFleur, "Mass Media Influences on Public Perceptions of Social Problems," *Social Problems* 23 (1975): 22–34.

3. Sandra Ball-Rokeach and M. L. DeFleur, "A Dependency Model of Mass-Media Effects," *Communication Research* 3 (1976): 3–21.

4. Ralph H. Turner, "Collective Behavior," in *Handbook of Modern Sociology*, ed. Robert E. L. Faris (Chicago: Rand McNally, 1964), p. 398.

5. Tamotsu Shibutani, *Improvised News: A Sociological Study of Rumor* (Indianapolis: Bobbs-Merrill, 1966), p. 17.

6. Gordon W. Allport and Leo Postman, *The Psychology of Rumor* (New York: Henry Holt, 1974), p. 34.

5: What Have They Learned After All?

1. The salience incorporated in this graph is salience of the earthquake threat as described in chapter six, not salience of the uplift as discussed earlier in chapter five.

2. Each of the indexes is briefly described in the text, generally in the chapter where it is of primary concern. For example, the measures of attitude toward science are described in chapter ten, and the measures of earthquake communication have already been described in chapter three.

3. H. J. Friedsam, "Older Persons in Disaster," in *Man and Society in Disaster*, ed. George W. Baker and Dwight W. Chapman (New York: Basic Books, 1962), pp. 155–157.

4. Zero-order Pearson correlations with awareness of the uplift are as follows: being Anglo, .243; educational attainment, .222; socioeconomic status, .186; household income, .167.

5. Pearson correlations are as follows: index of earthquake experience, .172; earthquake loss to close friends and relatives, .122.

6. Pearson correlations with predictions heard are as follows: earthquake loss to close friends and relatives, .149; educational attainment, .139; index of earthquake experience, .114; being Anglo, .101; socioeconomic status, .096.

6: Are the People Really Concerned?

1. Harry E. Moore, *. . . and the Winds Blew* (Austin: University of Texas, Hogg Foundation for Mental Health, 1964), p. 196.

2. In further analysis of these data, K. Jill Kiecolt and Joanne M. Nigg developed a model to explain people's decisions to move based on their perceptions of earthquake hazards. They found no evidence that past earthquake experience, living in especially vulnerable areas of the county, or awareness of forecasts and warnings affected the likelihood that people would consider moving. See "Mobility and Perceptions of a Hazardous Environment," *Environment and Behavior* 14 (March 1982): 131–154.

3. Hirotada Hirose, *Survey of People's Reactions to Predictions of a Tokai Earthquake in Northern Shizuoka Prefecture, Japan* (Tokyo: Tokyo Woman's Christian University, Department of Psychology, 1983).

4. Samuel A. Stouffer, *Communism, Conformity, and Civil Liberties* (New York: John Wiley, 1955), pp. 58–70.

7: Are They Looking Out for Themselves?

1. Emile Durkheim, *Suicide: A Study in Sociology*, trans. John A. Spaulding and George Simpson, ed. George Simpson (New York: Free Press, 1951; originally published in French in 1897).

2. Irwin Deutscher, "Words and Deeds: Social Science and Social Policy," *Social Problems* 13 (Winter 1966): 235–253.

8: Let Government Do It

1. Samuel H. Prince, *Catastrophe and Social Change: Based upon a Sociological Study of the Halifax Disaster* (New York: Columbia Univer-

sity, 1920), pp. 46–58; Martha Wolfenstein, *Disaster: A Psychological Essay* (New York: Free Press, 1957); Charles E. Fritz, "Disaster," in *Contemporary Social Problems*, ed. Robert K. Merton and Robert A. Nisbet (New York: Harcourt, Brace and World, 1961), pp. 651–694; Ralph H. Turner, "Types of Solidarity in the Re-forming of Groups," *Pacific Sociological Review* 10 (Fall 1967): 60–68; Allen H. Barton, *Communities in Disaster: A Sociological Analysis of Collective Stress Situations* (Garden City, N.Y.: Doubleday, 1969).

2. National Research Council, Panel on Public Policy Implications of Earthquake Prediction, *Earthquake Prediction and Public Policy* (Washington, D.C.: National Academy of Sciences, 1975).

3. The term *cooperative altruism* was proposed by Charles K. Warriner in "The Altruistic Impulse and the Good Society," in *Voluntary Action Research: 1972*, ed. David H. Smith (Lexington, Mass.: Lexington Books, 1972), pp. 343–355.

4. Allen H. Barton popularized the term *therapeutic community* to describe the integrative community response to natural disaster. See *Communities in Disaster*, pp. 216 ff.

5. Attitudes toward science are more fully examined in chapter ten.

6. Los Angeles City Task Force on Earthquake Prediction, *Consensus Report of the Task Force on Earthquake Prediction* (Los Angeles: Office of the Mayor, 1978).

7. $X^2 = 543.99$, 8 $d.f.$, $p < .001$.

9: Support and Obstruction

1. The groups included in this analysis held at least one meeting or discussion between January 1, 1976, and June 30, 1977. This eighteen-month period coincides with the greatest media coverage of the earthquake threat and with active community concern about earthquake predictions. No new groups in Los Angeles County emerged after this date, and the number of group meetings held were very few in number. None of our resource agencies reported more than a handful of requests after this date.

2. Because of the several sources used to gather this sample, some groups were located through two different sources, indicating that adequate search procedures were being employed to find as many sponsoring groups as possible located throughout the county. Although the sample was not randomly drawn, it is believed to reflect adequately the patterns and processes that were important in sensitizing groups to earthquake-related topics and in determining the extent to which different types of groups were mobilized. Because of the nonrandom sampling techniques used and the small numbers of cases in some categories, statistical measures of significance will not be used in the analysis. However, whenever applicable, descriptive data have been included to substantiate the conclusions that have been drawn.

3. Although this technique did not result in a large number of additions to the sample, it provided additional confidence that the three primary sampling sources were not overlooking any major categories of meeting activities.

4. Occasionally, the identified organizer fulfilled merely the perfunctory obligation of setting up the meeting or program and had no knowledge about the actual meeting. In those cases, additional interviews were conducted with "knowledgeable informants," people identified by the organizer as "knowing what went on" or as having been present at the meeting.

5. Robert W. Kates, "Hazard and Choice Perception in Flood Plain Management," Department of Geography Research Paper no. 78 (Chicago: University of Chicago, 1962).

6. Ian Burton and Robert W. Kates, "The Perception of Natural Hazards in Resource Management," *Natural Resources Journal* 3 (1964): 412–441.

7. Charles Fritz, "Disaster," in *Contemporary Social Problems*, ed. Robert K. Merton and Robert A. Nisbet (New York: Harcourt, Brace, and World, 1961), pp. 651–694; Charles Fritz and Eli Marks, "The NORC Studies of Human Behavior in Disaster," *Journal of Social Issues* 10 (1954): 26–41; Harry E. Moore, . . . *And the Winds Blew* (Austin: University of Texas. Hogg Foundation for Mental Helath, 1964); Anthony F. C. Wallace, *Tornado in Worchester*, National Research Disaster Council Study no. 3 (Washington, D.C.: National Academy of Sciences, 1956).

8. William A. Anderson, "Disaster Warning and Communication Processes in Two Communities," *Journal of Communication* 19 (1969): 92–104.

9. Charles Fogelman and Vernon Parenton, "Disaster and Aftermath: Selected Aspects of Individual and Group Behavior in Critical Situations," *Social Forces* 38 (1959): 129–135.

10. Harry E. Moore et al., *Before the Wind: A Study of the Response to Hurricane Carla* (Washington, D.C.: National Academy of Sciences, National Research Council, 1963).

11. Thomas Drabek, "Social Processes in Disaster: Family Evacuation," *Social Problems*, 16 (1969): 336–349.

12. Harry B. Williams, "Human Factors in Warning-and-Response Systems," in George H. Grosser et al., eds., *Threat of Impending Disaster* (Cambridge, Mass.: MIT Press, 1965), pp. 79–104.

10: Understanding and Respect for Science

1. Coefficient of reproducibility $= .79$; minimum marginal reproducibility $= .67$; percent improvement $= .12$; coefficient of scaleability $= .36$.

2. John A. Moore, "Creationism in California," *Daedalus* 103 (Summer 1974): 173–183; Lawrence Boadt et al., "Creationism," *Academe* 68 (March-April 1982): 7–36.

3. For a recent review, see Melvin L. DeFleur and Sandra J. Ball-

Rokeach, *Theories of Mass Communication*, 4th ed. (New York: Longman, 1982).

4. David Perlman, "Science and the Mass Media," *Daedalus* 11 (Summer 1974): 209.

5. Robert S. Morison, "Science and Social Attitudes," *Science* 165 (July 11, 1969): 151.

11: Neighborhood Makes a Difference

1. Harry E. Moore, . . . *And the Winds Blew* (Austin: University of Texas. Hogg Foundation for Mental Health, 1964); Dennis E. Wenger and Jack M. Weller, "Disaster Subcultures: The Cultural Residue of Community Disasters," Preliminary Paper no. 9 (Columbus, Ohio: Disaster Research Center, Ohio State University, 1973); Dennis E. Wenger, "Community Response to Disaster: Functional and Structural Alterations," in *Disasters: Theory and Research*, ed. Enrico L. Quarantelli (London and Beverly Hills: Sage Publications, 1978), pp. 17–47.

2. For a detailed explanation of the oversampling procedure and weighting procedure, see Ralph H. Turner, Joanne M. Nigg, Denise H. Paz, and Barbara Shaw, *Community Response to Earthquake Threat in Southern California* (technical report to NSF, 1980), Part Seven, pp. 4–8. (This can be obtained in paper or microfiche by writing to: National Technical Information Service, 5285 Port Royal Road, Springfield, VA 22161.)

3. Residents of the San Fernando earthquake impact zone are not significantly different from the control sample in age or in any of the three indicators of social stratification, so it is unnecessary to employ the analysis of covariance procedure used with the old-building and combined-hazard zones. However, the San Fernando zone is ethnically distinctive in being overwhelmingly white Anglo in composition. The most satisfactory way to control for ethnic distinctiveness of this sort is simply to eliminate from the analysis all except white Anglos in both the San Fernando zone and the control sample. The resulting sample sizes are 182 in the San Fernando zone and 348 in the control sample.

4. Ralph H. Turner, "Life Situation and Subculture: A Comparison of Merited Prestige Judgments by Three Occupational Classes in Britain," *British Journal of Sociology* 9 (December 1958): 299–320.

5. Harry E. Moore, op. cit., pp. 195 and 212–213.

6. John J. Cove, "Survival or Extinction: Reflections on the Problem of Famine in Tsimshian and Kaguru Mythology," in *Extinction and Survival in Human Populations*, ed. Charles D. McLaughlin, Jr., and Ivan A. Brady (New York: Columbia University Press, 1978), pp. 231–244.

7. Dennis E. Wenger and Jack M. Weller, op. cit.; Wenger, op. cit.

8. Carey McWilliams, "The Folklore of Earthquakes," *American Mercury* 29 (June 1933): 199–201.

9. Our characterizations of the natural areas are based principally upon intimate personal familiarity with the Los Angeles metropolitan area rather than on data assembled in the course of this investigation.

12: Waiting and Looking for Omens

1. Leslie Kish, *Survey Sampling* (New York: John Wiley, 1965).
2. *Chi-square* = 40.953, 4 *d.f.*, p < .001.
3. Paul Slovic, Howard Kunreuther, and Gilbert White, "Decision Processes, Rationality, and Adjustment to Natural Hazards," in *Natural Hazards: Local, National, Global,* ed. Gilbert White (New York: Oxford University Press, 1974), pp. 187–205.
4. *Chi-square* = 15.892, 2 *d.f,* p < .001.

13: Test of Time

1. For the sake of economy, the four follow-up interview waves and the New Year's Day earthquake interview (chapter fourteen) were conducted by telephone, with sampling by random-digit dialing within regions of the county paralleling those used in the sampling design for the field survey. The possibility must therefore be considered that differences between the February 1977 basic field survey and subsequent waves might be consequences of the changed interview or sampling mode. After a comprehensive review of all the time-series findings, we conclude that they cannot be explained in this way. Most telling is the frequent observation that a trend found between the basic field survey and the first follow-up wave is continued during the next time interval. Another relevant observation is that the New Year's Day earthquake restores certain key variables to the basic field survey level. For these and other reasons we are satisfied that the time series can be accepted at face value.

2. On the first three occasions, interviewers were instructed to record up to five separate answers and space was provided on the interview schedule for five corresponding sets of follow-up questions. To prevent an overly long interview and because respondents seldom offered more than three answers, only three announcements were recorded in the two final interview waves. In order to establish comparability, we have included only the first three announcements from each of the interview waves in the analysis of change and stability. For that reason there will be slight differences in the findings from the initial survey as reported earlier.

3. F = 2114.56; 1,3 *d.f.;* p < .001.

4. For pseudoscientific announcements: F = 56.52; 1,3 *d.f.;* p < .01; exponential curve. For prophetic announcements: F = 14.29; 1,3 *d.f.;*

$p < .05$; exponential curve. For general announcements: $F = 18.53$; 1,3 *d.f.*; $p < .05$; linear trend.

5. $F = 72.03$; 1,3 *d.f.*; $p < .01$.
6. $F = 29.48$; 1,3 *d.f.*; $p < .05$.
7. $F = 21.03$; 2,2 *d.f.*; $p < .05$.
8. $F = 23.89$; 2,2 *d.f.*; $p < .05$.
9. $F = 29.48$; 1,3 *d.f.*; $p < .05$.

14: New Year's Day Surprise

1. Waverly J. Person, "Earthquakes: January-February 1979," *Earthquake Information Bulletin* 11 (July-August 1979): 143–144.
2. The contrast may be exaggerated. Neither of the comparison questions coupled the term *upset* with the standard term *frightened*.
3. Tomatsu Shibutani, *Improvised News: A Sociological Study of Rumor* (Indianapolis: Bobbs-Merrill, 1966).
4. *Chi-square* = 7.150, 1 *d.f.*, $p < .01$.
5. *Chi-square* = 7.999, 1 *d.f.*, $p < .01$.
6. *Chi-square* = 10,048, 1 *d.f.*, $p < .01$.
7. Allen H. Barton, *Communities in Disaster: A Sociological Analysis of Collective Stress Situations* (Garden City, New York: Doubleday, 1969), pp. 205–279.
8. *Chi-square* with one *d.f.* = 14.391, 12.534, and 12.918, respectively; *Chi-square* for sensed change with two *d.f.* = 14.923. In all four instances, $p < .001$.
9. *Chi-square* = 7.543, 2 *d.f.*, $p < .05$.
10. We assume that this hypothesized lack of relationship applies only until the quake seems about to occur, when fear would surely increase. We suggest a *J*-curve relationship between sense of imminence and fear.
11. For safety codes, chi-square = 39.380, 1 *d.f.*, $p < .001$; for loans, *chi-square* = 8.898, 1 *d.f.*, $p < .01$.
12. For flashlights, *chi-square* = 18.091, 1 *d.f.*, $p < .001$; for radios, *chi-square* = 11.582, 1 *d.f.*, $p < .001$; for first-aid kits, *chi-square* = 4.934, 1 *d.f.*, $p < .05$.

15: Patterns of Change

1. Unfortunately, time limitations made it impracticable for us to include earthquake fatalism in the New Year's Day tremor study.
2. Haicheng Earthquake Study Delegation, "Prediction of the Haicheng Earthquake," *EOS: Transactions, American Geophysical Union* 58 (May 1977): 236–272.

3. Because of space limitations, we have not reported the tabulations supporting this relationship here.

4. Newspaper frequencies are plotted by four-week periods and include all items in the six monitored papers. The three types of newspaper coverage have been plotted in the same scale to permit comparison of absolute levels of attention. Each of the response variables has been plotted using a different scale, so trends, but not absolute levels, can be compared.

Index

Action: and affect, 18, 402; and awareness, 147–148, 185–186, 364–365; and fear, 187; and risk, 186–187; support for governmental, 212–218

Alarm-and-reassurance pattern, 40–41, 43–44, 50, 58–59, 377, 418

Alexander, George, 38, 39, 44–45, 47

Allen, Clarence, 41, 46, 99

Allport, George, 107

Alquist, Alfred, 27

Altruism, 12, 56, 195–203, 365–367

Apathy, 4, 411

Attitudes: and action, 17–18; fatalism, 18, 132, 167, 172, 175–178, 184, 198–199, 217, 365; spectator attitude, 185; toward prediction capability, 216, 354–356, 384; toward science, 132, 137–138, 172, 217, 254–259; withholding prediction information, 102–103, 257–258, 356, 385, 410–411

Awareness, 17–18; and action, 147–148; and cognition, 164–166; and fear, 158–164 passim; of predictions, 119–127, 136–139, 346–348; quality of, 118; as subcultural theme, 311–312; of uplift, 116–118, 130–136

Barton, Allen, 244

Bounded rationality, 17

Bradley, Tom, 31

Building safety: media coverage of, 53–54. See also Issue-oriented groups; Seismic safety ordinance

California Earthquake Prediction Evaluation Council, 28–29, 36, 110

Citizens' Committee to Save the Littlerock Dam, 240, 242, 247. See also Issue-oriented groups

Clowes, Richard, 30

Cognition: and affect, 134; and awareness, 164–166

Communication, 13–15. See also Informal discussion; Mass media

Community integration, 132

Concern. See Fear

Cranston, Alan, 30, 38

Creative Home Economics Consultants, 31, 239

Dam safety: media coverage of, 54–56. See also Issue-oriented groups

Designer: U.C. Press Staff
Compositor: Prestige Typography
Printer: Edwards Bros.
Binder: Edwards Bros.
Text: 10/13 Melior
Display: Melior